British Romanticism and the Critique
of Political Reason

British Romanticism

AND

the Critique
of Political Reason

•

TIMOTHY MICHAEL

Johns Hopkins University Press

Baltimore

© 2016 Johns Hopkins University Press
All rights reserved. Published 2016
Printed in the United States of America on acid-free paper
2 4 6 8 9 7 5 3 1

Johns Hopkins University Press
2715 North Charles Street
Baltimore, Maryland 21218-4363
www.press.jhu.edu

Library of Congress Cataloging-in-Publication Data

Michael, Timothy, 1980–
British Romanticism and the critique of political reason / Timothy Michael.
pages cm
Includes bibliographical references and index.
ISBN 978-1-4214-1803-2 (hardcover : acid-free paper) — ISBN 978-1-4214-1804-9
(electronic) — ISBN 1-4214-1803-7 (hardcover : acid-free paper) —
ISBN 1-4214-1804-5 (electronic)   1. Romanticism—Great Britain.   2. English
literature—Philosophy.   3. Politics and literature—Great Britain—History—18th
century.   4. Literature and society—Great Britain—History—18th century.
5. Politics and literature—Great Britain—History—19th century.   6. Literature
and society—Great Britain—History—19th century.   I. Title.
PR448.P5M53 2015
820.9'145   dc23
2015005808

A catalog record for this book is available from the British Library.

Special discounts are available for bulk purchases of this book.
For more information, please contact Special Sales at 410-516-6936 or
specialsales@press.jhu.edu.

Johns Hopkins University Press uses environmentally friendly book materials,
including recycled text paper that is composed of at least 30 percent
post-consumer waste, whenever possible.

To Mariam, Samir, and Daniel

CONTENTS

It is with great pleasure that I express my gratitude to the many people who have assisted in the writing of this book. My first thanks are to James Engell, who has been a source of knowledge of both means and ends. He has been, for me and for many others, a model teacher, mentor, and scholar. The virtues of this book are his. Leo Damrosch and Elaine Scarry offered invaluable guidance in the early stages of composition, lending their considerable expertise to the project when it was most needed. To Laurence Lockridge I am profoundly indebted for initiating me into the mysteries of Coleridge studies and for demonstrating the importance of philosophical criticism.

A number of colleagues and critics have read the manuscript, in whole or in part, and offered sound advice: Christoph Bode, James Chandler, Stephen Gill, Nicholas Halmi, Charles Mahoney, Richard Moran, Seamus Perry, Ann Rowland, Fiona Stafford, and David Womersley. The book is inestimably stronger for their suggestions and insights.

Daniel Moore at the University of Chicago and Rumur Dowling at the University of Oxford were outstanding research assistants. I would also like to thank the students in my graduate seminars at Oxford, who helped me clarify the ideas contained here and explain their significance.

For the lasting influence of their teaching: Homi Bhabha, Matthew Boyle, Louis Cassella, Roger Deakins, Jacques Derrida, Denis Donoghue, Dustin Griffin, John Guillory, Barbara Lewalski, Louis Menand, Paul O'Connor, Leah Price, Avital Ronell, Gertrude Schneider, Gabrielle Starr, Gordon Teskey, Friedrich Ulfers, and Helen Vendler.

For various forms of support and intellectual companionship: David Bevington, Matthew Bevis, Frederick Burwick, Graham Davidson, Sascha Ebeling, Marilyn Gaull, Melissa Girard, Richard Gravil, Noel Jackson, David Jacobson, Freya Johnston, Jacob Jost, Robert Lehman, Giuseppina Lobo, Julius Lobo, Paul Lukacs, Erica McAlpine, Gayla McGlamery, Nicholas Miller, Robert Miola, Kathryn Murphy, Brian Norman, Matthew Ocheltree, Mark Osteen,

Jacob Risinger, Andrew Stauffer, Richard Strier, and all of the Harper-Schmidt Fellows in the Society of Fellows at the University of Chicago.

I am grateful to the many close friends who discussed these ideas with me informally over the years: Katherine Chenoweth, Margaret Doherty, Erin Fehskens, Marcella Frydman, Nicholas Gaskill, Stephen Hequembourg, James Horowitz, Robert Huntington, Amelia Klein, Jason Manoharan, Maia Mc-Aleavey, Benjamin McKean, Julie Orlemanski, Brian Perkins, David Plunkett, Daniel Shore, and Hannah Sullivan.

I would like to thank the Rector and Fellows of Lincoln College, Oxford, for their support of my research. I would especially like to thank my colleagues in English: Peter McCullough, Daniel Starza Smith, and Mark Williams.

Matthew McAdam, Catherine Goldstead, Hilary Jacqmin, and Juliana McCarthy at Johns Hopkins University Press have been enormously helpful. Thanks to Beth Gianfagna for her expert copyediting and to Susan Storch for the index.

Research for the book was made possible by generous assistance from the Department of English at Harvard University, the Dexter Travel Fund at Harvard, the Society of Fellows at the University of Chicago, the Michael Zilkha Fund at Lincoln College, and the Faculty of English at the University of Oxford. A version of chapter 5 appeared as "Coleridge, Hume, and the Principles of Political Knowledge," in *Studies in Romanticism* (Fall 2010): 445–75.

For reading and commenting on much of what follows—and for countless acts of kindness and intelligence—I am especially grateful to Stacey McDowell.

I reserve my deepest thanks for my mother, father, and brother, to whom this book is dedicated.

*British Romanticism and the Critique
of Political Reason*

Problems of Knowledge and Freedom

The governing idea of this book, to which every detail of literary or intellectual history is ultimately subordinate, is the promise of enlightenment after revolution and terror—that is, the idea that one can impose some small measure of order on an often violent and chaotic world through the assertion of human reason and that it is through rational activity that things like liberty and justice cease to be merely ideas. This is not as uncontroversial a position as it might seem. There are philosophical problems, all addressed over the course of this study. How are we to define liberty and justice? How are we to determine the claims of reason? What constitutes rational activity? Under what conditions can we claim to "know" anything in a field as complex as politics? There are also practical concerns. It is not exactly clear, for example, how one makes the leap from the realm of ideas to the real world of human beings, as S. T. Coleridge was quick to realize (hence his distinction, borrowed from Kant, between reason and the understanding). The world of politics seems all too immune to the exhortations of reason, which is powerless, according to one view, in the face of class interests, dominant institutions, and the seemingly universal desire of individuals and groups to hold on to power. David Hume adopts something like this attitude in the middle of the eighteenth century when, regarding the alleged origins of the social contract, he skeptically asks if there is anything discoverable in the entire human record except force and violence; the attitude, we might add, persists into the twenty-first century, on both the left and the right. There are historical objections of another kind. Political theorists from

Burke to Oakeshott have argued that reason has played *too much* of a role in history: instead of being powerless against other social forces, rationalism in politics has been directly responsible for atrocities like the Terror of revolutionary France and the concentration camps and gulags of the twentieth century. What is needed, for these theorists, is *less* rationalism in politics.

The realization of ends like freedom and justice though rational activity, then, does not seem to be an unequivocal good, universally acknowledged. It is for this reason that the figures covered in this study were all, in some way or another, so deeply invested in it. If the governing idea of this book is the promise of enlightenment after revolution and terror, then the argument of the book is this: much of the literature at the heart of British Romanticism is a reconsideration, a trial, and a critique of reason in its political capacities and of the kinds of knowledge available to it. There are a number of subsidiary arguments, but they all derive from and develop this overarching one. The Romanticism of this book is an extension and modification of a certain brand of Enlightenment rationalism, one that suffered a setback by the French Revolution and its aftermath, for which it was held by some to be responsible. The narrative of enlightenment, revolution, and terror—a narrative at times resisted, at times reinforced in Romantic literature—demanded, for a particular group of poets and theorists, that we reassess the nature of human reason, its relationship to historical forces and social power, and its role in aesthetic creation.

The alliance of Romanticism and reason I present here has never been intuitive, despite a number of attempts over the years to revise our understanding of the period's place in the history of ideas and culture. It remains a truism of literary history to say that Romantic literature represents an unprecedented defense and celebration of the creative imagination. This is the case for good reason: the role of the imagination is the inevitable theme of much poetry and prose in the late-eighteenth and early-nineteenth centuries. What standard narratives of literary history often neglect, however, is how the defense of the imagination in the Romantic period is simultaneously a critique or a vindication of particular forms of reason.[1] The codependence of the two faculties—indeed, their identity—would be climactically revealed to Wordsworth in the Mt. Snowdon episode of *The Prelude* (1805), where the imagination is triumphantly hailed as "reason in her most exalted mood" (13.170).[2] The conflict between the imagination and reason is in many ways a post-Romantic construction.

By the "critique" of reason, then, I do not mean its rejection—so that the critique of one faculty is a way to make room for another—but the opposite: the self-grounding of reason, the determination of its own scope and limits, so that it may more legitimately justify its claims to knowledge. The sense of "critique" I invoke is that of the German *Kritik*. As Kant describes the first, monumental work of his critical system, *The Critique of Pure Reason* (1781) is a tribunal, an epistemological "court of justice, by which reason may secure its rightful claims while dismissing all its groundless pretensions."[3] The critique of pure reason in Kant, like the critique of political reason in Romanticism, is its greatest possible defense. Writing at the dawn of Romanticism in Europe—the publication of his critical system spans the period 1781–90, years encompassing both the death of Johnson and the initial phases of the French Revolution—Kant remarks that "our age is the genuine age of criticism, to which everything must submit."[4] The influence of Kant, direct and indirect, runs throughout this study, and I propose a revitalized version of Kantian Romanticism insofar as I see the literature of the period as an extension of transcendental self-criticism: an assessment of what can be rescued from Enlightenment models of rationality and an evaluation of how what remains of them might be deployed in postrevolutionary political contexts.

Romanticism, including its earliest manifestations in Britain, has its origins in the "age of criticism" Kant describes, and it shares its basic orientation: overcoming a set of impasses characteristic of late-Enlightenment thought through a self-conscious meditation on the mind itself. If the essence of Romanticism consists in its inward turn, then this turn is not the withdrawal it has often been assumed to be. The essence of the Romantic turn to the mind consists rather in establishing the subjective conditions of objective freedom (and, as Shelley would recognize more than any of his contemporaries, the objective conditions of subjective freedom). It is *The Prelude*, again, that most forcefully describes one reason that the reconciliation of subject and object was of such profound significance, and it does so in an extended critique of political reason in book 10. After dismissively recalling the appeal of Godwin's *Political Justice* to the young mind looking to ground the revolutionary hopes of man in the "purer element" of reason, Wordsworth claims to adopt a more sympathetic retrospective view:

> But, speaking more in charity, the dream
> Was flattering to the young ingenuous mind,
> Pleas'd with extremes, and not the least with that
> Which makes the human Reason's naked self
> The object of its fervour: what delight!
> How glorious! in self-knowledge and self-rule
> To look through all the frailties of the world
> And, with a resolute mastery shaking off
> The accidents of nature, time, and place
> That make up the weak being of the past,
> Build social freedom on its only basis,
> The freedom of the individual mind,
> Which, to the blind restraint of general laws

Superior, magisterially adopts
One guide, the light of circumstances, flash'd
Upon an independent intellect.   (10.814–29)

The "independent intellect" lines originate in *The Borderers* of 1797, a play designed "to shew the dangerous use which may be made of reason when a man has committed a great crime."[5] It is easy enough to dismiss, as Wordsworth seems to do even in his more charitable mood, the central idea of the passage: the only real basis of social freedom is the freedom of the individual mind. History, with its materialist bias, seems to argue otherwise. The idea, though, ought to be taken seriously, if only because of the noticeable effort Wordsworth takes to distance himself from it in 1797 and then again in 1805. The rationalist "dream" of predicating social on individual freedom is, in fact, one that Wordsworth could never fully renounce; it would continue to inform the importance he grants to retirement and tranquillity in his later work.

In the context of this book, the idea is at the center of the Romantic critique of political reason. The engineering impulse of these lines recurs in the other writers studied here, each of whom explicitly seeks to "build" social freedom on some basis or another. Similarly, they are all concerned with what they, from Burke to Shelley, called "rational liberty," a conception of freedom grounded in the self-regulating powers of human reason. The concept of "rational liberty," given its fullest philosophical treatment in Kant, is among the most important (and most overlooked) means by which subject and object are brought together in Romanticism. The foundation of objective freedom, reflected in social structures and political institutions, in subjective freedom is, like the concept of rational liberty itself, far from self-evident. It is perhaps a stranger idea to us now than it was at the end of the eighteenth century. One purpose of this book is to reintroduce the concept of rational liberty, and others like it, and to suggest why it was of such importance for this particular group of writers. The lines from *The Prelude* quoted above, to which I shall return periodically, indicate why a critique of reason seemed to be a necessary precondition of political regeneration.

I focus on the critique of *political* reason, then, for a few reasons. On the most basic level, the version of Romanticism I present here is the synthesis of two revolutions, Kant's "Copernican" revolution in philosophy and the revolution in France. The relationship between these two revolutions is the conceptual substratum of British Romanticism, the foundation from which a set of authors began to imagine alternative possibilities in material and immaterial domains—both concrete projects of reform and metaphysical projects geared toward the emancipation of the subject. There are also more purely inductive reasons, addressed throughout the work, for focusing on political reason: as discussed in this introduction, debates about "political knowledge" became increasingly intense as the eighteenth century progressed, culminating in the heated debates of the 1790s that forged the political sensibility of Romanticism; the conditions of "political knowledge" would in fact be at the center of the most systematic exposition of Coleridge's political thought and would play an important role in Shelley's philosophical view of political history; the definition of "political reason" and the possibility of "political metaphysics" were explicit concerns of Burke and his critics; and, as a final inductive reason, it became increasingly evident to me that questions of knowledge in the Romantic period were almost always coupled with questions of freedom (it is difficult to find a consideration of one that is not, in some way, also a consideration of the other). Epistemological questions were pursued by the Romantics with such force and persistence because they were seen as vitally connected to issues of liberty and justice. Finally, the focus on political reason is motivated in part by a gap in Romantic studies: an explanation of how Romantic theories of the mind and knowledge relate to Romantic politics. While there has been no shortage of work done in either subfield, there is not yet a study devoted to the mutually constitutive relationship between Romantic politics and Romantic epistemology. This study of the Romantic critique of political reason—the phrase, to be clear, refers not to a homogenous or consistent body of work, but to a shared set of concerns and terms—is an attempt to bridge that divide.

What I propose in this book, though, is to do more than suggest that two fields—Romantic politics and Romantic epistemology—bear some relation to each other, but to make a few specific claims that I hope tell a particular story when viewed together. In the most direct terms, then, I argue for the following: first, a conception of British Romanticism that sees in it the synthesis of two major revolutions originating on the Continent; second, an understanding of Romanticism that accounts both for its attempts to overcome the rationalism-empiricism impasse and its attempts to come to terms with the perceived terror of political rationalism (and that sees both of these attempts as part of the same project); third, a reading of Romanticism's reading of the history of ideas that is skeptical of the notion of the autonomous intellectual or poet, emphasizing instead the constant mediation between material conditions and cultural activity; fourth, an account of how the conflict (and potential reconciliation) of subject and object, the central philosophical theme of Romanticism, is mediated by issues of political knowledge and reason; finally, a revised account of the inward turn of Romanticism that sees it not as a withdrawal from history and politics, but an attempt to determine how far liberty might be founded on a secure and rational basis.

The terms "Romanticism" and "Romantic" recur frequently in these arguments. Still, I refrain from venturing something like a definition of Romanticism, at least at this point. "I do not propose to walk into that particular trap," Isaiah

Berlin remarks at the beginning of his study of the roots of Romanticism.[6] If pressed, I might say that it has to do with the collaborative work of Wordsworth and Coleridge near the turn of the century, though even here objections arise. To take another route, recalling F. W. Bateson's pronouncement, echoing Auden, that "literature is memorable words or it is nothing," one might say that Romanticism is philosophical verse written in response to the French Revolution or it is nothing, though, again, objections are audible by the time philosophy is invoked. The past century of criticism has indicated that attempting a definition of Romanticism is bound to be a fraught enterprise. If for this reason alone, we should not give up on the term, any more than we should give up on other general terms to describe the history of culture. Insofar as these are pragmatic, not metaphysical, terms—designed to give order to an immeasurable body of texts, ideas, and historical events—they are indispensable.[7] What I mean by "Romanticism" can only become clear over the course of this work, which treats only a few figures associated with it. Three of them are central figures by almost all accounts, so the use of the term has some justification on that basis. Others are less commonly included under the category of British Romanticism. By including the philosophy and political prose of the period—by those typically designated "Romantics" and by those who wrote in the crucial years between the French Revolution and the publication of the *Lyrical Ballads*—alongside its poetry, I hope to expand what we mean by the term. Like political reason itself, Romanticism is largely what generations of critics have determined it to be. And, as we shall now see, the histories of political reason and Romanticism in Britain converged in late-eighteenth-century debates about the possibility and importance of, as it was called at the time, "political knowledge."

The Discipline of Political Knowledge: Invention, Development, Crisis

In 1795, two years into Britain's decades-long war with revolutionary France and at the height of Pitt ministry repression, William Godwin wrote:

> The great problem of political knowledge, is, how to preserve to mankind the advantages of freedom, together with an authority, strong enough to controul every daring violation of general security and peace. The prize of political wisdom is due to the man, who shall afford us the best comment upon that fundamental principle of civilization, Liberty without Licentiousness.
>
> Great is the error, or sinister and alarming the policy, of those, who tell us that politics is a simple science, where the plainest understanding is in no danger of a fatal mistake. Politics, especially if we understand that term as relating to such societies of men as at present divide the earth, is the masterpiece of human sagacity.[8]

The register of Godwin's remarks, in which the stakes of political epistemology are alarmingly high, reflects the tone of much 1790s radicalism and the intensity of 1794–95 in particular. Mary Wollstonecraft attacked in 1794 the "pseudo-patriots" of France as "men without principles or political knowledge, excepting what they had casually gleaned from books, only read to while away an idle hour not employed in pleasure."[9] Samuel Taylor Coleridge, in a Bristol lecture the next year, criticized the "professed Friends of Liberty"—he had Godwin himself in mind—who feel no urgency in forming concrete plans of action: "theirs is not that twilight of political knowledge which gives us just light enough to place one foot before the other," using for the first time the phrase under which he would collect his most systematic political thought.[10] Godwin, Wollstonecraft, and Coleridge, in fact, joined a number of contemporary writers in their concern with "political knowledge," a category that became increasingly prevalent as the eighteenth century progressed.

"Political knowledge" is not in general part of our present vocabulary, even if the two constitutive terms of the phrase very much are. Outside of epistemological or meta-ethical contexts, we tend to speak of politics and knowledge as inhabiting two separate spheres: one defined by the organization of objective power relations and the other defined by the organization of subjective mental events, both their coherence with each other and their correspondence with an objective world. Furthermore, questions of freedom have been decoupled from questions of knowledge for good reason: given the nature of modern political and social justice movements around the globe—struggles that typically depend on popular mobilization around basic and widely shared moral principles—it might seem strange, even perverse, to insist on the close relationship between political and epistemological questions. It is difficult, for instance, to see how problems like war, poverty, and environmental degradation bear any relation at all to debates about how to justify political propositions. Hume, again, adopts this attitude in his essay "Of the Original Contract" (1748) when he asks if there is anything discoverable in the entire human record but "force and violence," echoing in his own way Thucydides's eternal maxim that large nations do what they wish, while small nations suffer what they must.[11] From this perspective, knowledge as such seems to play little role in the history of politics; emphasis on the conditions of knowledge in political contexts may seem fruitless at best, antidemocratic at worst.

The hard distinction, though, between political and epistemological concerns has not always been present. One aim of this book is to reintroduce the discourse of "political epistemology"—by which I mean, in its broadest sense, a discourse concerned with the relationship between knowledge and freedom—by examining the period of its greatest crisis.[12] The separation of questions of knowledge and freedom is ours, a contingent phenomenon with its own history, including the late-twentieth-century effort to rethink the relationship in the work of Foucault and others. Even Hume, who in 1748 saw little in the course of human events but coercion—all power, no knowledge—was able to ask a different sort of question in his 1742 essay, "That Politics May Be Reduced to a Science."[13] Despite his skeptical reservations, Hume is optimistic about such an enterprise, reflecting a confident Enlightenment belief that everything, potentially, may be "reduced" to a science. The question of whether politics may be reduced to a science, which Godwin suggests above should be handled with great care, includes the question of whether human beings may be studied like birds and trees, resulting in knowledge on a par with the knowledge produced by the natural sciences. In the most ambitious logic of the eighteenth century, there is no reason to think that human beings, including their organization into social and political units, are immune in any way to the techniques of scientific inquiry.

The modern category of "political knowledge" begins, like many epistemic categories, with Francis Bacon, who by the nineteenth century would be hailed as a "great prophet of political knowledge."[14] In *De Augmentis Scientiarum* (1623), Bacon writes, "If my leisure time shall hereafter produce anything concerning political knowledge, the work will perchance be either abortive or posthumous. In the mean time, now that all the sciences are ranged as it were in their proper seats, lest so eminent a seat should be left entirely vacant, I have determined to mark as deficient only two parts of civil knowledge, which do not belong to the secrets of Empire, but have a wider and more common nature."[15] The two deficiencies of political knowledge as it then existed, he says, pertained to the expansion of empire (an obviously worthy goal for Bacon) and the foundation of justice. The phrase also appears in Locke's "Some Thoughts concerning Reading and Study for a Gentleman" (dictated 1703, published 1720), which recommends that the pursuit of political knowledge be undertaken by patriotic gentlemen and not scholars "who would be universally knowing."[16] The questions of what political knowledge is, how it is attained, who is best suited to acquire it, and whose interests it serves would be the dominant questions of political epistemology in the eighteenth century.

The phrase "political knowledge" appears in over a thousand published texts between 1700 and 1800, with a steady increase in use as the century progresses and with the highest concentration of use in the decade following the French Revolution. In the largest digital collection of eighteenth-century texts, just three published texts use the phrase in the first decade of the century; more than five hundred do so in its last decade.[17] The total number of publications in the period grew, of course, as literary culture became more widespread. Still, as a percentage of the total number of published texts, publications that use the phrase grew fivefold. More important than the frequency of its use, though, are the contexts in which it occurs. At the beginning of the century, political knowledge is associated with the most rudimentary forms of commercial knowledge, that is, with enough arithmetic to conduct transactions involving cattle, and so forth. As mercantilism becomes more fully established as a crucial component of British imperialism, the value placed on this commercial knowledge grows, as does its perceived complexity. A member of the Royal Society in 1734 proposes *A New Political Arithmetic: Containing Some Considerations Concerning Public Roads*, in which the author promises to show "to what a prodigious degree, a diligent inquirer, by pursuing it to a due extent, may carry the political knowledge of any kingdom, and the true secret of raising it to its greatest height of wealth and power."[18] In 1757, soon after the "Black Hole of Calcutta" and other imperial disasters, economist Malachy Postlethwayt writes in *Great Britain's True System* that he has "taken Occasion to shew, that if ever *Britons* will attain to the Mastery of Trade, and support the *commercial Dominion*, they must do it by their superior Skill and Address in the practical Arts, as well as in the political Knowledge of Commerce; and that more depends upon these than upon the sword."[19]

Though the association with commercial knowledge would persist throughout the century, "political knowledge" would eventually be seen as a legitimate branch of science in its own right, typically alongside categories such as "ecclesiastical," "historical," "metaphysical," and "natural" knowledge. By the middle of the century, there is a discernible sense that political knowledge is something capable of being systematized. Hume, as noted, is an early advocate of the project in his 1742 essay. A little more than a decade later, and three years after the first English translation of Montesquieu's *Spirit of the Laws* (1748, trans. 1750), he sounds an even more optimistic note: "The laws have, or ought to have, a constant reference to the constitution of government, the manners, the climate, the religion, the commerce, the situation of each society. A late author of genius, as well as extensive learning, has prosecuted this subject at large, and has established, from these principles, the best system of political knowledge, which, perhaps, has ever yet been communicated to the world."[20] By 1775, the discourse of political knowledge is sufficiently established for a *Politician's Dictionary; or, a Summary of Political Knowledge* to be published.[21] William Paley, the natural theologian important to the intellectual development of both Wordsworth and Coleridge, includes in his *Principles of Moral and Political Philosophy* (1785) a book on "The Elements of Political Knowledge," which addresses the standard issues of late-eighteenth-century political philosophy: the origin of civil government, the nature of political obligation, the different forms of government, the British constitution, and the nature of liberty and justice.[22]

Debates about political knowledge ranged from practical questions like who is best suited to acquire it (the radical *North Briton* claims in 1763 that the merchants of London "possess more honest, useful, political knowledge . . . than all the ministers of state ever discovered")[23] to aesthetic questions about the importance of the "political knowledge of the poet" (*The Sequel to the Congress of the Beasts: or, the Northern Election*, 1749)[24] to philosophical questions about whether political knowledge was speculative or not (Joseph Priestley, for example, insisted it was not).[25] There were also debates about whether political knowledge was inherently allied with the interests of particular political parties. Agriculturalist and politician George Dempster contends in 1760: "Since political knowledge began to extend itself, and since the publication of some ingenious works in that science, it is plain that the tide has run very high in favour of Whiggism" (*Reasons for Extending the Militia Acts to the Disarmed Counties of Scotland*),[26] registering an apparent alliance between the new science and the traditional sources of Whig support (proponents of parliamentary power, the aristocracy, and nonconformist Protestants). From the beginning of the century through 1790, the subject of "political knowledge" is addressed in the writing of a diverse array of eighteenth-century literary figures: John Arbuthnot, Lord Bolingbroke, John Trenchard and Thomas Gordon, Henry Fielding, Laurence Sterne, Hugh Blair, James Boswell, Tobias Smollett, Edward Gibbon, and Charlotte Smith, among others.

Throughout the century, questions of political knowledge are bound to questions of British national identity in general and to the British Empire and constitution in particular. The association with wealth and empire begins with the modern birth of the category in Bacon, as we have seen, and intensifies in the second half of the eighteenth century. The association with the English constitution is emphasized by writers like Joseph Priestley, Samuel Johnson, and, later, Edmund Burke. Johnson argues in *The Idler* (1761) for the unique suitability of the English constitution for the cultivation of political knowledge: "Political knowledge is forced upon us by the form of our constitution, and all the mysteries of government are discovered in the attack or defence of every minister. The original law of society, the rights of subjects, and the prerogatives of kings have been considered with the utmost nicety, sometimes profoundly investigated, and sometimes familiarly explained."[27] Johnson would also say in other contexts that "questioning is not the mode of conversation among gentleman," and his sense of decorum typically carried over into his views about investigations into the "mysteries of government." It would be a mistake, that is, to regard him as a champion of political vigilance and scrutiny. In the *Idler*, political knowledge is "forced upon us" by the very form of the English constitution, rendering the human and political subject passive in its acquisition. Like Priestley, Johnson distinguishes political knowledge from metaphysical speculation, which for both requires a subject that is both more active and more at leisure.

It is in the decade following the French Revolution, though, that the literature of political knowledge attains its most serious and urgent tone. The leading figures of 1790s radicalism—Thomas Hardy, Thomas Paine, John Thelwall, John Horne Tooke, William Godwin, William Frend, and other members of the London Corresponding Society and the Society for Constitutional Information—repeatedly assert the possibility of political knowledge and insist on its dissemination in their attempts to alter the fundamental structures of British society. At the same time, conservatives of the period insist, as Burke ultimately would, on its impossibility: in the words of one West Yorkshire preacher, "the reasons and motives; the hinges upon which most of the political movements turn, can be known only to those who are initiated in the mysteries of state."[28]

Among those who think that it is indeed possible, there is still, after at least a century of conceptual development, debate as to what political knowledge is exactly (a healthy sign for any discipline or branch of knowledge). In an argument for the dissemination of political knowledge, the American Tench Coxe in 1789 identifies political knowledge simply with the ability to distinguish between "proper and improper measures of government."[29] David Williams, founder of the Literary Fund, associates it in the same year with inquiries into "the construction of societies, the formation of laws, and the origin of public principles, passions, and manners."[30] Thomas Beddoes distinguishes it from medical knowledge, which concerns the powers of good or evil—"for what are temporal good and evil but the sum of painful and pleasurable sensations felt during life?"—and identifies it with "the knowledge of institutions, productive of good and evil."[31] Maria Edgeworth asserts in *Practical Education* (1798) that "the causes of the rise and fall of empires, the progress of human knowledge, and the great discoveries of superior minds, are the real links which connect the chain of political knowledge."[32]

Alongside Beddoes's confidence-inspiring specificity—political knowledge is "no other than the knowledge of institutions, productive of good and evil"—there are still formulations at the end of the century as ambiguous, and portentous, as those of Bacon and Locke in the seventeenth century. Thomas James Mathias, satirist and Italian scholar, writes in the preface to his *The Shade of Alexander Pope on the Banks of the Thames: A Satirical Poem* (1799): "With political knowledge, well or ill understood, is now involved everything which is valuable and worth preservation. Morality, religion, the laws, literature, our domestick safety, and individual property must perish in the common shipwreck."[33] The possible subsumption of every kind of valuable knowledge under the category of "political knowledge" is a noteworthy facet of much postrevolutionary writing, a precondition for the Romantic elevation of serious literature through its intimate alliance with political knowledge. Even in 1800, one finds assessments such as that of John Penn, grandson of William Penn: "Political knowledge is certainly the most valuable of all similar kinds of acquisition; but for that very reason we ought to ascertain precisely what it is; and we may find, that much of what has made Englishmen, during many years, decry and appear to hate their country, as well as extol its most determined enemies, is no more political, than the jargon of the schools before Bacon's time was philosophical, knowledge."[34] The category of political knowledge does indeed undergo development throughout the eighteenth century, but one important story is the fluctuating interests, assumptions, and attitudes that govern the interrogation of the concept itself. By the end of the century, inquiry into the concept seems to have come full circle, as in Penn's earnest attempt to ascertain exactly what political knowledge is; and there are also those, like Mathias, who sense that everything of value seems capable of being subsumed under the category. That the question of how to define it is still being posed, with more urgency than ever in the 1790s, is worth remembering.

In addition to persistent questions about how to define the field of political knowledge, there is an intensification of meta-debate in the period around other sorts of philosophical questions: the conditions of its possibility, its legitimacy as a science, and the methods of its acquisition. The conservative position, for the most part, remains simply to deny its possibility. In his sermon, *The Danger of Political Innovation and the Evils of Anarchy* (1792), clergyman and schoolmaster Thomas Bancroft insists that "the fancied possession of political knowledge is an idea, which cannot but be flattering to popular vanity."[35] On the other side of the Atlantic, Alexander Hamilton takes a different, though epistemologically modest, view in *The Federalist* (1787): "Though it cannot be pretended that the principles of moral and political knowledge have in general the same degree of certainty with those of mathematics; yet they have much better claims in this respect, than to judge from the conduct of men in particular situations, we should be disposed to allow them."[36] The standard of mathematical knowledge, the Archimedean point of Kant's first *Critique*, recurs in texts like Tunis Wortman's *Treatise, concerning Political Enquiry, and the Liberty of the Press* (1800): "If education can form the lawyer, mathematician, and divine, why cannot attention and application, render us proficient in political knowledge?"[37] This kind of comparative interdisciplinarity is characteristic of the age. It informs, for instance, the attention Wordsworth pays, in the same year as Wortman's treatise, to the knowledge of the "Man of science, the Chemist and Mathematician" in relation to the knowledge of the poet in the 1800 Preface to the *Lyrical Ballads*.

The legitimacy of political knowledge as a systematic and scientific discipline remains a noticeable concern for a number of other writers through the

1790s. "Political knowledge is, no doubt, in its infancy," writes Godwin in his *Enquiry concerning Political Justice* (1793), reiterating a sense of newness present at virtually every stage of the discipline's development.[38] There is still confusion as what to call "that science . . . which tends most to promote, both the good of the individual, and the prosperity of the state," a science Sir John Sinclair "venture[s] to give the name of Statistical Philosophy" in his 1793 *Specimens of Statistical Reports.*[39] Sinclair refers to a 1788 *Political Survey of the Present State of Europe* by Eberhard Zimmermann and observes of its antecedents: "It is now about forty years . . . that a branch of political knowledge, which has for its object the actual and relative power of the several modern states, the power arising from their natural advantages, the industry and civilization of their inhabitants, and the wisdom of their governments, has been formed, chiefly by German writers, into a separate science."[40] (Shelley, twenty-six years later in *A Philosophical View of Reform*, would echo this account of an emergent Germany, "rising with the fervor of a vigorous youth, to the assertion of those rights for which it has that desire arising from knowledge.")[41]

One witnesses here the self-conscious emergence of political science as a modern discipline, though the meaning of the term has changed considerably since the end of the eighteenth century (Sinclair's emphasis on statistical models has been preserved, with greater reference perhaps to what he calls measurable "prosperity" than to abstract "good"). In his *Rudiments of Political Science* (1796), Angus Macaulay argues against those, like Burke, who "indiscriminately reprobate all abstract reasoning in politics" and contends that "without [abstract] discussion, our political knowledge cannot be termed Scientific."[42] The conflict within the discipline, whatever one chooses to call it, between how things are and how things ought to be is one possible cause of its dissolution, or its division into quantitative and humanistic branches: there is, as Hume famously put it, simply no way to get from an "is" to an "ought." Throughout the Romantic period, though, there is, as we shall see, a palpable faith among many writers in the integrity of the discipline and in its ability to reconcile the claims of scientific description with those of ethical or political normativity.

Concurrent with the heightened sense in the 1790s of political knowledge as a legitimate branch of scientific knowledge is increased attention to the methods of its acquisition. Reflecting the primary split within eighteenth-century epistemology in general, debates about political knowledge predictably divide along rationalist and empiricist lines; or, as with Priestley, in terms of "speculative" as opposed to "non-speculative" knowledge. As early as the 1740s, there are those, including the staunchly empiricist Hume, who think that "the different operations and tendencies of . . . two species of government might be made apparent even *a priori*."[43] By the 1790s, this would be the minority position.

Writing on the subject in Britain is overwhelmingly empiricist, stressing the need for both personal and historical experience in the acquisition of political knowledge. In a sermon by Richard Valpy, published in 1793 "at the request of the High Sheriff and Grand Jury of the County of Berks," the schoolmaster warns against "metaphysical abstraction in a science like that of legislation" and insists that "political knowledge can only be the slow and progressive result of experience."[44] Valpy's remark is representative of an accommodationist strain of conservative thought on the subject: if one concedes the possibility of political knowledge at all, it is far preferable to argue for the more laborious empiricist route, which seems less threatening than the apparently quick gains of rationalist speculation. In the preface to an anonymous drama of the same year, *Modern Politics, or, the Cat Let out of the Pock: A Dialogue* (1793), the author complains of the want of "political knowledge in these pretended Friends of the People" and stresses the importance of history, "by which the sage and judicious composer of Political Institutions, is enabled to form notions of the future conduct of mankind, by his observation of the past, and thereby to fix his system upon experience, instead of trusting to untried theories."[45] The language of "untried theories" is a staple of postrevolutionary conservative discourse, indebted most of all to Burke and profoundly influential in subsequent conceptions of conservatism on both sides of the Atlantic (recall, for example, Lincoln's definition of conservatism as "adherence to the old and tried, against the new and untried").

The dominant issue by far in debates about political knowledge in the 1790s is its "dissemination," or "diffusion," regarded by some as the necessary precondition of global political emancipation and by others as the most serious threat to the established social order. The English response to the French Revolution, occurring at a time when they were still celebrating the centenary of their own revolution, accelerated the formation of reformist or revolutionary societies whose primary goal was almost always something like the "dissemination of political knowledge." The Society for Constitutional Information, founded by Major John Cartwright, asserted in 1790 that "the communication of sound political knowledge to the people at large must be of great national advantage; as nothing but ignorance of their natural rights, or inattention to the consequence of those rights to their interest and happiness, can induce the majority of the inhabitants of any country to submit to any species of civil tyranny."[46] The Society of Friends of the People, promoted by Charles James Fox to advance Whig principles, resolved in 1792 "that a Society be formed in Southwark for the cultivation and diffusion of Political Knowledge."[47] The Birmingham Society for Constitutional Information, founded in 1792, similarly resolved "that our immediate object be the acquisition and dissemination of political knowledge."[48] The Revolution Society, based in London and affiliated with the Norwich Revolution Society, looked back in the same year to the achievements of 1688 and encouraged its members to act "till political knowledge and the love of liberty shall be so general, that the prostitution of the public press to the united purposes and corrupting wealth of the worst men in this country, and the wretched fugitives from France, shall no longer be able to excite the ignorant fury of a misguided mob," indicating an association between knowledge and liberty that would become increasingly prevalent in the 1790s.[49] The York Society for Political Information in 1795 asserted "that the more ignorant men are of the nature of civil and political government, the more will they be in danger of suffering by imposition and oppression; and, that society must derive considerable benefit from the propagation of political knowledge amongst its members."[50] In the same year, the Friends of Liberty United for Promoting Constitutional Information resolved to work "for the purpose of disseminating political knowledge, and by that means obtaining a peaceful, but radical reform, in the Common's House of Parliament." They affixed their declaration of principles to a reprint of Richard Price's seminal 1776 pamphlet *Observations on the Nature of Civil Liberty and the Principles of Government* (Price, a liberal Dissenter and, for a time, the instructor of Mary Wollstonecraft, would famously spark the "Revolution Controversy" with his 1789 sermon, *A Discourse on the Love of Our Country*).[51]

The best known of these societies is the London Corresponding Society, which linked together many of the smaller societies and vigorously opposed the war with France. After crackdowns by the Pitt ministry in late 1793 and early 1794, the Society began to reconsider its tactics. By 1795, it was debating whether to confine its efforts solely to the dissemination of political knowledge as the most effective means of attaining a redress of grievances, especially the demands for universal suffrage and annual parliaments. The Society notes in 1795 that "the avidity of the public mind for political knowledge continues to increase, insomuch, that we find there is scarcely an individual, especially in towns and cities where men are pressed together, so that minds can come into contact; that is not in some degree animated with the desire of political enquiry."[52]

Opposition to these societies, especially in their disseminating capacities, was on the rise, from both traditional centers of state power and among certain segments of civil society. Thomas Paine in 1792 remarks upon the "dread [the court in which he was tried] felt at the progressive increase of political knowledge" resulting from the cheap edition of the *Rights of Man* (1791).[53] Lawyer and politician Patrick Duigenan charged the Whigs with distributing the same work "partly gratis, and partly at the low price of one penny; this they stiled 'disseminating political knowledge.'"[54] Duigenan's dismissal—reiterating a very real Tory concern about the association of political knowledge with Whig, to say nothing of radical, principles—works by calling into question the semantic content of the idea itself. The same strategy recurs in a 1799 report from the Committee of Secrecy of the House of Commons, in which a society of United Scotsmen was imputed with "disseminating what they termed, 'political knowledge.'"[55] Conservatives of the period shared a particular fondness for this kind of radical critique of language: a phrase consisting of two ordinarily intelligible words occasions a rudimentary hermeneutics of suspicion. It is a telling historical fact, and an ambiguous honor conferred upon philosophy, that an epistemic category should receive so much public attention and state scrutiny. Societies were formed with the avowed purpose "strenuously to oppose the establishment of societies for promoting the diffusion of political knowledge,"[56] though their efforts were largely belated. "The poor man has tasted the apple from the tree of political knowledge," an anonymous "lover of peace" writes in his *Comments on the Proposed War with France* (1793). Opposition to the dissemination of political knowledge would be allied with the "spirit of despotism" by figures like Vicesimus Knox, compiler of the *Elegant Extracts* important to Wordsworth and others in his generation.[57]

Civil society opposition to dissemination, then, was present but limited. It was from the state, in the 1794 treason trials, that the category of political knowledge faced its most serious challenge. The case of Thomas Hardy, founder of the London Corresponding Society, is representative. In the case for high treason made against him, the prosecution noted that "you will find [men like Hardy] inflaming the people under the pretence of enlightening them; debauching their principles towards their country, under pretence of infusing political knowledge; addressing themselves to those who, in the eye of the law, are as valuable as any, but who, from the nature of their education, are ignorant, and not able to distinguish between truth and misrepresentation."[58] A letter of correspondence exchanged among the various constitutional societies, allegedly in the hand of John Horne Tooke, would be used as evidence in the trials of both Tooke and Hardy. It contained the following radical profession of faith: "We believe that instructing the people in political knowledge, and in their natural and inherent rights as men, is the only effectual way to obtain the grand object of reform; for men need only be made acquainted with the abuses of government, and they will readily join in every lawful means to obtain a redress."[59]

Such faith, the philosophical roots of which are in Godwin, would be essential to early Romanticism. The association, though, between knowledge and liberty in 1790s political epistemology would persist long after the reputed loss of faith in the teleological Godwinian narrative. The self-reckoning among the radical left in the 1790s is the self-reckoning of Romanticism itself. The doubts raised by the professed friends of liberty in the last decade of the eighteenth century, in terms of both long-term tactics and fundamental principles, are the doubts of Romantic poetry. Letters such as this one to the London Corresponding Society, signed "*Vice Cotis*," indicate the tone and trajectory of this self-reckoning:

> How far your Society may, in any instance, have mistaken its own object, or individuals, by misunderstanding your principles, may have deviated into imprudent conduct, I neither know nor inquire. The advancement of political knowledge, the professed object of your society, should at all times be the leading wish of every generous heart. Mankind should consider it as that enlivening, yet trembling dawn, that precedes the more glorious period, when liberty shall shine with a steady lustre, and human happiness be raised on a durable basis.[60]

The final clause anticipates the political and epistemic engineering of book 10 of the 1805 *Prelude*, noted above. The "advancement of political knowledge," and its correlation with the advancement of liberty, would remain a central concern for the Romantics studied here, though they would at the same time continue the interrogation of the concept and the conditions of its possibility begun in the eighteenth century and given new life through Kant's transcendental philosophy.

What Eliot says of Tennyson's poetry is equally true of Romanticism's relationship with political knowledge and the faculty responsible for its acquisition: it is remarkable not because of the quality of its faith but because of the quality of its doubt. Such doubt can easily turn into stupidity (recall Auden's criticism of Tennyson as the "stupidest" of English poets), cynicism, solipsism, or reaction. These are real aspects of Romanticism, and the narrative of apostasy has been pursued, over the past few decades, by critics from E. P. Thompson to Charles Mahoney.[61] My interests here lie slightly further afield: how early Romanticism inherits a problem of knowledge that was already a problem of freedom; how the rhetoric of the Revolution controversy is conditioned by particular epistemological assumptions; how political knowledge affects our understanding of Romantic faculty psychology; how the relationship between knowledge and freedom governs some of the period's most ambitious poems; and, as I shall turn to now, how the Romantic critique of political reason, the stage for which was set by the eighteenth-century debates about political knowledge just discussed, has had a rich afterlife in the history of ideas, the social sciences, and literary criticism.

Contexts: Intellectual History, Political Theory, and Romantic Studies

"Since the nineteenth century, Western thought has never stopped laboring at the task of criticizing the role of reason—or the lack of reason—in political structures."[62] This is Foucault in 1979, from the opening of his Tanner lectures at Stanford University. (Foucault's focus in these lectures is on the classical and early modern roots of political rationality; the role of Romanticism in facilitating such a preoccupation is not addressed.) Just as Romantic critiques of political reason took many, often contradictory, forms, so has subsequent commentary surrounding political reason been voluminous and varied. I can provide here only a partial sketch of the relevant literature, which includes figures as diverse as Max Horkheimer and Michael Oakeshott. With that in mind, I organize the most germane interlocutors and texts under three headings: intellectual history, political theory and sociology, and Romantic studies.

Within a domain as large as the history of ideas, one is bound to adopt something like an arbitrary method of presentation. In this case, it is to work through a series of intellectual pairs that have something to say to each other, within each pairing, and as a pair to the narrative of political reason and Romanticism I am attempting to sketch. The first is Michel Foucault and Noam Chomsky, whose 1971 debate on human nature marked out the distinct approach to knowledge and politics each would pursue for the rest of his career. The debate centers on a disagreement about the notion of creativity in the history of knowledge. Near the beginning of the debate, Chomsky alludes to the concept of internalized form, or free creation within a system of rule, developed by Wilhelm von Humboldt. Foucault, not inclined to let the concept of free creation go unchecked, discerns two directions of analysis: one that sees the construction of knowledge in terms of collective and complex transformations in institutions, practices, and rules and one that is based on an original inventor discovering the truth, a view he associates in this debate with "a certain 'romanticism' about the history of science."[63] Chomsky clarifies that he means a more mundane kind of creativity than Foucault imagines: not the achievements of a Newton but the kind of ordinary human creativity a child exhibits in adapting to new situations or learning a language. Chomsky had developed von Humboldt's notion of free creation within a system of rule earlier that year in his Cambridge lectures in honor of Bertrand Russell, published as *Problems of Knowledge and Freedom* (1971). Chomsky's Cambridge lectures, discussed in greater detail in the next chapter, emphasize a concept of freedom he sees at the heart of Russell's work and, he suggests, at the heart of a strain within early Romanticism.

For his part, Foucault developed his model of political rationality throughout the 1970s, giving it its fullest expression in his 1979 Tanner lectures cited above, *"Omnes et Singulatim*: Toward a Critique of Political Reason." Acknowledging the evident relationship between rationalization and excesses of political power, Foucault rejects both the Kantian approach of putting reason on trial and the Frankfurt School approach of investigating the origins of political rationalism in the Enlightenment. He proposes instead to outline the origin of a "pastoral modality of power" in ancient and early modern texts and describes the specific kinds of knowledge on which pastoral power depends. These are large issues about which much could be said, but I would like, for now, merely to note the following: the affinity between the concept of free creation within a system of rule developed by Chomsky and the notion of freedom as self-legislation formulated by Kant; Foucault's criticism of a "romanticism" in the history of knowledge that places undue emphasis on free creation; and, finally, the correlation between rationalism and excessive political power that Foucault joins the figures covered in this study in recognizing as an evident and pressing problem.

The problems discussed by Chomsky and Foucault have long been debated by intellectual historians, a group that has traditionally had an unusually strong interest in Romanticism.[64] Two such historians, in particular, are relevant here: Bertrand Russell and Isaiah Berlin. Russell devotes a substantial portion of his *History of Western Philosophy* (1945) to the Romantic period. As his chapter on Byron demonstrates, Russell's attitude toward Romanticism is essentially hostile, seeing in its tendencies toward irrationalism the roots of modern nationalism and totalitarianism. Romanticism, he says, is characterized above all by a "substitution of aesthetic for utilitarian standards."[65] In Russell's damning assessment: "It is not the psychology of the Romantics that is at fault; it is their standard of values. They admire strong passions, of no matter what kind, and whatever may be their social consequences. . . . Hence the type of man encouraged by Romanticism, especially of the Byronic variety, is violent and anti-social, an anarchic rebel or a conquering tyrant."[66] Russell's assessment is insufficient for a number of reasons, as I hope will become clear in what follows. As we shall see, the standard of utility persists through second-generation Romanticism, so that Shelley can observe with approbation in his *Philosophical View of Reform* that the result of political philosophy has been to establish "the principle of Utility as the substance & liberty & equality as the forms, according to which the concerns of human life ought to be administered."[67] More fundamentally, this study challenges Russell's association of Romanticism, even of the Byronic variety, with irrationalism. Like other purported members of what used to be called the "Satanic" School of Romanticism, Byron modifies an inherited model of reason that he does not seek to do away with altogether. Like his great predecessor in satire, Swift, he is inclined rather to attack the abuse of reason in order to defend it, or in Kant's terms, to "secure its rightful claims while dismissing all groundless pretensions." The critiques of political reason undertaken by other Romantics similarly seek to correct the abuses of rationalism in order to ground certain political values more squarely on it.

Where Russell is quite obviously hostile to the general project of Romanticism—with the possible exception of Shelley, with whom he, like Friedrich Engels, was obsessed as a young man—Isaiah Berlin has a more conflicted relation to it. Attracted to its emphasis on positive liberty yet ultimately suspicious of the forms positive liberty might take, Berlin sees Romanticism as irreducibly double-edged. Like Russell, Berlin discerns epistemological roots in Romantic conceptions of freedom. For Berlin, though, these roots lie not in Romanticism's alleged irrationalism, but in its nondescriptive idealism. It was not until the end of the eighteenth century, he contends, that it became clear that "certain questions, about what men should be or do, might differ logically from questions of fact; and that the methods of obtaining answers to them were in principle not like scientific inquiries, voyages of discovery, however peculiar and unique." In his 1952 Bryn Mawr lectures, posthumously published as *Political Ideas in the Romantic Age* (2006), Berlin argues: "It is during [the Romantic period] that, for the first time, there begins to emerge the notion that perhaps value judgments are not descriptive propositions at all, that values are not discoverable, that they are not ingredients of the real world in the sense in which tables or chairs or men or colours or past events are, that values are not discovered but invented—created by men like works of art, of which it is senseless to ask where they were before they were conceived."[68] The aesthetic creation of values, ends, and purposes—not their scientific discovery a priori or a posteriori—is for Berlin how Romanticism overcomes the rationalist-empiricist divide. In this, he is in accord with Russell's emphasis on the Romantic substitution of aesthetic for other standards.

But just as Russell's Romanticism is essentially Byronism, so is Berlin's Romanticism essentially German Romanticism, with Fichte as its most representative figure. The British Romantics, though, are, in everything but their most abstruse musings, not thoroughgoing idealists, and certainly not in their political prose and major poetry. Knowledge and value are not simply thought into existence, nor do they exist in the world like tables and chairs. The Romantics studied here adopt a more nuanced and less dogmatic view. The things of the highest value, Wordsworth suggests in "Tintern Abbey," are half-created and half-perceived, a reciprocity at the heart of the "spousal verse" the poet aspires to create; in the similarly reciprocal language of Coleridge's "Dejection" ode, "we receive but what we give, / And in our life alone does nature live" (47–48), lines that suggest a more delicate transaction between subject and object than the self-positing of Fichte or the *Naturphilosophie* of Schelling. The freedom offered by post-Kantian idealism was too extreme for the English Romantics, who retained enough of an empirical sensibility—and who had a sufficiently troubled relationship with the French Revolution—to approach with care extreme reconfigurations of what subjects and objects were in the first place. While sympathetic in their most radical moods to the creation of value out of self-positing consciousness that Berlin associates with German

Romanticism, the English Romantics on the whole work within models of political reason and rational liberty more rooted in eighteenth-century theories of knowledge and more responsive to the political circumstances differentiating Britain from Jena at the turn of the century.

The final pair of intellectual historians—as with Foucault and Chomsky, the term is used loosely—I wish to introduce here is in some ways the strangest: Michael Oakeshott and Max Horkheimer. Oakeshott's influential essay "Rationalism in Politics" appeared in the same year as Horkheimer's *Eclipse of Reason* and the revised edition of the *Dialectic of Enlightenment* (1947).[69] Together, these texts constitute a significant moment in the history of political reason and its critique. Oakeshott's essay joined a wave of conservative attacks, from a variety of intellectual traditions, against instrumental reason in the 1940s. His Burkean argument in "Rationalism in Politics" is that all of politics has become "rationalist," by which he means based on the kind of knowledge one can find in books, and that this is a cause of great concern: rationalism is a "disease" that destroys all sense of what Burke describes as the partnership between the present and the past. The argument is premised on a distinction between two types of knowledge: "technical" knowledge, which is capable of formulation, and "practical" knowledge, which is not. In Oakeshott's view, rationalism asserts that technical knowledge is the only true type of knowledge and attempts to govern accordingly. It neglects the kind of practical knowledge that is inexpressible (though he insists he refers to nothing like "esoteric" knowledge). The essay opens with a portrait—really a caricature—of "the Rationalist" Oakeshott has in mind, who among other abhorrent characteristics "has no sense of the cumulation of experience" and exhibits a "deep distrust of time."[70]

Godwin, Bentham, Marx, and Engels are for Oakeshott the great representatives of the type, though it has its roots in Descartes and Bacon. The knowledge of the Rationalist, in Oakeshott's opinion, will never be more than "half-knowledge," because "like a foreigner or a man out of his social class, he is bewildered by a tradition and a habit of behavior of which he knows only the surface."[71] Oakeshott's classist dismissal of half-knowledge is strange given his earlier remark in the essay that the Rationalist "has none of that *negative capability* (which Keats attributed to Shakespeare), the power of accepting the mysteries and uncertainties of experience without any irritable search for order and distinctness."[72] Setting aside the fact that Keats's politics would have made him unsympathetic to Oakeshott's diluted Burkeanism, Keats approvingly uses the term "half-knowledge," in his letter to George and Tom Keats, immediately after the description of negative capability alluded to by Oakeshott. The "half-knowledge" Oakeshott ridicules is part of the literary tradition he seeks to enlist. That Keats is making a claim about the poet, and not the statesman or citizen, under ideal circumstances does not seem to matter to Oakeshott. The caricature of political rationalism he condemns exists largely within the parameters of his own polemic.[73]

In the same year that Oakeshott diagnosed an excessive faith in reason as the most pressing political problem of the time, Max Horkheimer mounted a more radical critique of reason in his *Eclipse of Reason* and, with Theodor Adorno, in the revised edition of the *Dialectic of Enlightenment* (1947). Whereas Oakeshott had posited a model of political reason vitiated beyond recognition as a way to discredit it in general, the central figures of Frankfurt School never abandoned their fundamental commitment to the social value of Enlightenment reason, even as they were intensely critical both of its self-destructive tendencies and of what passed for reason in the modern era. As early as his 1942 essay on "Reason and Self-Preservation," Horkheimer reflected on the separation of subject and object as the epistemic precondition of capitalism: "Since Descartes, bourgeois philosophy has been a single attempt to make knowledge serve the dominant means of production, broken through only by Hegel and his kind."[74] In the *Eclipse of Reason*, Horkheimer differentiates "objective" reason, concerned with ends, from "subjective" reason, concerned with self-preservation, self-realization, and utility. The task of philosophy, he says, "is not stubbornly to play the one against the other, but to foster a mutual critique and thus, if possible, to prepare in the intellectual realm the reconciliation of the two in reality."[75] Horkheimer frequently stresses the privileged role of *Vernunft* in reconciling contradictions. The contradiction between subject and object is especially important for Horkheimer, as the irrational domination of the object by the subject—the problem, we might note in passing, at the core of "The Rime of the Ancient Mariner"—extends beyond humans' domination of nature into their relations with other subjects, who, as Kant had worried in his *Critique of Practical Reason* (1788), would be treated as means, objects, or commodities themselves. The philosophical problem is a real, political one, though Horkheimer argues in the *Eclipse of Reason* that rationality can provide no concrete plans for political action. Classical liberalism and Burkean conservatism were obviously not viable alternatives for the Frankfurt School, who, as Martin Jay notes, were forced to confront the fact that "the union of freedom as reason and as self-realizing action was split asunder. The Frankfurt School, following its initial instincts, could only choose reason, even in the muted, negative form in which it might be found in the administered nightmare of the twentieth century."[76] The administered nightmare of the twentieth century, of which concentration and internment camps are only the most extreme manifestations, is, with Robespierre's Reign of Terror, a standard reference point for critics of political reason, the point at which the faculty promising enlightenment and freedom becomes the vehicle of terror and cruelty.

I have grouped the above figures under the heading of intellectual history because, despite having roots in fields like linguistics or social research, each of them frames his ideas about reason in politics largely within the context of the history of philosophy. This is less true of Régis Debray and Andreas Glaeser, who adopt approaches more firmly rooted in the social sciences and who address the categories of political reason and political epistemology more directly. Régis Debray is an unusual figure: a former student of Louis Althusser, he traveled to Cuba in 1961, where he wrote on guerrilla strategies and taught philosophy, and then to Bolivia in 1967, where he collaborated with Che Guevara and was consequently sentenced to thirty years in prison (he was released after three years in 1970). Debray's *Critique of Political Reason* (1981) is a strange, at times trenchant, work of political theory. It argues, following Althusser, that political practice can only exist in and under ideology, but adds that knowledge of the ideological order is to be sought within the religious order, which Debray claims traditional political science has failed to do. "The classical political science of regimes and institutions has shown itself to be as powerless before the internal logic of politics as the old psychology of the faculties of the soul was in the face of the realities of mental life."[77] The realities of mental life and the realities of political life are analogous for Debray, who introduces, in the same year as Jameson's seminal study, the "political unconscious" as a way to describe the social dreams of which "religions and their ideological substitutes are the most obvious symptoms." Part of this political unconscious, Debray suggests, is the Prometheus myth, the crucial facts of which have been elided in its Romantic retellings (Shelley, Byron, and Longfellow all tried their hand at it, and it was the favorite myth of Marx). "The pious imagery of the Promethean spirit of conquest, which the nineteenth century found so intoxicating, misses this detail: in the original myth, the theft of fire is a stop-gap measure and Prometheus is the ambiguous hero of a partial success."[78] In the narrative of Protagoras, Prometheus failed in his original intention to steal the art of politics from the gods to give to man; Zeus's subsequent pity for humankind led him to provide them with a sense of justice, but he reserved for himself the secrets of managing power. "Everything in the myth hangs together," Debray says, "and it is still hanging around our necks."[79] The albatross of political reason in the Romantic period is in many ways the Prometheus myth, in its Protagorean form the story of the limits of emancipating knowledge when divorced from the art of politics. Romantic retellings of the myth such as Shelley's are, like the mariner's blessing of the water-snakes, the means by which the subject seeks to unburden itself.

The "political epistemology" proposed by Andreas Glaeser in *Political Epistemics: The Secret Police, the Opposition, and the End of East German Socialism* (2010) takes a more empirical approach than Debray's earlier *Critique of Political*

Reason, though it is similarly reluctant to inquire abstractly into the conditions of political knowledge. Rather, like Debray, Glaeser wishes to investigate how people in particular historical contexts "actually form and interrogate what to them *appears* as valid understanding."[80] Noting that while the component terms of "political epistemology" are familiar enough, their conjunction is not, Glaeser describes it as a field that brings together three trajectories within the social sciences: the sociology of knowledge (in the traditions of Marx, Durkheim, and Mannheim); post-Mertonian sociology of science; and "archaeologies" and "genealogies" of knowledge in the tradition of Foucault. In Glaeser's analysis of East German socialism, power holders are compelled to restrain their desire to manipulate the validation of knowledge that is the source of their power, and knowledge-producers are compelled to act on the basis of imperfect concepts and methods, "lest their desire to constantly refine and qualify knowledge suffocate any possibility to renew knowledge experientially."[81] The present study is an effort, in part, to understand the Romantic prehistory of the political epistemology Glaeser describes.[82] In their interest in the conditions or principles of political knowledge, figures like Coleridge and Shelley formulated an incipient sociology of knowledge—one that sought to integrate shared epistemological concerns with shared concerns about liberty, justice, and the effects of social and political institutions on the imaginative life.

Finally, Romanticists have long been interested in both the politics and epistemology of the period, though, as suggested above, typically in isolation. The philosophical current within Romantic studies is among the most distinguished and coherent lines of twentieth-century criticism and requires little exposition here: Northrop Frye, Earl Wasserman, M. H. Abrams, Alfred Cobban, Geoffrey Hartman and other members of the Yale School, Thomas McFarland, Laurence Lockridge, and James Engell, among others, all share a commitment to the history of philosophy, especially philosophies of the mind and knowledge, as an indispensable tool in the study of Romanticism. More recent works have sharpened the intellectual focus of the field on specific traditions within the history of philosophy—on, for instance, aesthetics, materialism, and pragmatism—in their examinations of the period's major figures.[83] Historically oriented critics—from Marilyn Butler and Nicholas Roe to David Bromwich and James Chandler—have grounded the drama of ideas in Romanticism in social and political contexts, providing a salutary corrective to what can be a kind of intellectual formalism. The present work builds on both traditions, philosophical and historical, though its emphasis remains on the self-grounding of Romantic theories of the mind in the concrete realities of power, right, authority, obligation, and freedom. The Romantic critique of political reason is in many ways a Kantian enterprise, though, as I hope to show, it takes from the "age of criticism" that Kant describes what it needs to confront the political and aesthetic circumstances of the moment. The chapters on philosophy and political prose are not a bracketing of aesthetic concerns, but an analysis of the conditions under which aesthetic creation, among other sorts of freedom, is considered possible. Of the authors studied here, Wordsworth and Shelley are the most sensitive to the political conditions of artistic vibrancy—and to the correlations between political and cultural debasement—though it is a concern for each figure (even in Burke, the encroachments of political reason threaten to disrupt the conditions of stability necessary for cultural activity). In short, this work aims to bridge two pillars of Romantic criticism by examining a critique of political reason that is foundational to both.

Cases of Romanticism

The first chapter, "Kant and the Revolutionary Settlement of Early Romanticism," is a conceptual introduction to the topic and addresses the connection between Romantic politics and Romantic epistemology by examining the relationship between the two revolutionary traditions that Romanticism inherits. Kant's critical system of the 1780s and the revolution begun in France in 1789 initiate two trajectories that would cross many times throughout the Romantic period. The energy of early Romantic literature, of which I take Wordsworth's *Prelude* of 1805 to be exemplary, largely derives from how it assimilates and synthesizes these two traditions. The trial of political reason staged in the later books of *The Prelude* is an imaginative extension of the trial of pure reason staged in Kant's *Critique of Pure Reason* (1781, 1787), a work its author describes as a "court of justice, by which reason may secure its rightful claims while dismissing all its groundless pretensions."[64] Just as Kant often describes his Copernican revolution in philosophy in the terms of freedom and justice, so does the political literature of the period represent the French Revolution as an epistemological break, a new claim about what kinds of knowledge are available to the political subject. Kant's own views on the revolution in France, contained in *The Conflict of the Faculties* and other texts, suggest other important links between the historical event and Kant's own philosophical project—for example, through his reflections on the "a priori" and "terroristic" manners of representing history. The a priori had by the end of the eighteenth century become a political concept: independence from experience would become both the dream and the nightmare of early Romantic poetry. As one of the most ambitious forms of Romantic freedom, independence from experience is at the center of the period's various critiques of political reason. The Kantian orientation introduced in this chapter runs throughout the study: in Coleridge's distinction between reason and understanding, in Shelley's dramatic representation of the forms of human thought, in Wollstonecraft's vindication of political reason, even in Burke's consideration of the possibility of a priori political knowledge and the limits of political reason.

Following the conceptual orientations of part 1, the rest of the book is structured according to genre and chronology: the second part examines a public debate in the "high rhetorical" tradition and a philosophical treatise of the 1790s; the third part, political prose, with a focus on middle-period texts of the first-generation Romantics; the fourth part, poetry and poetics, with a focus on poems published in 1814 and 1820.

"The Rhetoric of Hurly-Burly Innovation" studies the most immediate origins of Romanticism's critique of political reason in the "Revolution Controversy." The first two chapters in the section examine the debate between Edmund Burke and Mary Wollstonecraft. These two figures develop the terminology and contours of an argument that would persist throughout the Romantic period (often, as with Wordsworth and Coleridge, within a single author's career). The concept of "political knowledge" is unintelligible for Burke, whose *Reflections on the Revolution in France* (1790) vigorously contends that politics is not an a priori science and criticizes any operation of "political reason" that exceeds the bounds of induction and computation; it is an argument against what he dismissively refers to as "political metaphysics." The things of the highest value, for Burke, remain immune to the leveling impulse of political rationalism. Burke's *Reflections* has a conflicted, even contradictory, attitude toward the faculty of reason, a tension reflected in the essay's frequent use of paradox. The Burke of the *Reflections*, though, is one Burke of many. The chapter begins with a treatment of his 1783 speech on Fox's East India Bill, discerning in the hypotactic language of that speech the judicious temperament that for Burke always stops short of knowledge in political contexts.

Wollstonecraft's reply to Burke, the *Vindication of the Rights of Men* (1790), mounts an impassioned defense of political reason. The passions are the "necessary auxiliaries of reason" for Wollstonecraft, who, in contrast to what she sees as the empty sentimentality of Burke, grounds her vindication in a conception of knowledge bound to feeling, or the "rational affections." The rational affections are constructed by looking inward. Wollstonecraft's first *Vindication* sets a political and epistemic course for an inward turn that would persist in British literature for decades. The implications of that turn in this text, building in part on a set of associations developed in Burke's earlier *Enquiry* (1757), extend to aesthetics, gender relations, class hierarchy, and the sources of authority and obligation. Many of the predominant concerns of Romanticism begin here, in a vindication of rights that is simultaneously a vindication of reason. Coleridge's elaborate reconfiguration of the mental faculties, Wordsworth's provisional embrace of empiricism in politics and his emphasis on the objective value of subjective tranquillity, Shelley's philosophical narrative of British history and his dramatic representation of the mutability of human thought—all of these have their roots in a larger debate about knowledge and freedom, evident in the exchange between Burke and Wollstonecraft, occasioned by the French Revolution.

The third chapter in this part, "The Government of the Tongue: Godwin's Linguistic Turns and the Artillery of Reason," begins with an account of the political rationalism of the climactic text of eighteenth-century political epistemology, *An Enquiry concerning Political Justice* (1793, 1796, 1798). Godwin offers the most thorough and systematic argument in the period for the necessarily conjoined progress of knowledge and freedom. Even as he adheres to empiricism in strictly epistemological contexts, he wishes to emancipate political knowledge from the limits placed on it by experience, sensation, habit, and sentiment. An autonomous reason, for Godwin, is the only faculty that can provide us with the kind of knowledge that brings with it liberty and justice. The turn to the mind in *Political Justice* is accompanied by a simultaneous turn to language, a strategy continued in *Cursory Strictures* (1794). "There is no branch of virtue," Godwin writes, "more essential than that which consists in giving language to our thoughts," and, therefore, the "virtuous economy of speech" is "our perpetual affair."[85] In both texts, Godwin pays special attention to the various ways in which speech is governed and sees in this government of speech—both its virtuous cultivation and its vicious abuse—the determination of opinion that is the basis of his system. *Cursory Strictures* tests some of the core principles of *Political Justice*, but it maintains its insistence on the frank language of sincerity as the precondition of political reform.

The next part, "The Literature of Justice and Justification," examines the political prose of Coleridge and Wordsworth. Both chapters in this part demonstrate how middle-period texts like *The Friend* (1809–10, 1818) and *The Convention of Cintra* (1809) complicate a critical narrative of apostasy that tends to focus on the first and last political statements of each author. The section of *The Friend* titled "On the Principles of Political Knowledge" is the most systematic exposition of Coleridge's political thought, arguing that each major development in the history of political philosophy corresponds to a distinct set of assumptions about the human mind. The first chapter in this part demonstrates how Coleridge, particularly through his deep engagement with Hume, develops a conception of the understanding as the central faculty of his own political epistemology, with important effects on his conception of the conditions of knowledge more generally. For the mind to know certain things—more precisely, for the mind to have an idea of any real importance, such as substance, God, property, obligation, contract, or the perfect state—it must rely on the mediating capacity of the understanding, defined in *The Friend* as the expedient faculty of "suiting measures to circumstances." In its emphasis on the significance of the understanding, this chapter challenges the idea that the fundamental dialectic in the Romantic hierarchy of mental faculties is between reason and the creative imagination. The understanding may fit uneasily into this dialectic—where, in a Blakean context, the struggle between Urizen and Orc contains the most drama—but it is nevertheless, for Coleridge, essential to the art of governing and being governed.

In the same year that Coleridge was writing *The Friend*, Wordsworth was writing the *Convention of Cintra* (1809), a work that has been rightly recognized as one of the masterworks of English Romantic prose. The second chapter in this part, "The State of Knowledge: Wordsworth's Political Prose," places *Cintra* in the context of the poet's other major political writings, the *Letter to the Bishop of Llandaff* (1793) and the *Two Addresses to the Freeholders of Westmorland* (1818). It argues that the political crisis Wordsworth presents is ultimately an epistemological crisis: a failure on the part of statesmen to attain what he calls "higher knowledge." Wordsworth's argument that "it is plain *à priori* that the minds of Statesmen and Courtiers are unfavorable to the growth of this knowledge" involves a distinction between empirical knowledge "which must be *met*" and other kinds of knowledge "which may be *brought*." If it is to be just, political knowledge, he suggests, must be exercised through knowledge founded upon sensation. Wordsworth here displays the same distrust of political rationalism exhibited by Coleridge in *The Friend* and, earlier, in Burke's *Reflections*. Like Coleridge's emphasis on the understanding, Wordsworth's emphasis on a particular kind of empiricism in politics is an attempt to construct the kinds of epistemic precautions that would have prevented the perceived mistake of his own radicalism and perhaps even the excesses of the French Revolution itself. Wordsworth's most penetrating political writing does not renounce "French principles" altogether but discriminates between early and late revolutionary principles and advocates an active empiricism in the subject's understanding of them.

The poetry and poetics of the Romantic critique of political reason, as represented in the works of Wordsworth and Shelley, are the subjects of the final part, "Poetry and Poetics of the Excursive and Unbound Mind." The first chapter in this part, "The Dwellers of the Dwelling: Wordsworth and the Poetry of Recompense," begins with the poet's most precise epistemological formulation, stated in the 1802 Preface to *Lyrical Ballads*: pleasure is the condition of all knowledge. The chapter, then, addresses the following questions: what kind of pleasure does poetry produce, and how does this pleasure produce politically relevant forms of knowledge? Wordsworth's *Recluse* poetry, I argue, revolves around a kind of pleasure directly linked to Hellenistic conceptions of tranquility. *Home at Grasmere* (composed 1800–1806) offers Wordsworth's fullest meditation on how the achievement of tranquil pleasure is an act of justice or recompense; *The Excursion* (1814), a poem about the limits of philosophy and the promise of poetry in the face of political disappointment, examines how the tranquil pleasure offered by the schools of Hellenistic philosophy is both a right and an obstacle when isolated from other ends. The chapter illustrates how tranquillity is for Wordsworth, as it was for the Epicureans, a kind of pleasure and how it is, as it was for the Stoics, the only true source of liberty. Freedom becomes identical with a certain kind of rational submission, and, in Lucretian terms, the "inner citadel of the spirit" becomes the only true freedom because it is incapable of invasion. Wordsworth's *Recluse* poems continue to think about the premise (and the promise) of *The Prelude*: that social freedom might be built on the freedom of the individual mind, marked here by the pleasures of tranquillity and the freedom offered by the mind's "excursive power."

The excursive mind represented in Wordsworth's poetry is pushed to its limits in the more radically unbound mind of Shelley's poetry and prose, the subjects of the next chapter, "P. B. Shelley and the Forms of Thought." Beginning with a reassessment of a commonplace of Shelley criticism—that the poet is a skeptical idealist—I propose a richer conception of Shelley's theory of the mind that is grounded in the conjunction of politics and epistemology evident in his prose. Just as Coleridge had argued in *The Friend* that each division of political philosophy is accompanied by a set of assumptions about the human mind, so does Shelley contend in *A Philosophical View of Reform* (composed 1819–20) that the history of politics and the history of philosophy are inextricably linked. In a virtuosic history of what he calls "political knowledge," again echoing Coleridge, Shelley suggests the limits of skeptical idealism, especially as a philosophical position somehow "suited" to the project of reform. The doctrine of skeptical idealism, still the default philosophical position assigned to Shelley by critics, offers us little help in contending with a poem as complex as *Prometheus Unbound*, written around the same time as *A Philosophical View of Reform*. Intended by Shelley to familiarize the imagination with "beautiful idealisms of moral excellence," the poem is perhaps the most ambitious of the period's many epistemological courts of justice. The constitutive movements of the poem—collection and dispersion, or condensation and evaporation—derive from Shelley's picture of the mind, given shape here in the protean "atmosphere of human thought" that pervades the entire poem. The movement of the poem revolves around the knowledge of necessity, exchanged between Prometheus and mortals in reciprocal acts of emancipation.

It should be evident from the preceding chapter descriptions what sort of book this is: a study that integrates intellectual history, literary history, and, at times, formal analysis to offer an account, or a reading, of certain currents within British Romanticism, namely politics and epistemology, with a special emphasis on where and how those currents converge. It is perhaps necessary at this point to note as well what this book is not. It is not a comprehensive account of Romanticism or of philosophical or political writing during the Romantic period. Even for the story I wish to tell, there are a number of important figures who do not receive sustained attention here: Thomas Paine, John Thelwall, William Blake, Thomas De Quincey, William Hazlitt, John Keats, and, in truth, any number of the poets and thinkers we have come to associate with British Romanticism, to say nothing of their contemporaries in Germany, France, or America. I have focused on this particular set of authors because they seemed to me to be the most relevant and because the literature they produced is, I think, especially rewarding to study together. This is also not a book about Romantic criticism. I have kept references to other critics to a minimum for a number of reasons, not the least of which is the hope that this book will appeal to nonspecialists whose primary interests lie outside the current state of Romantic studies. When I refer to other critics, it is because I think their work is valuable and because I am indebted to them.

The following chapters, viewed together, show that the singular "critique" of the book's title applies only in a broad sense, insofar as this group of writers shared a set of terms and concerns in their reassessment of the roles that reason and knowledge are to play in public life: they all "put reason on trial" in some way or another. But, as will become clear, they do so in strikingly different terms. What we see are multiple critiques of political reason in the period, from a variety of ideological positions. We may place, according to convention, Burke on one end of the spectrum and Godwin, Wollstonecraft, and Shelley on the other; Wordsworth and Coleridge occupy middle positions. It is true enough to say, also according to convention, that Wordsworth and Coleridge begin their careers as radicals and end them as conservatives, though, as I hope to show, Wordsworth is not entirely deluded when he says in 1816, "In nothing are my *principles* changed" (Coleridge would similarly emphasize the consistency of his principles around the same time). It is for this reason that Wordsworth and Coleridge are perhaps the most nuanced, interesting political thinkers studied here. I hope that what follows brings out the complexity of each figure's conception of the connections between issues of knowledge and issues of freedom, between the project of enlightenment and the project of emancipation. Most of all, I hope that what follows does justice to the seriousness and urgency with which they thought and wrote about them.

CONCEPTUAL ORIENTATIONS

CHAPTER ONE

Kant and the Revolutionary Settlement of Early Romanticism

•

If the basis of a popular government in peacetime is virtue, its
basis in a time of revolution is virtue and terror—virtue, without
which terror would be barbaric; and terror, without which virtue
would be impotent.
                    —*Robespierre, "Report on the Principles of Political Morality,"*
                                                    February 5, 1794

Thoughts without content are empty, intuitions without concepts
are blind.
                    —*Kant,* The Critique of Pure Reason, *1781*

The possibility and legitimacy of "political knowledge" were, as we have seen,
intensely contested issues in eighteenth-century Britain: by the end of the
century, the dissemination of this knowledge was seen by some as "the only
effectual way to obtain the grand object of reform" and by others as the surest
way to debauch the people's feelings toward their country. Despite the volume
of attention it received, and despite occasional efforts to think about it in critical or abstract terms, political knowledge for these British writers remained
fairly straightforward: it included knowledge of things like institutions, history,
and rights (even if the "knowledge" of rights presents epistemological problems that institutional or historical knowledge does not). In Oakeshott's terms,
it consisted of the kind of "technical" knowledge capable of being expressed
in books. On the Continent, though, the association of knowledge and politics
had assumed a historically different cast. It was part of a larger and more systematic exploration of the relationship between human reason and human
freedom, an association that had been reintroduced by Renaissance humanists
such as Pico della Mirandola and Pietro Pomponazzi.[1] This more systematic
exploration of reason and freedom reached a high point in Kant, who dramatically
extended the range and significance of the faculty as it had been formulated in
the dominant Wolffian paradigm of the time.

   Late-eighteenth-century debates about "political knowledge" in Britain,
that is, provided one way of thinking about the conjunction of epistemology
and politics in the period. The purpose of this chapter is to think about their

convergence in the early Romantic period through the philosophical achievement of Kant in the 1780s and through the political achievement of France in 1789. "Early Romanticism" in Britain—a phrase, to be clear, I use simply as shorthand for whatever the 1805 *Prelude* is emblematic of, and for the literary project undertaken by Wordsworth and Coleridge during their collaborative years—is in this argument a kind of settlement, an assimilation of two revolutionary traditions it inherits and a tacit compromise between political and epistemic ideals: absolutism in all its forms is rejected, and an institutional arrangement, in which shared knowledge is the test of power, is embraced. The thirteen-book *Prelude* is the greatest product of this settlement, a process begun, for Wordsworth, fifteen years earlier with his first trip to revolutionary France in 1790 and continued in subsequent trips in 1791–92 and 1802. The trip by Wordsworth and Coleridge to Germany in 1798 is also relevant in this context, though that journey had different implications for the two poets: what propelled a lifelong study of German philosophy for Coleridge resulted in an inward turn, of which the two-part *Prelude* is the fruit, for Wordsworth. That Wordsworth does not seem to have studied Kant in any depth makes the affinities between the 1805 *Prelude* and Kantian philosophy more, not less, remarkable. The trial of reason staged by Wordsworth in *The Prelude* had been long in the making, in ways the poet could have been conscious of only in part.

The question this chapter considers, then, is this: how can we understand the relationship between Kant's self-styled "Copernican" revolution in philosophy and the French Revolution in such a way as to illuminate the project of early Romanticism in Britain? This is an immense question, and there are perhaps objections to the form of the question itself. But an account of how the most significant philosophical and political revolutions of the late eighteenth century converge is, I think, a potentially powerful and even necessary tool in understanding the diverse commitments of early Romantic literature: to knowledge and freedom, mind and body, imaginative autonomy and historical experience, lyric meditation and narrative description. The central importance of the French Revolution in British Romanticism needs no argument; the significance of Kantian and post-Kantian philosophy has not always been so secure. The attention paid here to the Continental revolution in philosophy is justified not merely by its direct relevance to the intellectual development of Coleridge or Wollstonecraft, or, more indirectly, to that of Wordsworth or P. B. Shelley. It is ultimately justified by a certain, insistently Romantic view of intellectual and literary history—deterministic in the most capacious sense of the term— that sees in particular creative achievements the distillation of assumptions and concerns that constitute the spirit of an age. The development of Kant's critical system from 1781 (*The Critique of Pure Reason*) to 1790 (*The Critique of Judgment*) is in this view the conceptual foundation of European Romanticism. No approach to Romanticism—metaphysical, ethical, or aesthetic—can afford to ignore it.[2]

What does it mean to offer a "Kantian" version of Romanticism? In its most modest sense, it is to situate Romanticism in a contemporary philosophical discourse with which it had, on some basic levels, a direct historical connection. In its more interesting and provocative senses, it is to say: (1) that the poetry and prose of British Romanticism may—indeed, should—be understood as both a middle way *between* and a transcendence *of* the competing claims of rationalism and empiricism (a tendency explicit in books 10 and 11 of the 1805 *Prelude* and virtually the whole of Coleridge's poetry and prose); (2) that what earlier critics like Geoffrey Hartmann called the "drama of consciousness" in Romanticism is also a drama of knowledge, predicated on a distinction, represented at times as a conflict, between subject and object; (3) that in its focus on self-consciousness, the self-regulating powers of human reason, and the creative imagination, Romanticism offers itself as an emancipating discourse; and (4) that British Romanticism is all of these things because it *presents itself* as all of these things (this is a Kantian claim insofar as it restricts real knowledge to a world of appearances that it does not pretend to see through). The details and implications of this account of Romanticism will become clearer in the following chapters. What I propose to do in this chapter is to think about how the Copernican revolution relates to a political revolution it both justified and held at a distance. There is a staggering multiplicity of ways to think about the relationship between Kant's philosophical revolution and the liberal, bourgeois revolution in France. In the interests of space and time, I shall limit myself to the following: the language used by both events to represent their respective achievements, Kant's own writing on the French Revolution, and the status of the a priori as a political problem at the end of the eighteenth century, with reference to the poetry of Wordsworth throughout.

Revolutions, Copernican and French

"Revolution" is a word—like the political designations of "radical" and "conservative," "left" and "right"—that comes into its etymological own at the end of the eighteenth century and during the Romantic period. As Raymond Williams has noted, the French Revolution solidified the shift in meaning of "revolution" from an older sense of the cyclical restoration of lawful authority to the modern sense of the linear and necessary innovation of a new order.[3] It is an important fact about both the Kantian and French revolutions that they so thoroughly conceived of themselves as "revolutions" in the first place. Here is Kant's famous description of the historical significance of the first *Critique*:

> Up to now it has been assumed that all our cognition must conform to the objects; but all attempts to find out something about them *a priori* through concepts

that would extend our cognition have, on this presupposition, come to nothing. Hence let us once try whether we do not get farther with the problems of metaphysics by assuming that the objects must conform to our cognition, which would agree better with the requested possibility of an *a priori* cognition of them, which is to establish something about objects before they are given to us.[4]

Kant tells us that this "would be just like the first thoughts of Copernicus," who made greater progress understanding celestial motion once he made the observer revolve and left the stars at rest. As Kant sees it, the reconception of the a priori is not a minor adjustment but a fundamental change to the philosophical tradition: "for after this alteration in our way of thinking we can very well explain the possibility of a cognition *a priori,* and what is still more, we can provide satisfactory proofs of the laws that are the *a priori* ground of nature, as the sum total of objects of experience—which were both impossible according to the earlier way of proceeding."[5] This is both a necessary advance and a return to the roots of modern philosophy, that is, "revolutionary" and "radical" in the literal senses of both terms. *The Critique of Pure Reason*, as its modern editors put it, "belongs to a main tradition in modern philosophy, beginning with Descartes, that tries to provide an *a priori foundation* for the methods and broad features of a modern scientific view of nature by an examination of the suitability of human cognitive faculties for the kind of knowledge of nature that modern science aims to achieve."[6] Kant's revolution in philosophy demonstrated that our mind is structurally suited to the kinds of knowledge we presumed we already had, but that had been called into doubt by the questions of skeptical empiricism, on one hand, and the irresponsible assertions of speculative metaphysics, on the other.

Suitability is likewise a key category for the British Romantics covered in this study, who elevated the term from the decorum of eighteenth-century aesthetics to a metaphysical condition of the most profound significance. The "spousal verse" of Wordsworth's *Home at Grasmere*, discussed in a later chapter, expresses the joy produced by the "great consummation" of an almost providentially suited subject and object:

> How exquisitely the individual Mind
> (And the progressive powers perhaps no less
> Of the whole species) to the external world
> Is fitted; and how exquisitely too—
> Theme this but little heard of among men—
> The external world is fitted to the mind;
> And the creation (by no lower name
> Can it be called) which they with blended might
> Accomplish: this is my great argument.[7]

Blake, the great enemy of deism in all its forms, found the idea behind these lines abhorrent: in his 1826 marginalia to these lines as they appeared in the "Preface" to Wordsworth's *Excursion*, he notes cuttingly, "You shall not bring me down to believe such fitting and fitted." The idea, however, is absolutely crucial to Wordsworth, whose poetry of compensation depends on an exchangeable currency between two roughly equal trading partners: between the individual consciousness and the world it inhabits (as in the lines above), between the individual consciousness and some larger consciousness (the "two consciousnesses" of book 2 in *The Prelude*), or between the individual consciousness and itself (with Robert Jones at the beginning of the ascent of Mt. Snowdon, "silently we sunk / Each into commerce with his private thoughts" [13.18–19]).[8]

The theme of suitability is sounded also in book 10 of the 1805 *Prelude*, a book containing some of the poem's most inspired verse and largely devoted to the claims of reason in politics. Here Wordsworth describes the point in his life—the summer of 1792 when firsthand experience of the French Revolution deepened his theoretical interest in it—when he began

> To think with fervour upon management
> Of Nations, what it is and ought to be,
> And how their worth depended on their Laws
> And on the Constitution of the State.   (10.685–89)

This introduces the famous "Bliss was it in that dawn to be alive" passage. Less frequently quoted is what follows, in which Wordsworth describes two personality types, both enraptured by the historical process the French Revolution seems to have set in motion: there are those of bold imaginations who, in terms echoing those of Kant quoted shortly, live "Among the grandest objects of the sense / And deal with whatsoever they found there / As if they had within some lurking right / To wield it" (10.713–16), and there are those of milder dispositions who "Had watch'd all gentle motions, and to these / Had fitted their own thoughts" (10.717–18). Wordsworth's bifurcation of the revolutionary or post-revolutionary subject would continue in *The Excursion*, where the dangers of the grandly imaginative are represented in the Solitary and the virtues of gentle accommodation are represented in the Wanderer. Here in *The Prelude*, though, Wordsworth reiterates, as he would throughout his poetry, the trope of a mind and world fitted to each other, a trope central to Kant's project of establishing the a priori grounds of modern science.[9] The high argument of both Kant's critical system and Wordsworth's major verse is to say that our most valued forms of knowledge are no mistake: we are not merely lucky to happen upon knowledge, like examples in epistemological Gettier cases, but certain kinds of knowledge are guaranteed by the suitability of the mind to the objective world—an increasingly pervasive idea across disciplines toward the end of the eighteenth century.

It was bliss in that dawn to be alive for many reasons, only one of which was the "attraction of a country in romance" (there is a noticeable elision here, of course, as the young Wordsworth himself joined the country in romance at this time). In addition to being swept up by run-of-the-mill revolutionary fervor and postadolescent *amour*, there was a philosophical dalliance, related to both, from which Wordsworth would never completely extricate himself.

> O times,
> In which the meagre, stale, forbidding ways
> Of custom, law and statute took at once
> The attraction of a Country in Romance;
> When Reason seem'd the most to assert her rights
> When most intent on making of herself
> A prime Enchanter to assist the work
> Which then was going forwards in her name: (10.693–700)

If *The Prelude* is the paradigmatic Romantic poem, it is because it transforms the genre of romance into something like a philosophical position—one about the promise and limits of reason, which assumes in this poem the roles Prospero or Archimago had played in previous romances (the association of reason with Prospero would be made explicit in book 11, where Wordsworth describes the power of "syllogistic words" and "charms of logic" to "unsoul" the mysteries of passion).[10] Like its Shakespearean and Spenserian antecedents, and indeed like Milton's Satan, reason in *The Prelude* is a "prime enchanter" of others and a shape-shifter itself. Kant similarly speaks in the first *Critique* of a deceptive faculty of reason that "does not merely forsake us but even entices us with delusions and in the end betrays us!"[11] The conception of reason as a pathological faculty is eventually, though with difficulty, overcome in Kant, through an appeal to reason's own capacity to limit itself to the world of appearances. The redemption of reason in Wordsworth, on the other hand, is achieved only through one final self-transformation in the Mount Snowdon episode of book 13, when the imagination is revealed to be "reason in her most exalted mood" (13.170).

The dream of pure reason—autonomous, legislative, and creative in her most exalted mood—is the great theme of early Romanticism, in England and in Germany. Wordsworth's language of the "rights" of reason in the above passage echoes the juridical language used by Kant to describe his *Critique of Pure Reason*. In the well-known metaphor with which he begins that work, Kant describes his project as "a court of justice, by which reason may secure its rightful claims while dismissing all its groundless pretensions, and this not by mere decrees but according to its own eternal and unchangeable laws; and this court is none other than the critique of pure reason itself,"[12] by which Kant means a critique of a priori cognition. Kant uses the same language shortly afterward to describe the power of a priori knowledge: "Reason, in order to be taught by nature, must approach nature with its principles in one hand, according to which alone the agreement among appearances can count as laws, and, in the other hand, the experiments thought out in accordance with these principles—yet in order to be instructed by nature not like a pupil, who has recited to him whatever the teacher wants to say, but like an appointed judge who compels witnesses to answer the questions he puts to them."[13] There are limits, though, to what the a priori can do. Pure reason for Kant results in an antinomy: the thesis that causality is in accordance with the laws of nature and freedom, for example, is opposed by the antithesis that "[t]here is no freedom, but everything in the world takes place solely in accordance with the laws of nature."[14] Kant's antinomies result from reason's failure to comprehend its own limits; their solutions arise when reason learns to confine itself to the world of experience, not things-in-themselves.

We shall return to the antinomy of freedom later, but I would like to note in this context Kant's inherited language of justice, the particular ways in which he puts reason on trial. The form of the "antinomy" itself has legal roots: it was widely used in seventeenth-century jurisprudence to point to differences between laws arising from clashes between legal jurisdictions (Kant keeps up the analogy by referring to opposed arguments within these antinomies as "parties").[15] The juridical language of the first *Critique* is most clearly on display in the Transcendental Deduction, which establishes our *right* to apply the a priori categories to objects. It begins: "Jurists, when they speak of entitlements and claims, distinguish in a legal matter between the questions about what is lawful (*quid juris*) and that which concerns the fact (*quid facti*), and since they demand proof of both, they call the first, that which is to establish the entitlement or the legal claim, the deduction."[16] There is something almost farcical about Kant's frequent recourse to the language of courts and justice to discuss epistemic questions—recall Chaucer's illiterate Summoner who cries, "*Questio quid juris* [the question is, what point of the law applies?]" whenever drunk—though it accords with his relentlessly sober attempt to rescue metaphysics from the battlefield of endless, and often pedantic, controversies. Judgment, for Kant, must itself be judged.

As we have begun to see, Kant is not alone in his attempt to put mental faculties and concepts on trial at this time. Wordsworth reimagines the courtroom drama of the Transcendental Deduction in book 10 of *The Prelude*. Having been led astray by a false, Godwinian reason "placed beyond / The limits of experience and of truth" (847–48) in his effort to "probe / The living body of society" (874–75), Wordsworth faces a moral and political crisis that is, at once, an epistemic crisis:

> Thus I fared,
> Dragging all passions, notions, shapes of faith
> Like culprits to the bar, suspiciously
> Calling the mind to establish in plain day
> Her titles and her honours, now believing,
> Now disbelieving, endlessly perplex'd
> With impulse, motive, right and wrong, the ground
> Of moral obligation, what the rule
> And what the sanction, till, demanding proof
> And seeking it in every thing, I lost
> All feeling of conviction, and in fine
> Sick, wearied out with contrarieties,
> Yielded up moral questions in despair.   (10.888–900)

Like Kant, who records feeling betrayed by the enticements and delusions of reason, Wordsworth records a sense of betrayal by a false version of dogmatic reason in his attempts to know—to understand in the fullest sense—the principles and consequences of the French Revolution (the feeling would linger with him for decades, so that his poetry is as much the record of being betrayed by reason as it is that of being disowned by memory). Kant views the elevation of human reason to the status of "an appointed judge" of nature as the essence of human freedom. Things are more complicated for the poet, who calls all passions, notions, and shapes of faith "like culprits to the bar," only to yield up in despair questions of freedom in the face of seemingly insurmountable antinomies or "contrarieties." *The Prelude* is, of course, a narrative poem with a temporal arc absent in Kant's systematic and synchronic *Critique* (though such an arc would reemerge in Hegel); the point here is that in book 10 of *The Prelude* Wordsworth represents an epistemic legal drama that follows the basic contours of Kant's *Critique* in general and of the Transcendental Deduction in particular, one designed to assess reason's assertions to its rights and to determine the legal entitlement of our concepts in their claims to objective validity (the question of legal entitlement was also a personal one for Wordsworth, as we shall see in a later chapter). The drama of consciousness in Wordsworth is grounded in a drama of knowledge taking shape in Britain, as discussed in the introduction, and on the Continent in more systematic and abstract ways.

The epistemological courts of justice staged by Kant and Wordsworth anticipated and reflected, respectively, a drama of knowledge that unfolded in France from 1789 to 1793. The intellectual ground for the Revolution had been prepared earlier in the century by the *philosophes*, and revolutionary documents make frequent and explicit use—most notably in the Declaration of the Rights of Man and of the Citizen (August 27, 1789) and the Constitutions of 1791 and 1793—of the vocabulary those philosophers had developed. The Declaration states: "No one is to be disquieted because of his opinions, even religious, provided their manifestation does not disturb the public order established by law," and "Free communication of ideas and opinions is one of the most precious of the rights of man."[17] These principles would be incorporated into the constitutions, along with variations of the remarkable claim in the Declaration that "ignorance, forgetfulness, or contempt of the rights of man are the sole causes of public misfortunes and of the corruption of governments."[18] It is important to remember that this idea, conceived in these specific terms, had been virtually unthinkable prior to the middle of the eighteenth century.

It was in opposition to an increasingly pervasive rationalist discourse that royal power appealed to conscience and sentiment. In the Regulation for Execution of the Letters of Convocation (January 24, 1789), Louis XVI expects "that the voice of conscience alone will be heard in the choice of deputies to the Estates General" (in the context of revolutionary rhetoric, a conspicuous, if implied, rebuke of the voice of reason).[19] In The King's Declaration concerning the Estates General (June 23, 1789)—three days after the Tennis Court Oath in which members of the National Assembly swore "not to separate, and to reassemble wherever circumstances require, until the constitution of the kingdom is established and consolidated upon firm foundations"—the monarch asserts: "If, contrary to the intention of the King, some deputies have taken the rash oath not to deviate from some particular form of deliberation, His Majesty leaves it to their conscience to consider whether the arrangements that he is about to order deviate from the letter or from the spirit of the obligation they have assumed."[20] The French nation deserves royal favor not because of its reason, as the revolutionaries might suspect, but because of its sentiments: "what other nation," the monarch exclaims, "has been more deserving because of its sentiments than the French nation!"[21]

The language of political rationalism had been sufficiently established by the start of 1789 that the Abbé Sieyès could protest against reason's limits in the face of revolutionary necessity. In his classic statement of radical principles, "What Is the Third Estate?" (January 1789), Sieyès locates the nation in the forty thousand parishes, which he argues should have been more speedily organized into *arrondissements* and then into provinces: "[I]t was not a question of negotiating with time, but of adopting the proper method of achieving the objective. A disposition to pay due regard to sound principles would have accomplished more for the nation in four months than the course of enlightenment and public opinion . . . could do in half a century."[22] All is to be subordinated to the general will: "It is useless to talk reason if, for a single instant, this first principle, that the general will is the opinion of the majority and not of the minority, is abandoned."[23] In the end, though, Sieyès maintains the same confidence in enlightened public opinion that marks most revolutionary writing of the time: "The third estate must perceive in the trend of opinions and circumstances that it can hope for nothing except from its own enlightenment and courage. Reason and justice are in its favor; . . . there is no longer time to work for the conciliation of parties."[24] The third estate, he argues, must be prepared to go it alone.

In the correspondence between the Revolution Society of London and the Constituent Assembly in late 1789, the Revolution itself becomes defined by an epistemic triumph in the arts and sciences. Responding to a letter of congratulation offered by the Revolution Society in early November, the Constituent Assembly remarks with satisfaction:

> The French nation has long been improving in knowledge and arts; and its government was directed by opinions derived from them even before the country governed itself by the laws which they dictated.
>
> The Nation pursued with ardor useful truths, and daily diffusing light over every branch of the administration, it appeared to be carried, as by an universal impulse, to those changes which now give it strength and stability.
>
> A King whom we may call the *best* of Men, and the *first* of Citizens, encouraged by his virtues the hopes of the Nation, and now, by universal concurrence, a durable Constitution is established, founded on the unalienable rights of Men and Citizens.
>
> It undoubtedly belongs to our age, in which reason and liberty are extending themselves together, to extinguish forever national hatred and rivalship.[25]

The terms of the letter mirror the language used by radical societies in Britain at the same time, discussed in the introduction. The inevitable and conjoined progress of liberty and reason is by now a revolutionary article of faith on both sides of the Channel.

Optimism in such progress became more intense in the early years of the Revolution precisely because it became more necessary, culminating in the public apotheosis of reason in 1793. In his proposed Declaration of Rights (April 24, 1793), Robespierre amplifies the claims made in the 1789 Declaration and the constitutions that followed: "The representatives of the French people, assembled in National Convention, recognizing that human laws which do not derive from the eternal laws of justice and of reason are only the outrages of ignorance or despotism against humanity; convinced that forgetfulness and contempt of the natural rights of man are the sole causes of the crimes and misfortunes of the world, have resolved to set forth in a solemn declaration these sacred and inalienable rights."[26] By the end of the year, revolutionary rationalism in France reached its peak under the dictatorship of the Committee of Public Safety: in a famous sequence of events, the Christian calendar was replaced by one beginning with the founding of the French Republic; the metric system was introduced; and the cathedral of Notre Dame was converted into a Temple of Reason, with a ceremony staged in honor of the Goddess of Liberty—moves that alienated a significant portion of the French population, especially Catholics, from the aims of the revolution. The success of Robespierre rested in part on his ability to capitalize on these feelings of alienation while at the same time insisting on his adherence to the original principles of the revolution.

To do this, he was forced to distance himself, most elaborately in the Festival of the Supreme Being in June 1794, from a political rationalism he had earlier exploited and to articulate, in his speech to the National Convention on December 25, 1793, his own narrative about the history of political knowledge:

> The theory of revolutionary government is as new as the Revolution that created it. It is as pointless to seek its origins in the books of the political theorists, who failed to foresee this revolution, as in the laws of tyrants, who are happy enough to abuse their exercise of authority without seeking its legal justification. And so this phrase is for the aristocracy a mere subject of terror or a term of slander, for tyrants an outrage and for many an enigma. It behooves us to explain it to all in order that we may rally good citizens, at least, in support of the principles governing public interest.[27]

Robespierre associates, as Shelley would for opposite reasons in *Prometheus Unbound*, political knowledge with the knowledge of necessity, an association that emerges in British writing at this time. In *The Measures of Ministry to Prevent a Revolution Are the Certain Means of Bringing It On* (1794), for instance, Irish nationalist and political theorist Arthur O'Connor describes the moment when "the mind has arrived at that state of political knowledge, by which it is enabled to discover the certainty of the immense Revolution which at this instant operates in civil society."[28] In the same year, an anonymous "old member of parliament," in *A Looking-Glass for a Right Honourable Mendicant*, writes: "It required but a moderate share of political knowledge and foresight to descry the approaching annihilation of the monarchy."[29] The prophetic tradition in Romantic literature and its broader modes of social criticism are rooted in the claims made about political foresight and historical necessity in the 1790s. Recall Blake's assertion, in his annotations to the bishop of Llandaff's *An Apology for the Bible* (1796), that prophecy is simply the honesty and intelligence to say "If you go on So / the result is So. . . . A prophet is a Seer not an Arbitrary Dictator."[30] The terms of Romantic prophecy—and of its various critiques of political reason—are in many ways forged here, in the competing epistemological contentions of monarchs, revolutionaries, dictators, and, as we shall now see, philosophers of terror such as Burke and Kant.

Prophetic History and Moral Terrorism:
The Conflict of the Faculties

Robespierre's remark in December 1793 that the phrase "theory of revolutionary government" itself is a "mere subject of terror" for the aristocracy would be prophetic: only three months later he would reclaim the term to say, "Terror is nothing else than justice, prompt, severe, inflexible." The kind of justice Robespierre had in mind would be clear from the end of 1793 to the middle of 1794, during which more than forty thousand people were executed across France. Terror, though, had not always been so bloody. It was a key term in Burke's aesthetic *Enquiry* (1757), where it is the ruling principle of the sublime; terror, or fear, would play a similar role in Kant's *Critique of Judgment* (1790) and, indeed, in the canonical moments of sublimity in Romantic poetry, in which fear is the condition not only of a certain kind of aesthetic experience but a certain kind of knowledge: the sublime knowledge, in Wordsworth's poetry, of the *un*-suitability of subject and object, or of the *lack* of legal entitlement. Before turning to the a priori and the fear of knowledge in the final section of this chapter, I would like to turn briefly to prophecy, terror, and other "revolutionary" concepts in the context of Kant's writings on the French Revolution.

The concept of revolution for Kant has, like the concept of freedom, both theoretical and practical senses, intimately related to each other. Theoretical revolutions of the mind are for Kant essential to the project of enlightenment, which he influentially defines as the human being's "emancipation from self-incurred tutelage" (the resonance with the "mind-forged manacles" of "London" is present, though Kant's emphasis on laziness and cowardice strikes a different tone than the pitiable "marks of weakness, marks of woe" of Blake's poem). The line between intellectual and political revolutions becomes blurred, however, when Kant, anticipating Godwin, discusses historical, *public* enlightenment, which can only happen slowly: "A revolution may well bring about a falling off of personal despotism and of avaricious or tyrannical oppression, but never a true reform in one's way of thinking; instead new prejudices will serve just as well as old ones to harness the great unthinking masses."[31] The gradual and historically necessary confluence of intellectual and political revolutions would be picked up (via Godwin) by Shelley, who turns it into the great theme of *Prometheus Unbound*.

Kant's reformism, which he would maintain in its essentials for his entire life, takes a middle path between the reformist positions of Godwin and

Burke. Like Godwin, he believes that people gradually work their way out of barbarism of their own accord through the use of reason, though only if there are no obstacles intentionally placed in their way. Kant is closest to the late Burke in the *Metaphysics of Morals* (1797), in which he declares that a change in a defective constitution can be carried out only through sovereign reform and not through popular revolution. He shares with Burke his horror at the French regicide, the idea of which he describes in the terms of a sublime *aporia* (Greek, impasse): "Like a chasm that irretrievably swallows everything, the execution of a monarch seems to be a crime from which the people cannot be absolved, for it is as if the state commits suicide."[32] Kant's opposition to radical or revolutionary activity is on the whole a more principled one than that of Burke, who frankly admits to a constitutional "dislike I feel to revolutions," as if the mere concept of popular resistance upsets his stomach (Burke has his principles, too, though they seem to derive from disposition rather than a sovereign faculty of reason, which he never believed in anyway). Both Kant and Burke refer at times to the people with condescension, though Kant's "unthinking masses" hits a more restrained pitch of disdain than Burke's "swinish multitude." In his most dogmatic and reactionary stance, Kant regards resistance to even an unjust government as contrary to right, however much one may be inclined to sympathize with its causes.

And Kant did indeed sympathize with the deepest ideals of the French Revolution, despite his objections to violence he joined virtually all of Europe in condemning. His sympathy with the Revolution persisted even after disenchantment set in among many of his contemporaries. It persisted at least as late as 1798, when his essay "An Old Question Raised Again" was published. The "old question" is whether the human race is constantly progressing, which he answers with optimism. Kant takes the French Revolution and its aftermath as a historical demonstration of the moral tendency of the entire human race. What is important about the Revolution, he says, is not its individual acts of villainy or heroism, or even the way in which political structures "vanish as if by magic while others come forth in their place as if from the depths of the earth."[33] Rather, it is "simply the mode of thinking of the spectators which reveals itself *publicly* in this great game of revolutions, and manifests such a universal yet disinterested sympathy for the players on one side against those on the other" that argues in favor of human moral progression. It is the status of the French Revolution as a kind of spectator-sport, a game requiring not action but impartial approbation or disapprobation, that most fully reveals the moral character of the species. Kant is indebted here to Smith's theory of moral sentiments, though his difference from Smith in this context is representative of his general departure from the empiricist picture of the mind:

The revolution of a gifted people which we have seen unfolding in our day may succeed or miscarry; it may be filled with misery and atrocities to the point that a right-thinking human being, were he boldly to hope to execute it successfully the second time, would never resolve to make the experiment at such cost—this revolution, I say, nonetheless finds in the hearts of all spectators (who are not engaged in this game themselves) a wishful *participation* that borders closely on enthusiasm the very expression of which is fraught with danger; this sympathy, therefore, can have no other cause than a moral predisposition in the human race.[34]

Kant offers a more ambitious conception of this moral predisposition than had his empiricist predecessors, whether Smith's innate principle of sympathy or the moral sense postulated by Francis Hutcheson and others. Kant's moral cause reveals itself in the *right* of a people to construct their own constitution and in the *end*, or "duty," of that constitution to be just and good itself, or "republican at least in essence."[35] The state for Kant is a rational necessity, a condition of possibility for a particular kind of human freedom.

"An Old Question Raised Again" was composed by Kant in 1795, when the moral fate of humanity seemed, for some at least, to hang in the balance (recall the previously quoted remarks by Godwin, Wollstonecraft, and Coleridge in 1794–95). The essay was not published, though, until after the death of King Frederick William II, to whom Kant had promised to cease writing on sensitive, specifically religious, subjects. It appeared as the middle essay in a collection of three, titled *Der Streit der Fakultäten* (1798), each of which dealt with the prerogatives of the "lower" faculty of philosophy in relation to one of the three "higher" faculties within the university: theology, law, and medicine. Kant's central argument is that the philosophical faculty ought to remain free of state regulation and university interference because it concerns the "public," not the "private," use of reason, a distinction introduced in "What Is Enlightenment?"(1784) to differentiate the use one makes of reason "as a *scholar* before the entire public of the *world of readers*" and the use one makes of reason in a civil post or office. This volley in an academic turf-war might seem an odd context for an argument about the rights of reason in shaping human history, though it is important to remember the dual sense of "faculty" (*Fakultät*)—a term of enormous significance for both Kant and the Romantics of this study—as both an institutional arrangement and a mental power or capacity. The modification of eighteenth-century faculty psychology into a driving force of transcendental idealism intersects here with the modern history of intellectual disciplinarity. Departmental autonomy in the German research university is for Kant an issue of the autonomy of public reason, which he insists "must always be free" and which "alone can bring about enlightenment among human beings."[36]

When read as an allegory of the drama between the various mental faculties, which Kant invites us to do, *The Conflict of the Faculties* reveals itself to be an especially illuminating work. Indeed, the middle essay, with which I am concerned here—nominally on the relationship between the faculties of philosophy and law in a university—contains in miniature some of the central problems of both Kantian philosophy and early Romanticism. Mirroring the wish to justify the possibility of metaphysics at the beginning of the first *Critique*, it begins with the question: "What do we *want* to know in this matter?"[37] Kant's Romantic answer, though, is unlike anything found in the earlier work: "We desire a fragment of human history and one, indeed, that is drawn not from past but future time, therefore a *predictive* history." In the next section, "How *can* we know it?," he recasts this divinatory historical narrative in coldly formal terms as "a possible representation a priori" of future events. This recasting seems less strange when Kant introduces yet another iteration of the question: "How is a history a priori possible?," this time unequivocally echoing the form of the inaugurating question of the first *Critique* ("How are synthetic judgments a priori possible?"). *The Conflict of the Faculties*, in other words, broadens the domain of Kantian formalism so that it encompasses historical judgment in addition to metaphysical, ethical, and aesthetic judgment.

The question of how a "history a priori" is possible is a reiteration and extension of the question of how synthetic a priori knowledge is possible: principles like "every event has a cause" predicate historical—though, if a priori, universal and necessary—propositions about the tendency of particular events. It makes sense, then, that Kant's explanation of how prophetic history a priori is possible mirrors the answer given in the first *Critique*: it is possible because of the contributions of the subject, in this case "if the diviner *makes* and contrives the events which he announces in advance."[38] Kant cites the example of the Old Testament prophets who had knowledge of the decadence and dissolution of the state because "they themselves were the authors of this fate." In Kant's reading, they had so "loaded their constitution with ecclesiastical freight" that the state became untenable. One need not look as far back, though, as the Hebrew prophets of the Old Testament. Kant refers to modern politicians who do much the same, establishing the conditions of the revolution they warn of by actively making the people what they are, "stubborn and inclined to revolt," through unjust constraint: "obviously then, if the government allows the reins to relax a little, sad consequences ensue which verify the prophecy of those supposedly sagacious statesmen."[39] A predictive history a priori is possible, it seems, only in the active construction of that history, by a subject freely establishing the conditions of historical necessity.

The Hebrew prophet and the modern statesman, though, are special cases, and Kant is not inclined to have a priori political knowledge depend on these contingent and extraordinary positions of social power. A priori knowledge cannot, of course, directly depend on any kind of experience whatsoever. Universal and necessary historical principles, such as the moral tendency of the species, are knowable not through experience, which offers us only a synthesis of potentially confusing or contradictory appearances, but through reason. The problem of political a priori knowledge thus follows the same basic pattern of a priori knowledge elsewhere in Kant, and the trope of the Copernican Revolution is deployed to similar ends: "If the course of human affairs seems so senseless to us, perhaps it lies in a poor choice of position from which we regard it. Viewed from the earth, the planets sometimes move backwards, sometimes forward, and sometimes not at all. But if the standpoint selected is the sun, an act which only reason can perform, according to the Copernican hypothesis they move constantly in their regular course."[40] Kant's analogy of planetary and historical movement is telling. Earlier in the essay, he calls the idea of a constant retrogression toward wickedness "moral *terrorism*" and calls his own view of constant progression a kind of *eudaemonism*. The use of "terror" in this context should be noted, as real terror for Kant consists not in the acts of the occasional Robespierre but in the unsympathetic response of the disinterested observer, that is, the "mode of thinking of the spectators which reveals itself *publicly* in this great game of revolutions." His concern with the "terroristic manner of representing human history" is that it denies human freedom in the worst possible way, toward the disintegration of the species. The context of self-fulfilling prophecies also suggests that the terroristic manner of representing history has the potential to create the history it envisions.

More important is the fact that the kind of a priori knowledge Kant has in mind here is related to the *legibility* of a particular historical sequence. The idea that the course of human affairs often appears senseless is not uncommon, but it was especially common in the last decade of the eighteenth century as the world, interested and disinterested parties alike, watched events unfold in France. It is difficult not to think of what E. P. Thompson calls the "Jacobinism-in-recoil" of Wordsworth and his contemporaries when reading Kant's description of the problems of intelligibility posed by contemporary historical events,[41] for it is precisely the predicament of reading or cognizing the French Revolution that Wordsworth articulates in the passage from *The Prelude* quoted earlier, in which the political spectator, demanding proof that experience is unable to provide, eventually yields up moral questions in despair. It is, again, no accident that book 10 of that poem is simultaneously devoted to political and epistemological questions. The French exchange of "a war of self-defence / For one of conquest" in the spring of 1794 challenged not merely a set of political beliefs—such as the belief in human perfectibility and historical progress shared by Godwin and Kant—but a particular notion of belief-formation itself, predicated on "One guide—the light of circumstances, flashed / Upon an independent intellect." It is a crisis occasioned by a loss of vision, an inability to see, in the fullest sense of the term, what is apparent to the senses. Alain Badiou has argued in more recent contexts that it is a feature of counter-revolutionary periods (such as the one he argues we are presently in) to render previous revolutionary sequences illegible. He points, for example, to how a key feature of the Thermidorean reaction was to "make illegible the previous Robespierrean sequence: its reduction to the pathology of some blood-thirsty criminals impeded any political understanding."[42] The political books of *The Prelude* tell the story of a historical sequence becoming inscrutable before one's eyes, a subjective blurring of vision that seems indistinguishable from the increasing complexity of objective events.

The impossibility of reading history a posteriori is a central problem of Kant's *Conflict of the Faculties*. The course of human affairs seems illegible or senseless when one relies on experience, yet, Kant contends, "the prophetic history of the human race must be connected to some experience." The importance of the French Revolution for Kant is that it functions as precisely this sort of experience, one capable of demonstrating the progressive trend of human freedom but only when viewed from a standpoint outside of experience. It requires an act of reason to establish such a standpoint, in which a priori knowledge is seen to have some connection with a form of experience on which it does not, strictly speaking, depend. Seen from this perspective, the French Revolution illuminates the entire historical record, "not itself as the cause of history, but only as an intimation, a historical sign (*signum rememorativum, demonstrativum, prognostikon*)."[43] The problem of the political books of *The Prelude*, similarly, is to establish a position from which these historical signs once again become legible.

Independence from Experience: The a Priori Aporia

I have already noted the sublime language of aporia that Kant uses to describe the French regicide—"Like a chasm that irretrievably swallows everything, the execution of a monarch seems to be a crime from which the people cannot be absolved, for it is as if the state commits suicide"—and I have noted some affinities between the attitudes of Kant and Burke toward the French Revolution. That event, however, raised more fundamental questions, and differences, about the possibility of what Burke dismissively calls "political metaphysics" in his *Reflections on the Revolution in France* (1790). Political knowledge is for Burke an unintelligible concept. In this he differs sharply from the English radicals discussed in the introduction, for whom political knowledge is not merely possible but its dissemination is a necessary condition of human emancipation.

Kant shares with Burke a skepticism of speculative metaphysics, but it must be remembered that the German philosopher's entire project in the first *Critique* is to rescue metaphysics, or a priori principles, from dogmatic debasement. This includes what Burke calls "political metaphysics," the possibility of which Kant seems to accept. In the preliminary notes to his essay "On the Common Saying: That May Be Correct in Theory, but It Is of No Use in Practice" (1793), Kant refers to August Wilhelm Rehberg's *Examination of the French Revolution* (1793), which made the then-controversial claim that "metaphysics" as such had brought about the Revolution. Kant mentions Rehberg's charge in his notes and asks whether this ought to be considered an achievement of metaphysics, because "men of affairs" had long made it their principle to banish metaphysics to the schools.[44] Kant's position is that while subjects do not have a right to rebel, they do have other rights, which the sovereign has a duty to respect by governing in conformity with reason. Political theory, based on rational not empirical grounds, is for Kant the *only* thing of use in practice.

When read in conjunction with the pamphlet wars of the 1790s, the arguments of Kant and Rehberg in 1793 form part of an unprecedented debate on both sides of the English Channel—among academic philosophers and members of Parliament, laborers and merchants, radicals and reactionaries—about the place of abstract thinking in political affairs, indeed about the possibility of "political reason" itself. The first, and perhaps the last, thing to note about this debate is that much of it took place in the context of the Terror. The years in which debates about political knowledge raged most intensely (1793–95) encompassed the period of mass executions in France.

There are some obvious ways in which terror intersects with the critique of political reason we have been tracking: (1) the reactionary narrative, articulated most influentially by Burke, that there is a direct line connecting the ideas of the *philosophes* with the violence of the guillotine or, later, with the imperial ambition of Napoleon (a narrative that persists even in Bertrand Russell, extending to his treatment of Byron and twentieth-century fascism); (2) the tempered liberal narrative, in which the excesses of the Revolution demonstrated, in some oblique fashion, the limits of pure reason in politics (this would essentially be the Kantian position of Wordsworth and Coleridge); (3) the Jacobin narrative, stated by Robespierre above, that what is called "terror" is "nothing else than justice, prompt, severe, inflexible," to which knowledge itself is subordinate; and (4) the communist narrative, voiced by Badiou above, that the Terror is unknowable because counterrevolutionary forces immediately rendered it unintelligible. Fear and terror, though, have emerged in the more surprising context of twenty-first-century epistemology. Paul Boghossian, for instance, titles his attack on postmodern relativism *Fear of Knowledge* (2006), and the recent collection *What Place for the a Priori* (2011) concludes with an essay by Ümit Yalçın titled "Terror of Knowing: Can an Empiricist Avoid Unwanted a Priori Knowledge?" It perhaps comes as no surprise that the first

decade of the second millennium, beginning as it did, would produce a renewed intellectual interest in terror, even in the domain of analytic epistemology. This has coincided with renewed philosophical interest in the *a priori*.[45]
These are not unrelated tendencies. Just as the epistemological impasse Kant intends to overcome in the 1780s revolves around the possibility of a priori knowledge, so does the Romantic critique of political reason—which Burke insists
cannot operate a priori, a possibility Wollstonecraft, Godwin, and the Romantic
poets are more inclined to consider—intend to overcome a political and epistemological impasse that takes the form of terror. In short, questions about the a
priori are questions about independence from experience, a state that, for the
figures covered here, either promises the only true kind of freedom or threatens the most real kind of subjective and objective terror.

One way of reframing the initial question about the relationship between the
Copernican and French revolutions, then, is to ask: to what extent is the a priori,
especially as it was conceived toward the end of the eighteenth century, a political concept? A pragmatist would say that this is like asking to what extent a
hammer or the number five is a political concept, and he or she would have a
point. Perhaps there is nothing necessarily political about independence from
experience, though it is difficult, on the other hand, to imagine that there is
not. Wordsworth suggests as much when he recalls his hopes of "shaking off /
The accidents of nature, time, and place" in the effort to build social freedom on
the freedom of the individual mind. Independence from experience is a paradigmatic form of Romantic freedom, the distillation and the ground of other forms
of autonomy.

In is simplest definition, a priori knowledge is knowledge that is prior to or
independent of experience (as opposed to a posteriori, or empirical, knowledge). Beyond this basic definition, there remains little agreement among philosophers as to what the a priori is in its details, what kinds of propositions
would fall under the category, how a priori and a posteriori knowledge relate to
each other, and even whether a priori knowledge is possible at all. Standard
examples of a priori propositions have included: "$2+3=5$," "A bachelor is an
unmarried man," "Every event has a cause," "No object can be red and green
all over at the same time," and "The shortest distance between two points is a
straight line." Some have extended the category to include basic ethical principles such as "It is wrong to torture infants to death just for the fun of it" or "It
is unjust to punish an innocent person." The idea of a priori knowledge is that
propositions such as these can be known to be true without any justification
from the character of the subject's experience. It is no objection to the a priori to
say that experience is required for the acquisition of some of the constitutive
concepts (though there is debate as to what exactly counts as "experience" in
this context): the a priori is a relation of entitlement, not causality. Experience

may be required to grasp the concepts of an a priori proposition, but, once known, the truth of the proposition itself does not depend on the evidence of experience. As Paul Boghossian and Christopher Peacocke put it in their introduction to *New Essays on the a Priori* (2000), "No particle accelerator, however powerful, can refute the proposition that $7 + 5 = 12$."[46]

A full treatment of the status of the a priori, at the present moment or at the end of the eighteenth century, is well beyond the scope of this work. What I would like to do, however, is suggest what is at stake in debates about the a priori and to argue that debates about political epistemology are at bottom debates about this basic form of knowledge. The primary aim, again, of *The Critique of Pure Reason* is to show how synthetic judgments a priori are possible. "Synthetic" judgments—like "Every event has a cause" or the axioms of geometry—differ for Kant from "analytic" judgments—"Every *effect* has a cause" or "A bachelor is an unmarried man"—which can be known as necessarily true through an analysis of the constitutive concepts. Synthetic judgments a priori pose epistemological problems in a way that analytic judgments do not because they depend on a rational intuition or insight not contained in the concepts themselves or in the logical form of the sentence in which they occur. Kant's solution to the problem of synthetic a priori knowledge is to say that such knowledge is possible because the mind itself contributes a few basic things to cognition, namely, the forms of intuition (space and time) and the pure concepts of the understanding (the "categories" of quantity, quality, relation, and modality). Insofar as these are entirely the contributions of the mind, a priori knowledge is "knowledge absolutely independent of all experience" (a claim that has been softened or complicated in subsequent discussions of the a priori). Kant's argument was revolutionary insofar as the passive empiricist subject of the earlier part of the eighteenth century, who merely receives the sense data of experience, was replaced by an active transcendental subject, whose mind is structured in such a way as to make experience possible in the first place. On the whole, the rationalist tradition, beginning with Descartes and Leibniz, tends to hold that there can be a priori knowledge of the world; the empiricist tradition, beginning with Hobbes and Locke, tends to deny it. Again, there seems to be nothing inherently emancipating—or, for that matter, anything inherently oppressive—about either epistemological position. And, strictly speaking, I do not think there is. In less strict terms, though, both theories of knowledge have been understood, by Romantics and non-Romantics alike, to bear some relation to freedom and oppression as they exist in the world of historical experience.

In his 1971 Cambridge lectures in memory of Bertrand Russell, collected as *Problems of Knowledge and Freedom*, Noam Chomsky proposes to discern some common elements in Russell's effort to examine the conditions of human knowledge and the conditions of human freedom. Russell, according to Chomsky, explored the limits of empiricism in an attempt to discover the principles of nondemonstrative inference that justify scientific inference, that is, a priori principles. Russell concludes that "part of empiricist theory appears to be true without any qualification," namely, that "words which I can understand derive their meaning from my experience." But he also concludes that another part of empiricism is untenable: our knowledge presupposes certain principles of inference that cannot be deduced from facts of experience: "either, therefore, we know something independently of experience, or science is moonshine," reiterating a Kantian identification of a priori knowledge with science or philosophy itself.[47] Chomsky notes that empiricists such as Hume and Quine have reached similar conclusions and recalls Leibniz's observation that by admitting reflection as a source of knowledge, Locke leaves the door open for a reconstruction of rationalist theory in another terminology. There is for Chomsky no way around some basic notion of a priori knowledge if philosophy or science is to be possible at all, even if the same innate principles of mind that make possible the acquisition of knowledge and systems of belief might also impose limits on scientific understanding of how knowledge and belief are acquired.[48] The lack of complete transparency regarding our own cognitive faculties need not preclude justified belief in their existence or activity. Chomsky refers to Kant's pregnant remarks on the "schematism of the understanding," which "in its application to appearances and their mere form, is an art concealed in the depths of the human soul, whose real modes of activity nature is hardly likely ever to allow us to discover, and to have open to our gaze."[49] Kant's section of the schematism of the understanding in the Transcendental Analytic is indeed one of the most cryptic of the entire work, as it is here that he argues that there "must be some third thing," the schematism of the understanding itself, that mediates between the categories and appearances (it was precisely this sort of mysterious fabrication of faculties in Kant that so infuriated Nietzsche). The opacity Kant uncharacteristically attributes to the schematism of the understanding, as "an art concealed in the depths of the human soul," is the last line of defense against empiricist encroachments on a priori principles.

The importance of all this for Chomsky is that these "intrinsic principles of mental organization permit the construction of rich systems of knowledge and belief on the basis of scattered evidence."[50] His narrative of the history of philosophy, in which even Hume and Quine are unwitting rationalists, supports of course the basic features of his own linguistic theory, in which an innate, a priori language faculty common to the species provides the framework for the interpretation of experience. Chomsky, though, relies on a more general argument that is only suggested in his writing on epistemological and political questions. The implied argument is that without some rudimentary notion of a priori knowledge, the human being is rendered a passive recipient of experience, a conception of the human subject with troubling political implications. The active Kantian subject is able to resist being a mere means, susceptible to external manipulation and control, and instead asserts itself as a complex end, capable of self-legislation and imaginative creation. In the conclusion to the epistemological half of his Russell lectures, Chomsky warns against the illusion of freedom that accompanies the empiricist picture of the mind. "The image of a mind, initially unconstrained, striking out freely in arbitrary directions, suggests at first glance a richer and more hopeful view of human freedom and creativity, but I think that this conclusion is mistaken. Russell was correct in titling his study *Human Knowledge: Its Scope and Limits.* The principles of mind provide the scope as well as the limits of human creativity. Without such principles, scientific understanding and creative acts would not be possible."[51] Chomsky, significantly, quotes Coleridge's Shakespeare lectures in this context: "The spirit of poetry, like all living powers, must of necessity circumscribe itself by rules," under laws of its own origination.[52] Coleridge, himself echoing Schlegel here, felt as keenly as any of his contemporaries the devastating effects that strict adherence to empiricist doctrine would have on the moral-aesthetic life of the human being, a feeling that informed both his subordination of the mechanical fancy to the creative imagination and his broader rejection of Hartleyan associationism in favor of Kantian and Schellingian idealism.[53] The poet, Coleridge writes in the *Biographia*, "brings the whole soul of man into activity, with the subordination of its faculties to each other, according to their relative worth and dignity."[54] The essence of human freedom consists in this activity, whereby the mind comes to realize its own structure, powers, and limits.

The notion of a kind of freedom that results from the human power of self-circumscription finds its greatest poetic expression in the period in Wordsworth's sonnets of 1802, written during his trip with Dorothy to France. The prefatory sonnet argues that just as "Nuns fret not at their Convent's narrow room," so does the poet rejoice in the emancipating limits imposed by the form of the sonnet.

> In truth, the prison, unto which we doom
> Ourselves, no prison is: and hence to me,
> In sundry moods, 'twas pastime to be bound
> Within the Sonnet's scanty plot of ground:
> Pleas'd if some Souls (for such there needs must be)
> Who have felt the weight of too much liberty,
> Should find short solace there, as I have found.   (8–14)[55]

In the "Miscellaneous Sonnets" and the "Sonnets Dedicated to Liberty" that follow in the 1807 *Poems in Two Volumes*, Wordsworth subjects the categories of lordship and bondage to a sustained kind of scrutiny unparalleled elsewhere in his poetry. The idea of independence is interrogated in these poems on multiple levels: formally, in the poet's assertion of independence from the "architectural" tradition of the Shakespearean sonnet and his allegiance to Milton's "spherical" unification of the Italian form; philosophically, in the speaker's desire to liberate himself from the seductions of the material world, sensation, and Fancy; and politically, in his meditations on the Haitian Revolution, Napoleonic expansion, and the need for a political prophet to assume the mantle of Milton. Throughout, Wordsworth delineates the contours of freedom and oppression with a discriminating eye trained on the mutual dependence of material and spiritual bondage. Liberty, he suggests, begins and ends with an act of self-limitation and self-legislation, though the poet is under no illusions about the material constraints placed on this kind of freedom.

Both Coleridge and Wordsworth posit robust, nuanced conceptions of freedom that, while not entirely congruent with Kant's, accord with the philosopher's insistence on true freedom as an act of self-legislation: "What, then, can freedom of the will be other than autonomy, that is, the will's property of being a law to itself."[56] The autonomy of the will, the freedom of the subject to legislate for itself, is the key component of practical freedom for Kant. Its theoretical analogue is spontaneity, or the power of reason to begin a state itself, "without needing to be preceded by any other cause that in turn determines it to action according to the law of causal connection."[57] Spontaneity, as opposed to receptivity, and autonomy, as opposed to heteronomy, are the defining characteristics of Kantian and early Romantic freedom. The ideas are not unique to the late eighteenth century—they respond to the early modern distinction between freedom "from" and freedom "to," and they anticipate Isaiah Berlin's later distinction between negative and positive liberty—but the extraordinary emphasis on a self-legislating subject is a feature of the period's literature, in Britain and on the Continent, that it is impossible to ignore.

The kind of Romantic self-legislation under consideration depends on innate principles of the mind that structure the experience of freedom, determining its scope and limits. Freedom in this view is not merely the liberal absence of restraint (allied with spontaneity and negative liberty) but free creation within a self-generated system of rule (allied with autonomy and positive liberty). It is in the nature of reason itself to determine the limits of freedom, which Kant notes is constitutionally disposed to pass into sublime terror, to "pass beyond any and every specific limit."[58] The significance of innate a priori principles in this context is that they provide freedom with form. If freedom is the self-realization of certain faculties or principles of the mind, then the structure of the mind will determine the nature of that freedom. Postulate a rich conception of the mind, capable of both self-government and imaginative creation, and one develops an equally rich, and self-limiting, conception of freedom; posit a blank slate of a mind, impotent in its ability to structure experience and seemingly unconstrained in its acquisition of knowledge, and one develops an equally emaciated, and potentially self-destructive, conception of freedom.

This, at least, is the kind of argument for which Chomsky enlists Coleridge's support in *Problems of Knowledge and Freedom*. The alliance is not as unnatural as it might seem: Chomsky represents a strain of anarchist thought with self-avowed roots, like Coleridge's early radicalism, in Godwin, and he is here making a Kantian argument against strict empiricism that Coleridge would have sympathized with at any point in his life. The turn to the mind for both is a precondition of an advanced notion of freedom premised on self-realization and self-legislation. If, as Russell frequently expressed it, the "true life" of the human being consists "in art and thought and love, in the creation and contemplation of beauty and in the scientific understanding of the world," then, Chomsky argues, "it is the intrinsic principles of mind that should be the object of our awe and, if possible, our inquiry."[59] Coleridge shared this attitude, and he consequently based his metaphysics, literary criticism, and poetry on a notion of the human mind divided according to the principles of eighteenth-century faculty psychology. As he says in the *Biographia* regarding the development of his own critical system, "I labored at a solid foundation, on which permanently to ground my opinions, in the component faculties of the human mind itself, and their comparative dignity and importance" (this, as it happens, in a defense of a "Universal Grammar," among other abstractions).[60] It is the distinguishing feature of Kant's philosophy, Coleridge notes elsewhere, "to treat every subject in reference to the operation of the mental Faculties."[61] The importance of Kantian philosophy in this view is not that it settles once and for all the question of whether the mind has nine or twelve categories, but that it delineates the conditions of human freedom in its most fully developed form. For certain inheritors of Kant, this is closely related to the project of realizing, in Russell's words, "a world in which the creative spirit is alive, in which life is an adventure full of joy and hope, based rather upon the impulse to construct than upon the desire to retain what we possess or to seize what is possessed by others."[62]

I am emphasizing the rule-bound nature of Kantian and early Romantic freedom—its character as free creation within a self-generated system of rule—because it is precisely this feature that would be made illegible in later Romanticisms (both post-Kantian idealism and second-generation British Romanticism) and even in later representations of Romanticism in criticism of a particular sort. Both Fichte and Schelling, Howard Caygill notes, "transformed spontaneity and autonomy into subjective and objective absolutes, a practice which Hegel was the first to criticize for positing absolutist and insatiable demands which remained empty and incapable of realization except through destructive terror, one which indeed passes 'beyond any and every specific limit.'"[63] In the section of *The*

Phenomenology of Spirit (1807) titled "Absolute Freedom and Terror," Hegel argues that the end of the eighteenth century witnessed the transformation of the Enlightenment notion of utility from a mere object and predicate into a subject, or "the new shape of consciousness, *absolute freedom*." The universal work of absolute freedom, though, can only result in *negative* action, "merely the *fury* of destruction": "The sole work and deed of universal freedom is therefore *death*, a death too which has no inner significance or filling, for what is negated is the empty point of the absolutely free self. It is thus the coldest and meanest of all deaths, with no more significance than cutting off a head of cabbage or swallowing a mouthful of water."[64] The destruction of the Terror was meaningless for Hegel—no more significant "than cutting off a head of cabbage"—because it was divorced from the general will or Spirit that is the only source of positive truth. The negation of Enlightenment utility is death without meaning, "the sheer terror of the negative," a phase of history that is overcome only when absolute freedom leaves "its self-destroying reality and pass[es] over into another land of self-conscious Spirit where, in this unreal world, freedom has the value of truth."[65] For those who did not share Hegel's optimism in the necessity of historical synthesis, the rigid formalism of Kantian freedom continued to raise doubts. As Nietzsche remarked, noting the origins of our moral discourse in the sphere of legal obligations, "the categorical imperative smells of cruelty."[66] Debates about how absolutist accounts of freedom are amenable to terror and domination would continue in the twentieth century in the work of Heidegger, Adorno, Horkheimer, and Sartre.

The a priori, then, presents a promise as well as a danger: independence from experience offers the possibility of freedom as self-realization at the same time that it removes the restraints that only experience can provide. The promise is allied with a rich conception of the human mind (including intrinsic principles), epistemological construction, ethical self-legislation, and aesthetic creation. The danger is allied with unchecked rationalism, metaphysical fabrication, asocial solipsism, artistic self-indulgence, and political terror. The problems of the a priori, in other words, are the problems of Romanticism itself. The solution offered by the Kantian tradition, with which I am associating early Romanticism in Britain, is to say that self-realization is also self-circumscription (in the terms of Coleridge, "the spirit of poetry, like all living powers, must of necessity circumscribe itself by rules"). The structure and limits of the mind structure and limit the experience of freedom, or, rather, they make the experience of freedom possible in the first place (a mere receptacle or processor of sense impressions could never experience the kind of freedom we are concerned with here). If Romanticism represents a drama of knowledge as well as consciousness, it is because it embraces a desire for universal knowledge, including political knowledge, at the same time that it confronts sheer epistemic terror, the fear of knowledge that is never fully adequate to present circumstances, knowledge that is capable of being determined for the passive subject by forces of repression and domination, or, worst of all for Wordsworth, the knowledge of a subject structurally unsuited to the objective world in which it lives. It is perhaps these fears that led some later Romantics to affect various renunciations of knowledge, whether in Keats's avowed, never realized, preference for a life of sensation over one of thought or Byron's resigned premise in *Manfred* that "Sorrow is knowledge." The Romantic poets covered in this study are on the whole more epistemically anguished, as repelled by the nightmarish metamorphoses of knowledge as they are drawn to its enlightening promise of freedom. The roots of this anguish, as we shall now see, lie in the controversy that raged in England immediately after the French Revolution, when the terror of political rationalism was still in the process of being formed and formulated.

THE RHETORIC OF
HURLY-BURLY INNOVATION

CHAPTER TWO

Burke and the Critique of Political Metaphysics

•

These things indeed you have articulate,
Proclaimed at market-crosses, read in churches,
To face the garment of rebellion
With some fine color that may please the eye
Of fickle changelings and poor discontents
Which gape and rub the elbow at the news
Of hurlyburly innovation.
And never yet did insurrection want
Such water colors to impaint his cause,
Nor moody beggars starving for a time
Of pell-mell havoc and confusion.
                                —Henry IV, Part 1, *5.1.73–83*

"Innovation" takes on its sense of radical political change or revolution around the same time that Shakespeare wrote his history of Henry IV; "hurly-burly," a contracted form of "*hurling and burling*," similarly makes its earliest literary appearance in the play. The king's innovative language, addressed to Worcester following his presentation of grievances, suggests a distaste for innovation as such. In addition to a scorn for the "fickle changelings and poor discontents" so easily seduced by the rhetoric of hurly-burly innovation. Among the ironies of the king's remarks is that they elide the violent, rebellious origins of his own power in the prior deposition of Richard II. Facing the most serious threat to his authority yet, Henry IV defends himself by attacking the emptiness and dangers of revolutionary rhetoric.

I begin with these lines from *Henry IV, Part 1* for a few reasons. First, the sense of "innovation" they help to inaugurate would become crucial in Burke's political philosophy, which famously revolves around a distinction between "innovation" and "reform." Second, the lines voice concerns about the rhetoric of innovation and its threat to established authority that would emerge on a wider scale and with greater vehemence in the political debates of the 1790s, including the debate between Burke and Wollstonecraft studied in this chapter and the next. The king's criticism of insurrectionary rhetoric reiterates a criticism as old as the rhetorical tradition itself: the capacity of beautiful language to disguise ugly truth. The trope of the "fine garment" of rhetoric would be suggested by Burke in his *Reflections on the Revolution in France* (1790)—in his criticism of radicals like Richard Price who clothe their arguments with the "air of novelty" and of the "literary cabal" of French *philosophes* who ultimately trade in fashion—and by Wollstonecraft, who repeatedly attacks the "specious garb" and "gorgeous drapery" of Burke's language in her public reply to Burke, *A Vindication of the Rights of Men* (1790). Third, the context of the passage in the broader narrative of the play anticipates Wollstonecraft's critique of Burkean history, which, as we shall see in the next chapter, is purported to elide the violent and unjust origins of the institutions it cherishes. Finally, I begin with these lines to emphasize the fact that the constitutional dislike toward revolutions so conspicuous in Burke's *Reflections*—he frankly admits to "the dislike I feel to revolution," as if it were a matter completely divorced from intellection—and even toward the people when they are assembled in particular configurations—as in the oft-quoted remark about "a swinish multitude" seduced by a reinvigorated rhetoric of innovation—are, of course, hardly new sentiments. They are neither the most original nor the most interesting aspects of Burke's political thought.

One aim of this chapter is to draw out what is original and interesting in Burke, which is often less in the principles he espouses than in the unprecedented manner of their exposition. Like Pope's philosophical verse, Burke's speeches and political writings contain few novel ideas (a point of pride for Burke); they are remarkable for how they give old ideas elegant and persuasive new forms, setting a standard for subsequent attempts in the genre. As his earliest critics recognized, Burke's rhetoric is a force to contend with, and any reduction of his political thought to a system of blind reaction does it an obvious injustice. In this, I am in accord with much of the renewed interest in Burke over the past decade or so, which displays greater sympathy with the thinker than he had enjoyed under the more radical critical programs of previous decades. The Burke of the *Reflections*, critics now recognize, is one Burke of many, and by many accounts hardly the most interesting. As this chapter's section on his speech on Fox's East India Bill suggests, Burke is at his most compelling when discussing historical events in all their specificity and complexity. It is here that he demonstrates a command of rhetorical strategies uncontaminated by the almost bodily revulsion he feels when discussing revolution or other abstract concepts. It should be remembered, though, that the *Reflections* is Burke's most systematic expression of mature political principles, containing what is perhaps the period's most influential critique of, in Burke's terms, "political reason" and "political metaphysics." The *Reflections on the Revolution in France* warrants continued attention not only because of its culminating position in Burke's political philosophy but also because of the profound effect it has had in determining the terms of modern political discourse. The founding text of modern conservatism, Burke's *Reflections* presents a model of political truth constituted by, to appropriate Nietzsche's famous phrase, "a mobile army of metaphors, metonyms, and anthropomorphisms" that very much remains with us. Insofar as what is now considered "conservatism" bears any relation at all to the argument of Burke's *Reflections*, an examination of this foundational text, alongside Wollstonecraft's reply to it, can help us understand the rhetorical strategies of our own political debates.

The more immediate aim of this section in the context of this study is to show how the Burke-Wollstonecraft debate cuts to the heart of many of the issues surrounding political reason toward the end of the eighteenth century. The intention of the present chapter is not to draw out the complexity of Burke's thought for its own sake—or, for that matter, the often mind-numbing simplicity of which both he and his interlocutors on the left were extremely capable—but to organize the complexity of his ideas and sentences in accordance with the political and epistemological terms we have been tracing. I take a rhetorical approach in this section because, again, what seems most interesting about Burke and the responses of his critics is how old ideas are given new life through a new kind of persuasive language—language that persists to the present moment, often in debased forms. I propose, then, reading the following texts according to what I consider to be their distinctive rhetorical strategies or modes: *hypotaxis* in Burke's speech on Fox's East India Bill; *paradox* in his *Reflections*; *ratiocinatio* in Wollstonecraft's first *Vindication*. The hypotactic syntax of Burke's East India Bill speech, a speech as much about language and style as it is about politics, performs the principle of subordination at the root of his social, political, and philosophical thought. Taken together, Burke's *Reflections*, Wollstonecraft's first *Vindication*, and Godwin's *Political Justice* bring eighteenth-century debates about political reason to a head, and they delineate the terms through which subsequent meditations on the subject, including the inward turn of Romanticism, understand the stakes of those debates.

Hypotaxis: Burke's Speech on Fox's East India Bill

Just as he was for Wordsworth, Coleridge is perhaps Burke's earliest and greatest true critic. Among the most astute of his many observations on Burke is this assessment from the *Biographia*: "Edmund Burke possessed and had sedulously sharpened that eye, which sees all things, actions, and events, in relation to the *laws* that determine their existence and circumscribe their possibility. He referred habitually to *principles*. He was a *scientific* statesman; and therefore a *seer*. For every *principle* contains in itself the germs of a prophecy; and as the prophetic power is the essential privilege of science, so the fulfillment of its oracles supplies the outward and (to men in general) the *only* test of its claim to the title."[1] Burke is a "*scientific* statesman" in that he habitually refers to principles, the strategy Coleridge would conspicuously adopt in his own exposition of political theory in *The Friend*. The science of politics for Coleridge consists in being able to see the relationship between the historical event and, in terms reflecting Kant's continued influence, the laws that circumscribe its possibility. And it is precisely because of this scientific impulse that Burke is a prophet in the Romantic sense. In the terms of Blake quoted previously, a prophet is a "Seer," not an "Arbitrary Dictator."[2] In Coleridge's view, Burke's particular strength lies in the power of his historical vision and in his ability to discern in pure principles the seeds of prophecy properly understood.

The structure of Burke's historical vision, for Coleridge, is mirrored in the structure of his rhetorical language. Just as he is able to see that principles contain in themselves the germs of prophecy, Burke's style consists in "the unpremeditated and evidently habitual *arrangement* of words, grounded on the habit of foreseeing, in each integral part, or (more plainly) in every sentence, the whole that he then intends to communicate."[3] Again, there is the emphasis on habit, a concept appropriated and revalued by Burke and Coleridge from the empiricist tradition of Hobbes and Hume. Habit is no longer an impediment to genuine knowledge, but the means of its acquisition and the condition of its possibility. Habit allows one to see and to foresee: to see in syntactical parts the truth of the whole and, in doing so, to foresee the consequences of first principles. It is in this spirit of rhetorical and historical metonymy that I approach Burke's speech on the East India Bill, a speech designed to show how the existing conditions of British imperialism contained the seeds of future disasters. The prophetic model of political reason implicit in this speech would be, as we shall see, heavily qualified and even subverted in the later *Reflections*.

England's imperialist economic presence in India began in 1600, when Queen Elizabeth I granted the East India Company a royal charter, offering the company a monopoly on trade with India for a period of fifteen years (the monopoly would be effectively maintained until the Charter Acts of 1813 and 1833). Soon after the Restoration, Charles II gave the company a broad set of legal, military, judicial, and economic rights, transforming it into the de facto imperial government in India. As the company recognized the profitability of governance and expanded its control of the country in the eighteenth century, it encountered serious financial troubles, demanding a set of government bail-outs to rescue it from ruin.[4] Internal problems, however, remained, and new reforms were needed by the early 1780s. Growing public awareness of the extravagant wealth of returning nabobs, and of the atrocities that generated this wealth, spurred calls for reform with even greater urgency.

Fox's East India Bill—Burke's in all but name, as Bromwich reminds us—was the Fox–North coalition's leading instrument for the reform of imperial policy.[5] Burke, who began his career as a political theorist with a failed attempt at irony in the *Vindication of a Natural Society* (1756), had by the early 1780s already established his reputation in the House of Commons as an exceptionally skilled orator and an expert on Indian affairs. His speech on Fox's East India Bill (1783) stands as one of his finest, combining a modern conception of state regulation with a humanitarian defense of colonized subjects. The regulatory component of the bill is straightforward: the authority of the shareholders would be replaced by the more regular oversight of two commissions, answerable to Parliament. The humanitarian argument, constituting the bulk of the speech, features a meticulous history of the British East India Company and concludes that this history consists of nothing other than systematic injustice and domination. The bill eventually would be defeated in December 1783, one of its provisions being that the first set of sixteen commissioners, named in the bill, all be loyal Foxites.

The speech derives its structure from Burke's answers to four objections to the bill: that the bill is an attack on the chartered rights of men; that it increases the influence of the monarch; that it decreases the influence of the monarch; and that it affects national credit. All three special topics of classical rhetoric are present in the work: it is deliberative, or legislative, in its exhortation to pass the bill; judicial, or forensic, in its accusation of the company in general and Warren Hastings, the governor-general of Bengal, in particular; and epideictic, or ceremonial, in its concluding panegyric to Fox. Similarly, the speech makes, by turns, logical, ethical, and emotional appeals. The style of the speech alternates between the middle style (*genus temperatum*), the style appropriate for the general tenor of Burke's political thought, and the high style (*genus grande*), the style appropriate for the subjects of human dignity and national identity.

Burke's response to the first objection—that the bill is an attack on the chartered rights of men—is as close to formal political theory as he will get in the largely pragmatic speech. He finds in the language of the objection itself an unwarranted assumption about the political status of corporations: "I must observe that the phrase 'the chartered rights *of men*,' is full of affectation"[6] and, he notes, rare in discussions about corporate charters.

> The rights of *men*, that is to say, the natural rights of mankind are indeed sacred things; and if any publick measure is proved mischievously to affect them, the objection ought to be fatal to that measure, even if no charter at all could be set up against it. If these natural rights are further affirmed and declared by express covenants, if they are clearly defined and secured against chicane, against power, and authority, by written instruments and positive engagements, they are in a still better condition: they partake not only of the sanctity of the object so secured, but of that solemn publick faith itself, which secures an object of such importance. Indeed this formal recognition, by the sovereign power, of an

original right in the subject, can never be subverted, but by rooting up the holding radical principles of government, even of society itself.[7]

Paine's *Rights of Man* would not be published for another eight years, and Burke in 1783 can still speak of "the rights of men" without grimacing (so long as they are of the restrained English kind and not the excessive French kind). Burke is unambiguously opposed in the speech to what is now called "corporate personhood," the debate over which would be continued a decade after Burke's speech by Hamilton and Jefferson in the United States. "Political power and commercial monopoly are *not* the rights of men," Burke argues; it is "fallacious and sophistical" to argue otherwise, that is, to argue that the Magna Carta of 1215 and the royal charter of 1600 share something in excess of a merely linguistic affinity.

In the above passage, Burke's habitual hypotaxis is evident, with the abundance of subordinated clauses indicating the judicious discrimination that marks virtually all of his writing. The rights of men, for Burke, require definition, immediately provided in the appositive clause following the introduction of the subject. There are only *natural* rights, applicable to human beings and not to concentrations of wealth and power, which may be *further* affirmed when formalized in contracts and charters. Rights are recognized, not created. Insofar as they are "sacred," they are secured against violation (short of political and social revolution) and, implicitly, against inquiry (an inquiry into the foundation of right would, for Burke, be a fruitless exercise). The defense against charges of legislative mischief in the prolepsis following the first semicolon is effective, forestalling objections that the bill does not take rights seriously *enough*. Two parallel and passive if-clauses follow so that the introduction of the subject pronoun ("they") referring to "natural rights" appears late. "They" reappears almost immediately, but this time with a different antecedent ("written instruments and positive engagements") and at the head of a particularly elegant construction: "they partake not only of the sanctity of the object so secured, but of that solemn publick faith itself, which secures an object of such importance." The delayed object is the genuine object, governing more immediately perceptible relations: these charters partake not only of the sanctity of *x*, but of *y*, which itself makes *x* possible. The material subject (the written document) is here subordinated to the relationship between immaterial objects (a contractual agreement itself subordinated to the public faith guaranteeing that agreement). The chiastic structure of the passage (subordination:subject:: subject:subordination) relies, then, on one pronoun ("they") with two antecedents ("natural rights" and what the next sentence terms "formal recognition"). The movement of the passage is into the concept of right only to realize its independence from formal state recognition.

As part of his response to the objection that the bill is an attack on chartered rights, Burke adumbrates four conditions that, if met, would justify a government takeover of the East India Company: the object affected by the abuse is "great and important"; the abuse itself is one of "great atrocity"; the abuse is "habitual, and not accidental"; and, finally, the abuse is incurable in the body as it was then constituted. Burke devotes almost three-quarters of his speech to these four justifying conditions; more than half of it to the second one alone. Demonstrating that the East India Company's conduct in India has been an atrocity rests, he thinks, on three propositions: that there is not a single prince, state, or potentate in India whom it has not sold; that there is not a single treaty it has ever made that it has not broken; and, lastly, that there is not a single prince or state who ever placed any trust in the company who is not utterly ruined.

The third proposition—that there are none who ever confided in the English who have not been ruined—occasions some of the speech's most impressive language. Burke proceeds from the premise that, unlike the merely "mischievous" Tartar invasion ("mischief" is one of Burke's favorite terms of abuse, used to describe crimes both great and small), "it is our protection that destroys India."[8] The paradox of the premise results from England's failure to appreciate the dynamics, or contradictions, of colonial control—that previous conquerors such as the Arabs, Turks, and Persians "rose or fell with the rise and fall of the territory they lived in." Sated on the "intoxicating draught of authority and dominion," the young Englishmen who currently govern there "have no more social habits with the people, than if they still resided in England." There is nothing, in fact, "before the eyes of the natives but an endless, hopeless prospect of new flights of birds of prey and passage, with appetites continually renewing for a food that is continually wasting." The image could, of course, easily predicate a larger argument about what is now referred to as "hearts and minds"—that what is required is merely a minor modification of imperial policy so that it is less blatantly offensive to the natives—but this is not Burke's argument, which sees in England's colonial presence in India a violent disruption of established order. Order is a kind of substance for Burke, an independent thing persisting through time upon which other things depend; it justifies but stands itself in no need of justification. No right—natural, chartered, or divine—to disturb this order exists. It is this principle, above all else, that gives consistency to Burke's diverse positions on British, French, American, and Indian affairs.

Burke's rhetorical consistency, though, lies primarily not in ideology or principle, but in the penetration of his "moral imagination" (a phrase originating with Burke himself). In the speech on the East India Bill, he is able to argue from a position sensitive to Indian and British moral concerns. Just as he had addressed the justified Indian vision of predatory British rapacity, Burke acknowledges that it is "an arduous thing to plead against abuses of a power which originates from your own country, and affects those whom we are used to consider as strangers." In preparing his audience to hear something unpleasant, Burke assumes a middle position that he alone occupies. He will not, however, be *too* unpleasant, as the temperament of his audience must dictate the tone of his argument: "I shall certainly endeavor to modulate myself to this temper; though I am sensible that a cold style of describing actions which appear to me in a very affecting light, is equally contrary to the justice due to the people, and to all genuine human feelings. I ask pardon of truth and nature for this compliance. But I shall be very sparing of epithets either to persons or things."[9] Burke does not ask pardon of his audience for necessary candor (*parrhesia*) but, in an adept inversion, begs pardon of truth for necessary modulation. He thus claims to adopt, despite his own inclination and the demands of justice, a "cold" (non-abusive) style for his descriptions of people, actions, and things (an aspiration that would soon be challenged in his depiction of Warren Hastings). He observes that two masters of the "cold style," Tacitus and Machiavelli, are open to charges that they approve of the enormous crimes they relate:

> [It has been said] that they seem a sort of professors of the art of tyranny, and that they corrupt the minds of their readers, by not expressing the detestation and horrour that naturally belong to the horrible and detestable proceedings. But we are in general, Sir, so little acquainted with Indian details; the instruments of oppression under which the people suffer are so hard to be understood; and even the very names of the sufferers are so uncouth and strange to our ears, that it is very difficult for our sympathy to fix upon these objects.[10]

Burke thus transforms a basic demand of neoclassical aesthetics, the congruity of form and content, into an ethical and political issue. The indecorum of describing horrific acts in non-horrific terms is an offense to justice and, Burke implies, the audience's own moral sense. This seemingly artless style serves the "art of tyranny"; Burke's self-consciously artful rhetoric, in contrast, serves only what he would elsewhere call "natural liberty." He suggests that he must sometimes break from the cold style because he has the added challenge of relating unfamiliar crimes and unfamiliar names. Sympathy, Burke suggests, is the product of intimate acquaintance, the absence of which demands a greater representation of detail if the imagination is to perform its sympathetic work. As it was for Smith, and as it would be for the Romantics covered in this study, the creative imagination is for Burke a moral faculty, the means by which one is able to envision, however imperfectly, a relatable situation. The English imagination is both animated and thwarted in its engagement with India, the exoticness of the methods and objects of its oppression calling it into action aesthetically and, at once, setting limits on its operation ethically. Burke's claim that the "instruments of oppression under which the people suffer are so hard to be understood" seems unnecessarily accommodating (domination is domination, and Burke's home country across the Irish Sea provided ample analogies), but this excessive accommodation (*epitrope*) has its own rhetorical advantages. Having been made simultaneously aware of their liberty and their dullness, his audience in the House senses perhaps that they must engage new faculties, or use existing faculties in new ways.

Burke's implication that the "uncouth and strange" names of "the sufferers" may likewise be an obstacle to sympathy is notable. It is an odd attitude to have toward proper names, one Burke entertains with patient condescension. "Uncouth" did not always have a pejorative connotation, but in the eighteenth century it typically did. The very strangeness of the names makes the "objects" to which they refer themselves somehow distasteful or unpleasant, thereby obstructing sympathetic identification. Strangeness, Burke had argued in the aesthetic *Enquiry* of 1757, produces not sympathy but terror, the ruling principle of the sublime. Terror—in government, religion, or art—relies on obscurity, a quality especially well suited for affecting the imagination. "It is our ignorance of things that causes all our admiration, and chiefly excites our passions. Knowledge and acquaintance make the most striking causes affect but little."[11] And the medium most capable of affecting the imagination through obscurity is language, "so that poetry with all its obscurity, has a more general as well as more powerful dominion over the passions than any other art."[12] Obscure, strange language, like the names of our "sufferers," affects the passions not in the direction of sympathy, but toward fear (the passion, Burke notes, that is the foundation of all despotic government). His expressed aims in the speech are to clarify what is obscure and to supply knowledge where it is absent. Clarity and familiarity are, in the *Enquiry*, the enemies of passion; in the speech on Fox's bill they are the friends of reason and, perhaps, even of the kind of sociability-promoting natural laws discoverable through reason. These positions would be inverted in the later *Reflections*, where it is disruptive forms of reason and knowledge that are associated with sublime terror.

Immediately after his admission that the House is "so little acquainted with Indian details"—the instruments of oppression and the unfamiliar names that refer to its objects—Burke makes a stunning declaration:

> I am sure that some of us have come down stairs from the committee-room with impressions on our minds, which to us were the inevitable results of our discoveries, yet if we should venture to express ourselves, in the proper language of our sentiments, to other gentlemen, not at all prepared to enter into the cause of them, nothing could appear more harsh and dissonant, more violent and unaccountable, than our language and behavior. All these circumstances are not, I confess, very favourable to the idea of our attempting to govern India at all. But

there we are; there we are placed by the Sovereign Disposer; and we must do the best we can in our situation. The situation of man is the preceptor of his duty.[13]

It is a strange confession, lacking the kind of calculated transparency that is, for the most part, characteristic of Burke. What impressions and what discoveries? What language, sentiments, and behavior? Presumably he refers to the kind of matter that follows the passage, the lengthy story of the East India Company's mistreatment of the Wazir of Oudh, Asaf al-Daula, under the Treaty of Faizibad.[14] These are no doubt unfamiliar names to eighteenth-century English ears, but Burke's language of strange impressions, discoveries, sentiments, and behavior suggests something more unspeakable than this piece of colonial drama, namely, the kind of rationalized atrocities Burke usually associates with the revolutionary impulse. The secrecy of the committee-room is translated here into the opacity of Burke's prose. If his diction points to what may not be said—for those answers we are directed *upstairs*—Burke's syntax reveals a plenitude of signification. His hypotaxis runs its course in the long first sentence, the discursivity of his reason given enough space to account for the conditions of "unaccountable" language and behavior. The subordination that defines *hypotaxis* (Greek, subjection) depicts here two epistemologically unequal social groups: the committee-room men whose scientific ideas are the product of necessity ("impressions . . . the inevitable results of our discoveries") and the well-intentioned but ill-informed "other gentlemen, not at all prepared to enter into the cause of them." The epistemic difference (informed and uninformed) is also an aesthetic difference ("the proper language of our sentiments" and "harsh and dissonant" language). These refer to the *same* language: what is proper for one acquainted with Indian details is distasteful to one who is not. Burke, belonging naturally to the "some of us" acquainted with these details, reserves the right to reduce a difference of principle to a difference of taste, about which, he suggests, there can be no arguing.

That these basic differences exist at all, Burke argues, does not inspire confidence in Britain's ability to govern India. "But there we are." The reassuring brevity of the statement itself seems to argue in its favor: no statement of such unshakeable simplicity could be a faulty foundation for legislative deliberation. It would become the unspoken premise of subsequent debates about foreign occupation: the question is less frequently by what right "we" occupy another nation or state, but rather what to do once "we" are there, a presence assumed to be inevitable: as Wollstonecraft would say about Burkean history in general, violent, impure origins are erased in order to perpetuate unjust practices. "But there we are," presumably by the same kind of natural and historical necessities that produce sunsets and riots. In Burke's argument, though, it is above all providential necessity: "there we are placed by the Sovereign Disposer; and we must do the best we can in our situation." Once one accepts the metaphysical premise, the unobjectionable do-the-best-we-can approach follows effortlessly. Burke is not on the whole an apologist for imperialism, just as he is not opposed to it in principle; but the force of his arguments for the reform of colonial policy rests on his ability to accommodate its basic assumptions. "The situation of man is the preceptor of his duty"—this assertion is itself the guiding precept of Burke's, and later Coleridge's, politics of expedience. The digression on style, then, moves with ease through an analogy (Tacitus and Machiavelli), a highly subordinated illustration ("I am sure . . . language and behavior"), a strategic confession, a brief statement of fact, an exhortation, and a concluding maxim. Burke's artful digression on style is also a statement on political expedience: knowing when to use polite language is an essential part of political knowledge, which, in this speech, is to be derived only from experience.

Once he has accommodated the imperialist assumptions of his audience, Burke returns to the third proposition (there is not a partner they have not ruined) of the second justifying condition (the abuse is a great atrocity). Here he presents the story of the Wazir of Oudh, Asaf al-Daula, and appears to chafe immediately under the constraints of the cold style. To protect himself from the kind of language he thinks the matter warrants, he allows al-Daula to speak for himself through his written complaint to Hastings. Al-Daula protests, justifiably according to Burke, about the number of the East India Company's troops stationed in his territory in excess of the number stipulated in the treaty. These troops, he argues in language Burke himself emphasizes, "bring nothing *but confusion* [including general famine] *to the affairs of my government, and are entirely their own masters*" (Burke's emphasis here and throughout).[15] Burke bites his tongue in presenting the wazir's complaint, allowing emphasis to perform the work of commentary. He does the same in presenting Hastings's insensitive response, declaring only that Hastings falls into a "violent passion; such (as it seems) would be unjustifiable in any one who speaks of any part of *his* conduct." Burke thus quotes Hastings's criticism of the style of the wazir's complaint: "[T]he *demands*, the *tone* in which they were asserted, and the *season* in which they were made, are all equally alarming, and appear to him to require an adequate degree of firmness in this board, in *opposition* to them." Hastings proceeds, Burke says, to administer "very unreserved language, on the person and character of the nabob and his ministers," declaring that in the contest between him and the nabob "*the strongest must decide.*" Burke continues to quote Hastings, stressing every disreputable word and phrase along the way, concluding: "Here, Sir, is much heat and passion; but no more consideration of the distress of the country, from a failure of the means of subsistence, and (if possible) the worse evil of an useless and licentious soldiery, than if they were the most contemptible of all trifles. A letter is written in consequence, in such a style of lofty despotism, as I believe has hitherto been unexampled in the records of the East."[16]

This is a political dispute carried out entirely on the level of rhetorical style. Burke begins by defending his own dispassionate language (the "cold style") in describing issues about which he feels strongly; he defends the plain, "humble, and almost abject" style of al-Daula; and he attacks (coolly, practically through emphasis alone) the "violent passion," the "very unreserved language," and the "heat and passion" of Hastings's warm style. Disinterestedness and sentimentality compete here as rhetorical standards. The rhetoric of detachment is allied in Burke's speech with liberty and justice; the rhetoric of passion with despotism. This kind of passion, though, is not the sensibility of giving in to refined emotions, but the unrestrained sentimentality of allowing one's feelings to predominate in excess of reason or taste. Burke continues the strategic conflation of political and aesthetic matters begun in the 1757 *Enquiry*, a conflation that would be used to great effect in the 1790 *Reflections*, where revolutionary feeling seems to be most damningly a symptom of poor taste.

The cold style is of course a rhetorical stance, temporarily adopted by Burke to discredit Hastings's heated stance (a variant of Gorgias's advice that we should "kill our opponent's seriousness with our ridicule and his ridicule with our seriousness"). Burke, like his contemporaneous theorists of rhetoric, never abandons Aristotle's third mode of persuasion, the emotional appeal. "The coolest reasoner," observes George Campbell in *The Philosophy of Rhetoric* (1776), "always, in persuading, addresseth himself to the passions some way or other. . . . So far, therefore, is it from being an unfair method of persuasion to move the passions, that there is no persuasion without moving them."[17] Richard Whately, the nineteenth-century English rhetorician, would similarly argue in his *Elements of Rhetoric* (1828) that the appeal to reason (*logos*) persuades the listener of the appropriateness of the means; the appeal to emotion (*pathos*) of the desirableness of the end. Burke does not stray far from this central line of classical and neoclassical rhetoric, but it is important to note the appearance of deviation. Passion for Burke must be properly channeled (the "proper language of our sentiments"); a rhetoric that is all "heat and passion," without principle, is the rhetoric of revolutionaries and tyrants.

The rest of the speech consists of a catalogue of the company's crimes—a comprehensive recapitulation of which would be "too fatiguing to you, too disgusting to me, to go through with"—as Burke repeatedly plays the Blakean prophet ("The invariable course of the company's policy is this . . ."; "In all this there is nothing wonderful . . ."; "This is the uniform strain of their policy . . .").[18] The prophetic strain of Burke's rhetoric, which Coleridge is only among the first to appreciate, runs throughout the speech. In every principle, Burke sees the germ of prophecy ("If you go on so, the result is so"); in every one of his sentences, one sees the whole he intends to communicate. There is little out of place in the lengthy speech, and every set piece within it contains the principles animating the whole, an instantiating logic present in Burke's argument itself:

> In effect, Sir, every legal regular authority in matters of revenue, of political administration, of criminal law, of civil law, in many of the most essential parts of military discipline, is laid level with the ground; and an oppressive, irregular, capricious, unsteady, rapacious, and peculating despotism, with a direct disavowal of obedience to any authority at home, and without any fixed maxim, principle, or rule of proceeding, to guide them in India, is at present the state of your charter-government over great kingdoms.[19]

Here, again, is Burkean hypotaxis, with one highly subordinated sentence broken into parallel constructions separated by a semicolon. In both constructions the subject is separated from the verb by multiple subordinate clauses ("every legal regular authority . . . is laid level;" and a "despotism . . . is at present the state"), and the two subjects exist in antithesis. Burke elicits the listener's indignation through an amplification of objects in the first construction and through an amplification of subject modifiers in the second. The "of" repetition lends formality to the first construction, within which there is an even greater sense of discrimination in the minor *symploce* "of criminal law, of civil law" (a combination of *anaphora* and *antistrophe*, repetition at the beginning and end of successive phrases). It is an extremely well balanced construction, conspicuously embodying the kind of principled order British government in India lacks.

The "subjection" at the root of Burke's rhetoric, the hypotaxis of his syntax, bridges the concepts of passion and right developed in the *Reflections*, to which I shall presently turn. As he argues there, government is the means of providing for human wants. Among these wants, he says, is the want of sufficient restraints upon human passion. "Society requires not only that the passions of individuals should be subjected, but that even in the mass and body as well as in the individuals, the inclinations of men should frequently be thwarted, their will controlled, and their passions brought into subjection."[20] This apparently illiberal position—sharing more affinities with Rousseau's *Social Contract* (1762) than Burke would care to admit[21]—is, however, immediately qualified. The subjection of human passions, Burke contends, can only be done "*by a power out of themselves*; and not, in the exercise of its function, subject to that will and to those passions which it is its office to bridle and subdue. In this sense the restraints on men, as well as their liberties, are to be reckoned among their rights."[22]

Subjection (or, in the language of some of his contemporaries, "subordination"), then, is one of the "*real*" rights of men. Just like his contemporary and friend, Samuel Johnson, and later Henry James, Burke in his hypotactic prose performs the kind of subordination he thinks is the appropriate form of social organization, at home and abroad. Classical and eighteenth-century hypotaxis suggests the virtues of balance and order; biblical and twentieth-century parataxis (Hemingway, Salinger, McCarthy) suggests a democratic leveling and an inversion of natural power relations (the voice of the expatriate, the disillusioned, the outlaw). Hypotaxis is the structure of sober refinement and discrimination; parataxis the structure of intoxication and divinely inspired utterance. The paratactic mode, Erich Auerbach observes of Augustine, "has something urgently impulsive, something human and dramatic" about it.[23] Burke's prose can be "human" and "urgently impulsive," but it is more often social in orientation, concerned with historical trends and systematic abuses, and impulsive upon reflection. It takes its origin, as Wordsworth would say of poetry generally, from emotion recollected in tranquillity. Burke's speech on Fox's East India Bill exhibits an extraordinary balance of passion and tranquillity—a balance, the speech makes clear, that is a political, epistemic, and rhetorical virtue.

Paradox: *Reflections on the Revolution in France*

The speech on Fox's East India Bill reveals Burke's moral imagination in its most specific mode: general principles are subordinated to particular circumstances, and the sharpness of Burke's historical vision is reflected in the judicious subordination of his sentences. Larger questions of political knowledge or political reason are typically not addressed as such, as the circumstances he addressed there seemed explicable through other means. This would not be the case seven years later in his *Reflections on the Revolution in France*, which on its most fundamental level is about the limits and scope of, in Burke's terms, "political reason." The French Revolution brought out an epistemological strain in Burke that had been largely dormant since his earlier *Enquiry*. Burke, who saw the Revolution as a consequence of an unjustifiable faith in the powers of human reason, challenges abstract reasoning in politics, what he calls "political metaphysics," and champions a reliance on custom and inherited institutions that is to be felt, not known.

Burke justifies this preference through a skeptical assessment of individual knowledge and through a confident belief in the providential guidance of certain historical events. Collective institutions, Iain Hampsher-Monk has observed, fulfill for Burke the epistemic functions formerly granted to individual reason: the family, private property, the aristocracy, state religion, and what Burke calls "corporations" are all "vehicles for the trans-historical accumulation and perpetuation of human knowledge."[24] The assumption that the individual has a right to judge or act on the wisdom of inherited experience is "an act of epistemological and volitional original sin—pride."[25] The epistemic implications of Burke's argument were clear to Coleridge, who in the first issue of *The Watchman* (1796) criticizes William Godwin for possessing too much faith in human reason and Edmund Burke for possessing too little. Godwinian rationalism is the product of "detached metaphysical systematizers"; Burke, by contrast, is guilty of a kind of anti-intellectualism in his aversion to metaphysics and "French principles" derived from reason.

Burke's *Reflections* was a reply to Dr. Richard Price's *A Discourse on the Love of Our Country* (1789), the Dissenting sermon celebrating the centenary of England's revolutionary settlement of 1689 and expressing great enthusiasm at the prospect of thirty million French people "indignant and resolute, spurning slavery, and demanding liberty with an irresistible voice."[26] The ecstatic millennial vision of Price is an apocalyptic nightmare for the aging Burke, who responded with a combination of fear and faith in his *Reflections*: fear about the threat posed to established order, which critics such as Wollstonecraft would quickly condemn as a euphemism for property and patriarchy, and faith in the wisdom of the past and the providential course of English history. Price's sermon is a classic statement of late Enlightenment political epistemology: it argues for a "just and rational principle of action," the "diffusion of knowledge" that distinguishes civil society from the state of nature, the union of knowledge with virtue, and the inseparability of liberty from both.[27]

Burke's *Reflections* sought to redefine the terms of Price's arguments, specifically the meanings of "knowledge" and "reason" as they related to political liberty. The "reflection" was an established prose subgenre by the end of the eighteenth century, offering authors an opportunity to write on serious subjects in a desultory way: other examples around the time of Burke's piece include Joseph Galloway's *Historical and Political Reflections on the Rise and Progress of the American Rebellion* (1780), adapted by John Wesley in a similarly titled text the same year; Thomas Day's *Reflections on the Present State of England* (1782); and Priscilla Wakefield's *Reflections on the Present Condition of the Female Sex* (1798). Still, Burke's *Reflections* is aptly named, as Hampsher-Monk notes, "for the multiple ambiguities about its identity, what it is that it is supposed to shed light on and for whom."[28] The public "reflection" is an Enlightenment mode: it suggests the redirection of internal illumination outward. "Reflection" is an important term in the philosophical tradition as well, its status as a possible source of knowledge a point of contention between empiricists and rationalists. The philosophical inheritance of "reflection" ought to be remembered in the context of Burke's tract, which presents itself as an argument against rationalism—and an argument for inductive empiricism—in political contexts.

According to Burke, the rationalism of the French *philosophes*, and the English radicals indebted to them, went astray in trying to derive the rights of men from political reason.

> The pretended rights of these theorists are all extremes; and in proportion as they are metaphysically true, they are morally and politically false. The rights of men are in a sort of *middle*, incapable of definition, but not impossible to be discerned. The rights of men in governments are their advantages; and these are often in balances between differences of good—in compromises sometimes between good and evil, and sometimes, between evil and evil. Political reason is a computing principle: adding, subtracting, multiplying, and dividing morally, and not metaphysically or mathematically, true moral denominations.[29]

Burke's critique of political reason is less nuanced than that of the Romantics covered in this study: it is a negating criticism of it, premised on a suspicion of metaphysics in general. What is true in metaphysics—and Burke is not ready to admit that this amounts to much—is not necessarily true in morals and politics. It is this distinction, in part, that justifies the paradoxical language found throughout the work. In the passage above, the rights of men are both true and false, depending on the philosophical discipline from which one approaches them. Moreover, they are discoverable and, at the same time, indefinable. Because they exist in "a sort of *middle*," political rights can seem to be two opposed things at once. In this case, the metaphysical truth of rights and the mere existence of political reason itself seem part of a strategy designed to anticipate the arguments of rationalist critics.

At the heart of Burke's argument is the idea that states may not be thought into existence—an argument against political idealism in the philosophical sense. It is also an argument against political rationalism, the idea that reason operating independently is sufficient in constructing, reforming, or even destroying the state. Because the constitution of the state is "a matter of the most delicate and complicated skill" and "because it requires a deep knowledge of human nature and necessities," Burke prescribes serious limits for abstract reasoning in practical politics. In one of the *Reflections*' less prophetic moments, he asks, "What is the use of discussing a man's abstract right to food or to medicine?"—a question, he says, merely about methods of procuring and administering. "In that deliberation I shall always advise to call in the aid of the farmer and the physician, rather than the professor of metaphysics."[30] The recognition of the ethical complexity of modern political organization, in which sympathy or a sense of duty must somehow extend far beyond the field of immediate sense experience, is betrayed here by a vision of premodern social relations. Like Smith's brewer, butcher, and baker, Burke's farmer and physician perform the roles of their precapitalist pasts (Smith's argument in *The Wealth of Nations*, it should be noted, was for perfect liberty under conditions of perfect equality, conditions to which Burke would never assent). Burke misperceives here a trend that has become even more salient since his time: as social life becomes more complex and concentrations of private and state power become more entrenched, the question of rights in relation to food or medicine becomes more, not less, pressing.

The fate of the farmer and physician, perhaps, Burke could not have known. But his hostility toward the "professor of metaphysics" is real, rooted in a fear that the traditions and institutions that constitute national identity are under threat. Rationalism, especially in its political form, is the fullest realization of this threat; strict empiricism the last line of defense. Knowledge that is independent of experience is, of course, the great prize of rationalism, and Burke consequently addresses the possibility of a priori knowledge in politics.

> The science of constructing a commonwealth, or renovating it, or reforming it, is, like every other experimental science, not to be taught *à priori*. Nor is it short experience that can instruct us in that practical science; because the real effects of moral causes are not always immediate, but that which in the first instance is prejudicial may be excellent in its remoter operation, and its excellence may arise even from the ill effects it produces in the beginning. The reverse also happens; and very plausible schemes, with very pleasing commencements, have often shameful and lamentable conclusions. In states there are often some obscure and almost latent causes, things which appear at first view of little moment, on which a very great part of its prosperity or adversity may most essentially depend.[31]

If the argument fails, it is not on logical grounds. Few people would deny that the state is like a complex machine or organism, in which there are all sorts of unexpected consequences. Likewise, few would conceive of political science as an entirely a priori science, operating completely outside of experience. The craftsmanship of Burke's rhetoric remains impressive here as well: the *conduplicatio* (repetition of a word in succeeding clauses) of "or" and then "very"; the conjunction of philosophical ("*a priori*," "moral causes") and affective ("pleasing," "shameful," "lamentable") diction; most of all, the extraordinary sense of balance resulting from internal division and antithesis (not *a*, nor *b*; not *b* because *c*; *c* because either *d* or *e*; finally *f*). If the argument fails to persuade, it is because of an implicit and unjustified appeal to reverence for authority and traditional values (*argumentum ad verecundiam*). The argument from authority is the dominant mode in the *Reflections*, whereas it plays a more subordinate role in Burke's more nuanced writings on India, America, Ireland, and slavery, in which emotional appeals to concepts like justice and liberty predominate (and not to tradition or authority as such). Burke sums up this most theoretical section of his most theoretical work with the following hypotactic, utterly Burkean sentence:

> The science of government being therefore so practical in itself, and intended for such practical purposes, a matter which requires experience, and even more experience than any one person can gain in his whole life, however sagacious and observing he may be, it is with infinite caution that any man ought to venture upon pulling down an edifice which has answered in any tolerable degree for ages the common purposes of society, or on building it up again, without having models and patterns of approved utility before his eyes.[32]

Burke shares the eighteenth-century, Humean faith that "politics may be reduced to a science," though the method of Burke's science seems to consist solely of observation. The hand of reform should be uncertain, so uncertain in fact that it is withdrawn almost as soon as it is extended. The method of the science of government seems here to be a kind of radical empiricism—radical less in its exclusion of any kind of knowledge not derived from sense experience (although it shares with positivism a rejection of almost all metaphysical speculation) than in the impossibly immense amount of experience it demands ("more experience than any person can gain in his whole life"). When it comes to political knowledge, Burke is epistemologically skeptical, even more skeptical than Hume, for whom political principles may at times be deduced a priori.[33] One simply cannot acquire enough knowledge to begin tampering with political institutions. Political philosophy for Burke begins in wonder and ends there.

Burke's, though, is ultimately a half-hearted empiricism: like his recognition of political reason as a computing principle, his embrace of induction in politics provides cover for the kind of anti-intellectualism Coleridge discerned in him in 1796 (and Wollstonecraft and others discerned even earlier). Knowledge derived from experience is fine for Burke, as long as it does not interfere with existing structures in any fundamental way. Knowledge is finally subordinate to other forms of justification; the faculty of political reason is not sovereign, but answerable to a sensibility that generates affection for existing institutions. This is a half-hearted, not a thoroughgoing, empiricism because it is hard to imagine Burke's argument being controverted by other kinds of empirical evidence: the violent details of Hume's *History of England* or the degraded condition of women, slaves, and the poor presented in Wollstonecraft's two *Vindications* make no mark on the edifice of Burke's argument. Knowledge is an irritant for the Burke of the *Reflections* (not so, it should go without saying, for the earlier Burke or for the Burke known to Johnson and other members of the British literati). The empirical "science of government" begrudgingly conceded by Burke is so overburdened with qualification as to render it stationary and impotent. "The nature of man is intricate; the objects of society are of the greatest possible complexity; and therefore no simple disposition or direction of power can be suitable either to man's nature, or to the quality of his affairs."[34] Burke's arguments for caution and complexity, like arguments made in the name of security, can be difficult to oppose on their own terms, a fact not lost on some of his most ardent present-day acolytes. The recognition of complexity so vaunted by conservative disciples of Burke is almost always an argument to keep things as they are. It would be up to Burke's best critics on the left, such as Wollstonecraft and Mackintosh, to argue that complexity knows no party.[35]

Given Burke's frequent animadversions on the "mazes of metaphysic sophistry," one might think that, while society is necessarily complex, the language of philosophy (and especially political philosophy) ought not to be. His self-representation as a philosopher in the empiricist tradition naturally allies him with the "historical, plain method" of Locke that eschews unnecessarily metaphorical or paradoxical language. We have seen at least one instance where Burke resists the constraints of the noncontradictory plain style—in arguing for rights that are true in one sense yet false in another, discoverable yet indefinable—because the "middle" ground of the subject demanded such fine distinctions. And, as we shall see in the next chapter, Burke's "slavish paradoxes" were a source of great exasperation for Wollstonecraft. The hypotaxis of his earlier work does not go away, but it is conjoined in the *Reflections* with language that often seeks to do two opposed things at once.

Paradox (Greek, contrary to opinion or expectation) works on multiple levels in the *Reflections*. It operates in terms of principle, so that it is difficult, for instance, to reconcile the "old settled maxim, never entirely nor at once to depart from antiquity" with Burke's retrospective endorsement of past events that no doubt seemed like major disruptions to established order at the time (the Glorious Revolution, the Reformation, or even, as Wollstonecraft would point out, the establishment of the Christian religion itself). It occurs in declarations like "the essence of property . . . is to be *unequal*" (neither the etymology nor the concept of property, of course, entails its unequal distribution); in assertions that, in joining civil society, man "abdicates all right to be his own governor" (none of the major contract theorists goes quite this far, though Hobbes comes close); in the contention that "the restraints on men, as well as their liberties, are to be reckoned among their rights" (this is the sort of sophistical cant Burke condemns in the *philosophes*); and in his argument that "prejudice" in religious matters, far from being antithetical to reason, may contain "profound and extensive wisdom."[36] None of these claims is obviously false—they are not patent contradictions—and Burke offers persuasive arguments for some of them. They do, however, run counter to certain forms of opinion or expectation: the most ardent defenders of the Church of England, for instance, would hesitate to style themselves champions of "prejudice." Burke wishes to revise some of his audience's most basic concepts, a project that in the *Reflections* often demands counterintuitive language.

It is when discussing ethical virtues, though, that Burke's tendency toward paradox is most evident. Consider, for example, this passage near the end of the work's well-known rhapsode on Marie Antoinette. The inaction of the crowd on one of the "October days"—protesting rising bread prices, a fact Burke thinks it unnecessary to mention—as some entered the queen's bedchamber reveals a kind of moral obtuseness:

> Never, never more, shall we behold that generous loyalty to rank and sex, that proud submission, that dignified obedience, that subordination of the heart, which kept alive, even in servitude itself, the spirit of an exalted freedom. The unbought grace of life, the cheap defence of nations, the nurse of manly sentiment and heroic enterprize is gone! It is gone, that sensibility of principle, that chastity of honour, which felt a stain like a wound, which inspired courage whilst it mitigated ferocity, which ennobled whatever it touched, and under vice itself lost half its evil, by losing all its grossness.[37]

All of this suggests to Burke that "the age of chivalry is gone" and "that of sophisters, oeconomists, and calculators, has succeeded."[38] The passage gains its force through a series of virtues modified in unexpected ways: "generous loyalty," "proud submission," "dignified obedience." These are terms best kept separate according to the ethical tradition of liberalism of which Burke is a product: generosity, pride, and dignity are the marks of independence; loyalty, submission, and obedience the marks of tyranny. Burke's salient conjunction of the terms—his idea that the spirit of freedom may be found in servitude itself— challenges a liberal tradition that, as he sees it, has lost its capacity for moral discrimination.

For Burke this loss of moral imagination is related in some basic way to the looming shift from British empiricism to French rationalism as the center of philosophical gravity: the cautious and moderate empiricism of Locke and, in certain moods, Hume seems threatened by the unsubmissive epistemological pride of Helvétius and Holbach. The shift is not likely to make it across the Channel, Burke says, owing to English stubbornness.

> Thanks to our sullen resistance to innovation, thanks to the cold sluggishness of our national character, we still bear the stamp of our forefathers. We have not (as I conceive) lost the generosity and dignity of thinking of the fourteenth century; nor as yet have we subtilized ourselves into savages. We are not the converts of Rousseau; we are not the disciples of Voltaire; Helvetius has made no progress amongst us. Atheists are not our preachers; madmen are not our law-

givers. We know that *we* have made no discoveries; and we think that no discoveries are to be made, in morality; nor many in the great principles of government, nor in the ideas of liberty, which were understood long before we were born, altogether as well as they will be after the grave has heaped its mould upon our presumption, and the silent tomb shall have imposed its law on our pert loquacity.[39]

This is Roman rhetoric, existing, like the principles of liberty to which he refers, long before Burke and persisting long after him. For those sympathetic to Burke, its rhythms and repetitions seem direct indications of the truth and dignity of its sentiments; for others, including Wollstonecraft, it is precisely the kind of "turgid bombast" that stands in the way of progress. The question on which the passage turns—whether there are any discoveries to be made in morals and politics—similarly has a long history extending into ancient philosophy, and Burke's negative answer in the *Reflections* would exert a powerful influence on the political discourse of Romanticism and beyond.

If there are no discoveries to be made in morals and politics, then at least two paths seem open: an inward turn loosely associated with liberal individualism and a communitarian impulse, premised not on rational and democratic deliberation but on a shared sense of inheritance and a shared sense of fear. The inward turn—toward either the creative life of the mind or toward the satisfaction of desires—would for the most part be the strategy of Romanticism, even as it largely holds on to the optimistic attitude toward political knowledge characteristic of the eighteenth century. This, at least, is the case I have been trying to make. In its most exalted moments, Romanticism adopts, to borrow the words of Russell, a vision "based rather upon the impulse to construct than upon the desire to retain what we possess or to seize what is possessed by others," an attitude, I suggest, with an epistemological correlative in Kantian constructivism: the turn to the mind reveals it to be richer and more active than previously imagined, the source of cognition, freedom, and even experience itself. For the Romantics covered in this study, the revelation of the inward turn does not end in withdrawal, but in a sustained commitment to building social freedom on the freedom of the individual mind.

Burke's response to the impasse of political knowledge, on the other hand, obviates any such inward turn. His sympathies in the *Reflections* lie with a kind of constrained communitarianism, marked not by the political power of collective decision making but by the solace offered to otherwise atomized individuals through the paternal institutions of church, state, and private property. "We are afraid to put men to live and trade each on his own private stock of reason; because we suspect that the stock in each man is small, and that the individuals would do better to avail themselves of the general bank and capital of nations, and of ages."[40] Reason is socialized; property is privatized. The analogy between reason and capital is telling: advanced capitalism, for both Smith and Marx, tends toward monopoly (for Smith, monopolies "derange" the natural distribution of stock in a society and are maintained by the unjust laws of the state; for Marx, they indicate a form of sovereignty in which the worker is reduced to "the most wretched of commodities"). Burke's argument for the capital accumulation of reason is not immune to the logic of late capitalism: the limits of political reason in individuals necessitate its concentration in more impersonal forms. Burke is a proponent of representative government, but the fear of individual reason he expresses in the *Reflections* raises questions about the logic of representation itself. Reason as accumulated and shared capital is, in Marxist terms, a kind of reification: it is an abstraction given material reality, precisely the kind of rhetorical fallacy Burke claims to abhor in French philosophy. "Reason has always existed," Marx says in an early article, "only not always in reasonable form."[41] The simultaneous confidence in a collective and hypostasized political reason and the disavowal of political reason as it exists in the individual is among the most fundamental of Burke's paradoxes.

It is Marx himself who offers the most stinging assessments of Burke's paradoxes, typically characterized by critics in the less charitable terms of ideological inconsistency or worse. After tracing the history of the phrase "labouring poor" in English legislation, Marx challenges the good faith of Burke in calling the phrase "execrable political cant": "This sycophant, who, in the pay of the English oligarchy, played the part of the romantic opponent of the French Revolution, just as, in the pay of the North American colonies at the beginning of the troubles in America, he had played the liberal against the English oligarchy, was a vulgar bourgeois through and through. 'The laws of commerce are the laws of Nature, and therefore the laws of God.' No wonder then, that, true to the laws of God and Nature, he always sold himself in the best market!"[42] Marx repeats criticisms that had been leveled at Burke throughout his political career. Accusations that Burke was the recipient of a secret government pension began as early as 1774 and continued through the end of his life.[43] Given new life after a meeting between Paine and Burke in May 1790, the rumors were, the evidence suggests, false. They were nevertheless used repeatedly in attempts to discredit Burke, who had pushed for the abolition of certain pensions and sinecure appointments in his position as paymaster-general. Wollstonecraft accuses Burke, as Marx would, of enjoying the "wages of falsehood"—secretly receiving a "pension of fifteen hundred pounds per annum on the Irish establishment"—while displaying a clear "contempt for the poor" (Marx's characterization of Burke as a "romantic" opponent of the French Revolution also begins with Wollstonecraft). Paine would continue the allegations in his *Rights of Man* (1791), in which Burke is "accustomed to kiss the aristocratical hand that hath purloined him from himself" and, again, in his *Letter Addressed to the Addressers* (1792).[44] The attack would be renewed by prominent Whigs when Burke did indeed receive a pension upon his retirement from Parliament in 1794, prompting him to defend himself finally against charges of inconsistency and sycophancy in the extraordinary *Letter to a Noble Lord* (1796).

The myth of the secret pension had such staying power partly because critics of Burke have discerned few alternative explanations for what seemed to be an outright betrayal of earlier principles. One could argue for a consistency in the structure of Burke's rhetoric whereby, as Coleridge suggested, he foresees in each aspect of his language the whole he intends to communicate. In this broad sense, we see the same elements throughout Burke's rhetoric: balance, parallelism, antithesis, repetition, amplification, concession, deliberation, and subordination. Burke's language performs the principles of his political thought: perfect paratactic equality is neither sublime nor beautiful, and perfect political knowledge—any kind that can be expressed in a declaration or manifesto, indeed any kind that can be articulated in a single, written constitution at all—is neither possible nor desirable. Similarly, the paradoxes of the *Reflections* reveal a curiously capacious ethical vision, in which the spirit of liberty is to be found even in servitude, just as they reveal a political reason that, in its public and historical functions, does what individual political reason cannot. The power, and at times contradictions, of Burke's thought would exasperate more than one critic. Wollstonecraft, whose reply to Burke I now turn to, nearly gave up the enterprise midway through its composition, recording her frustration in the finished text itself. Even Samuel Johnson, who made a pastime of tossing and goring people in conversation, approached his friend with uncharacteristic caution: "That fellow calls forth all my powers," Boswell records him as saying. "Were I to see Burke now, it would kill me."[45] Burkean rhetoric, in both its pure and debased forms, remains formidable in the present moment, in ways perhaps that even he himself at his most prophetic could not have foreseen.

CHAPTER THREE

Wollstonecraft and the Vindication of Political Reason

The Rights of Men

•

> Coherence, without some pervading principle of order, is a
> solecism.
> —*Wollstonecraft,* A Vindication of the Rights of Men

> This is what makes it a more spiritual event than our Revolution,
> an event of much more powerful and worldwide interest, though
> practically less successful; it appeals to an order of ideas which
> are universal, certain, permanent. 1789 asked of a thing, Is it
> rational?
> —*Arnold, "The Function of Criticism at the Present Time"*

Insofar as it existed at all, "political reason" was for the later Burke a "comput-ing principle" of moral denominations that cannot be derived "metaphysically or mathematically." The science of constructing a commonwealth is "like every other experimental science, not to be taught *a priori*," though, in the *Reflec-tions*, he would just as well do away with the application of science to politics altogether. Society is an object of the greatest possible complexity, unknowable to even the most advanced scientist or philosopher. In his reluctant reliance on inductive, or "experimental," philosophy in political contexts, Burke parts ways with the Romantics covered in this study, all of whom express serious doubts about the limits of purely inductive empiricism and concerns about its disas-trous consequences for the human being's political and imaginative life.

Mary Wollstonecraft, who uses the term "romantic" itself with ambivalence, anticipates Coleridge, Wordsworth, and Shelley in their suspicion of strict empiricism in political contexts. She goes further than they do, however, in ar-ticulating an enlightened and radical conception of the role of reason in politi-cal affairs. Her public reply to Burke, *A Vindication of the Rights of Men* (1790), is a monument of late Enlightenment political rationalism. In opposition to Burke's designed appeal to various kinds of *pathos* in the *Reflections*, Wollstone-craft makes a self-conscious appeal to *logos*, with *ratiocinatio*, as both a rhetori-cal mode and philosophical abstraction, at the center of her argument. Critics have long noted the emphasis on reason in Wollstonecraft's critique of Burke, but her association of reason with emancipation is worth studying in greater detail. It is here—in her conception of the revolutionary capacity of the rational faculty itself—that Wollstonecraft makes one of the most important contributions to late eighteenth-century political epistemology. In what follows, I examine Wollstonecraft's revolutionary conception of ratiocinatio, the rhetoric through which it is mediated, and the relationship between the aesthetic categories she inherits and the argument for rational freedom she proposes. The critique of political reason contained in her *Vindications* is premised on a liberating inward turn that reveals the most basic forms of knowledge; the abuse of rhetoric she discerns in Burke reveals, she suggests, a fundamental lack of self-knowledge.

Ratiocinatio: Building Affection on Rational Grounds

Wollstonecraft's was the first of forty-five answers to Burke written in the year following publication of his *Reflections* (a cause of some concern for William Godwin and others on the left). These replies to Burke constitute one of the great movements in British political writing, producing such radical professions of faith as Catharine Macaulay's *Observations on the Reflections of the Rt. Hon. Edmund Burke* (1790), Thomas Paine's *Rights of Man* (1791), James Mackintosh's *Vindiciae Gallicae* (1791), and Joseph Priestley's *Letters to the Right Honorable Edmund Burke* (1791). In the context of these other replies, Wollstonecraft's stands out for a few reasons. As David Bromwich argues, she seems a more original moral thinker and a deeper reader of Burke than many of her contemporaries.[1] Two other attributes of her work should also be noted: it attains a level of philosophical abstraction, ranging from epistemology to aesthetics, not present in other works of its kind, and it is, rhetorically, as passionate a work as one will find in 1790s radicalism.

The role of reason in political affairs is an essential point of difference between Burke and Wollstonecraft in their debate on revolution. In the simplest terms, Burke sees the dogmatic application of reason in politics as a source of violence, anarchy, and discontinuity; Wollstonecraft sees the reflective application of reason in politics as the only possible solution to revolutionary violence, anarchy in its underdeveloped form, and the related ideologies of class hierarchy, sexism, and racism. Some critics have sought to soften the difference between the two on this score. R. R. Fennessy, for instance, insists that Burke was not simply a critic of reason: "Burke's anti-rationalism is not a rejection of reason but a protest against the application of a particular method of reasoning to the study of society and the state," a method James Conniff specifies as "a kind of crude a priorism which is out-of-touch with experience."[2] These sorts of claims, though, do not tell us much: few would argue that Burke is an out-and-out anti-rationalist in the tradition of Hamann, distrustful of reason in all its forms, and even fewer would profess "a crude a priorism which is out-of-touch with experience." These general objections to debased forms of rationalism are truisms, arguing essentially that Burke joined the rest of the philosophical community in condemning bad forms of rationalism. If Burke's postrevolutionary position is to be meaningful at all, it must be understood for what it is: an unapologetic objection to the authority of reason in political contexts. Similarly, one should not weaken Wollstonecraft's position in efforts to demonstrate its complexity. Conniff is right to say that Wollstonecraft saw reason and sentiment as intimately related, but this assertion is too mild. What is interesting about Wollstonecraft's position is its emphasis on the sovereignty of reason in political affairs, even as it bridges the claims of reason and sensibility in an idea of the "rational affections." The proper function of reason is a real point of divergence for Burke and Wollstonecraft, not merely a difference in emphasis.

It is worth taking a closer look, then, at the role of reason in the *Vindication of the Rights of Men*, which is as much a vindication of the rights of reason as it is one of the rights of man ("man" and "reason" are the two most frequently used keywords in the text). Wollstonecraft begins her work by claiming to "contend for the rights of men *and the liberty of reason*," though the latter phrase has received far less scrutiny than the former. In what does the "liberty of reason" consist, and under what conditions does it make sense to think of mental faculties in political terms? As seen throughout this study, the discourse of faculty psychology became increasingly politicized toward the end of the eighteenth century, the residue of which may be seen in Romantic poetry and prose. The Romantic conception of reason's autonomy has its roots in Kant, not only in his critical system but also, as we have seen, in works like "What Is Enlightenment?" (1784) and *The Conflict of the Faculties* (1798). It should be remembered that Wollstonecraft, a translator of German and French, was familiar with the German philosophical tradition from Leibniz to Kant.[3] In her *Vindication of the Rights of Men*, published in the second year of the French Revolution and a mere month after Burke's *Reflections*, a politicized faculty psychology is dominated by reason, which she says in another work "should cultivate and govern those instincts which are implanted in us to render the path of duty pleasant."[4] Wollstonecraft's addition of pleasure to the duties demanded by reason represents her most significant departure from Kantian ethics and anticipates Wordsworth's later alliance of pleasure and knowledge in the poetics of the 1802 Preface to the *Lyrical Ballads*. The "liberty of reason" for Wollstonecraft consists in its sovereignty over a cluster of related concepts: experience, history, authority, custom, habit, passion, sentiment, and sensibility. This, again, is a substantial departure from the highly qualified "rational reform" of Burke.

Wollstonecraft's argument against Burke is that he has allowed his attachment to these other sources of justification, especially history and sensibility, to dominate the only true source of political and epistemic justification, the God-given and humanizing faculty of reason. The psychological factors contributing to such a renunciation were of considerable interest to Wollstonecraft, as they were to many of Burke's contemporaries, who wondered why the aging member of Parliament would devote himself to aristocratic propaganda. At bottom, she suspected unreflective ambition and vanity in the generally well-intentioned Burke, a "scrupulous anxiety" to revive his shining reputation whereby "his reason, the weather-cock of unrestrained feelings, is only employed to varnish over the faults which it ought to have corrected."[5] She even suggests a "mortal antipathy to reason" in the *Reflections*; the abuse of reason to provide a varnish, cloak, or facade for political injustice is a dominant motif of the work. The ad hominem attacks on Burke's abuse of reason, though, constitute only one aspect of Wollstonecraft's general treatment of the faculty, which may be divided into positive, negative, and synthetic parts. In positive terms, Wollstonecraft argues for reason as a legitimate source of moral and political knowledge. In negative terms, she defines it against a range of other faculties and sources of knowledge, especially sensibility. In synthetic terms, she argues for a conception of the "rational affections" in which duty more or less coincides with inclination.

The Vindication of the Rights of Men endorses reason as a valid source of moral and political knowledge, including knowledge of the right to "a degree of liberty, civil and religious, as is compatible with the liberty of every other individual with whom he is united in a social compact." The liberal component of Wollstonecraft's argument—reiterating the basic elements of the natural law and social contract theories developed by Hobbes, Locke, and Rousseau—should be remembered, as should the fact that it serves as the basis for more radical claims:

> Liberty, in this simple, unsophisticated sense, I acknowledge, is a fair idea that has never yet received a form in the various governments that have been established on our beauteous globe; the demon of property has ever been at hand to encroach on the sacred rights of men, and to fence round with awful pomp laws that war with justice. But that it results from the eternal foundation of right—from immutable truth—who will presume to deny, that pretends to rationality—if reason has led them to build their morality and religion on an everlasting foundation—the attributes of God?[6]

Wollstonecraft repeatedly emphasizes the harmful effects of private property, which she argues, encourages blind self-love, crushes the contemplative faculties of the mind, and impedes the progress of civilization (she stresses the role of cities in the advancement of knowledge). Wollstonecraft singles out two species of property in particular, inherited and church property, for special censure. These are offenses against nature and reason, as "the only security of property that nature authorizes and reason sanctions is, the right a man has to enjoy the acquisitions which his talents and industry have acquired."[7] The language of encroachment and "fencing round" evokes the still palpable and, in some cases, accelerating effects of land enclosure, which she attacks later in the *Vindication* as a form of class robbery made worse by the complicity of the state.

The argument for reason as a source of moral, political, and even religious knowledge is developed here in the terms of philosophical rationalism, whereby experience may initiate the acquisition of knowledge or subsequently confirm its validity but is finally subordinate to reason as the sovereign, or "sanctioning," cognitive faculty. Reason is imagined here in its largest sense, subsuming moral and aesthetic judgment, often at the same time. Wollstonecraft provides the example of the "poor wretch, whose *inelegant* distress extorted from a mixed feeling of disgust and animal sympathy present relief"—a jab at Burke's conflation of morality and taste and at the general substitution of benevolent impulses for principles of justice—to argue for a morality constructed on the basis of reason, or conscience, which she argues are synonymous terms. In this, Wollstonecraft joins a rationalist tradition of conscience, emphasizing its etymological roots "with knowledge," including Coleridge's later definition of conscience as the level of agreement between free will and reason.

After the identification of reason with conscience, Wollstonecraft's argument takes a particularly effective turn. She asks if "Mr. Burke will be at the trouble to inform us, how far we are to go back to discover the rights of men, since the light of reason is such a fallacious guide that none but fools trust to its cold investigation?"[8] It is a Humean question—recall Hume's questions regarding an allegedly original contract ("Is there anything discoverable in all these events but force and violence? Where is the mutual agreement or voluntary association so much talked of?")—to which she gives a Humean reply. Her reply is true not only to the letter of Hume, relying as it does on appropriately barbarous selections from his *History of England* (1754–62), but also to the spirit of the debunking empiricist, who would have similarly asked Burke from what impressions he derives his idea of ancient virtue. Wollstonecraft, however, poses and answers her own question—the technique of *hyperphora* so often used by Burke himself—to discredit the claims of Humean empiricism in political contexts. The termination of empiricism in skepticism is not a viable path for Wollstonecraft, who adopts an optimistic, enlightened idiom to affirm the light of reason as a trustworthy guide in human affairs.

The essential thing to note in this context is that the light of reason for Wollstonecraft is perceptible only when one turns inward. Burke's great error, she suggests, is ultimately an insufficient degree of introspection, an irritable hankering after the imagined facts of the past to compensate for an intellectual cowardice in confronting the inconvenient truths of the present, in which one is more immediately implicated. Were he to look into his own soul, Burke would find that power and right are synonymous for him, an identification, she suggests, from which he has personally profited:

> But in fact all your declamation leads so directly to this conclusion, that I beseech you to ask your own heart, when you call yourself a friend of liberty, whether it would not be more consistent to style yourself the champion of property, the adorer of the golden image which power has set up?—And, when you are examining your heart, if it would not be too much like mathematical drudgery, to which a fine imagination very reluctantly stoops, enquire further, how it is consistent with the vulgar notions of honesty, and the foundation of morality—truth; for a man to boast of his virtue and independence, when he cannot forget that he is at the moment enjoying the wages of falsehood.[9]

Wollstonecraft alludes here to a pension Burke would not in fact receive until 1794, as discussed in the previous chapter. Her iconoclasm suggests what she sees as the irreligious tendencies of Burke's veneration of established power, but it also has a subjective correlative: just as she hopes to break the idols of the past, so does she promote an act of introspective ratiocination designed to dismantle inconsistencies and rob them of their power. Her pointed reference to "mathematical drudgery" recalls Burke's arguments that political knowledge is not, like mathematics, an a priori science, and that political reason is at best a "computing principle" that deals with moral, not metaphysical or mathematical, denominations. For Wollstonecraft, the project of examining the coherence of our ideas, though it may bring displeasure, is a political and potentially emancipating act for those with and without power. It is crucial to stress here the political significance of her argument for ideational coherence, which appears to be an uncomplicated or unobjectionable end as long as moral principles are separated from instrumental reason. Once these are understood in some relation to each other—the possibility of which is the great promise of political reason broadly conceived—the problem of coherence assumes greater proportions. Incoherence describes not merely relatively rare cases of strict propositional conflict or contradictory sense data, but how political beliefs fail to align with "vulgar notions of honesty" or basic moral principles (Orwell would have called it "doublethink," and it is the dark side of Romantic "negative capability"). The turn to the mind—or the "heart," as they amount to nearly the same thing in Wollstonecraft's account of rational sensibility—is the precondition for ideological and moral coherence, a subjective state with objective conditions and consequences.

The exhortation to turn inward is a dominant strategy in the *Vindication*. Injunctions to Burke such as "Go hence, thou slave of impulse, look into the private recesses of thy heart"[10] are also, of course, challenges to the unreflective reader, who is invited to discover for him- or herself what intrinsic principles or innate faculties belong to the mind and what things must be learned or acquired. The substance of Wollstonecraft's philosophical argument is that Burke's moral instinct is an illusion, one which, intentionally or not, justifies the status quo. Virtue is not innate but acquired with the exertion of reason (which is innate), a fact Burke would recognize were he to examine, for instance, his own inconsistency in hastily stripping Louis XVI of his hereditary honors: "Where then was the infallibility of that extolled instinct which rises above reason? was it warped by vanity, or *hurled* from its throne by self-interest? To your own heart answer these questions in the sober hour of reflection— and, after reviewing this gust of passion, learn to respect the sovereignty of reason." "Respect" is the key term here, as the *Vindication* is largely an effort to undermine the aesthetic premise of Burke's *Enquiry* (1757): the masculine sublime commands respect and terror; the feminine beautiful inspires affection and love. Wollstonecraft is intent on challenging this distinction because respect in Burke's *Reflections* is reserved not for rational principles of justice but for the sensible authority of patriarchal tradition. The inward turn of the *Vindication* is designed to reverse this orientation:

> I reverence the rights of men.—Sacred rights! for which I acquire a more profound respect, the more I look into my own mind; and, professing these heterodox opinions, I still preserve my bowels; my heart is human, beats quick with human sympathies—and I FEAR God!
>
> I bend with awful reverence when I enquire on what my fear is built.—I fear that sublime power, whose motive for creating me must have been wise and good; and I submit to the moral laws which my reason deduces from this view of my dependence on him.—It is not his power that I fear—it is not to an arbitrary will, but to unerring *reason* I submit.[11]

In an important sense, the inward turn of Romanticism begins here, in Wollstonecraft's postrevolutionary exhortation to examine the contents of one's own mind. While there are clear seventeenth- and eighteenth-century precedents for Romantic inwardness—in the retirement or country-house poem, descriptive-meditative verse, the poetry of sensibility—subsequent inward turns in Romantic poetry and prose would retain the political inflection so distinctly pronounced in Wollstonecraft. The turn to the mind is a turn to the source of knowledge itself and a turn away from the sovereignty of history and experience. Sublime awe is properly reserved for the human mind (awe that would turn into terror in Wordsworth's "Prospectus" to the *Recluse* and Coleridge's "Dejection" ode); the orientation of sublime wonder in Burke toward the wisdom of the past is a renunciation of the spontaneity and autonomy Kant had argued are essential to human freedom. The essence of early Romantic freedom, again, is not the mere absence of restraint but the voluntary submission to a moral law deduced by reason, which for Wollstonecraft is also an aesthetic act in the broadest sense (both bodily in its congruity with the affections and artistic in the power of human creativity to circumscribe itself by rules of its own making).

The negative and synthetic parts of Wollstonecraft's argument about reason have already been suggested, though I consider them briefly here because these moments, too, reveal important aspects of her criticism of Burke. Reason in the *Rights of Men* is represented at times as the faculty that does what the others cannot and that must resist the encroachment of their claims to cognition. In this view, reason regulates the activities of fancy, imagination, instinct, and sensibility. As far as her quarrel with Burke goes, it is the deference to sensibility that is her most serious concern.

> [T]hroughout your letter you frequently advert to a sentimental jargon, which has long been current in conversation, and even in books of morals, though it never received the *regal* stamp of reason. A kind of mysterious instinct is *supposed* to reside in the soul, that instantly discerns truth, without the tedious labour of ratiocination. This instinct, for I know not what other name to give it, has been termed *common sense*, and more frequently *sensibility*; and, by a kind of *indefeasible* right, it has been *supposed*, for rights of this kind are not easily proved, to reign paramount over the other faculties of the mind, and to be an authority from which there is no appeal.[12]

In contrast to Burke's sentimental jargon is Wollstonecraft's own rationalist prose, and there is a performative element in her rhetoric that requires little explanation. The passage, though, operates through a telling set of alliances (between sentiment and jargon, royal authority and reason, sensibility and right) and oppositions (leisurely intuition vs. laborious ratiocination, supposition vs. justification, authority vs. resistance). The compactness of Wollstonecraft's style relies, in eighteenth-century terms, on the associative faculty. One becomes habituated to associate certain terms in her writing because there is, as in Burke, a set of master distinctions under which other major oppositions may be organized. In the early Burke, the distinction between the sublime and the beautiful seemed capable of subsuming every aesthetic and even philosophical distinction of importance; in the later Burke, reform and innovation (or order and disorder) do much the same. In Wollstonecraft, these associations and oppositions are deployed with equal skill, though eventually overcome in a way that they are not in her less dialectical interlocutor.

The synthetic element of Wollstonecraft's rationalism ought not to be overlooked, as it is here that she most effectively navigates between the anarchic urgings of sensibility and the authoritarian rule of reason. The passions, she says, are the "necessary auxiliaries of reason," and reflection, in turn, "must be the natural foundation of the *rational* affections."[13] Burke's refusal to see these truths is the cause of his unjustified affection, "real or artificial," for an imperfect English constitution. His affection resembles the "blind, indolent tenderness" weak characters feel for their relations, one "that *will not* see the faults it might assist to correct, if their affection had been built on rational grounds."[14] Wollstonecraft is not the first to argue for a conjunction of reason and sensibility, but the politicization of faculty psychology toward the end of the century, and the immediate context of the French Revolution, distinguishes Wollstonecraft's claims for an associated, rational sensibility.

Affection built on rational grounds is the subjective analogue of objective political conditions, namely, the radical reconstruction of society such that duty merges most fully with inclination—thus her vision of an intermediate stage of society, short of egalitarian, consisting of larger landowners "whose duty and pleasure it was to guard" the happiness of smaller landowners.[15] In Wollstonecraft's larger vision, the coincidence of duty and inclination entails a revolution in social relations, especially between the sexes, and in property. Misogyny and private property are evils because they encourage irrational habits overcome only by antiquated notions of chivalry and benevolence. The chivalry of Burke's set piece on Marie Antoinette, in which ten thousand swords should have leaped from their scabbards to avenge so much as a threatening look, is an ethical code expressing the contradictions of feudal society. Wollstonecraft looks forward to a different mode of social organization, in which a *sense* of duty—at once bodily and rational—informs the principles of justice on which society is founded, instead of gallantly rushing in to conceal the symptoms of its contradictions.

Stale Tropes and Cold Rodomontade

Not only is the *Vindication of the Rights of Men* among the most spirited defenses of political rationalism of the period, it is, like the text to which it responds, a remarkable rhetorical achievement. This is not an uncontroversial position. Critics have disparaged Wollstonecraft's prose style since the late eighteenth century, describing it, Christine Skolnik has noted, variously as "incoherent, unselfconscious, and inherently contradictory."[16] Horace Walpole called the author a "hyena in petticoats" for her attack on Marie Antoinette; Godwin "was displeased, as literary men are apt to be, with a few offences against grammar and other minute points of composition" and regretted that it should be the first argument to counter Burke's; Burke claimed not to have read it, though that did not prevent him from describing Wollstonecraft in a 1795 letter as one of "that Clan of desperate, Wicked, and mischievously ingenious Women, who have brought, or are likely to bring Ruin and shame upon all those that listen to them."[17] Skolnik herself claims to have no intention of championing

Wollstonecraft as a stylist, though it is difficult to leave her analysis without a greater admiration for Wollstonecraft's gifts as a rhetor. The first *Vindication* may not be as polished as the responses to Burke by Paine, Mackintosh, Macaulay, or Godwin (it was written quickly and sent to press before it was finished), but, more often than not, this augments its appearance as the spontaneous outpouring of sincere conviction.

The "vindication" is an appropriate mode for the defense of political reason. "Vindication" (Latin, *vindicatio*: claiming, defending, punishing) has both political and philosophical roots. By the early seventeenth century, it had developed the sense of "deliverance" or "emancipation"; by the end of that century, it had developed the sense "justification by proof or explanation." As a prose subgenre, the "vindication" enjoyed considerable popularity toward the end of the seventeenth century and throughout the eighteenth century. Wollstonecraft's vindications of the rights of men and women joined an often volatile tradition of justice and justification: noteworthy examples include Anne Wentworth's 1679 vindication of herself, Swift's satirical 1709 vindication of "Isaac Bickerstaff" (John Partridge), Sewell's 1716 vindication of the English stage, and Warburton's 1740 vindication of Pope. The man who would have been Wollstonecraft's son-in-law, P. B. Shelley, would vindicate vegetables in 1813; her antagonist, Burke, had composed his own *Vindication of Natural Society* in 1756. Wollstonecraft's two *Vindications*, along with Thomas Paine's *Rights of Man*, would be mocked by Thomas Taylor in his 1792 *Vindication of the Rights of Brutes*.

Wollstonecraft's first contribution to this tradition in 1790, the *Vindication of the Rights of Men*, is thus a belated entry to the field—the mode seems to have become less popular in the nineteenth century, the prose of which tended toward a more explicit moral didacticism—and the author makes full use of an accumulated stock of techniques developed within the mode and elsewhere in eighteenth-century rhetoric. Julia Allen has documented Wollstonecraft's knowledge of rhetorical theory, paying special attention to the adaptation of Hugh Blair's *Lectures on Rhetoric and Belles Lettres* (1783), in the two *Vindications*.[18] Much of the work done on Wollstonecraft's style emphasizes her rhetorical performance of gender, her strategic appropriation of "manly rhetoric." There is, again, undoubtedly a performative element to her work, and, given that the field was, like many other spheres of literary production in the eighteenth century, dominated by men, it is inevitable that the use of almost any rhetorical device might be deemed an appropriation of masculine technique. The appropriation of the "manly" style and the performance of gender are important aspects of Wollstonecraft's rhetoric, though they are not the only ones.

When turning to Wollstonecraft's specific modes of persuasion in the *Rights of Men*, one soon notices how many of its most effective passages are on the topic of rhetoric itself and its abuse in the hands of Burke (an old strategy, to be sure, but especially conspicuous here). The abuse of rhetoric is equated with an abuse of reason, which for Wollstonecraft is a degradation of character and a moral failing ("the loss of reason appears a monstrous flaw in the moral world").[19] Wollstonecraft was quick to recognize paradox in particular as an abused form of reason and rhetoric in the *Reflections*. Paradox for her is not the natural expression of wisdom that pushes the prohibitive boundaries of logic, grammar, or common sense, but a reflection of weakness and vanity: weakness in the failure of the author's reason to assert its rightful sovereignty and vanity in the author's infatuation with his own language. These rational and moral failures, revealed in the structure of Burke's sentences themselves, push Wollstonecraft into her highest registers of contempt:

> I glow with indignation when I attempt, methodically, to unravel your slavish paradoxes, in which I can find no fixed first principle to refute; I shall not, therefore, condescend to shew where you affirm in one page what you deny in another; and how frequently you draw conclusions without any previous premises:—it would be something like cowardice to fight with a man who had never exercised the weapons with which his opponent chose to combat, and irksome to refute sentence after sentence in which the latent spirit of tyranny appeared.[20]

The exasperated Wollstonecraft will not able to resist the urge for long, as she draws out Burke's alleged contradictions over the course of her tract: his chivalrous response to Marie Antoinette as he tramples the poor women of France underfoot, his earlier position on American conciliation and his opposition to the French Revolution, the extension of his principles to what would be a retroactive renunciation of the Reformation, and so on.

There is something paradoxical in Wollstonecraft's own mixture of indignation and method, present throughout the work, though her doctrine of the rational affections argues for their compatibility. Her criticism of Burke's cowardice is likewise present throughout the tract, an attempt to out-man Burke by beating him on his own terms (Burke repeatedly invokes the idea, common in the eighteenth century and in Wordsworth's political prose and poetry, of a "manly" love of freedom). She does this, it should be noted, as she claims to refrain from discursive combat because of Burke's inexperience with rational weaponry. Most interestingly, she registers the same sense of instantiating metonymy—in which "the spirit of tyranny is latent in every sentence"—that Coleridge had detected in Burke, whose style, again, consists in "the unpremeditated and evidently habitual *arrangement* of words, grounded on the habit of foreseeing, in each integral part, or (more plainly) in every sentence, the whole that he then intends to communicate."[21] This is the wonder of Burke's rhetoric, and it is the challenge to the critic who seeks the premises and conclusions that his avowed allegiance to methodical induction suggests. Burke's paradoxes are "slavish" because they, wittingly or not, serve the interests of power: in their simultaneous representation of conflicting images or ideas, they clothe reactionary sentiments in impenetrable garb.

Just as Wollstonecraft sees paradox as Burke's preferred means of semantic obfuscation, so is the rhythm of his highly periodic prose (owing in large measure to the hypotaxis discussed in the previous chapter) a kind of syntactic obfuscation. Wollstonecraft begins her reply to Burke by conceding that she has "not yet learned to twist my periods, nor, in the equivocal idiom of politeness, to disguise my sentiments, and imply what I should be afraid to utter."[22] Wollstonecraft's concession is ironic and strategic: she has learned all too well how to twist her periods, as her own hypotactic and periodic prose elsewhere shows. Her argument in the first *Vindication*, though, depends on an initial separation between the embowered darkness of the "flowers of rhetoric," with which she associates Burkean sensibility, and the light of reason, with which she associates the knowledge of right. Burke's rounded periods obscure the light of reason and reveal his religious hypocrisy. Responding to Burke's "affectation of holy fervor" in condemning Price's enthusiasm for the National Assembly, she declares: "Observe, Sir, that I called your piety affectation.—A rant to enable you to point your venomous dart, and round your period."[23] Wollstonecraft was only the first to note how the language of Burke's *Reflections* circumvents the labor of ratiocination and feeling (Paine, for instance, would later echo her in his remark on Burke's "periods, with music in the ear, and nothing in the heart"). Anxiety about the abuse of rhetoric is here, as it is so prominently in Augustine, philosophical and religious: the dramatic conflict between content and form allegorizes a more universal conflict between unadorned truth and seductive falsehood.

Concerns about the abuse of rhetoric are also aesthetic. For Wollstonecraft, Burke is, counterintuitively perhaps, the quintessential "romantic" insofar as he holds onto beliefs and feelings antithetical to reason. "Romantic" she confines here to one definition—"false, or rather artificial feelings"—and it is a spirit on the wrong side of history: "Whether the glory of Europe is set, I shall not now enquire, but probably the spirit of romance and chivalry is in the wane; and reason will gain by its extinction."[24] This is revolutionary rhetoric, an early intimation of the teleological narratives that would flourish in the nineteenth century in Shelley, Marx, and the Whig historians. It gains part of its force, as Burke's rhetoric does, through an appeal to aesthetic judgment: "In modern poetry the understanding and memory often fabricate the pretended effusions of the heart, and romance destroys all simplicity; which, in works of taste, is but a synonymous word for truth. This romantic spirit has extended to our prose, and scattered artificial flowers over the most barren heath; or a mixture of verse and prose producing the strangest incongruities. The turgid bombast of some of your periods fully proves these assertions; for when the heart speaks we are seldom shocked by hyperbole, or dry raptures."[25] "Romanticism" as a term denoting an aesthetic movement would not become current for at least another three decades, but the genre on which the term is based is governed, according to Wollstonecraft, by hopelessly antiquated notions of truth and beauty. Burke is "romantic" because he uncritically applies the aesthetic standards of a fictional feudal past to present circumstances, which are intelligible only through the labor of ratiocination in conjunction with basic moral principles. The "turgid bombast" of his periods reflects a baroque sensibility at odds with beauty in its simplest, and consequently truest, form. Burke, she thinks, must realize this on some level, and it is on these grounds that she doubts his sincerity, supposing "that you have said many things merely for the sake of saying them well," a suspicion that would become a fixture in later criticisms of Burke.[26]

The turgid bombast of Burke's rhetoric is marked by a lack of what Wollstonecraft calls "concatenation," the linking together of sentences in a coherent order. The "best turned conceits" fall short of eloquence, which might have been achieved "if the sparkling periods had not stood alone, wanting force because they wanted concatenation."[27] This is perfectly natural, she says, in certain forms of impassioned poetry. Poetry rightfully draws the language of passion from the imagination in the moment of composition. "And, during this 'fine phrensy,' reason has no right to rein-in the imagination, unless to prevent the introduction of supernumerary images; if the passion is real, the head will not be sacked for stale tropes and cold rodomontade. I now speak of the genuine enthusiasm of genius, which, perhaps, seldom appears, but in the infancy of civilization; for as this light becomes more luminous reason clips the wing of fancy—the youth becomes a man."[28] Burke is no poet, and certainly not a genial poet in the infancy of civilization. He has come late to the party, Wollstonecraft suggests, and his intoxicated utterances seem less profound than they would have earlier. His passion, unlike the poet's, is hollow, an emptiness reflected in the stale figures and vainglorious boasting of his language. The conspicuously French *rodomontade* is appropriate here, an inspired word choice born of genuine enthusiasm for the French Revolution and a brief indulgence in fancy, clipped on both sides in these lines by the more sober qualifications of reason.

Concatenation is the rightful property of reason, which Wollstonecraft argues has been fooled by the imagination in Burke. In the unforgiving climax of her conclusion, Wollstonecraft voices her suspicion that "depth of judgment," allied with the logical concatenation of thoughts and sentences, "is, perhaps, incompatible with the predominant features" of Burke's mind:

> Your reason may have often been the dupe of your imagination; but say, did you
> not sometimes angrily bid her to be still, when she whispered that you were de-

parting from strict truth? Or, when assuming the awful form of conscience, and only smiling at the vagaries of vanity, did she not austerely bid you recollect your own errors, before you lifted the avenging stone? Did she not sometimes wave her hand, when you poured forth a torrent of shining sentences, and beseech you to concatenate them—plainly telling you that the impassioned eloquence of the heart was calculated rather to affect than dazzle the reader, whom it hurried along to conviction? Did she not anticipate the remark of the wise, who drink not at a shallow sparkling stream, and tell you that they would discover when, with the dignity of sincerity, you supported an opinion that only appeared to you with one face; or, when superannuated vanity made you torture your invention?—But I forbear.[29]

The passage, representative of Wollstonecraft's most spirited rhetoric, operates through a concatenation far removed from Burkean hypotaxis. Here is a string of rhetorical questions, each one reiterating the same basic premise: Burke has renounced the counsel of reason. It is not the hierarchical, hypotactic subordination of *A*, *B*, and *C* so frequently found in Burke, but the leveling, paratactic coordination of A^1? or A^2? or A^3? Wollstonecraft's interrogation is itself an act of insubordination: clauses within the sentences may be subordinated to each other (Wollstonecraft, like most eighteenth-century prose stylists, is on the whole a hypotactic writer), but the force of the passage consists in the elaboration of a single conceit in a series of syntactically equal and reiterative questions. Concatenation, Wollstonecraft argues, ought to be governed by reason; its absence is justified on the strength of the passion animating the thought. The weak, paratactic concatenation of questions in the above passage expresses, and is justified by, the force of its motivating passion. Helen Vendler has remarked, in the context of Keats's poetry, on enumeration as the trope of exterior plenitude; reiteration as the trope of inner intensity. The idea applies here as well, where the reiteration of the passage bespeaks an inner intensity requiring increasingly pitched elaborations of a single principle.

The issue of concatenation demands our attention not only as a rhetorical or aesthetic problem, but also, as Wollstonecraft is able to see, as a political one. Her sense of the danger of Burke's purported lack of concatenation—in the way his torrent of shining sentences pours forth, each one resplendent in isolation but empty in connection with the rest—prefigures later arguments about the politically corrosive effects of certain forms of speech and thought. In the twentieth century, both Benjamin and Adorno detected an erosion of true experience (*Erfahrungen*) in modern life, but Benjamin, in his 1939 essay "On Certain Motifs in Baudelaire," locates it particularly in the replacement of coherent narration by dissociated information. As one becomes more habituated to working with discrete units of information at the expense of larger discursive structures, one forsakes a politically significant, and potentially emancipating, element of human experience or cognition. Wollstonecraft recognizes this in her repeated emphasis on concatenation, and her attack on Burke's language in general should be understood in a similar context. In stressing the intimate connection between speech, thought, and political well-being, she anticipates the kind of argument Orwell makes in "Politics and the English Language" (1946): if one gets rid of certain bad habits in speech and writing, "one can think more clearly, and to think clearly is a necessary first step towards political regeneration."[30] Her attack on the "stale tropes and cold rodomontade" of Burke would be echoed in Orwell's attack on dying metaphors, pretentious diction, and meaningless words. Reliance on these devices, for both Wollstonecraft and Orwell, indicates a malfunction in the cognitive faculty, one that needs to be addressed if conditions of freedom are to obtain.

It is in this context of rational and rhetorical coherence that we are able to feel the full force of the epigraph at the opening this chapter: "Coherence, without some pervading principle of order, is a solecism." We recall that Wollstonecraft appropriates, as Shelley would, Hume's *History of England* to demonstrate the barbarity, not the wisdom, of English political history. The ancient foundations of authority and right so cherished by Burke are revealed to consist in acts of arbitrary power and human cruelty. In the infancy of English society—the moment, incidentally, when Wollstonecraft allows for the unrestricted imaginative play of the impassioned poet—customs were established "by the lawless power of the ambitious individual" or by the weakness of a prince who "was obliged to comply with every demand of the licentious barbarous insurgents," historical contingencies that cannot compete with the necessary dictates of reason. "Are these the venerable pillars of our constitution? And is Magna Charta to rest for its chief support on a former grant, which reverts to another, till chaos becomes the base of the mighty structure—or we cannot tell what?—for coherence, without some pervading principle of order, is a solecism."[31] *Solecismus* (Greek, speaking incorrectly)—the misuse of cases, genders, and tenses—originates as a term with the corruption of the Attic dialect by Greek colonists at Soloi in Cilicia; it is related to barbarism (initially it referred to words in combination, while *barbarismus* referred to an error in a single word). Wollstonecraft's claim that "coherence, without some pervading principle of order, is a solecism" is remarkable not only because of its brevity, but also because of how it prefigures larger arguments in the *Rights of Men* about ideational coherence and rhetorical concatenation. Burke's misuse of language is more than a rhetorical or aesthetic failure; it reflects an ahistorical and, as in his use of paradox, an irrational view of human freedom. To suggest a prior historical coherence without the order that reason is only now beginning to provide is a barbaric abuse of language, mirroring the violence that prevailed in the infancy of society and that Burke refuses to admit into his system.

Our Ideas of the Sublime and Beautiful

The engagement of the *Vindication of the Rights of Men* with the aesthetics of Burke's *Philosophical Enquiry into the Origin of Our Ideas of the Sublime and Beautiful* (1757) is evident from the beginning of the tract. It opens with a modification of Burke's distinction, declaring truth in morals the essence of the sublime and simplicity in taste the only criterion of the beautiful; it is on these grounds that the author would object to Burke's baroque sensibility in politics. As other critics have noted, Wollstonecraft repeatedly "dislocates" Burke's masculine sublime and turns it against him.[32] In her opinion, the truly sublime character acts from principle, "and governs the inferior springs of activity without slackening their vigour."[33] This is not the case, she argues, in the feverish Burke. If respect chills love, as Burke contends in his *Enquiry*, then "it is natural to conclude that all your pretty flights arise from your pampered sensibility."[34] We have seen that Wollstonecraft's argument operates through a series of alliances based on this principle: on one hand, sensibility, femininity, chivalry, feudal subordination, beauty, and the "flowers of rhetoric;" on the other, reason, masculinity, duty, equality, sublimity, and poetic language justified by the strength of genuine passion. These alliances would not remain firmly in place throughout the work—reason, for instance, would be synthesized with sensibility in the "rational affections," and the gendering of the terms would be qualified, though never fully challenged, in the argument for female education—but they determine its contours. The distinction between beauty and sublimity frames the argument and provides Wollstonecraft with an irresistible opportunity to deploy Burke's aesthetics against his politics.

The point on which this deployment turns is the sensibility of "gothic beauty," which Wollstonecraft attributes to Burke. It is this effeminate, pampered sensibility that leads her to suspect "a mortal antipathy to reason" in him. If his *Reflections*, she says, contains anything like an argument, it is this: "[T]hat we are to reverence the rust of antiquity, and term the unnatural customs, which ignorance and mistaken self-interest have consolidated, the sage fruits of experience: nay, that, if we do discover some errors, our *feelings* should lead us to excuse, with blind love, or unprincipled filial affection, the venerable vestiges of ancient days. These are gothic notions of beauty—the ivy is beautiful, but, when it insidiously destroys the trunk from which it receives support, who would not grub it up?"[35] The author of the first *Vindication* does not hesitate to "grub it up," attacking Burke's argument root and branch, even as she agrees with him on basic principles like the necessity of reform in other contexts. Whether or not the above is a fair characterization of Burke's argument—with a few minor substitutions and modifications, it essentially repeats the terms of the *Reflections* itself—is a separate matter.[36] The important thing to note here is that just as Burke appeals to standards of taste in his condemnation of radical principles, so does Wollstonecraft appropriate Burke's basic aesthetic categories to condemn their misapplication in political contexts: "Man preys on man; and you mourn for the idle tapestry that decorated a gothic pile."[37] The sensibility of Gothic beauty is a symptom of a barbaric age, exhibiting the same infatuation with glittering surface that marks Burke's rhetoric; adherence to the austere rationality of sublimity demands the creative destruction, in both politics and aesthetics, that Shelley would later associate with the west wind.

In Wollstonecraft's view, Burke's Gothic aesthetics stand in the way of just social relations in general and enlightened sexual relations in particular. Among the many treatises written on the beautiful and the sublime in the eighteenth century, Burke's is distinguished by how thoroughly gendered the terms are. The sublime inspires admiration, reverence, and respect; its ruling principle is terror; Milton is its greatest exemplar in literature, though Job and Virgil are also sublime; it is characterized above all else by strength and power. The beautiful, on the other hand, inspires love and affection; it is small, smooth, and delicate; its association with women, Burke suggests in his *Enquiry*, practically goes without saying. "I need here say little of the fair sex, where I believe the point will be easily allowed me. The beauty of women is considerably owing to their weakness, or delicacy, and is even enhanced by their timidity, a quality of mind analogous to it."[38] "Women," he says, "are very sensible of this; for which reason, they learn to lisp, to totter in their walk, to counterfeit weakness, and even sickness."[39]

Wollstonecraft would attack these sentiments most directly in her *Vindication of the Rights of Woman* (1792), but the seeds of her later argument are contained in the first *Vindication*, where she laments the sensibility that "makes those beings vain inconsiderate dolls, who ought to be prudent mothers and useful members of society."[40] In an ironic appropriation of Burke's voice, Wollstonecraft suggests that these are the aesthetics and ethics of a libertine:

> Nature, by making women *little, smooth, delicate, fair* creatures, never designed that they should exercise their reason to acquire the virtues that produce opposite, if not contradictory, feelings. The affection they excite, to be uniform and perfect, should not be tinctured with the respect which moral virtues inspire, lest pain should be blended with pleasure, and admiration disturb the soft intimacy of love. This laxity of morals in the female world is certainly more captivating to a libertine imagination than the cold arguments of reason, that give no sex to virtue.[41]

Wollstonecraft's irony is on the whole more dexterous than that of Burke, who had clumsily adopted the style of Bolingbroke's rationalism in his *Vindication of Natural Society* (1756). In contrast to what Bromwich terms Burke's "empiricist-dandyish style" in some passages of the *Enquiry*, Wollstonecraft adopts in passages such as this a rationalist-egalitarian tone allied with a kind of sansculotte aesthetic. The author is here at her most self-assured, an intimation of the voice that would emerge even more sharply in the second *Vindication*. Wollstonecraft's rhetoric is warmest when defending the cold arguments of reason; the sense of balance produced by this tension is an essential element of her style (heated arguments in defense of passion, it might be said, contain about as much dynamism as purely formal or abstract defenses of reason). Burke, we have seen, claims to adopt the "cold" style in his criticism of Hastings in his East India Bill speech, a strategy successful in part because it is balanced by the obvious warmth of his sentiments.

The political implications of Burke's gendered conceptions of the sublime and the beautiful were immediately apparent to Wollstonecraft. Indeed, they were made clear in Burke's *Enquiry* itself, in which the author notes how we respect, not despise, natural strength or power: "the power which arises from institution in kings and commanders, has the same connection with terror."[42] Burke notes how sovereigns are frequently referred to as "dread majesty" (the kind of appellation abhorred by Wollstonecraft and her radical contemporaries) and quotes the Book of Job as an example of natural timidity in the face of power: "*When I prepared my seat in the street, the young men saw me, and hid themselves*" (Job 29:7). Job says this as he recalls his past happiness, just after he had expressed, in the most sublime chapter of the book, the limits of human understanding in relation to divine majesty. Burke echoes the idea in an epistemological aside on "the Godhead merely as he is an object of the understanding," a complex idea of power, wisdom, justice, and goodness that, by itself, falls short of knowledge. Burke introduces the example into "an argument so light as this" with some hesitation, but he does so because he knows that this is not only an aesthetic matter. Job's timidity in the face of divine power, he suggests, is the natural attitude of the political subject in relation to worldly authority, the sublimity of which differs from divine authority only in degree.

Sublimity, in other words, is associated in Burke's *Enquiry* with a kind of epistemological skepticism, or at least modesty; it is unknowable in a way that finite beauty is not and for this reason is immune to rational critique. It is associated with an unknowable law of the father, given religious expression in the Book of Job but applicable to the political conditions of modernity as well. Wollstonecraft's sensitivity to Burke's aesthetic distinction is largely predicated on her realization of this association; her discussions of familial relations and paternal authority in the first *Vindication* are invested with the epistemic, political, and religious implications of Burke's *Enquiry*. Real virtue in any of these spheres, she suggests, is impossible in a system designed to preserve private property and existing power relations.

> A brutal attachment to children has appeared most conspicuous in parents who have treated them like slaves, and demanded due homage for all property they transferred to them, during their lives. It has led them to force their children to break the most sacred ties; to do violence to a natural impulse, and run into legal prostitution to increase wealth or shun poverty; and, still worse, the dread of parental malediction has made many weak characters violate truth in the face of Heaven; and to avoid a father's angry curse, the most sacred promises have been broken. It appears to be a natural suggestion of reason, that a man should be freed from implicit obedience to parents and private punishments, when he is of an age to be subject to the jurisdiction of the laws of his country.[43]

Wollstonecraft demonstrates a complex understanding of how power is established, maintained, and regulated outside of the official apparatus of the state. The "barbarous cruelty" of some familial relations, whereby parents are free to punish their children for misdemeanors that do not come under the "cognizance of public justice," is an unjustified violation of liberty, which for Wollstonecraft extends beyond the formal, state-sanctioned rights emphasized by liberal reformers (including the reformist Burke). The correspondences between familial, political, and divine authority suggested by Burke in his *Enquiry*—united, again, by a sublime law of the father beyond the limits of understanding—are picked up by Wollstonecraft, who was quick to perceive the family as a mediator of social values and as a class system subject to similar forms of conflict. The crucial role of the family in mediating between base and superstructure would be a theme pursued by later critics who, following Marx, saw the bourgeois family as a manifestation of dehumanized alienation. Horkheimer would argue in his contribution to the Institute for Social Research's monumental *Studies on Authority and Family* (1936) that with the decline of the father's authority in advanced capitalism went a transfer of his metaphysical aura to social institutions outside the family. Such a transfer had not yet occurred in Wollstonecraft's time, which, for the Frankfurt School, was an era of bourgeois liberalism in which the family still fulfilled a mediating and instantiating function. The "dread of parental malediction" for Wollstonecraft is a primitive but consequential form of terror, itself a symptom of the fear of loss of property and violent death at the root of the liberal conception of the state (as we shall now see, Coleridge objected to political theories, such as Hobbes's, founded upon such fears).

Drawing on the sexual and aesthetic distinction of Burke's *Enquiry*, and applying it to the thinly veiled defense of paternal authority in the *Reflections*, Wollstonecraft makes an extraordinary argument in the *Vindication of the Rights of Men* about the complex system of relationships, across social units and discursive spheres, that perpetuates unjust institutions. Reform that does not address the roots of injustice, but in a belated show of gallantry conceals its symptoms, is contrary to reason and right; the radicalism of the first *Vindication* consists in the largeness of its vision, in the way it detects offenses to reason across various aspects of social life. The narrowness of Burke's vision is an insincere affectation, for, as she says, he has, as a member of Parliament, "been behind the curtain."[44] The obscurity granted to the sublime in Burke's aesthetics is a precondition of his political paternalism. The illuminating and sovereign faculty of reason, which gives neither sex nor class to virtue, is for Wollstonecraft the most powerful antidote to the rhetoric of excess, asymmetry, and terror.

CHAPTER FOUR

The Government of the Tongue

Godwin's Linguistic Turns and the Artillery of Reason

•

If any man among you seem to be religious, and bridleth not
his tongue, but deceiveth his own heart, this man's religion
is vain.

—*James 1:26*

No question can be conceived more important than this. In the
examination of it philosophy almost forgets its nature; it ceases to
be speculation, and becomes an actor.

—*William Godwin,* Enquiry concerning Political
Justice *(3rd ed., 1798)*

The question to which Godwin refers in his *Enquiry concerning Political Justice, and Its Influence on Morals and Happiness*—in the examination of which philosophy almost forgets its nature—is the question of political resistance: under what conditions is it justifiable for political subjects to resist, by force, oppression or abuse? It is simultaneously a question about the limits of language: "what is the nature of the abuse, which it would be pusillanimous to oppose by words only, and which true courage would instruct us was to be endured no longer."[1] The answer of *Political Justice* is that resistance by force should almost always subordinate itself to the power of discourse: "writing and speech are the proper and becoming methods of operating changes in human society, and tumult is an improper and equivocal method."[2] Godwin was a revolutionary insofar as he sought a gradual revolution in opinion as the necessary precondition of political change culminating in the eradication of the state. The foundational premise of Godwin's position comes directly from Hume, who concludes in "Of the First Principles of Government" (1742) that it is "on opinion only that government is founded."[3] Hume's conclusion, which assumes that force is always on the side of the governed, reintroduced into the main current of political philosophy the problem of how consent can be manufactured and the crucial roles reason and knowledge are to play in the construction of a free and just society. These are Godwin's master themes, and they are inseparable, in *Political Justice*, from questions about the legitimate use of language.

For Godwin, if people are not ready to be free, they cannot, as Rousseau had supposed, be forced to be free. The readiness for freedom, according to Godwin, consists in the state of "political knowledge," a more epistemologically assertive form of Humean "opinion": "In a word, either the people are unenlightened and unprepared for a state of freedom, and then the struggle and the consequences of the struggle will be truly perilous; or the progress of political knowledge among them is decisive, and then every one will see how futile and short-lived will be the attempt to hold them in subjection, by means of garrisons and a foreign force."[4] The aim of *Political Justice* is to inquire into and contribute to the state of political knowledge and thus to accelerate the already necessary advance of liberty and truth.

In the broader context of this study, Godwin and his circle, including Mary Wollstonecraft and P. B. Shelley, constitute one pole of the critique of political reason that occurred in the late eighteenth and early nineteenth centuries; Burke, I have argued, occupies the other pole (though, as we shall see, Godwin had more in common with Burke, whom he greatly admired, than might be supposed). We might situate the Godwinian critique on the left and the Burkean critique, on this issue, on the right. The first-generation Romantics, Wordsworth and Coleridge, occupy middle positions, offering nuanced, dynamic considerations concerned with delimiting the proper scope of particular forms of knowledge and reason. Their critiques, synthesizing elements of Godwin and Burke in different proportions over time, are sensitive to both the promise of political reason and to the dangers it poses when not operating under certain constraints.

The emphasis Godwin places on reason in politics is evident: what is occasionally submerged or complicated in the political books of *The Prelude* or in *The Friend* is plainly on the surface of *Political Justice*. The purpose of this chapter is twofold: to provide a brief account of political rationalism in Godwin's most important philosophical work and, in accordance with the focus in this section on rhetoric, to provide an account of Godwin's frequent turn to language, in *Political Justice* and in the *Cursory Strictures* of 1794, as a way of developing the connections between knowledge and freedom. These connections for Godwin are, on the whole, abstract and theoretical, but it is necessary to see their relation to the world of men and women—the world of authority and obedience, rights and duties, taxation and treason, labor and human dignity. "Nothing can be more improbable than to imagine, that theory, in the best sense of the word, is not essentially connected with practice."[5] While theory and practice are essentially connected for Godwin, it is a mistake to erase the distinction entirely. It is an easy and even enticing mistake to make—so much so that Godwin can speak of a philosophy that "almost forgets its nature" with a touch of solemn awe—but, as we shall now see, reason terminates in freedom and justice even as it, strictly speaking, does nothing.

The Power of Mere Proposition: *Political Justice*

Epistemology and the philosophy of mind play crucial roles in Godwin's major work of political philosophy, in ways perhaps more natural to eighteenth-century and Romantic than to subsequent modes of thought. A basic premise of *Political Justice* is that political institutions have a more powerful influence than has been commonly ascribed to them, particularly in the formation of men's opinions. "But we can never arrive at precise conceptions relative to this part of the subject, without entering into an analysis of the human mind,"[6] one of many turns to the mind in the text. Godwin seeks to demonstrate two things in this respect: (1) human action is the result of circumstances and events, not any "original determinations" that subjects bring into the world (a position as opposed to innate ideas as it is to Kant's categories) and (2) our voluntary actions depend not on the impulses of sense but on the decisions of the understanding. If he can demonstrate these two aspects of the mind, Godwin can, he thinks, more easily demonstrate that the opinions of men are "for the most part, under the absolute control of political institution."[7] He prefers the term "political institution" to "government" because it expresses the various mechanisms, some more overt than others, through which an individual is compelled to subordinate his or her obedience to the only authority that matters, the independent intellect, to external forms of authority. Godwin's inquiry is finally concerned with whether these external forms of authority have any justification. It is an inquiry into how political institution "insinuates itself into our personal dispositions, and insensibly communicates its own spirit to our private transactions."[8] An inquiry into the legitimacy of political institutions demands for Godwin, as it would for Coleridge, an inquiry into the nature of the mind; an inquiry into the nature of the mind reveals the profound effect political institutions have in forming the very opinions that legitimize and perpetuate them.

Reason, the mental faculty with which Godwin is most concerned, receives a surprisingly modest definition toward the beginning of *Political Justice*: it is "merely a comparison and balancing of different feelings."[9] Godwin begins by offering such a humble definition of reason because he wants to divorce it at the outset from the "tumult and violence" he worries might accompany a misunderstanding of the faculty or of his inquiry into it: reason, he insists, "is not an independent principle, and has no tendency to excite us to action."[10] The idea is repeated later in the work, in an analysis of the purposes of punishment. "Coercion has nothing in common with reason, and therefore can have no proper tendency to the cultivation of virtue. It is true that reason is nothing more than a collation and comparison of various emotions and feelings; but they must be feelings originally appropriate to the question, not those which an arbitrary will, stimulated by the possession of power, may annex to it."[11] Godwin's twice-repeated disarming of reason, it should be recognized, goes against the general thrust of *Political Justice*, in which reason is typically "omnipotent" and "irresistible."

We ought to note, however, the language of sentiment that attends Godwin's most formal descriptions of reason ("sentiment" in *Political Justice* is allied with sensation, affection, and passion). In the above definitions, reason is a comparison of unspecified emotions and feelings (presumably, feelings of what is right, just, and true). He speaks elsewhere of the "sentiments of reason"[12] in terms similar to Wollstonecraft's and, later, Wordsworth's examinations of rational sentiments and affections. Even as he maintains that our only task is to discover what form of civil society is "most conformable to reason," he addresses the possibility that reason is inadequate to the task, in which case it may be necessary to call in "mere sensible causes,"[13] the visible signs of distinction that accompany other forms of authority—a possibility entertained and promptly dismissed. The language of sentiment recurs throughout this emblematic work of political rationalism, with Godwin opposed to "unfeeling logic" and convinced that the "first sentiment of an uncorrupted mind" is entirely consistent with the final determinations of reason.[14]

Despite, though, Godwin's occasional reference to the "sentiments of reason" and his definitions of reason as merely the comparison of various emotions and feelings, sentiment and reason tend to be distinguished in *Political Justice*, with the former subordinate to the latter. Godwin introduces the example of a man at the height of sensual enjoyment ("Passion is in this case in its full career") who is told that his father is dead, at which point the indulgence becomes impossible: "So vast is the power which a mere proposition possesses over the mind of man" (this, it might be noted, is no "mere" proposition, conveying as it does the death of a parent).[15] Our sensual and sentimental attachments, Godwin suggests in opposition to Burke, are more easily overcome than we might expect. "Is it to be supposed that the power of sensual allurement, which must be carefully kept alive, and which the slightest accident overthrows, can be invincible only to the artillery of reason, and that the most irresistible considerations of justice, interest and happiness will never be able habitually to control it?"[16] The point is part of Godwin's larger argument that the voluntary actions of men originate in their opinions and that, once opinion is wrested away from the control of political institutions, the progress of reason and justice would be irresistible.

Throughout *Political Justice*, then, Godwin argues against a political philosophy that relies too heavily on the senses, what we might call "political empiricism." He argues against the idea that "[a]dvantage must be taken of the imperfection of mankind. We ought to gain over the judgments through the medium of their senses, and not leave the conclusions to be drawn, to the uncertain processes of immature reason."[17] Godwin associates this position with Burke, who had famously argued in the *Reflections* that the private stock of reason in each man is small and that "individuals would be better to avail themselves of the general bank and capital of nations, and of ages."[18] This view of the human mind is for Godwin a cover, an apology for established practices and institutions. "[T]he adherents of the old system of government affirm 'that the imbecility of the human mind, is such as to make it unadviseable, that man should be trusted with himself; that his genuine condition is that of perpetual pupillage; that he is regulated by passions and partial views, and cannot be governed by pure reason and truth. . . .' "[19] Godwin argues against political empiricism—the doctrine that men are governed from within by their senses and that they ought, therefore, to be governed from without in similar fashion—at the same time that he upholds empiricism in strictly epistemological contexts: "The human mind, so far as we are acquainted with it, is nothing else but a faculty of perception. All our knowledge, all our ideas, every thing we possess as intelligent beings, comes from impression."[20] Knowledge, too, is defined in conventional Lockean terms: "The knowledge of truth, lies in the perceived agreement or disagreement of the terms of a proposition."[21] But while it is true that all of our knowledge derives from experience, it would be a mistake to construct one's politics around this epistemological premise. To do so would be to close oneself off from "the only method according to which social improvement can be carried on," which occurs when "the improvement of our institutions advances, in a just proportion to the illumination of public understanding."[22] It is, in other words, to close oneself off from what Godwin regards as the highest form of knowledge, which is political—that is, social in nature and related to systems of power and authority: knowledge pertaining to issues such as obligation, duty, resistance, liberty, and equality.

In this way, Godwin joins and brings to a climax the eighteenth-century discourse of political knowledge discussed in the introduction. I noted there his sense that the science of politics—and Godwin insists, with Hume, that politics may be reduced to a science—has only just begun: "Political knowledge is, no doubt, in its infancy."[23] The project now, articulated by Godwin with unprecedented force and supported by a philosophical system other radicals of the time failed to achieve, is to diffuse "in every possible mode, a spirit of enquiry" and to embrace "every opportunity of increasing the stock, and generalizing the communication, of political knowledge!"[24] The significance of such a project, he repeatedly stresses, is that the reformation of a society's political institutions must "keep pace" with its advancement in knowledge: "the legitimate instrument of effecting political reformation is knowledge."[25] Knowledge brings with it, as it does for Wordsworth, pleasure, tranquillity, and virtue. And, as for the early Wordsworth, true political knowledge is opposed to habit or custom, which Godwin in *Political Justice* conceives of as a priori knowledge that has been emptied of its justifying logic. So the man who attends church because it is routine is akin to the "scholar who has gone through a course of geometry, and who now believes the truth of the propositions upon the testimony of his memory, though the proofs are by no means present to his understanding."[26] This is one danger of a priori knowledge, the status of which was, I have suggested, a political problem at the end of the eighteenth century: the a priori can liberate us from the tyranny of sensory experience—an extension of what Wordsworth and Coleridge would refer to as the "despotism of the eye"—at the same time that its authority, especially in moral or political matters, can become mediated or assumed.

Godwin often speaks of the progress of knowledge in general and of political knowledge in particular as objective historical forces, inexorable and totalizing. His concern, later appropriated by Shelley in *A Philosophical View of Reform*, is with the general "state of political knowledge," which advances independently and through which one can explain particular historical events. In his discussion of political associations, Godwin considers the possibility that in a "moment of convulsion," in the "terror of general anarchy," some degree of political association, generally proscribed in *Political Justice*, may be necessary for the general welfare. But even here the state of political knowledge, in conjunction with specific circumstances, should direct individual human action: "In a crisis really auspicious to public liberty, it is reasonable to believe that there will be men of character and vigour, called out on the spur of the occasion, and by the state of political knowledge in general, who will be adequate to the scenes they have to encounter."[27] In his willingness to grant something approaching objective reality to abstractions such as the states of knowledge, reason, truth, and mind, Godwin develops an almost Hegelian language to explain the historical unfolding of mind: "Mind, though it will perhaps at no time arrive at the termination of its possible discoveries and improvements, will nevertheless advance with a rapidity and firmness of progression, of which we are, at present, unable to conceive the idea."[28] This is the language that appealed to the young Wordsworth, who sought in *The Prelude* to trace in the growth of his own mind the historical progression of human society toward greater degrees of freedom and virtue, what Kant referred to as the "moral tendency of the species."

Godwin's faith in the irresistible and necessarily conjoined advance of knowledge and freedom—and his faith that the "conviction of the understanding

[is] a means fully adequate to the demolishing [of] political abuse"[29]—is predicated in *Political Justice* on a particular conception of knowledge. I have already noted the definition in the section "On the Right of Private Judgment": knowledge is the perception of agreement or disagreement of the terms of a proposition. In "Of Revolutions," Godwin returns to the definition of knowledge, this time offering a less conventional understanding of the term. He notes what he regards as a widely held belief: that men may have an adequate knowledge of the error of their conduct and yet may still be disinclined to forsake it.

> This assertion however is no otherwise rendered plausible, than by the vague manner in which we are accustomed to understand the term, knowledge. The voluntary actions of men originate in their opinions. Whatever we believe to have the strongest inducements in its behalf, that we infallibly choose and pursue. It is impossible that we should choose any thing as evil. It is impossible that a man should perpetuate a crime, in the moment that he sees it in all its enormity. In every example of this sort, there is a struggle between knowledge on one side, and error or habit on the other. While the knowledge continues in all its vigour, the ill action cannot be perpetrated. . . . Knowledge in this sense, understanding by it a clear and undoubting apprehension, such as no delusion can resist, is a thing totally different from what is ordinarily called by that name, from a sentiment seldom recollected, and, when it is recollected, scarcely felt or understood.[30]

This is the epistemic heart of Godwin's system. "The beauty of the conception here delineated, of the political improvement of mankind, must be palpable to every observer."[31] The beauty of the system consists, first, in the revised definition of knowledge as, simply, a "clear and undoubting apprehension," a reversion from Lockean to Cartesian epistemological language. The beauty of the system also consists in the strict necessity with which knowledge leads to the highest ethical and political virtues. Throughout *Political Justice*, knowledge inevitably leads to virtue, pleasure, tranquillity, freedom, justice, and equality. In the above passage, personal vice and social injustice are epistemic failures: one thinks one has knowledge of something, but one does not. Knowledge, for Godwin, is the precondition of reform; enlightenment entails emancipation (the centrality of awareness- and consciousness-raising in modern political activism have their philosophical origins here). Social change that does not proceed from knowledge results in "tumult and violence"; social change predicated on knowledge cannot go wrong. Such is the power of "mere proposition."

The beauty of the system consists, finally, in the simplicity of the political arrangement it prescribes. In "the simple scheme of political institution which reason dictates,"[32] the state will disappear because it will be shown to be inherently allied to war, inequality, and other injustices; manual labor will be minimized because it will be shared by all who are able; property will be equal because disparities in private property—disparities that enjoy the "positive protection of the state"[33]—will be seen as antithetical to human dignity and because egalitarianism will be regarded as "the true republicanism"; and social relations will be simplified and strengthened because people will speak to each other with sincerity and candor, on equal footing, marked by the consciousness that one is, in Godwin's phrase, "a man speaking to a man."[34] All of the above necessarily follows the cultivation of "clear and undoubting apprehension," or knowledge, in a mind free from political interference. "Freedom of institution is desirable, chiefly because it is connected with independence of mind."[35] Here is the most direct source of Wordsworth's Godwinian meditation on the relationship between objective and subjective freedom in book 10 of *The Prelude*. Building social freedom on the freedom of the individual mind is the high argument of *Political Justice*, and it is an argument, we have already begun to see in his analysis of "knowledge," that required Godwin to turn to the nature of language itself.

Constructing a Form of Words: *Political Justice*

The turn to language in *Political Justice* takes three forms: philosophical remarks about the nature of language in general, analysis of specific terms, and, most important, arguments about sincerity and the government of particular forms of speech. After offering a brief conjectural history of the origins of language in standard eighteenth-century fashion toward the end of book 1, Godwin includes a lengthy footnote on abstraction that marks his first major break with Burke in the book. In the note, he argues that the human mind is capable of forming abstract ideas, even if it were denied the use of speech. He suspects, moreover, that the mind is incapable of forming anything but general ideas and that the opposition to the doctrine of abstract ideas has arisen from an ambiguity in the term "idea" itself. Godwin claims to use "idea" in its Lockean sense to refer to any conception that can exist in the mind and not merely to a mental image. He divides ideas into four classes, the last of which—"imperfect" ideas that have "no resemblance to an image of any external object"—is his primary concern. These ideas include the perception produced in us by the words such as "river" and "field," which, he suggests, "have no more resemblance to the image of any visible object, than the perception ordinarily produced in us by the words, conquest, government, virtue."[36] There is something admittedly strange about Godwin's argument here, as one might be justified in thinking that the perception produced by a word such as "river" does indeed have more of a resemblance to an image than the perception produced by a word such as "government."

The argument becomes less strange in light of the reference to Burke that immediately follows it.

The subject of this last class of ideas is very ingeniously treated by Burke, in his *Enquiry into the Sublime*, Part V. He has however committed one material error in the discussion, by representing these as instances of the employment of "words without ideas." If we recollect that brutes have similar abstractions, and a general conception, of the female of their own species, of man, of food, of the smart of a whip, &c. we shall probably admit that such perceptions (and in all events they are perceptions, or, according to the established language upon the subject, ideas) are not necessarily connected with the employment of words.[37]

In part 5 of the *Enquiry*, Burke distinguishes between three classes of words: "aggregate" words that "represent many simple ideas *united by nature* to form some one determinate composition" (man, horse, tree, castle, etc.); "simple abstract" words that stand only for one simple idea (red, blue, round, square, etc.); and "compound abstract" words that are formed by an "*arbitrary* union of both the others" (virtue, liberty, honour, persuasion, docility, etc.). According to Burke, compound abstract words come with no ideas or images attached to them. "As compositions, they are not real essences, and hardly cause, I think, any real ideas."[38] Such words, for Burke, "are in reality but mere sounds," but they are sounds that produce powerful responses because they are closely tied to our affections and to our habits. Because they so easily produce powerful responses and because they can so easily turn into bombast, it requires "much good sense and experience to be guarded against the force of such language."[39] Burke even suggests that, under normal circumstances, most language, not just compound abstract language, does not produce distinct ideas or images in the mind. He writes that he finds it "very hard to persuade several that their passions are affected by words from whence they have no ideas; and yet harder to convince them, that in the ordinary course of conversation we are sufficiently understood without raising any images of the things concerning which we speak," even as he recognizes the peculiarity of the enterprise: "It seems to be an odd subject of dispute with any man, whether he has ideas in his mind or not."[40] It is a dispute, we shall see later, that Coleridge enters into with Hume, but in *Political Justice* it is a linguistic dispute that prefigures a broader ideological one. It is no accident that Burke's examples of compound abstract words are "virtue, liberty, and honour" and that Godwin's examples of the same class of words are "conquest, government, and virtue."

If Burke contends that we can have—indeed, most of the time, we *do* have—words without ideas, then Godwin contends that we, like the "brutes," can have ideas without words. The relationship between abstraction and language, for Godwin, is one of both priority and reciprocity: "Abstraction, which was necessary to the first existence of language, is again assisted in its operations by language."[41] By subordinating language to abstraction, Godwin suggests that general terms like government and virtue are ideas operating according to reason—not, as Burke had suggested, simply words exciting sympathy according to habit—and are thus capable of gradual reformation. Godwin looks with wonder at the nearly miraculous development of language from the inarticulate cries of our ancestors to the variety and complexity of current modes of speech and writing, an "acquisition of slow growth and inestimable value" that is still being carried to even higher perfection.[42] "This," Godwin says with a glance back to Burke, "is the temper with which we ought to engage in the study of political truth. Let us look back, that we may profit by the experience of mankind; but let us not look back, as if the wisdom of our ancestors was such, as to leave no room for future improvement."[43] The study of language reveals its subordination to abstraction: it is to ideas, even in the absence of accompanying language, that we owe our allegiance. Burke's skeptical caution regarding "words without ideas" renounces the authority of reason by subjecting abstract words—in the examples of both Burke and Godwin, the language of politics—to the laws of affect and habit.

Because language is, for Godwin, an emblem of human perfectibility and because it is so closely bound to the mutually constitutive progress of reason and freedom, it ought to be used, studied, and, where necessary, reformed with attention and care; hence, the frequent and often extended analysis in *Political Justice* of terms such as "mind," "passion," "nature," "nation," "necessity," "king," and "aristocracy." Godwin typically aims to resolve an ambiguity in the use of the term that is not necessarily built into the idea itself. Once we have an adequate grasp of the idea to which a term refers, we can immediately and independently judge the validity of someone else's use of the term or, more to the point, the validity of the thing itself. "Mind," for example, is shown to be a coherent concept and is thus redeemed as a legitimate part of philosophical and political discourse; "passion" is "extremely vague in its signification," but when, properly understood, is not nearly as powerful as is commonly supposed; "nation" is an "arbitrary term" that all governments necessarily abuse, and so forth.[44] Godwin at times seeks to break the spell cast by particular words, such as "king" or "aristocracy," by inquiring into their meaning. "Let us not be seduced by a mere plausibility of phrase, nor employ words without having reflected on their meaning."[45] Rather, "let us bring these ideas to the touchstone of reason," upon which, of course, many ideas reveal themselves to be impure, a strategy continued in *Cursory Strictures*. Just as one cannot knowingly choose evil, one cannot continue to grant integrity to an incoherent term once its meaning has been exposed in the plain light of day. An incoherent term, for Godwin, is an unjust term; coherence is a kind of justice.

In addition to general statements related to the philosophy of language and case studies of individual words, linguistic issues play a crucial role in *Political*

Justice insofar as they are so deeply embedded in the institutions the work interrogates. In his examinations of promises, political associations, national assemblies, tests, oaths, libels, and constitutions, Godwin situates the legitimate use of language at the center of his political inquiry. In his view, the doctrine of the social contract depends, as it does for many contract theorists, on a promise: we have promised obedience to government and are therefore bound to obey. Promises, though, can never serve as the foundation of morality, a title that only justice can claim. It is not, Godwin contends, because of something so slight as a promise that we are bound to promote the general welfare, an obligation that must be constantly discerned by reason. To bind oneself to a prior performative utterance, or to the hypothesis of such an utterance, is to renounce one's rational autonomy. Godwinian sincerity—a model of social engagement in which we speak to each other with truth and candor in practically every circumstance—rests on similar grounds:

> It is not on account of any promise or previous engagement, that I am bound to tell my neighbor the truth. Undoubtedly one of the reasons why I should do so, is, because the obvious use of the faculty of speech is to inform, and not to mislead. But it is an absurd account of this motive, to say, that my having recourse to the faculty of speech, amounts to a tacit engagement that I will use it for its genuine purposes. The true ground of confidence between man and man is the knowledge we have of the motives by which the human mind is influenced; our perception, that the motives to deceive can but rarely occur, while the motives to veracity will govern the stream of human actions.[46]

The only reason we have to obey our promises is because it "tends to the welfare of intelligent beings."[47] Sincerity promotes the general welfare because the faculty of speech is directed into its proper channel, in which neighbors inform each other of "how they ought to be employed, and how to be improved."[48] Sincerity, in Godwin's system, is coupled with public inspection: "Men would act with clearness and decision, if they had no hopes in concealment, if they saw, at every turn, that the eye of the world was upon them."[49] This social vision is, of course, a nightmare for liberal individualists, but for Godwin it represents an end to the "cold reserve, that keeps man at a distance from man" and an end to social vices aggravated by anonymity.[50]

The belief that the proper use of the faculty of speech is to inform and not to mislead, the basis of Godwinian sincerity, is also a premise in Godwin's arguments against political associations and national assemblies, bodies that tend to place limits on sincerity and that make a mockery of the attention to language that he elsewhere wishes to promote. An inevitable feature of meetings of political associations is "contentious dispute and long consultation about matters of the most trivial importance."[51] In the event that a document needs to be drafted

in the name of the whole, Godwin, with some insight into the workings of com-
mittees, protests: "Commas are to be adjusted, and particles debated. Is this an
employment for rational beings? Is this an improvement upon the simple and
inartificial scene of things, when each man speaks and writes his mind, in such
eloquence as his sentiments dictate, and with unfettered energy . . . ?"[52] The
same objection is made against the procedure of voting on a measure in national
assemblies, which requires "constructing a form of words" that expresses the
uniform opinion of a multitude. "What can be conceived, at once more ludicrous
and disgraceful, than the spectacle of a set of rational beings, employed for hours
together, in weighing particles, and adjusting commas?"[53] Such scenes are for
Godwin sources of embarrassment, disavowals of autonomy and sense. Political
meetings, at the local or the national level, promote conformity; private judgment, which ought to be inviolable, is made to yield to general sentiment. The
force of Godwin's commitment to the priority of private judgment, often at the
expense of other liberal or leftist values, ought to be felt here. In his opposition to
political associations (indeed, to most forms of what we would call "organiz-
ing"), to national assemblies (which introduce "the evils of a fictitious unanim-
ity"),[54] and to certain forms of voting ("that flagrant insult upon all reason and
justice, the deciding upon truth by the casting up of numbers"),[55] Godwin presents an uncompromising, enlightened anarchism based, in every instance, on
the autonomy of reason and the right of private judgment.

Laws against heresy—the object of which is plainly "to prevent men from
entertaining certain opinions, or, in other words, from thinking in a certain
way"[56]—present an overt challenge to the autonomy of reason and the right of
private judgment, but there are, Godwin says, other mechanisms through
which political institutions determine opinion. Book 6 of *Political Justice*, "Of
Opinion Considered as a Subject of Political Institution," is especially concerned with how political power establishes itself in the regulation of speech.
Tests and oaths, for instance, typically involve a suspension of reason and an
abuse of language. Godwin's example is the French oath, introduced early in
1790 to suppress libel and specified by the constitution of September 3, 1791,
"to be faithful to the nation, the law and the king." The earlier argument
against promises applies here as well and remains just as straightforward: what
if I should change my mind in twelve months? Assuming one is sincere when
one makes them, promises and oaths leave no room for the subsequent reformation of opinion, which it is our duty to cultivate. The French oath also demands allegiance to three distinct, potentially opposed, interests. Even if one
were to provide a liberal interpretation of the oath—so that when one swears
fidelity to "the nation, the law and the king," one means so far as those au-
thorities agree with each other and so far as they, collectively, agree with the
general welfare—one really means something like, "I swear that I believe it is

my duty to do everything that appears to me to be just." Who, Godwin asks, "can look without indignation and regret, at this prostitution of language?"[57] Under the light of reason, the oath becomes, at best, a moral truism and, at worst, an intolerable manipulation of language and thought.

Oaths in general, moreover, take for granted a set of religious beliefs, namely, the existence of "an invisible governor of the world, and the propriety of our addressing petitions to him."[58] What, Godwin asks, "are the words with which we are taught, in this instance, to address the creator whose existence we have thus recognized? 'So help me God, and the contents of his holy word.' It is the language of imprecation. I pray to him to pour down his everlasting wrath and curse upon me, if I utter a lie.—It were to be wished that the name of that man had been recorded, who first invented this mode of binding men to veracity."[59] Binding men to veracity is precisely what Godwin would like, but it must not feel too much like binding; or, rather, it is to be a binding so strong that it is indistinguishable from freedom. Thus, in the discussion of free will and necessity in book 4, the "advocate of liberty in the philosophical sense" must recognize that "all the actions of men are necessary."[60] Freedom and necessity are commonly opposed because the "established language of morality has been so universally tinctured" with the errors of contingency and accident.[61] Freedom, properly examined, is nothing other than necessity, properly examined. "Accuracy of language," here and throughout *Political Justice*, "is the indispensible prerequisite of sound knowledge."[62]

Like laws against heresy and like the administration of tests and oaths, laws against libel are opposed in principle to the cultivation of accurate language: "Laws for the suppression of private libels are, properly speaking, laws to restrain men from the practice of sincerity."[63] Private libel should not, according to Godwin, be corrected by force because sincerity cannot flourish under repressive conditions. In a society marked by sincerity and public inspection, libels will be recognized for what they are because people will be in the habit of promoting truth and correcting error. "From the collision of disagreeing accounts," Godwin writes, echoing Milton, "justice and reason will be produced."[64] Public libel, which Godwin defines as "any species of writing in which the wisdom of some established system is controverted," is more complicated because of its potential to be associated with tumult and violence. It is important, though, to distinguish between "a libel the avowed intention of which is to lead to immediate violence," which for Godwin may warrant forceful intervention, and a publication designed to assess the legitimacy of an institution, which should be encouraged. In all cases, though, truth and sincerity ought to be cultivated. "There is no branch of virtue more essential, than that which consists in giving language to our thoughts,"[65] and none more fraught with danger.

Courage consists more in this circumstance than in any other, the daring to speak every thing, the uttering of which may conduce to good. Actions, the performance of which requires an inflexible resolution, call upon us but seldom; but the virtuous economy of speech is our perpetual affair. Every moralist can tell us, that morality eminently consists in "the government of the tongue." But this branch of morality has long been inverted. Instead of studying what we shall tell, we are taught to consider what we shall conceal. Instead of an active virtue, "going about doing good," we are instructed to believe that the chief end of man is to do no mischief. Instead of fortitude, we are carefully imbued with maxims of artifice and cunning, misnamed prudence.[66]

Among those who stressed the morality of the "government of the tongue," Joseph Butler and Richard Allestree would have been familiar to Godwin. A diary entry for August 20, 1795, includes a reference to Butler's *Fifteen Sermons Preached at the Rolls Chapel* (1726), one of which is devoted to the "government of the tongue" and begins with the verse from James used as an epigraph to this chapter.[67] Allestree is the likely author of the anonymously published *The Whole Duty of Man* (1658) and *The Government of the Tongue* (1674). Godwin owned a 1709 edition of *The Whole Duty of Man*; *The Government of the Tongue*, also reissued throughout the eighteenth century, asserted that "the due managery therefore of this unruly member, may rightly be esteemed one of the greatest mysteries of Wisdom and Vertue," exactly the sort of commonplace that Godwin thinks distorts morality by substituting prudent silence for intrepid speech.[68]

In light of the 1794 treason trials that occasioned the *Cursory Strictures*, to which I presently turn, the "courage" of which Godwin speaks in *Political Justice* is no mere abstraction. And, as Isaac Kramnick has observed, Godwin's preoccupation with sincerity, "his quaint insistence that one must not have one's butler lie when one is in but not eager to see company, is more than simply the eccentricity of a bookish crank."[69] The kinds of courage and sincerity Godwin has in mind have material consequences. The depressingly vast array of social and political injustices—from the dishonesty between neighbors to the inevitable tendencies of the state to protect inequality and wage war—have, for Godwin, a common cause: the failure to tell the truth. Opportunities for direct action are rare and ultimately undesirable; there are, however, innumerable opportunities for truth-telling. The "virtuous economy of speech" is, in this way, "our perpetual affair." Telling the truth demands, of course, knowing what the truth is—hence the desire throughout *Political Justice* to liberate opinion from various forms of state interference. Book 6, on how opinion is shaped by political institutions, revolves around an analysis of speech acts such as heresies, tests, oaths, and libels because it is here that the "government of the tongue" is most clearly on display. Some form of consent, though, is manufactured in every abuse of speech, even the most quotidian, that interferes with private judgment. The social transformation Godwin envisions begins with a discursive shift. This is not a theoretical platitude, but a principled, realistic commitment to writing and speech as "the proper and becoming methods of operating changes in human society." Godwin's position involves a reappropriation of the "government of the tongue" so that it no longer refers to matters of occasional discretion or to the preservation of orthodoxy, but to the regular cultivation of language into its proper—that is, its informative and emancipating—channels.

Resisting "Incroachment": *Cursory Strictures*

Beginning in May 1794, just over a year after the publication of *Political Justice*, members of the London Corresponding Society and the Society for Constitutional Information were arrested on charges of treason and "misprision of treason," that is, the offense of neglecting to disclose or intentionally concealing a treasonable design. Like many of the other radical groups in the 1790s with which they were affiliated—such as the Manchester Constitutional Society, the Norwich Revolution Society, the Sheffield Constitutional Society, and the Whig Association of the Friends of the People—the London Corresponding Society and the Society for Constitutional Information pushed for annual parliaments, universal suffrage, and parliamentary reform. Godwin knew most of the accused and was friends with three of those indicted for high treason. After the indictment in October of Thomas Holcroft, his closest friend, Godwin decided to act. The result was *Cursory Strictures on the Charge Delivered by Chief Justice Eyre to the Grand Jury*, published in October 1794. Personal allegiances aside, Godwin felt that this was an issue of justice and that even the most impartial spectator, a figure often invoked in *Political Justice*, would feel that the trial, as it was proceeding, was an offense to reason and fairness. The public celebrations that followed the acquittals in November and December 1794 suggested that much of the London populace shared the sentiment.

At the same time, the London Corresponding Society and the Society for Constitutional Information stood for much of what Godwin argued against in *Political Justice*. There, Godwin argued against political associations; now, in *Cursory Strictures*, he found himself defending two of the most prominent radical societies in England. In the earlier work, he had argued against immoderate or inflammatory speech; now he was defending groups that spoke with far greater urgency ("what is moderation of principle, but a compromise between right and wrong," Thelwall wrote in the *Tribune* in May 1795). In the earlier work, Godwin had argued against placing too much faith in the distant past, in medieval modes of social organization; now he was defending groups that appealed to the ancient constitution "freed from its Norman Yoke" and individuals who signed their communications "Anglo-Saxon." Most of all, *Political Justice* had repeatedly argued against direct political action, which for Godwin tends to disorder and violence; these societies sought more immediate political reforms than those that come about through the gradual enlightenment of human reason. The profound differences between Godwin's philosophical anarchism and the Jacobin politics of radical agitation came into even sharper focus after the acquittals—acquittals, according to at least one of the accused, in which Godwin's *Cursory Strictures* played no small role.

In "The Charge, Delivered by the Right Honourable Sir James Eyre," the chief justice writes that the alleged occasion for the commission is: "That a traitorous and detestable Conspiracy has been formed for subverting the existing Laws and Constitution, and for introducing the System of Anarchy and Confusion which has so lately prevailed in France."[70] Eyre then refers to the Statute of Treasons of 1352 ("25 Edward III")—which declares treason to occur "when a man doth compass or imagine the death of our lord the king" (*Statutes at Large*, 2:51)—and suggests, through a liberal interpretation of the statute, that an association for the reform of parliament does indeed threaten the life of the king. In making the charge, Eyre appeals to the discourse of political reason and knowledge that, we have seen, developed throughout the eighteenth century and peaked in the 1790s.

> But if we suppose these Associations to adhere to the professed Purpose [parliamentary reform], and to have no other primary Object; it may be asked, is it possible, and (if it be possible) by what Process is it, THAT AN ASSOCIATION FOR THE REFORM OF PARLIAMENT CAN WORK ITSELF OF THE CRIME OF HIGH TREASON? All men, nay, all Men must, if they possess the Faculty of thinking, reason upon every Thing which sufficiently interests them to become Objects of their Attention; and among the Objects of the Attention of free Men, the Principles of Government, the Constitution of particular Governments, and, above all, the Constitution of the Government under which they live, will naturally engage Attention, and provoke Speculation. The Power of Communication of Thoughts and Opinions is the Gift of God, and the Freedom of it is the Source of all Science, the First Fruits and the ultimate Happiness of Society; and therefore it seems to follow, that human Laws ought not to interpose, nay, cannot interpose to prevent the Communication of Sentiments and Opinions in voluntary Assemblies of Men; all which is true, with this single Reservation, that THOSE ASSEMBLIES ARE TO BE SO COMPOSED, AND SO CONDUCTED, AS NOT TO ENDANGER THE PUBLIC PEACE AND GOOD ORDER OF THE GOVERNMENT UNDER WHICH THEY LIVE; and I shall not state to you that Associations and

Assemblies of Men, for the Purpose of obtaining a Reform in the interior Constitution of the British Parliament, are simply unlawful; but, on the other Hand,
I must state to you, that they may but too easily degenerate, and become unlawful, in the highest Degree, even to the enormous Extent of the Crime of High
Treason.[71]

Much of this could have been written by the author of *Political Justice*. Here, as
in Godwin's inquiry, the unrestricted communication of opinion about the
principles of government is an indispensable and salutary element of life in a
free society (even if we sense that Eyre grudgingly concedes what Godwin en-
thusiastically endorses), but assemblies that endanger the public peace are to
be avoided because they "too easily degenerate" ("Who knows not that?" Godwin asks after quoting Eyre's claim, "Was it necessary that the Chief Justice
should come in 1794, solemnly to announce to us so irresistible a proposition?").[72] For Eyre, the faculty of thinking demands that individuals reason
about anything that captures their attention or interest, including the principles of government, but such thinking in organized bodies must remain within
certain bounds: it must not threaten what he calls, elsewhere in the charge,
"that glorious fabric which it has been the work of ages to erect, maintain, and
support, which has been cemented with the best blood of our ancestors."[73]
This is Burkean language, used by Godwin himself in *Considerations on Lord
Grenville's and Mr. Pitt's Bills concerning Treasonable and Seditious Practices
and Unlawful Assemblies* (1795):

> He that deliberately views the machine of human society, will, even in his spec-
> ulations, approach it with awe. He will recollect, with alarm, that in this scene,
>   —Fools rush in, where angels fear to tread.
>   The fabric that we contemplate is a sort of fairy edifice, and, though it con-
> sist of innumerable parts, and hide its head among the clouds, the hand of a
> child almost, if suffered with neglect, may shake it into ruins.[74]

Godwin bestowed effusive praise on Burke on a number of occasions, including in the "Letters of Mucius" and throughout *Political Justice*, and he shared
his reverence for the delicate fabric of society. Godwin simply thought that
Burke's reverence was misdirected in that it was oriented toward the habits and
institutions of the past whereas it should have been oriented toward the rational demands of the present and toward a future in which the fabric of society
need not be held together by the state.

Godwin quotes Eyre's passage about the "glorious fabric" in *Cursory Strictures* but does not comment on it. Instead, he moves directly to this particular
case of high treason, which he would like to divorce, for the moment, from
philosophical abstraction—both Eyre's and, in a way, his own from the previ-

ous year. Godwin argues what he claims Eyre already implies in his charge: that the case under consideration does not fall within the letter of 25 Edward III, "one of the great palladiums of the English constitution" and defined in *Cursory Strictures* as "levying war against the king within the realm, and the compassing or imaging of the death of the king," nor does the case fall under any clear precedent.[75]

Among the rhetorical strategies of *Cursory Strictures*, the frequent turn to language—Eyre's, Godwin's, the language of statutes, the language of French conventions, the terms of rhetoric—is among the most prominent. Godwin first notes the abundance of conjectural language in Eyre's charge: "things likely," "purposes imputed," "measures supposed," and "imaginary cases."[76] The obvious reason for this, Godwin contends, is that Eyre knew that there was no legitimate basis for the charge of treason: "He is therefore obliged to leave the plain road, and travel out of the record."[77] Knowing that these associations for parliamentary reform do not fall under existing laws or precedents, the chief justice is compelled to imagine new forms of treason. "Every paragraph now presents us with a new treason, real or imaginary, pretendedly direct, or avowedly constructive . . . his whole discourse hangs by one slender thread," which Godwin claims is a treason of his own creation, a conspiracy to subvert the monarchy.[78] "Upon this self-constituted treason he hangs his other conjectures and novelties as well as he is able, by the help of forced constructions, of ambiguous and deceitful words, and the delusions of a practiced sophister."[79]

There is no evidence at all, according to Godwin, to suggest that these associations for parliamentary reform were engaged in a conspiracy to subvert the monarchy (again, Eyre's own definition of treason). Godwin here takes the conclusion of *Political Justice* for granted, already an accepted piece of political knowledge: "If any man in England wishes the subversion of the Monarchy, is there a man in England that does not feel, that such subversion, if effected at all, can only be effected by an insensible revolution of opinion?"[80] This is a dangerous move, as the radical societies clearly did seek a revolution of opinion, most evident in their repeated emphasis on the "dissemination" or "diffusion" of political knowledge. Godwin, though, wants at the very least to clear the societies of conspiracies to murder the king or the royal family, which should appear to any spectator as an unfounded charge. "But the authors of the present prosecution probably hope, that the mere names of Jacobin and Republican will answer their purposes."[81] Again, injustice is allied with an abuse of language, a cynical use of metonymy to exploit popular prejudice and fear. The contest Godwin stages is largely between the "mere names" that, as Burke had argued in part 5 of his *Enquiry*, so easily excite passion and the "mere propositions" that, in book 1 of *Political Justice,* are capable of overpowering even the strongest passions.

Without direct evidence of a conspiracy to murder the king or the royal family, Eyre, Godwin suggests, has to introduce, under other names, the possibility of "constructive treason," described by Hume in his *History of England* (1754) as:

> a kind of *accumulative* or *constructive* evidence, by which many actions, either totally innocent in themselves, or criminal in a much inferior degree, shall, when united, amount to treason, and subject the person to the highest penalties inflicted by the law. A hasty and unguarded word, a rash and passionate action, assisted by the malevolent fancy of the accuser, and tortured by doubtful constructions, is transmuted into deepest guilt, and the lives and fortunes of the whole nation, no longer protected by justice, are subjected to arbitrary will and pleasure.[82]

This, Godwin suggests, is the kind of treason Eyre hopes to introduce into the case when he instructs the jurors:

> In the course of the evidence *you will probably hear* of bodies of men having been collected together, of violent resolutions voted at this and other meetings, of some preparation of offensive weapons, and of the adoption of the language and manners of those Conventions in France, which have possessed themselves of the government of that country. I dwell not on these particulars, because I consider them not as substantive treasons, but as circumstances of evidence, tending to ascertain the true nature of the object which these persons had in view.[83]

Eyre's charge, Godwin thinks, perfectly matches Hume's description of constructive treason, a "loose and fluctuating" interpretation of treason that is bound to produce terror among anyone suspected of it. The "hasty or unguarded word" and the "rash and passionate action" to which Hume refers might, in this case, easily encompass the adoption by the accused of "the language and manners of those Conventions in France"—language and manners that, Eyre admits, are not crimes themselves, but that, under a theory of constructive treason, may constitute evidence of a criminal tendency.

Eyre's distinction between conventions in imitation of French models designed to "usurp the government of the country" and conventions that seek only parliamentary reforms prompts Godwin to examine the term "convention" itself: "There lurks a memorable ambiguity under this word *Convention*."[84] He points to two recent conventions that were "considerably more formidable in their structure" than the convention in question, which was "simply of delegates from the different societies, voluntarily associated for the purpose of Parliamentary Reform."[85] It is clear, in other words, that the meetings under consideration in the trial do not fall under the first category of those trying to "usurp the government of the country." This, though, is precisely what Eyre suggests in his charge, through a special abuse of language that demands a new rhetorical term. "There is a figure in speech, of the highest use to a designing and treacherous orator, which has not yet perhaps received a name in the labours of Aristotle, Quintilian, or Farnaby. I would call this figure *incroachment*. It is a proceeding, by which an affirmation is modestly insinuated at first, accompanied with considerable doubt and qualification; repeated afterwards, and accompanied with these qualifications; and at last asserted in the most peremptory and arrogant terms."[86] Godwin goes through Eyre's charge, noting how what began as a possible treason that clearly does not fall within the statue of Edward III nor under any existing law or precedent gradually becomes a convention in the French style, "a case of no difficulty, and the clearest High Treason." Eyre's claim is actually that *if* the convention were of the usurping French sort, then it "would be" a clear case of high treason. Having just quoted this part of the charge, Godwin would have been familiar with the original language. Dropping the conditional "would be" is strategic. Godwin's broader argument, though, highlights an important aspect of Eyre's charge: just as it relies at times on a notion of "constructive" or "accumulative" treason, so is there an accumulative quality to Eyre's rhetoric, which begins cautiously and becomes gradually more assertive.

Godwin's assault on Eyre's abuse of language continues throughout *Cursory Strictures*: "Can any play upon words be more contemptible . . ."; "Nothing can be more gross to the view of any one who will attentively read this paragraph, than its total want of all definite and intelligible meaning"; "What is here intended by the words *power* and *force*?"; "This word is still more ambiguous than any of the rest"; "This is a sort of language which it is impossible to recollect without horror, and which seems worthy of the judicial ministers of Tiberius or Nero."[87] Godwin twice translates Eyre's sophistical language into the unadorned language of truth: "The plain English of his recommendation is this . . ." and "If therefore he address them in the frank language of sincerity, he must say . . . ."[88] If Godwin is inclined at times toward hyperbole in *Cursory Strictures*, it is because "[t]his is the most important crisis, in the history of English liberty, that the world ever saw."[89] The treason trials are a crisis because they threaten to undermine the unrestricted construction and communication of opinion that Godwin thinks, with some caveats, are indispensable elements of the conjoined projects of enlightenment and emancipation. The kind of stateless society envisioned in *Political Justice* can exist only when the individual use of reason has been sufficiently developed such that it can offer independent principles of self-legislation and social organization. The manner in which the treason trials were proceeding was troubling because, personal allegiances aside, it was precisely the kind of political interference in the formation of opinion that posed the most serious threat to the development of reason. In *Cursory Strictures*, Godwin suspends his reservations about political associations, which interfere with private judgment in their own way, and radical agitation, which too easily leads to violence, because state interference was, in this case, so direct and so consequential.

Eyre's charge to the jury, then, constitutes an abuse of language in two important respects. First, it involves the kind of sophistical language that for Godwin is often allied with injustice. In its specious interpretation of 25 Edward III, in its"forced constructions" and "ambiguous and deceitful" words, and in its rhetorical strategies of insinuation and "incroachment," the charge commits a number of unpardonable linguistic sins. Second, the charge represents the "government of the tongue" in the worst possible sense. It represents not the kind of discretion Godwin prescribed in *Political Justice*, in which it is the duty of discoverers of truth to "exercise a rigid censure over themselves" precisely because it is inappropriate for the state to do so, but a coercive silencing operating under the names of law and morality.[90] It is a moral commonplace, Godwin had asserted, to stress the importance of the government of the tongue, but the regulation of speech and writing must be the rational product of individual judgment. When censure is externalized, the unstated object is always to prevent people from thinking in a certain way, which is, for Godwin, intolerable.

"The tendency of all false systems of political institution," Godwin writes in *Political Justice*, "is to render the mind lethargic and torpid."[91] The political value of the active mind is perhaps Godwin's most important contribution to first-generation British Romanticism, to which I now turn. The principle of the active mind remained a cornerstone of Coleridge's philosophical thought—not only in his politics (in which the active mind must submit to a particular ordering of the faculties), but also in his theology, metaphysics, and epistemology— and it did so long after Coleridge renounced Godwin for Burke (who could only offer such a principle in action, not, doctrinally, as an end unto itself). "Torpor," a keyword in *Political Justice*, would become an important term for Wordsworth, whose poetics and politics sought to distinguish between savage torpor and enlightened tranquillity. For Godwin, "Whenever government assumes to deliver us from the trouble of thinking for ourselves, the only consequences it produces are torpor and imbecility."[92] For Wordsworth, this torpor, which has cultural as well as political roots, is the distorted reflection of tranquillity, a political virtue that is actively achieved. "Truth," Godwin says in *Political Justice*, "dwells with contemplation. We can seldom make much progress in the business of disentangling error and delusion, but in sequestered privacy, or in the tranquil interchange of sentiments that takes place between two persons."[93] Above all, Godwin provided a rigorous philosophical system designed to demonstrate what would become a fundamental Romantic intuition: political problems are epistemological problems; problems of freedom are problems of knowledge. In other words, if we are to understand the complexities of a postrevolutionary world or to realize the noblest of revolutionary aspirations, it is necessary that we understand basic elements of our mental life—that we account for our knowledge, its conditions, and the means by which it is acquired. This also means accounting for how knowledge, or opinion, is impeded in its progress—how it is bluntly shaped by coercion, violence, or law and how it is subtly shaped by habit, sentiment, or sophistry. "Freedom of institution," in Godwin's formulation, "is desirable chiefly because it is connected with independence of mind." Wordsworth's troubled dream of building social freedom on the freedom of the individual mind was first Godwin's vision, the most radical and the most affirmative critique of political reason of its time.

THE LITERATURE OF JUSTICE
AND JUSTIFICATION

CHAPTER FIVE

Coleridge and the Principles of Political Knowledge

•

> Reserving then the expression "Idea" (*Idee*) for the objective or
> real Notion (*Begriff*) and distinguishing it from the Notion itself
> and still more from mere pictorial thought, we must also reject
> even more vigorously that estimate of the Idea according to
> which it is not anything actual, and true thoughts are said to be
> *only* ideas.
>
> —*G.W.F. Hegel,* Science of Logic

> Being impelled or inspired by an image is not the same as
> knowing a world. We do not need to postulate a world beyond
> time which is the home of such images in order to account for
> their occurrence, or for their effects on conduct.
>
> —*Richard Rorty,* Contingency, Irony, and Solidarity

The conditions of knowledge were, for S. T. Coleridge, the conditions on which the practical affairs of this world were required to stand. What sorts of things counted as knowledge, and how the human mind comes to know certain things, determined both the legitimacy of social structures and the nature of political obligation. In his mature political prose, Coleridge denies the autonomy of epistemological discourse, emphasizing instead the necessary connection between how the mind functions, on one hand, and the validity of particular political arrangements, on the other. This belief in the social reality of what constitutes knowledge led him to pursue a relatively sustained, at least by Coleridgean standards, analysis of what he calls the "principles of political knowledge." It is under this heading that the political essays of the 1818 edition of *The Friend*, Coleridge's first real attempt to formulate his own political philosophy in a systematic way, are gathered. Political knowledge, like any other form of knowledge, must satisfy certain conditions if it is to be trusted as any sort of guide in practical affairs, especially those in which the welfare of large numbers of people is concerned. Coleridge's specific interest is in the source of this knowledge, and he thus engages with the faculty psychology of the period (in both its British form and as modified and extended by transcendental thought). The relationships among the various mental faculties form the basis of his theory of political knowledge, just as they form the basis of his literary criticism, his metaphysics, and much of his best poetry.

I argue in this chapter for the centrality of the understanding in Coleridge's mature political thought. A faculty often overlooked in Romantic studies, which tends to focus on the dialectic between reason and the imagination, the understanding is for Coleridge the operative faculty in judging and applying the principles of political knowledge.[1] I first examine Coleridge's relationship to Hume, arguing that Coleridge's rejection of Humean epistemology reveals what is perhaps the most essential aspect of Coleridge's own theory of knowledge, the status of the "idea." The political consequences of Humean epistemology provide more problems for Coleridge, whose ideas of the social contract and political obligation differ sharply from Hume's. I then provide a reading of *The Friend* (1809–10, 1818), with attention also paid to *The Statesman's Manual* (1816) and the *Lectures on the History of Philosophy* (1818–19), pursuing the implications of Coleridge's revaluation of the understanding as the faculty of "suiting measures to circumstances" and the foundation of all political knowledge.[2] The significance accorded to the understanding is shown to have the following related purposes: (1) to address the possibility of metaphysics in the face of Hume's critique of causality; (2) to demonstrate the necessity of the unequal distribution of property; (3) to secure the autonomy of the moral will in the context of political obligation; (4) to establish that a philosophy reliant on the senses is no longer suited to the material conditions of the nation; and, finally, (5) to define knowledge in such a way as to make room for particular kinds of faith.

The terms of this argument require some clarification, as "epistemology" is our word, entering the language near the middle of the nineteenth century, and not Coleridge's. The most direct justification for its use is the fact that Coleridge is explicitly concerned with the "principles of political knowledge" in the sense of the grounds or conditions of this knowledge. The necessary condition of political knowledge is, for Coleridge, a particular configuration, or hierarchy, of the mental faculties under the chairmanship of the understanding. In presenting us with a theory of how the mind functions, Coleridge presents us with a theory of knowledge. Until the late nineteenth century, the two projects were typically connected, if not coextensive: forming an idea of what constitutes knowledge usually demanded forming an accurate picture of the mind. It is not until Frege's, and then Husserl's, rejection of "psychologism" from philosophy that the two projects formally diverge.

What, then, is given to us in an analysis of "the *principles* of political knowledge?" Beginning in the fourteenth century, "principle" in English signified much the same as its root (Latin, *principium*), that is, "origin" or "source." "Principle" develops a secondary sense of "general law or rule" in the sixteenth century (a general law or rule "of nature" in the nineteenth) and another sense of "elementary constituent" in the seventeenth century.[3] Coleridge invokes these related meanings of "principle" in *The Friend* when he speaks of his desire "to refer men to PRINCIPLES in all things,"[4] to "refer men's opinions to their absolute principles"[5] and when he speaks of principles as "fundamental truths"[6] and "fundamental doctrines"[7] of "ABSOLUTE PRINCIPLES or necessary LAWS"[8] and of "scientific principles (or laws)."[9] Coleridge also uses "principle" in *The Friend* to signify "ground" or "condition": "a man's principles, on which he grounds his Hope and his Faith, are the life of his life;"[10] in the important epigraph to *The Friend* from Spinoza (to be discussed later), "to demonstrate from plain and undoubted principles, or to deduce from the very condition and necessities of human nature, those plans and maxims which square the best with practice;"[11] "the full exposition of a principle which is the condition of all intellectual progress;"[12] "the *grounds* and essential *principles* of their philosophic systems;"[13] and "the conditions and principles of method."[14] These kinds of principles, then, are quite clearly distinguished from "maxims" or general rules of conduct: "[God] gave us PRINCIPLES, distinguished from the maxims and generalizations of outward experience by their absolute and essential universality and necessity."[15] These are, in effect, *pure* principles, the formal a priori grounds or conditions of knowledge generally.[16]

The other relevant definition of "principle" in *The Friend*, here a kind of knowledge and not simply one of its conditions, is the kind Kant termed "practical": "Practical *principles* [*Prinzipen,* or *Grundsatze*]," according to Kant, "are propositions that contain a general determination of the will, having under it several practical rules."[17] They are subjective maxims "when the condition is regarded by the subject as holding only for his will"; they are objective laws "when the condition is cognized as objective, that is, as holding for the will of every rational being."[18] Coleridge adopts Kant's definition of *practical* principles (a kind of knowledge that may, in fact, take the form of a subjective maxim or an objective "general law or rule"), arguing in *The Friend* that political knowledge, to be discussed in greater detail below, is a form of propositional knowledge—specifically, inferential and demonstrative knowledge—that is not derived from either experience or reason alone, but from the mediating faculty of the understanding.

Romantic studies has, for the past three decades or so, been keen on subverting the "Kantian/Coleridgean" version of Romanticism, suggesting that we may be able to learn more about British literary culture following the French Revolution by focusing on its internal tensions and affiliations rather than its dubious importation of a foreign philosophic tradition (that Coleridge never quite "got" Kant is still, lamentably, a lingering suspicion in Coleridge studies).[19] At its best, critical resistance to the traditional Kantian/Coleridgean line provides a salutary corrective to monolithic interpretations of Romanticism that invariably return to, as Stanley Cavell puts it, "something called uniting subject and object."[20] The seminal works of Romantic criticism, though, and specifically in the Coleridge criticism that has historically related metonymi-cally to the larger field, are extraordinarily sensitive to the debt of the Roman-tics to native intellectual traditions. The primary purpose of this chapter is not to espouse a particular "version" of Romanticism, either Kantian/Coleridgean or, say, one focusing on Byron or Walter Scott, nor does it presume to negoti-ate between supposedly competing versions. Its aim is to follow a particular line of Kantian thought in Coleridge, revealed through his rejection of Hume, in order to understand his most fundamental epistemological and political assumptions.

In his contribution to *Scotland and the Borders of Romanticism*, "Coleridge, Hume, and the Chains of the Romantic Imagination," Cairns Craig argues that Coleridge, in the *Biographia*, neglects to engage fully with Hume's theory of association, focusing instead on Hartley, because Humean association makes room for the imagination in a way that Hartley's materialism does not. The Kantian imagination offered a way out of Hartley's materialism for Coleridge; but, according to Craig, "Humean associationism presents a very different and much more anguished conception of the imagination since, for Hume, the imagination is both the foundation of all our experience and, at the same time, its inevitable dissolution."[21] In his review of Craig's essay, Seamus Perry reminds us that, at least in terms of the personal philosophical development depicted in the *Biographia*, Hume simply does not play much of a role—that, in Craig's terms, the "historical and philosophical suppression involved in this substitu-tion of Hartley for Hume" may have less to do with Coleridge's anxiety regard-ing Hume (attracted to his theory of association and, simultaneously, repulsed by his alleged atheism) and more to do with the fact that Coleridge simply did not devote as much thought to Hume as to Hartley or, Perry notes, to Joseph Priestley.[22] Even if one were to grant the relative inattention to Hume in the *Biographia*, the vitriol with which Coleridge speaks of Hume throughout his prose suggests that there is much at stake here—namely, I argue, a picture of the mind with political consequences. Where Craig sees a historical and philo-sophical suppression of Hume for the sake of the transcendental imagination, at least in the *Biographia*, I argue for a more direct engagement with Hume on ideational and ideological grounds—in other words, one centered on the status of the idea and the social consequences of that status.

Hume and the Highest Problem of Philosophy

Evidence of Coleridge's antipathy toward Hume is not difficult to find. The tenor of the antagonism is perhaps best expressed in Coleridge's remark that, in his planned *History of Metaphysics*, Hume was to be given considerable at-tention and that he would be "besprinkled copiously from the fountains of Bitterness and Contempt."[23] Criticisms typically fall into three related categories: theological, philosophical, and cultural. Coleridge, like many others, objected to Hume's agnosticism in the strongest possible terms. The *Biographia Literaria* (1817) refers to "the impious and pernicious tenets defended by Hume, Priestley, and the French fatalists or necessitarians; some of whom had perverted metaphysical reasonings to the denial of mysteries and indeed of all the peculiar doctrines of christianity."[24] *The Statesman's Manual* (1816) unsympathetically refers to "the same Scotch philosopher, who devoted his life to the undermining of the Christian religion; and expended his last breath in a blasphemous regret that he had not survived it!"[25] The charge of blasphemy is repeated in the 1818–19 *Lectures on the History of Philosophy*, in which Coleridge dismisses, as he would throughout his *Marginalia*, the "spider" argument from Hume's *Dialogues concerning Natural Religion* (1779).[26]

These theological objections stem from more fundamental objections to Hume's philosophy, particularly his epistemology. Coleridge offers his most concise and direct statement of the link in the *Biographia*: "The process, by which Hume degraded the notion of cause and effect into a blind product of delusion and habit, into the mere sensation of *proceeding* life (nisus vitalis) associated with the images of the memory; this same process must be repeated to the equal degradation of every *fundamental* idea in ethics or theology."[27] The degrading ethical and theological effects of Hume's critique of causality are countered in *The Statesman's Manual*, where Coleridge contends that the necessity of causal relations "depends on, or rather inheres in, the idea of the Omnipresent and Absolute: for this it is, in which the Possible is one and the same with the Real and the Necessary."[28] For Hume, we remember, "necessity is something, that exists in the mind, not in objects."[29] While the necessity of causal relations in the idea of the "Absolute" is slightly obscure in its details—it is difficult to imagine such a process without resorting to something approaching Malebranche's occasionalism or Berkeley's idealism—Coleridge clearly and consistently posits God, the infinite I AM, as the ground or foundation of all reality. Coleridge is thus acutely aware not only of the standard skeptical arguments forwarded in Hume's *Dialogues concerning Natural Religion* and *Natural History of Religion* (1757), but he is also sensitive to how the reduction of causal knowledge to habitual belief in Hume's *Treatise* (1739–40) threatens every "fundamental" ethical and theological idea.

There are also more purely philosophical objections to Hume's epistemology, although these, too, almost always contain the trace of theological suspicion. Perhaps the most technical objection is found in the *Notebooks* (1804):

How opposite to nature & the fact to talk of the one *moment* of Hume; of our whole being an aggregate of successive single sensations. Who ever *felt* a *single* sensation? Is not every one at the same moment conscious that there co-exist a thousand others in a darker shade, or less light; even as when I fix my attention on a white House on a grey bare Hill or rather long ridge that runs out of sight each way (How often I want the german *unübersehbar?*) the pretended single sensation is it anything more than the *Light*-point in every picture either of nature or of a good painter; & again subordinately in every component part of the picture? And what is a moment? Succession with *interspace*? Absurdity! It is evidently only the Licht-punct [*punkt*], the *Sparkle* ~~of~~ in the indivisible undivided Duration.[30]

This notebook entry, from Christmas Day 1804, registers Coleridge's main philosophic complaint against Hume. The "copy principle" of Hume's *Treatise*—the notion, derived from Locke, that complex ideas are composed of simple ideas, which are fainter copies of the simple impressions from which they ultimately derive, to which they correspond and exactly resemble—was formulated so that irreducible complex ideas, such as the soul, God, or substance could be shown to lack cognitive content. Its premise is that one can reduce a complex idea into its constituent simple ideas and that these simple ideas, in turn, could be reduced to the simple impressions from which they derive. Coleridge repudiates the whole notion of a single impression, suggesting the indivisibility of what Kant would call the manifold of intuition, thus allowing the irreducibly complex idea of God to have some other epistemological basis.

Hume's critique of causality, Coleridge worries, threatens the possibility of metaphysics itself. In the *Biographia*, he writes that "after I had successively studied in the schools of Locke, Berkeley, Leibnitz, and Hartley"—a trajectory familiar to readers of Coleridge—and "could find in neither of them an abiding place for my reason," he began to ask whether "a system of philosophy, as different from mere history and historic classification, [is] possible?"[31] As Coleridge sees it, the possibility of metaphysics is threatened by the empirical claim, originating in Aristotle and finding its fullest expression in book 1 of Locke's *Essay*, that "there is nothing in the mind that was not before in the senses." It is also threatened by Hume's analysis of cause and effect, which, Coleridge argues, "will apply with equal and crushing force to all the other eleven categorical forms, and the logical functions corresponding to them."[32] Coleridge, Bate and Engell note, "is saying that once a strictly empirical premise is conceded, none of Kant's categories may be trusted as objective operations of the mind."[33] Coleridge will concede neither the foundational empirical premise nor Hume's claims regarding causality because, as he puts it, "Truth is correlative of Being," or "intelligence and being are reciprocally each other's Substrate."[34] Coleridge immediately makes it clear that "being" here refers specifically to a Supreme Being, the (possibility of the) idea of which dictated the philosophical development, described with proper names, he has just outlined. "An abiding place for my reason," offered by none of the philosophers mentioned, is above all a system in which the idea of God is able to rest.[35]

The status of the idea, so obviously crucial in Hume's philosophy, is precisely what is at stake in Coleridge's negotiations with Hume. It is, as Coleridge would say in the final sentence of *The Statesman's Manual*, "the highest *problem* of philosophy, and not part of its nomenclature."[36] Hume in the *Treatise* defines the "idea" as "faint images of [impressions] in thinking and reasoning." He explains in a note that he is restoring the word "idea" to its "original sense, from which Mr. Locke had perverted it, in making it stand for all our perceptions."[37] Coleridge shares with Hume his rejection of Locke's overly broad definition, and offers his own, poorly worded definition in *The Statesman's Manual*:

> A Notion may be realized, and becomes Cognition; but that which is neither a Sensation or a Perception, that which is neither individual (i.e. a sensible Intuition) nor general (i.e. a conception) which neither refers to outward Facts nor yet is abstracted from the FORMS of perception contained in the Understanding; but which is an educt of the Imagination actuated by the pure Reason, to which there neither is or can be an adequate correspondent in the world of the senses—this and this alone is = AN IDEA. Whether Ideas are regulative only, according to Aristotle and Kant; or likewise CONSTITUTIVE, and one with the power and Life of Nature, according to Plato, and Plotinus is the highest *problem* of Philosophy, and not part of its nomenclature.[38]

Coleridge claims that the appendix from which this passage comes is "by far the most miscellaneous and desultory of all my writings;" but, he adds, "it had a right to be such." It had a right to be such because, as one of his editors observes, this passage is perhaps "the best statement of Coleridge's philosophical position."[39] However much we may object to it on literary grounds, it condenses into a relatively short space the complexity of the Coleridgean idea. An idea, according to Coleridge, is a notion necessarily engaging with all three major faculties: it is abstracted from the understanding, an "educt" (i.e., an inference or development)[40] of the imagination actuated by the reason. Coleridge is intent on having the idea interact with as many aspects of the mind as possible because his desire is to widen the range of things that may possibly be considered "ideas." If the ideas of God or substance cannot exist in an empirical system of sense impressions, then surely they can exist in the slippery space known as the "play of the mental faculties."[41] Their status as regulative or constitutive is left undetermined, but, given Coleridge's theory of the symbol and his other writings on the idea in the *Biographia* and elsewhere in *The Statesman's Manual*, one may assume the latter.[42]

The *Biographia* offers a less definitive but more suggestive discussion of the idea. Its chapter on the history of associationism complicates and extends the claims made in the *Notebooks* regarding the indivisibility of sensation. Intending to demonstrate that Hobbes contributed nothing original or substantial whatsoever to this history, Coleridge describes Hobbes's theory of association in Humean terms: "Whenever we feel several objects at the same time, the *impressions* that are left (or in the language of Mr. Hume, the *ideas*) are linked together. Whenever therefore any one of the movements, which constitute a complex impression, are renewed through the senses, the others succeed mechanically."[43] Hobbes (and, Coleridge contends, the materialists such as Hartley who followed him) thus reduces all the forms of association to "the one law of time." This is an untenable philosophical position for Coleridge, for whom contemporaneity is only part of the law of association: "For the objects of any two ideas need not have co-existed in the same sensation in order to become mutually associable."[44] Memory, that is, works with sensation in providing the materials of association. More important, however, than the rejection of claims regarding Hobbes's lasting contributions to the history of associationism—a judgment not at all surprising for someone who had long since rejected materialism in all its forms—is what Coleridge says in a lengthy footnote appended to the sentence just quoted. In it, Coleridge grudgingly justifies his, and Hume's, use of the word "idea":

> I here use the word "idea" in Mr. Hume's sense on account of its general currency among the English metaphysicians; though against my own judgement, for I believe that the vague use of this word has been the cause of much error and more confusion. The word, *idea*, in its original sense as used by Pindar, Aristophanes, and in the gospel of Matthew, represented the visual abstraction of a distant object, when we see the whole without distinguishing its parts. Plato adopted it as a technical term, and as the antithesis to *eidola*, or sensuous images; the transient and perishable emblems, or mental words, of ideas. The ideas themselves he considered as mysterious powers, living, seminal, formative, and exempt from time.[45]

This Platonic use of the term is essentially the one Coleridge adopts in his most sustained and thorough writing on the subject, *The Statesman's Manual*: "But every principle is actualized by an idea; and every idea is living, productive, partaketh of infinity, and (as Bacon has sublimely observed) containeth an endless power of semination."[46] What is conspicuously absent here is the concept, the division of which into a priori and a posteriori classes by Kant left little room for the kind of idea Coleridge viewed as "exempt from time." "[A]n *Idea* is equidistant in its signification from Sensation, Image, Fact, and Notion: [it] is the antithesis not the synonyme of *eidolon*."[47] The operative relationship here is the actualizing one between the idea and the principle, to be discussed shortly.

The crucial issue, as far as Coleridge's relationship to Hume is concerned, is the possibility of an idea not derived from sense experience. The instances of the ideas of God and substance have already been mentioned, but the idea as it relates to political knowledge is Coleridge's other concern, and our primary one here. Coleridge warns against the abuse of the idea, speaking nostalgically of the "genial reverence" with which Algernon Sydney "commune[d] with Harrington and Milton on the *Idea* of a perfect state; and in what sense it is true, that the men (i.e. the aggregate of the inhabitants of a country at any one time) are made for the state, not the state for the men."[48] The influence of materialism and Lockean psychology, however, has produced a new breed of philosophers, "and these too have *their* Ideas!" They include those who have "an *Idea*, that Hume, Hartley, and Condillac have exploded all *Ideas*, but those of sensation." The suggestion is that the complex idea of a perfect state, here defined in illiberal terms, cannot rest on ideas derived from sensation, but must have some other source.

These assertions from *The Statesman's Manual*, in which an English literary and political tradition is threatened by Scottish and French influences (and from within by materialists such as Hartley and Priestley), reflect Coleridge's anxiety about the status of English literary culture, broadly defined, at the end of the eighteenth and beginning of the nineteenth century.[49] These "cultural" objections constitute the third major category of Coleridge's criticisms of Hume, existing alongside and frequently engaging with more purely theological and philosophical objections. Coleridge laments in his *Notebooks* that "the *flashy* moderns seem to *rob* the ancients of the honors due to them / & Bacon & Harrington are *not* read because Hume and Condillac *are*. This is an evil," a claim he would repeat in the *Biographia* thirteen years later.[50] In an entry from 1805, he says, "Let England be Sir P. Sidney, Shakespeare, Spenser, Milton, Bacon, Harrington, Swift, Wordsworth, and never let the names of Darwin, Johnson, Hume, *furr* it over!"[51] In his marginalia to Pepys's *Memoirs*, Coleridge observes: "But alike as Historian and as Philosopher, Hume has, meo saltem judicio, been extravagantly overrated.—Mercy on the Age, & the People, for whom Lock is profound, and Hume subtle."[52] Criticism is often directed toward Scotland and Scottish writers at large, reflecting an anti-Scottish sentiment that even Wordsworth would share at times. In his marginalia to Anderson's *British Poets* we find: "Damn this Scotch Scoundrel of a Biographer," and "Is it possible than a man should have written this?—O Lord! Yes! any thing is possible from a Scotchman."[53] In an 1816 letter to Thomas Boosey, Coleridge writes: "The Scotch appear to me dull Frenchmen, and superficial Germans.— They have no *Inside*."[54] Alexander Dyce, the Scottish editor and literary historian, suspected in Coleridge a "mortal antipathy to Scotchmen."[55] The source of this anti-Scottish sentiment is unclear, but there is, at best, an uneasiness, more than a century after the Act of Union, about the role Scotland is to play in British cultural life.

These objections by Coleridge to Hume on theological, philosophical, and cultural grounds are significant, and they form the basis of Coleridge's fundamental attitude toward Hume. Of equal importance and interest, however, are the rare moments when Coleridge defends Hume. In his *Lectures on the History of Philosophy* (1818–19), Coleridge argues that Hume has been attacked unjustly, singling out the opponents of Hume whom Kant dismisses in his *Prolegomena to Any Future Metaphysics* (1783): Joseph Priestley, James Oswald, and James Beattie. "No one will suspect me of being an advocate of Mr. Hume's opinions," Coleridge writes, "but I most assuredly do think that he was attacked in a very illogical, not to say unhandsome manner, both by Priestley and Oswald, and, I grieve to say for the beauty of the book in other respects, by Beattie."[56] Their attacks were "illogical" and "unhandsome" because they were too easily alarmed by the consequences of Hume's critique of causality: " 'Here is a man denying all cause and effect. What will become of all our religion?' If it stopped there, there would be some sense in it, but they went on. 'What was to become of all society? If such opinions were to prevail, men would not use their spoons to put their soup into their mouths!' "[57] Coleridge warns against this vulgarizing, overly literal interpretation of Hume. He is shrewd enough not to reduce Hume to the caricature of the skeptic—someone unable to avoid running into posts, as was said of Pyrrho. For Coleridge, a philosophy such as Hume's becomes "pernicious" when it serves as an epistemic foundation not only for theological claims (from what impression do we derive our idea of God?), but also for political claims (from what impression do we derive our idea of contract or right?). The relations between these branches of thought were clear enough for Hume. "The task he set for his political theory," Knud Haakonssen observes, "was to explain why [superstition and enthusiasm] were philosophically misconceived, empirically untenable, and, in their extreme forms, politically dangerous."[58]

Hume's political philosophy proceeds naturally from the same basic assumptions and premises he employs in the rest of his philosophy. Just as the *Treatise* confidently proposes a science of human nature, so do Hume's political essays contend "that politics may be reduced to a science": "So great is the force of laws and of particular forms of government, and so little dependence have they on the humors and tempers of men, that consequences almost as general and certain may sometimes be deduced from them as any which the mathematical sciences afford us."[59] The "universal axioms," "maxims," and "eternal political truths" of Hume's politics are uttered on this basis. In its negative component, Hume's politics deny the contract theory associated with Hobbes and Locke and its attendant claim that consent is the source of political obligation. "But would these reasoners look abroad," Hume writes in "Of the Original Contract," "they would meet with nothing that in the least corresponds to their ideas or can warrant so refined and philosophical a system."[60] Again, from what impression or impressions do we derive our idea of an original contract? "On the contrary, we find everywhere princes who claim their subjects as their property and assert their independent right of sovereignty from conquest or succession." Political obligation does not have its source in an original contract, real or imagined, but in historically situated power relations. "Is there anything discoverable in all these [historical] events but force and violence? Where is the mutual agreement or voluntary association so much talked of?"[61] The claim that the historicity of the contract is irrelevant—that it gains its force through a process of analogy (we have certain social obligations *as if* such a contract had existed)—is, for Hume, "false philosophy": we are thrown, as it were, into societies that are already subject to authority and find ourselves obliged to obey their laws, without the choice that is necessary in any contractual relationship.

In more positive terms, Hume's politics extend the empirical methods of experience and observation to make claims about property, law, and justice: "In general we may observe that all questions of property are subordinate to the authority of civil laws, which extend, restrain, modify, and alter the rules of natural justice, according to the particular *convenience* of each community. The laws have, or ought to have, a constant reference to the constitution of government, the manners, the climate, the religion, the commerce, the situation of each society."[62] Having demonstrated the insufficiency of the contract theory in his political essays, where he concludes that "some other foundation of government must also be admitted,"[63] Hume continues in the second *Enquiry* to argue for a foundation of interest: "Property is allowed to be dependent on civil laws; civil laws are allowed to have no other object, but the interest of society: This therefore must be allowed to be the sole foundation of property and justice. Not to mention, that our obligation itself to obey the magistrate and his laws is founded on nothing but the interests of society."[64] The assurance with which Hume reaches this claim about political obligation comes from the empiricist's faith in his own experience and observation (the unacknowledged origins of our impressions) as the bases of his ideas (no rationalist claim about the *volonté générale* is attempted with such sangfroid). The briefest reflection on our own experience, for Hume, indicates that our allegiance to governmental authority comes from a collective interest in the protection (specifically, of property and contracts) given to us by the administration of justice.[65] Hume's inspiration here is nonetheless French, as it is Montesquieu's *De l'esprit des loix* (1748) that has "prosecuted this subject [the fitness of the law to the historical circumstances of a society] at large, and has established, from these principles, a system of political knowledge, which abounds in ingenious and brilliant thoughts, and is not wanting in solidity."[66]

Hume's remark about "political knowledge" returns us to the "principles of political knowledge" that Coleridge examines in *The Friend*, to which I will presently turn my full attention. Hume's epistemology of impressions and ideas, and the strict correspondence between them, yielded a political philosophy that subordinates questions of property to questions of law, places the source of political obligation in interest, and maintains that basic social and political institutions are fundamentally artificial: "those impressions, which give rise to this sense of justice, are not natural to the mind of man, but arise from artifice and human conventions."[67] These are unacceptable premises for Coleridge, for whom the structure of the mind itself determines both political organization and the constitution of political knowledge. This is not to say that the ideas of justice, property, right, obligation, and the perfect state—in short, the most important and basic kinds of "political knowledge"—are, for Coleridge, innate to the mind; but rather that the structure of the mind, and not its impressions, determines their status as knowledge.

Structures of Mind and Government: *The Friend*

The earliest reference to what would become *The Friend* occurs in an 1804 note-book entry, where Coleridge writes, "I should *like* to dare to look forward to the Time, when Wordsworth & I with some contributions from Lamb & Southey—& from a few others . . . should publish *a Spectator*."[68] In a letter to Thomas Poole of the same year, he describes the work in noticeably different terms: "Consolations and Comforts from the exercise and right application of the Reason, the Imagination, and the moral Feelings, addressed especially to those in Sickness, Adversity, or Distress of mind, *from speculative Gloom*, &c."[69] This description, which would be repeated five years later in the Prospectus to *The Friend*, declares the renovating and fructifying purpose of the work. It is no accident that this project would be undertaken in the midst of Coleridge's so-called dark years, when the effects of his failed marriage, his strained relationship with Wordsworth, his persistent depression, his financial troubles, and his opium addiction demanded the assistance of some "friend" to rescue him from his dejection. Given that no friend—not Wordsworth, Southey, Gillman, or even the steadfast Poole—was capable of the task, Coleridge, in an impressive act of an often paralyzed will, assumed the role of aid-giver so that he might heal himself. The agent of this healing is not the idea or the concept, but the principle: "It is my object to refer men to PRINCIPLES in all things; in Literature, in the Fine Arts, in Morals, in Legislation, in Religion. Whatever therefore of a political nature may be reduced to general Principles . . . this I do not exclude from my Scheme."[70] *The Friend* is an effort to return to firm principles so that the detritus of false metaphysics may be discarded.

Twenty-eight numbers were produced between June 1809 and March 1810. An "1812 edition" reprinted the numbers in a single volume. The 1818 *rifacimento* altered and rearranged the essays so as to form a more coherent whole, divided into three volumes. All three volumes contain much that is interesting, covering a wide range of subjects with Coleridge's characteristic bursts of imaginative insight. Throughout there is an emphasis on the return to pure principles, an effort to establish a foundation for judgment more firm than the one provided by discursive reasoning. It is, however, the first proper section, beginning toward the end of the first volume and continuing all the way through the second, that is my primary concern. This section, "On the Principles of Political Knowledge," contains Coleridge's most sustained and explicit analysis of the relationship between political theory and the conditions of knowledge.

The first essay on the principles of political philosophy begins with an epigraph from Spinoza's *Tractatus Theologico-Politicus*. In it, Spinoza criticizes both the "mere practical Statesman" and the "mere Theorists" for neglecting to do the actual work of "conceiv[ing] a practicable scheme of civil policy." Spinoza proposes, in contrast, "simply to demonstrate from plain and undoubted principles, or to deduce from the very condition and necessities of human nature, those plans and maxims which square best with practice."[71] This, as we shall see, is essentially the political model of expediency espoused by Coleridge later on in the work. It is important, however, to note here the significance of beginning his most sustained discussion of political history with a lengthy epigraph from Spinoza. By the time Coleridge had begun writing *The Friend*, he had rejected the fundamental claims of Spinoza's *Ethics* and had already immersed himself in the Kantian-Schellingian phase that would dominate his mature philosophic thought. By beginning with Spinoza, Coleridge signals two central themes of *The Friend*: (1) a philosophically radical metaphysics such as Spinoza's may be consistent with a political philosophy that is far less radical (politically, Spinoza largely follows Hobbes, with some important qualifications regarding the theory of sovereignty); and (2) in many ways, the Coleridge of 1818 is much the same as the Coleridge of 1795. Nowhere is this more evident than in his decision to reprint some of his 1795 Bristol lectures in *The Friend*. As Barbara Rooke points out, "In republishing in 1818 a large section of his political lectures originally delivered in Bristol in 1795 during his period of pro-revolutionary enthusiasm, Coleridge was doing more . . . than trying to prove that, contrary to the satirists and caricaturists, he had been no seditionist at that time and was no reactionary now."[72] He is asserting his own fidelity to pure principles. Just as Burke had opposed the French Revolution while supporting

American conciliation, so had Coleridge maintained a consistent principle throughout his seemingly incongruous philosophic allegiances. The principle is ultimately pragmatic: a political proposition is justified as long as it proves useful in a specific set of circumstances, what Coleridge would call in *The Friend* the "theory of expediency." This pragmatic principle does not, to be sure, extend across the full range of Coleridge's philosophical thought; its application in *The Friend* is limited to what he calls "political knowledge." But as critics are beginning to appreciate, and as I hope to indicate here, the pragmatic strain in Coleridge's thought is perhaps stronger than previously assumed, inflecting his discussions of metaphysical ideas that are not overtly political.[73]

The political essays of *The Friend* are predicated on a division of "all the different philosophical systems of political justice, all the Theories on the rightful Origin of Government" into three classes. What is absolutely crucial, for our purposes, is that each class is attended by an assumption about how the mind functions or what it can know. The first class is the system of Hobbes, which ascribes the origin and continuance of government to fear, "or the power of the stronger, aided by the force of custom."[74] This theory corresponds to the view that "the human mind consists of nothing, but manifold modifications of passive sensation." Coleridge follows both Harrington and Cudworth here in objecting to Hobbes's debasement of men into brutes, possessing some degree of understanding but utterly devoid of the moral will.[75] The reality and legitimacy of the moral will is the first principle of Coleridge's ethics, just as the principle of irreducible unity is the first and guiding principle of his metaphysics. Any theory of government that denies it is therefore untenable. This objection aside, the whole theory is, Coleridge contends, "baseless" on more empirical grounds: "We are told by History, we learn from experience, we know from our own hearts, that fear, of itself, is utterly incapable of producing any regular, continuous and calculable effect, even on an individual; and that the fear, which *does* act systematically upon the mind, always presupposes a sense of duty, as its cause."[76] Fear may provide us with an inclination to behave in certain ways, but it is always preceded, and ideally subjugated, by a dominant sense of duty. Such a sanguine view of things, reaffirmed no doubt by his reading of Kant, does not inquire into the causes of the sense of duty. Knowledge of the sense of duty is not derived from any particular impressions, but, it seems, from more universal principles under which historical and personal particulars are subsumed. It is in this state that the conscience, which Coleridge defines earlier in *The Friend* as a "spiritual sense or testifying state of the coincidence or discordance of the FREE WILL with the REASON," may be said to operate.[77]

The individual "sense of duty" translates easily into a more general "Spirit of Law," the "true necessity, which compels man into the social state."[78] This is as close as Coleridge comes to asserting an original contract, which for him is an absurd theory insofar as it neglects to assign a "moral force" to the contract. In Coleridge's sense, the word "contract" simply is the "sense of duty acting in a specific direction, i.e. determining our moral relations, as members of a body politic": "If I have referred to a supposed *origin* of Government, it has been in courtesy to a common notion: for I myself regard the supposition as no more than a means of simplifying to our apprehension the ever-continuing causes of social union, even as the conservation of the world may be represented as an act of continued Creation."[79] The analogy Coleridge presents between the preservation of social union and the divine preservation of the world itself recalls not only the conclusion of Berkeley's argument of *esse est percipi*, but also the *Biographia's* definition of the primary imagination as a "repetition in the finite mind of the eternal act of creation in the infinite I AM."[80] The "origin" of government is not an isolated historical event but is continually created by the "moral force" of our "sense of duty."

This subjective sense of duty, and the objective "Spirit of the Law" to which it corresponds, is the guiding principle of the second theory of government, what Coleridge acknowledges as his own theory of expediency: "according to this theory, every institution of national origin needs no other justification than a proof, that under the particular circumstances it is expedient." The epistemic assumption of this theory is that the human being is an "animal gifted with understanding," defined here by Coleridge as "the faculty of suiting measures to circumstances."[81] This is the most prominent definition of the understanding in *The Friend's* analysis of the principles of political knowledge, although there are others. The political essays of *The Friend* are preceded by a section on the distinction between the reason and the understanding, a distinction on which Coleridge claims to base his entire metaphysics.[82] Coleridge here presents authentically Kantian definitions of the two faculties. The understanding is "the faculty by which we generalize and arrange the phenomena of perception; that faculty, the functions of which contain the rules and constitute the possibility of outward experience." In a note to the political section itself, Coleridge writes that "by the UNDERSTANDING, I mean the faculty of thinking and forming *judgments* on the notices furnished by the sense, according to certain rules existing in itself, which rules constitute its distinct nature."[83] For Kant, the understanding (*Verstand*), "whose province alone it is to make an objective judgment on appearances," compares perceptions and connects them in consciousness.[84] It is none other than the faculty of thinking, for thinking "is the same as judging, or referring representations to judgments in general."[85] In the first book of the Transcendental Analytic in *The Critique of Pure Reason*, Kant defines the understanding as the faculty of rules.[86]

Kant distinguishes the understanding from the reason in the Transcendental Dialectic: "here we will distinguish reason from understanding by calling reason [*Vernunft*] the *faculty of principles*";[87] and again, "If the understanding may be a faculty of unity of appearances by means of rules, then reason is the faculty of the unity of the rules of understanding under principles."[88] In *The Friend*, Coleridge defines reason as the "organ of Super-sensuous," that which subordinates the notions of rules of the understanding to "ABSOLUTE PRIN-CIPLES or necessary LAWS."[89] In the note to the political section, he explains: "By the pure REASON, I mean the power by which we become possessed of principle, (the eternal verities of Plato and Descartes) and of ideas, (N.B. not images) as the ideas of a point, a line, a circle, in Mathematics; and of Justice, Holiness, Free-Will, &c. in Morals."[90] As he does in the *Biographia*, he is careful to emphasize the Platonic idea in opposition to *eidola*, or "sensuous images," that are further removed from cognition and knowledge.

Coleridge begins to make stronger claims on behalf of reason with his intro-duction of Jacobi's definition of reason as the organ concerned with "spiritual objects, the Universal, the Eternal, and the Necessary." Reason, Coleridge in-sists, is in fact an organ *identical* with its objects: "Thus, God, the Soul, eternal Truth, &c. are the objects of Reason; but they are themselves *reason*."[91] He appeals to Milton: "We name God the Supreme Reason; and Milton says, 'Whence the Soul *Reason* receives, and Reason is her Being [*Paradise Lost*, 5.486–87]." Animals may possess understanding (what Hooker, Bacon, and Hobbes called "*discourse*, or the discursive faculty"), but they entirely lack rea-son: "an understanding enlightened by reason Shakespear gives as the contra-distinguishing character of man, under the name *discourse of reason*."[92] "The human understanding," he concludes, "possesses two distinct organs, the out-ward sense, and 'the mind's eye' which is reason." Coleridge appeals, then, to the authority of Milton and Shakespeare to argue for: (1) the identity of reason with its objects; and (2) the subsumption of the reason *under* the understand-ing. The section on "Reason and Understanding" does not simply distinguish between the two faculties along Kantian/Jacobian lines but, significantly, sub-ordinates reason (the only faculty capable of making Kant blush: "Since I am now to give a definition of this supreme faculty of cognition, I find myself in some embarrassment")[93] to the understanding.[94] What is to be gained by this subordination of reason to the higher faculty of understanding? Coleridge pro-vides a clue when he writes: "If the reader therefore will take the trouble of bear-ing in mind these and the following explanations, he will have removed before hand every possible difficulty from the Friend's political section."[95] The answer is that in redeeming the understanding from the penury of bureaucratic middle-management, elevating it to what Deleuze would call the "chairmanship" of the mental faculties, Coleridge provides a new necessary condition of political knowledge. Like the emphasis on active empiricism in Wordsworth's political writings, the emphasis on the understanding in *The Friend* is an epistemic precaution—one that, had it been in place earlier, might have averted the perceived mistake of his own radicalism and perhaps even the excesses of the French Revolution itself.

The Kantian definition of the understanding used by Coleridge—"the faculty of thinking and forming judgments"—does not by itself justify or explain the definition of the understanding in the political section as "the faculty of suiting measures to circumstances." These appear to be two vastly different operations, one being a basic act of perception (or a comparison of perceptions) and the other an active engagement with the objective world or even a refined skill in the art of policymaking. Kant suggests a link when he posits two species of judgment: theoretical and practical. Theoretical judgment applies a concept to a determinate *given* object; practical judgment determines how to *produce* an object (in this sense a goal or purpose). The understanding, though, is for Kant not responsible for practical judgment. Coleridge's placement of both of them in the understanding, suggesting that they are the same sort of thing, is perhaps justified by the impossibility of assigning these operations to any other faculty. The reason, we have seen, has its eye on the super-sensuous, operating outside the realm of "circumstances" altogether, and the imagination's duties, conspicuously absent in *The Friend*, are defined elsewhere in more vital and esemplastic terms. So to the understanding are left the relatively mundane tasks of making connections between appearances and forming judgments about them. Coleridge extends the sense of "forming judgments," allowing the phrase to signify the recognition of appropriateness or "suitability." It is essential for Coleridge that this function be denied to reason. Reason alone is insufficient in the art of governing and being governed. It can only provide principles that the understanding must apply to particular circumstances. The cautious moderation of this theory, the attitude prescribed by Hume toward the end of his *Treatise* and by Burke in his *Reflections*, is predicated on a critique of reason as the guiding faculty in political affairs. The position, though, is fundamentally Kantian: pure political ideas and ideals are not things that have validity in their own right, but are relevant insofar as they regulate an approach to politics that is grounded in experience. The understanding, furnished by sense experience and enlightened by reason, is the means of this regulation.

The third and final political system adumbrated by Coleridge in *The Friend* is the system of "pure rationality," that which "denies all rightful origins to government, except as far as they are derivable from principles contained in the REASON of Man, and judges all the relations of men in Society by the Laws of moral necessity, according to IDEAS."[96] The fundamental principle of the theory is that "[n]othing is to be deemed rightful in civil society, or to be tolerated as such, but what is capable of being demonstrated out of the original laws of the pure Reason." The assumption of the theory is that "[w]hatever is not *every where* necessary, is *no where* right." It is the system of Rousseau and the "French economists," presumably physiocrats such as Quesnay, Turgot, and de Nemours. It insists that the only rightful form of government "must be framed on such principles that every individual follows his own Reason while he obeys the laws of the constitution, and performs the will of the state while he follows the dictates of his own Reason."[97] Coleridge's objection to the theory of "pure rationality" is based on a suspicion of the general will. He sees no necessary reason why the general will must reflect either the reason or the best interests of the people from whom it supposedly originates. There is a "mere *probability*" that it does; "and thus we already find ourselves beyond the magic circle of the pure Reason, and within the sphere of the understanding and the prudence."[98] The apotheosis of reason in France, Coleridge argues, ended disastrously because pure reason, unaided by the understanding, is incapable of making judgments based on perception. It can provide only the principles that the understanding must apply to specific circumstances.

If all of this seems like the safe, common-sense politics of a former radical coming to terms with his own apostasy, it is because it is. There is, of course, limited political value in insisting that things must be judged in the specificity of their circumstances (the claim itself is so general and self-evident as to resist interrogation), and a prudential politics based on the understanding hardly makes for inspiring ideology, radical or reactionary. Throughout Coleridge's analysis is the suggestion that he is no longer prone to unmanly excess but is a mature, practical political thinker capable of suiting measures to circumstances. Behind this familiar, even predictable, rhetoric of moderation, though, is a hierarchy of mental faculties in political affairs that runs counter to both eighteenth-century rationalism and critical assumptions about the Romantic view of the mind. The reason and the imagination are here subordinated to a faculty almost all thinkers of the period acknowledged in animals and idiots. The privileging of the understanding in *The Friend* is part of a project to secure a moderate cast of mind and an increasingly conservative political agenda. As John Morrow observes, Coleridge develops in *The Friend* a philosophical defense of property-based politics.[99] This defense involves a remarkable link between the possession of property and the mental faculties. Coleridge writes in *The Friend*:

> [W]here individual landed property exists, there must be inequality of property: the nature of the earth *and the nature of the mind* unite to make the contrary impossible. . . . Now it is impossible to deduce the Right of Property from pure Reason. The utmost which Reason could give would be a property in the *forms* of things, as far as the forms were produced by individual power. In the *matter* it could give no property. . . . Rousseau himself expressly admits, that Property

cannot be deduced from the Laws of Reason and Nature; and he ought therefore to have admitted at the same time, that his whole theory was a thing of air.[100]

The passage makes explicit what is at stake in the hierarchy of faculties. One simply cannot deduce, Coleridge argues, the right of property from pure reason. The implied argument is that pure reason operates in an autonomous world of concepts and ideas, dealing with the objective world only through the mediation of the understanding and, in turn, sensation. The materialist critic may be tempted to view this conclusion—the impossibility of deducing the right of property from pure reason—as the first principle of Coleridge's entire analysis, the assumption motivating the whole system. In this view, Coleridge's mental hierarchy exists so that the right of property—that is to say, the necessity of the inequality of property—may have some other, more secure epistemological basis. The cynical view is not necessarily inaccurate, but it is limited insofar as it suggests that Coleridge's primary concern is the world of matter and not the world of spirit. At the same time, I do not wish to suggest that Coleridge's sole concern is with immaterial concerns, if only because Coleridge's place in the pantheist tradition indicates that he did not always find such a dualistic vocabulary useful, even if it was the dominant vocabulary of the time or the one most readily available to him. I do wish to suggest that Coleridge's philosophical defense of property-based politics may have been as much in the service of philosophy as it was in the service of property. An appeal to the material interests of his readers, in a work persistently charged with obscurity, is part of a larger strategy including the rejection of French rationalism and the exposition of a uniquely Coleridgean brand of English conservatism rooted in transcendentalism. Coleridge, we remember, declared that he had snapped his "squeaking baby-trumpet of Sedition" in 1798, the same year he began his life-long study of Kant.[101]

If one accepts, as Coleridge does, that the nature of the mind is such that it entails the inequality of property—or even more generally, that there exists a direct relationship between how the mind functions and how societies are structured—then one requires a sufficiently generative psychology, that is, one capable of producing changes in the physical world by virtue of its very structure. The partitioning of the mind in faculty psychology, essentially the construction of a set of mental enclosures, provided such a structure. Faculty psychology is in this way the "natural" psychology of property-based bourgeois culture. In Coleridge's version of it, the unequal endowment of mental faculties, the rejection of Rousseau's claim that "[r]eason is not susceptible of degree," makes the necessity of inequality more plausible. It is perhaps here that Coleridge's relationship to the Enlightenment, at least the pre-Kantian Enlightenment, is most evident. It is only from the reason that we can derive principles, and it is left to the understanding to apply these principles. "This however gives no proof that Reason alone ought to govern and direct human beings, *either as Individuals or as States*. It ought not to do this, because it cannot."[102] The laws of reason, Coleridge argues, are unable to satisfy the "first conditions of Human Society." The "first conditions" of human society must rely on the understanding, "enlightened by past experience and immediate observation, and determining our choice by comparisons of expediency."[103] This is the second, correct theory of government, only briefly discussed by Coleridge before he attacks the third theory of "pure rationality." The relative inattention given to this theory of expediency suggests that Coleridge's purposes are more proscriptive than prescriptive. The principles of political knowledge should not, because they cannot, be deduced from reason alone. Just as "Dejection: An Ode" exhibits something resembling a real fear of the imagination in its seventh stanza, so does *The Friend* exhibit something resembling a real fear of untethered political reason, a faculty with leveling consequences for both ideas and property.

Coleridge's apprehension about the potentially devastating effects of pure rationalism is occasioned not only by the threat it poses to private property, but also by the political consequences it had in France. The reliance on principles derived from reason alone, such as the general will, was for Coleridge, as it was for others, the precondition of the Terror and Napoleon's rise to power. "With a wretched *parrotry* [the National Assembly] wrote and harangued without ceasing of the *Volonté generale*—the *inalienable sovereignty* of the people: and by these high-sounding phrases led on the vain, ignorant, and intoxicated populace to wild excesses and wilder expectations, which entailing on them the bitterness of disappointment cleared the way for military despotism, for the satanic Government of Horror under the Jacobins, and of Terror under the Corsican."[104] The targets here are the framers of the 1791 constitution, although claims made on behalf of the *volonté générale* and the "natural, inalienable, and sacred rights of man" were voiced in considerably stronger terms in the 1789 Declaration of the Rights of Man and of the Citizen. The 1791 constitution is in fact a much more sober document than Coleridge suggests, with the debates leading up to it dominated, at least in the beginning, by the moderate *monarchiens*. Intoxication, "wild excesses and wilder expectations," may have been the result of the new political culture that emerged between 1789 and 1791, but one would be hardpressed to find them in the constitution itself.

Similarly, Coleridge's claim that the framers of the 1791 constitution "deduce, that the people itself is its own sole rightful legislator, and at most dare only recede so far from its right as to delegate to chosen deputies the power of representing and declaring the general will" is misleading.[105] The phrase "general will" is never explicitly mentioned in the document, the most objectionable article being perhaps the now modest republican claim that "the nation, from

which alone all powers emanate, may exercise [sovereignty] only by delega-
tion."[106] So Coleridge, in his effort to establish a direct link between the ideas of
philosophes such as Rousseau and the terror of the Robespierre-led Jacobins and
Napoleon, constructs a reading of the constitution in which phrases such as
"clear the way" perform a fair amount of work. Coleridge, following Burke, remains committed to the social and political efficacy of ideas, confident in their
ability to determine material conditions and not the other way around.

The displacement of reason by the understanding as the paramount political
faculty has ethical implications as well. Specifically, Rousseau's theory of pure
rationality, the idea that one can derive fundamental political principles from
the reason alone, seems to jeopardize the moral judgment. "Apply his principles
to any case, in which the sacred and inviolable Laws of Morality are immediately interested, all becomes just and pertinent."[107] This is so because each man
is compelled to act according to the dictates of his own conscience, which, as we
have seen, is no more than the "testifying state of the coincidence or discordance of the free will with the reason." Since neither free will nor reason is
susceptible of degree, the dictates of conscience are universally irreproachable.
Coleridge follows Kant in declaring the categorical imperative to be the "one
universal and sufficient principle and guide of morality." The justification of
this claim, Coleridge argues, is the fact that "the *object* of morality is not the
outward act, but the internal maxim of our actions." And, Coleridge concedes,
"so far it is infallible." Coleridge thus rejects consequentialist or utilitarian ethics in favor of a virtue ethics in which the inner "purity of our motives" is the
basis for all moral judgment. Laurence Lockridge, Coleridge's greatest ethical
critic, correctly situates this purity of motives—or, more broadly, the will—at
the center of Coleridge's thought. "Among the many foundational concepts in
Coleridge," Lockridge argues in his review of the *Opus Maximum*, "the most
fundamental is Will—the Absolute Will of God as the source of all that is, and
the finite personal Will of human beings, the source of our individuality and, if
conjoined with Reason, our goodness and wisdom."[108] The conjunction of the
finite personal will with the principles derived from reason results in "virtuous
habits," which, for Coleridge, are formed "by the very means by which knowledge is communicated."[109]

Coleridge devotes the majority of the first volume of *The Friend* to an attempt to "detail and ground the conditions under which the communication of
truth is commanded or forbidden to us as individuals."[110] The communication
of truth is, not surprisingly, commanded more frequently than forbidden, as the
conditions of communicating a "right though inadequate notion," or a "noble
lie," are few and rare. As he asserts in the essay titled "Virtue and Knowledge,"
"The essence of virtue consists in the principle" and "with clearer conceptions
in the understanding, the principle of action would become purer in the will."

Virtue and knowledge are so intimately linked that to take care of one is to en-
sure that the other will follow. There is a contradiction here, as Lockridge notes
in *Coleridge the Moralist*, between the "formalism" of an individual virtue ethics ("probable consequences and personal inclination are of little to no import
in determining what is right and wrong") and the prudential model of expediency Coleridge prescribes for the state: "In *The Friend*, he often seems to say that
the affairs of the state should proceed on the basis of prudence alone; the only
thing the state must consider is the outward act. This muddles, of course, his
position as a moral critic of social and political affairs. How can he continue to
denounce the expediency he seems in these instances to be recommending?"[111]
One resolution of the contradiction is to concede the incommensurability of
public and private morality. The "main office" of government is for Coleridge
the regulation of social organizations according to particular circumstances, a
responsibility that possibly demands no greater morality than that of its constituent members. "Public" morality, not far removed from the alleged interests
of the general will, may too easily slip into the "wretched parrotry" Coleridge
abhorred in the National Assembly.

To concede the incommensurability of public and private morality—or to
deny the existence of a public morality above and beyond a number of disparate
private moralities—does not, however, solve the problem of moral action in the
public sphere. Coleridge, as noted, admits the possibility that reason is capable of
formulating a principle of moral action, such as the categorical imperative. Yet, he
argues, it remains entirely incapable of deducing "the form and matter of a rightful Government, the main office of which is to regulate the outward actions of
particular bodies of men, according to their particular circumstances."[112] Rousseau, then, is mistaken in believing that reason, which Coleridge acknowledges
to be a sufficient guide in individual morality, is equally capable of determining
moral action in the public sphere. Coleridge tacitly invokes the traditional
morality-prudence distinction, arguing that the former is the domain of the
individual conscience (and therefore the reason) and the latter the domain of
public decision making (the understanding).[113] The two converge most conspicuously in the case of political obligation, in which the claims of the individual and those of the state must achieve some sort of rapprochement. As Morrow notes, obligation for Coleridge has a moral basis: it springs "from a sense of
duty which reflected an acknowledgment of the appropriateness of particular
arrangements."[114] In Coleridge's terms, "the whole duty of obedience to Governors is derived from, and dependent on" the *idea*, as opposed to the fact, of a
social contract. Again, "in my sense, the word Contract is merely synonimous
[*sic*] with the sense of duty acting in a specific direction, i.e. determining our
moral relations, as members of a body politic."[115]

That political obligation, described here and elsewhere as a "sense" or "feeling," should be derived from the "idea" of a contract may seem surprising; but Hume, for one, readily granted the ability of complex ideas (such as a social contract) to produce new impressions. For Coleridge, though, the word "contract" signifies merely this "sense of duty." There is an apparent tautology here, with the "whole Duty of Obedience to Governors" being derived from an idea of a contract, or "the sense of duty acting in a specific direction." Political obligation seems to be predicated on a particular form of political knowledge, namely, the idea of a contract. The "idea" of a contract and a "sense of duty" appear to arise contemporaneously. There is no impression from which we derive our idea of duty; rather, this "sense," or feeling, of duty simply is the "idea" we have of a contract. As we have seen, Coleridge rejects the entire notion that all our ideas are faint copies of our impressions, arguing instead that, as far as political knowledge is concerned, feelings, or impressions, and thoughts, or ideas, are not so easily distinguishable.

The political essays of *The Friend*, then, situate the understanding at the center of an epistemology appropriate to the application of the principles of political knowledge. It is only through the understanding that the theory of expediency, or prudential politics, may be said to operate. Coleridge's argument ultimately takes a middle ground on the status of the principle—that is, Coleridge is, as Lockridge puts it, "attracted to principles in principle," but is skeptical of thinkers, such as Rousseau (or even, one may say, people like Godwin and Thelwall), who rely exclusively on principles derived from pure reason—and grants priority to the idea. The principle, we have seen, merely actualizes the idea, and the idea itself "is living, productive, partaketh of infinity, and (as Bacon has sublimely observed) containeth an endless power of semination." By granting such a mysteriously generative power to the idea, as far removed from Hume's copies of impressions as possible, Coleridge makes room for a highly adaptable political system, one capable of applying principles to constantly changing circumstances.

The Symptom of Empiricism

It is precisely in light of this fact that we can begin to understand more fully Coleridge's rejection of Hume, with which I began and with which I shall conclude. Just as Coleridge had to repudiate Hartley in order to make room for the creative imagination, so does he have to reject Hume in order to make room for the endlessly disseminating idea. The status of the idea is strategically important in the formation of an epistemology that is to have political consequences. Because the structure of the mind is such that it demands a particular form of social organization, Coleridge is careful to delineate a mind that is capable of applying principles derived from pure reason and, at the same time, is not so utterly reliant on those principles as to impair its ability to react to changing circumstances. The Coleridgean idea, actualized by principles but not determined by them, is thus able to remain both living and autonomous. This autonomy is realized in the flexibility of the understanding, the faculty on which practical and political affairs must depend. The attitude that corresponds to the proper functioning of the understanding is one of cautious moderation, which, as I have noted, is the one Hume ultimately prescribes in the conduct of practical affairs. This, of course, would have resonated with the political attitudes Coleridge inherited from Burke.

Yet despite what Hume says at the end of his *Treatise*, Coleridge is unable to accept the political consequences of the theory of knowledge expounded in book 1, "Of the Understanding." Hume radicalized Locke's empiricism (thus making it ridiculous) and, in doing so, continued a tradition that was appropriate for a particular phase in English history insofar as it served the interests of "national pride." This phase, Coleridge suggests, is over. In his *Lectures on the History of Philosophy*, Coleridge refers to the beginning of Hume's essay on causality.[116] "Everywhere it is, you have no real truth but what is derived from your senses, it is in vain to talk of your ideas of reflection for what are they? They must have been originally in our senses or there is no ground for them."[117] This is a mostly fair assessment of Hume's position, though Hume readily admits the reality of ideas derived from "impressions of reflection."[118] What follows is of greater interest:

> So many circumstances combined together as to make it a kind of national pride in the first place, and secondly, the interest of almost each of the parties to cry [up] Mr. Locke. . . . I can therefore say this finally with regard to Locke, that it was at the beginning of a time when they felt one thing: that the great advantage was to convince mankind that the whole process of reacting upon their own thoughts or endeavoring to deduce any truth from them was mere presumption, and henceforward men were to be entirely under the guidance of their senses. This was most favourable to a country already busy with politics, busy with commerce, and [in] which yet there was a pride in nature [so] that a man would not like to remain ignorant of that which had been called the queen of sciences, which was supposed above all things to [elevate] the mind, which had produced a word which a man had overthrown, had . . . that of "philosopher." What a delight to find it all nonsense, that there was nothing but what a man in three hours might know as well as the Archbishop of Canterbury!
>
> This exactly suited the state of the nation, and I believe it was a symptom of that state of providential government of the world which observed the nearer union of the kingdoms of Europe to each other.[119]

Coleridge is especially prescient here, anticipating the symptomatic reading of the history of ideas that has come in and out of fashion since Marx. Coleridge sees the end of the seventeenth century, then, as the beginning of empiricism's dominance in British philosophy and attributes that success to two conditions: (1) the limited leisure time available to an incipient British middle-class in an increasingly commercial society and (2) a desire, the residue apparently of a theologically dominated superstructure, on behalf of that class to attain particular kinds of knowledge. Empiricism "exactly suited the state of the nation" because it required nothing other than the evidence of one's senses while granting that evidence the sort of solidity formerly granted to faith-based theological claims. It was a "symptom" of a state of European society in which a continentwide division of philosophical labor sponsored the growth of philosophies suited to the soil of individual nation-states, specifically empiricism in Britain, rationalism in France, and transcendentalism in Germany. Locke inaugurated the movement in England, and, Coleridge suggests, Hume carried it to its absurd and pernicious conclusion. Coleridge seems unsympathetic to the claim that Hume, in an important and direct sense, made German transcendentalism possible, focusing instead on his association with Locke and the overreliance on the senses.

Coleridge's reading of the history of philosophy is schematic, but it reveals his conception of how philosophies are "suited" to the needs of a nation, even if an explicitly causal relation is never established or specified. My repetition of Coleridge's "suited" here is deliberate, not least because it recalls the language used in his definition of the understanding in *The Friend*: the "faculty of suiting measures to circumstances." It also recalls his contention, cited above, that there is a correspondence between the structure of the mind and the structure of the social or political world: the mind is somehow structurally *suited* to the world (an idea that would find frequent expression in Wordsworth's poetry of "fitting and fitted"). The nature of this correspondence is perhaps necessarily vague, although I have attempted to sketch some of its outlines above. The correspondence, I have argued, hinges on the operation of the understanding, which is the only faculty capable of mediating between subject and object, the reason and the world of practical affairs. It is also the only faculty capable of resolving the theological doubts posed by Hume's skepticism, however mitigated it may finally be. These are the doubts with which we began: the precarious status of the idea of God in a system whereby all our ideas are derived from impressions, "which are correspondent to them, and which they exactly resemble." Hume and skeptics like him, Coleridge argues, take refuge in the claim that the "principle of Faith was utterly out of their scope."[120] This is not an option for Coleridge, and his response has at times been understood as an embrace of the certainty promised by the transcendental imagination. "The

Kantian/Coleridgean conception of the imagination," Craig argues, "is one which seeks—or, indeed, already assumes—the possibility of certainty."[121] It should be noted that Kant on the whole departs from the modern preoccupation, from Descartes to Hume, with certainty, restricting it to the "subjective validity of judgement" and that Coleridge tends to join him in this shift of emphasis. Insofar as it is possible for Coleridge, certainty does not apply to the kinds of knowledge he would refer to as "sacred truths."

In the face of Humean skepticism, Coleridge asks, in his lectures on the history of philosophy, "What shall we do?":

> It is most certain that the subjects most interesting to our best hopes, most entitled to our *Faith*, are not within the domains of faculties the stuff of which is given by the Senses—and if this be granted, how are we to distinguish dreams from sacred truths?—The mid way seems plain—. Congruity with Reason—that which the Understanding convinces itself to be above the Understanding, or beyond it—but not contradictory to it—Still it must be of universal validity—for instance, the Categorical Imperative of the Moral Law—not pretending to any nostrum, the Rule being this—We affirm that truths there are higher than those of the understanding deduced from experience of the senses; but that those who faithfully exert their Understanding without sophistication from passion & appetite will be the first to see and admit this—Hill above Hill—First surmount the first—& then/[122]

The halting, hesitant cadence of the passage—perhaps only partly explained by the transcription from Frere's shorthand—suggests an exhausted Coleridge, covering familiar, tiresome philosophic terrain so that the prospect of the next hill may become visible. It is as if only now, in 1818 and under financial duress, that Coleridge is able to overcome the charge laid against him by Carlyle: that instead of decidedly setting out, "he would accumulate formidable apparatus, logical swim-bladders, transcendental life-preservers and other precautionary and vehiculatory gear."[123] Here he has finally set out; but it is not with the dialectical zigzaggery of 1798, when Hazlitt anecdotally observed that "he continually crossed me on the way by shifting from one side of the footpath to the other."[124] Now, for Coleridge, "the mid way seems plain." The "mid way" is precisely that of the understanding, the faculty capable of recognizing what is above or beyond it, but not contradictory to it. The dispassionate exertion of the understanding is necessary in the acquisition of "sacred truths" above and beyond it.

These pedestrian metaphors appear to have led us from political to theological concerns, but Coleridge, in his philosophical lectures of 1818, broadens the centrality of the understanding from the kinds of political knowledge discussed above to sacred truths that are "most interesting to our best hopes." In short, Coleridge by 1818 had developed a conception of the understanding in which it is the central and dominant faculty of what one may call his political epistemology, with profound effects on his conception of the conditions of knowledge more generally. For the mind to know certain things—more precisely, for the mind to have an idea of any real importance, such as substance, God, property, obligation, contract, or the perfect state—it must rely on the essentially mediating capacity of the understanding. In this faculty, which is none other than the prudential faculty of "suiting measures to circumstances," the oppositional tensions that mark Coleridge's thought are suspended: subject and object, reason and imagination, principle and policy, individual and state. Coleridge's own self-representation as a transcendental thinker in the dialectical tradition is, in this view, subsumed into a larger picture of his thought attentive to the social consequences of epistemological assumptions. The critique of political reason represented in *The Friend* and other texts subsists in Coleridge's reading of the history of philosophy, in which human freedom is significantly circumscribed by the structure of the mind that conceives of it.

CHAPTER SIX

The State of Knowledge

Wordsworth's Political Prose

•

The state is not put together, but it lives; it is not a heap or a
machine; it is no mere extravagance when a poet talks of the
nation's soul.

                        —F. H. Bradley, Ethical Studies

Men at forty
Learn to close softly
The doors to rooms they will not be
Coming back to.

                        —Donald Justice, "Men at Forty"

Wordsworth wrote his greatest piece of political prose, *The Convention of Cintra*, in late 1808 and early 1809, when he was thirty-eight. The reviews of *Poems, in Two Volumes* (1807) were not good, and the increasingly withdrawn and irritable Wordsworth would not publish new poetry until 1814. His relationship with Coleridge continued to sour during this period, with the feelings of both hurt over *The White Doe of Rylstone* and the circumstances of its publication. Along with Mary Hutchinson and his sister Dorothy, he moved into the "uninhabitable" Allan Bank in 1808. The years between 1808 and 1814 were on the whole a dark period in Wordsworth's life, but from them came his most sweeping indictment of political power. *The Convention of Cintra* presents a more sophisticated defense of liberty than *A Letter to the Bishop of Llandaff* (1793) had fifteen years earlier, and it has none of the personal moral entanglements that mark the *Two Addresses to the Freeholders of Westmorland* (1818) ten years later. Wordsworth's de-radicalization had begun in 1797, but *Cintra* represents an effort to salvage and extend some of his first principles in politics. Wordsworth, that is, was still, in 1808–9, in the process of closing the doors on his radicalism. Like Coleridge's *The Friend*, written at approximately the same time, this statement of political principles is often lost in a narrative of apostasy that gravitates toward the extreme positions at both ends of their careers.

    This chapter places *The Convention of Cintra* in the context of Wordsworth's other political writings. It argues that the status of knowledge—who has it, what it consists of, and how it is gained—in each work is among the most important indicators of Wordsworth's developing ideological position. But, before we turn to his political prose, it is important to note the aesthetic orientation of Wordsworth's claims about knowledge, its effects, and its conditions, as this orientation would predicate some of his later political arguments. He had written on knowledge before *Cintra*, in the 1802 Preface to the *Lyrical Ballads*. There, as we shall see in the next chapter, it is repeatedly allied with pleasure; the force of both together constitutes a powerful check on what Wordsworth called, in the 1798 Advertisement, "our own pre-established codes of decision."[1] Knowledge that is accompanied by pleasure counteracts, throughout the Preface, an inferior knowledge that is bound to social opinion and taste. "[T]ruth which is its own testimony," the kind conveyed in the *Lyrical Ballads*, requires no social corroboration.[2]

There are other moments in the Preface, though, when Wordsworth discusses the operation of the mind without immediate reference to pleasure, or the pleasure that arises from tranquil recollection. The mind in these moments is significantly closer to a state of excitement or agitation. The object of his poetry, he says, is to make the incidents of common life interesting by tracing in them the laws "in which we associate ideas in a state of excitement."[3] The association of ideas, the philosophical issue on which our humanity seemed to stand or fall in the eighteenth century, is as important to his theory of poetry as it is to Coleridge's theory of the imagination. Wordsworth is animated on this point: "The subject is indeed important! For the human mind is capable of excitement without the application of gross and violent stimulants."[4] His insistence on the issue suggests a variety of causes. Wordsworth perceived, as Coleridge did, a threat to English culture in the degradation of public taste (he would lose almost all faith in public taste by the "Essay Supplementary to the Preface" of 1815)—hence the remark that the works of Shakespeare and Milton were being "driven into neglect by frantic novels, sickly and stupid German Tragedies, and deluges of idle and extravagant stories in verse."[5]

It is not, though, only for the sake of Shakespeare and Milton, or for English culture in general, that Wordsworth becomes so animated. The discriminating power of the mind is for him essential to ethical and political freedom. He would speak in *Cintra* of "the delicacy of moral honour" and "the apprehensiveness to a touch unkindly or irreverent" that characterizes a free people.[6] Aesthetic sensitivity is closely related to an awareness of encroachments on one's autonomy, whether in obvious forms like Napoleon's subjugation of the Iberian Peninsula or in subtler encroachments on one's intellectual autonomy (Wordsworth does not anticipate postmodern skepticism about the possibility of such autonomy). He detected, for example, threats to subjective freedom in the increasing "accumulation of men in cities," where the capacity for discernment is dulled through overstimulation. Wordsworth, then, claims in the Preface to discern a dangerous pattern whereby men are increasingly unable to discern patterns, making them more susceptible to becoming what Kant and others would call "commodities" in an industrial society.

The Preface argues for a different kind of agitation, one that arises from the most elemental of stimuli: ordinary language about ordinary objects and events. To this end, Wordsworth proposes a psychology and a poetics of flux: "our continued influxes of feeling are modified and directed by our thoughts, which are indeed the representatives of all our past feelings," and poetry is to "follow the fluxes and refluxes of the mind when agitated by the great and simple affections of our nature."[7] The primary meaning of "flux" is "flow" (the two share the Latin root *fluxus*), and these remarks on fluxes, influxes, and refluxes immediately follow the claim that good poetry is "the spontaneous overflow of powerful feelings." Godwin had used these terms in a central chapter of *Political Justice*, "Of Revolutions," in which he argued against the view that the progress of truth is not always progressive, "but subject, like other human things, to the vicissitudes of flux and reflux."[8] There is no doubt, Godwin writes, that "there is the appearance of flux and reflux in human affairs," but "the mass of truth seems too large a consideration, to be susceptible of these vicissitudes."[9] Wordsworth is less interested in the Preface with the irresistible "mass of truth" than he is in the workings of the mind, and he internalizes the fluctuation Godwin ascribes to the appearance of things, making it a real element of our mental life that poetry is obliged to follow. There are, then, two forms of agitation in the Preface: the agitation of the mind produced by the "great and simple affections of our nature" and that produced by "violent stimulants." The capacity to be agitated in the former sense is a mark of freedom. The kind of mental autonomy that Wordsworth presupposes in the Preface, as both the precondition and consequence of poetic pleasure, remains at the heart of his radical, and then his liberal, politics. In *Llandaff* and in *Cintra*, though, mental freedom is associated with "violent stimulants" of a different sort. In the *Two Addresses to the Freeholders of Westmorland*, the idea would be given up altogether.

Rational Resistance: *A Letter to the Bishop of Llandaff*

The full title of Wordsworth's first formal political statement, never published in his lifetime, is *A Letter to the Bishop of Llandaff on the Extraordinary Avowal of His Political Principles Contained in the Appendix to His Late Sermon by a Republican*. The bishop of Llandaff is Richard Watson, who in January 1793 published an unremarkable reactionary statement occasioned by the execution of Louis XVI. The statement may be regarded as "extraordinary" insofar as it came as a surprise to many who had known Watson's previous writings championing a variety of liberal causes. Wordsworth calls himself a "Republican" in the title, a term, as Owen and Smyser point out, that was anathematized on an almost daily basis in the English press of 1792–93.[10] The most noteworthy fact about the title, though, is its reference to "Political Principles." In calling Watson's composition, originally an appendix, an avowal of "Political Principles," Wordsworth situates the text in an eighteenth-century philosophical discourse that is not its most obvious home. There are principles, to be sure, in Watson's appendix—some of them sensible—but there is an equal amount of reflection, hope, hyperbole, conjecture, casuistry, and inherited rhetoric. "Before I take notice of what you appear to have laid down as principles," Wordsworth writes, "it may not be improper to advert to some incidental opinions found at the commencement of your political confession of faith."[11] This is to be contrasted with Wordsworth's more methodical approach ("I now proceed to principles . . ."). Wordsworth takes full advantage of the semantic development of "principle" discussed in an earlier chapter. His frequent reference to principle is consistent with the hyperrationalistic rhetorical stance that Wordsworth assumes throughout his *Letter.* The text's self-conscious rationalism has been pursued by James Chandler, who observes that Wordsworth's diction ("proofs" and "maxims," "causes" and "effects"), distinctions ("argument" as opposed to "assertion"), demands (for "sufficient reason"), and rhetoric (prolepsis, reductio ad absurdum, etc.) all reflect "an exemplary commitment to the procedures of enlightened inquiry." Wordsworth, though, is not merely displaying good Enlightenment manners here; his attitude toward knowledge informs the argument of the *Letter.* "The relation of free intellectual inquiry and social progress," Chandler observes, "lies at the ideological center of the *Letter to Llandaff.*"[12]

"Knowledge" figures prominently in the letter: in an assertion of one of his most fundamental political principles, in a justification of revolution, and then in a direct accusation of Watson. Wordsworth refers to the "unnatural" situation of the monarch, which requires more than human talent and virtue can provide and "at the same time precludes him from attaining even a moderate knowledge of common life and from feeling a particular share in the interests of mankind."[13] This is essentially the same point he would make about "Statesmen and Courtiers" fifteen years later in *The Convention of Cintra,* and it is a point Godwin stresses in book 5 of *Political Justice,* in his discussion of the "education of a prince." "Knowledge" in Wordsworth's political prose is almost always empirical knowledge of human nature and common life. Wordsworth goes on in the *Letter* to defend the excesses of the French Revolution, which at the time of composition was caught between the execution of Louis XVI and the dictatorship of the Committee of Public Safety, by attacking Watson's naive political hopes: "have you so little knowledge of the nature of man as to be ignorant, that a time of revolution is not the season of true Liberty."[14] This is the familiar claim of the revolutionary: in the extraordinary terms of the letter, "[p]olitical virtues are developed at the expence of moral ones."[15] Wordsworth, at the age of twenty-three, is cynical enough to realize the limits of moral virtues in political life, but not cynical enough to deny the existence of "political virtues" themselves.

Whereas the monarch's state of ignorance is, for Wordsworth, a necessary consequence of his unnatural position, popular ignorance is contingent on the direction, or misdirection, of opinion and inquiry. In the *Letter*, Wordsworth allies Watson with the "Infatuated moralist" Burke, who "by a refinement in cruelty superiour to that which in the East yokes the living to the dead" sought to persuade the people that they were "riveted to a constitution by the indissoluble compact of a dead parchment, and were bound to cherish a corse at the bosom, when reason might call aloud that it should be entombed"[16] (sentiments to be recanted in the 1850 *Prelude*: "Genius of Burke! forgive the pen seduced / By specious wonders" [7.512–13]). Watson commits a more grievous sin, "more criminal because more dangerous and insidious:"

> Attempting to lull the people of England into a belief that any enquiries directed towards the nature of liberty and equality can in no other way lead to their happiness than by convincing them that they have already arrived at perfection in the science of government, what is your object but to exclude them for ever from the most fruitful field of human knowledge? Besides, it is another cause to execrate this doctrine that the consequence of such fatal delusion would be that they must entirely draw off their attention not only from the government but from their governors; that the stream of public vigilance, far from chearing and enriching the prospect of society, would by its stagnation consign it to barrenness and by its putrefaction infect it with death. You have aimed an arrow at liberty and philosophy, the eyes of the human race.[17]

Wordsworth shares the Enlightenment faith in the possibility of a "science of government," a system of political rules and principles that may be derived through observation and logical inference. This particular field of inquiry— indeed the "most fruitful field of human knowledge"—is potentially open to the entire population and is here directly opposed by a cabal of unscrupulous interests. Wordsworth does not merely assert a kind of institutional or systemic opposition to the growth of this knowledge, but a conscious and deliberate effort to perpetuate popular ignorance. Public opinion that there is no more work to be done in the science of government—a prominent conclusion of Burke's *Reflections*, repudiated in Godwin's *Political Justice*—would result in the cessation of public vigilance, a critical attention not only to the form or structure of government but also to agents within it who may be held accountable.

The possibility of politics as a descriptive science underwrites the political principles articulated in the *Letter to the Bishop of Llandaff*, Wordsworth's own, abandoned attempt to contribute to the "science of government." The *Letter* contains a positive and a negative aspect: an argument for republicanism as the proper form of government and an argument against monarchy. There is not much original political philosophy in the *Letter*, as Wordsworth draws from Rousseau, Paine, and, behind them, seventeenth-century English republicans such as Milton, Harrington, and Sydney. The conclusion of the positive argument is that "a republic legitimately constructed contains less of an oppressive principle than any other form of government."[18] Wordsworth takes it as a "natural deduction" that whatever has a tendency to unite the interests of governors and the governed "must also in the same degree promote the general welfare." Since the size of nation-states prevents the creation of pure democracies, a system of universal representation is the best practicable alternative. Republicanism has the advantage of peace and stability, as laws would be the expression of the general will and "would be enacted only from an almost universal conviction of their utility." The negative arguments against monarchy rest mainly on its instability and the inequalities of wealth and power it necessarily creates.

While these may be familiar arguments, it is important to recognize the radicalism of the document: It calls for universal representation, universal suffrage, penal reform, annual parliaments, and the abolition of the nobility.[19] The distinctions enjoyed by the nobility are "absurd, impolitic, and immoral," and they have the effect of dishonoring labor: "the languid tedium of this noble repose must be dissipated."[20] The *Letter to the Bishop of Llandaff*, Alan Liu has argued, is "the single most violent work he ever attempted."[21] Just as *The Convention of Cintra*, as we shall now see, is at bottom a call for more war, the *Letter to the Bishop of Llandaff* justifies conflict on the grounds of revolutionary necessity. Political virtues are developed at the expense of moral ones; liberty and justice are purchased with violence.

The Limits of Experimental Philosophy: *The Convention of Cintra*

Fourteen years before composing *The Convention of Cintra* (1809), Wordsworth wrote to his Cambridge friend, William Mathews, who had recently visited the Iberian Peninsula. Wordsworth asks: "What rema[rks do] you make on the Portuguese? in what state is knowledge with them? and have the principles of free government any advocate there? or is Liberty a sound, of which they have never heard? Are they so debased by superstition as we are told, or are they improving in anything?"[22] Wordsworth would assume a more forgiving tone regarding Portuguese superstition in *Cintra*, but his interest in the "state of knowledge" with them, and with British statesmen, would remain undiminished. The state and status of knowledge are at the center of Wordsworth's political pamphlet. The immediacy with which Wordsworth inquires into the Portuguese state of knowledge, and the question's contiguity with a question about the "principles of free government," is telling. He premises the argument of *The Convention of Cintra* on an intimate connection between knowledge and liberty ("Wherever the heaving and effort of freedom was spread, [mental] purification must have followed it").[23] The pamphlet defines knowledge in such a way as to justify an aggressive, militaristic defense of freedom. Its argument is straightforward: in allowing the defeated French army to leave the Iberian Peninsula on favorable terms, the British generals who negotiated the treaty disgraced Great Britain and offended, in the vocabulary of the time, "the spirit of liberty." It is an extraordinary document, exhibiting a keen and undervalued political intellect, a prescient understanding of power relations in global politics, and remarkable rhetorical force. Critics have already noted the influence of Burke on Wordsworth's rhetoric in *Cintra*. Stephen Gill adds that "if Wordsworth has a model it is Milton rather than Burke, but again and again in images and manner of address the *Reflections* are evoked and *Cintra* is not damaged by the comparison."[24]

The stylistic indebtedness of *Cintra* to Burke and Milton raises the question of what kind of pamphlet it is, politically and ideologically. Gordon Kent Thomas, in the most extensive treatment of *Cintra* to date, situates the text in the tradition of English liberalism.[25] Thomas correctly dismisses charges that Wordsworth's doctrine of "National Happiness" in *Cintra* is an early manifestation of twentieth-century nationalism and rejects allegations that Wordsworth, in the words of one critic, "enunciated an anti-democratic doctrine of leadership which foreshadows the 'hero-worship' of Carlyle."[26] Wordsworth's doctrine of National Happiness, Thomas observes, should be understood in the context of his definition in *Cintra* of a nation as "nothing but aggregates of individuals." The charge of hero-worship is similarly difficult to maintain, as the tract argues for the necessity of challenging the authority of those who claim to speak on behalf of the people, and it belittles the souls and minds of men like Napoleon (". . . to what a narrow domain of knowledge the intellect of a Tyrant must be confined . . .").[27] *The Convention of Cintra* is often a robust statement of democratic principles: its repeated emphasis is the value of "a government which, being truly *from* the People, is faithfully *for* them."[28] Doctrinally, Wordsworth is considerably closer to Milton than he is to Burke. He commends the Spanish for respecting "established laws, forms, and practices," but, he argues, "when old and familiar means are not equal to the exigency, new ones must, without timidity, be resorted to."[29] Wordsworth praises the Spanish people, "whose failing of excess, if such there exist, is assuredly on the side of loyalty to their Sovereign, and predilection for all established institutions." *Cintra* ends, tellingly, with a passage from Milton's *History of Britain* (1670), criticizing "our ancestors" who were "valiant, indeed, and prosperous to win a field; but, to know the end and reason of winning, injudicious and unwise."[30]

The liberal, Kantian distinction between means and ends is, for Words-worth, one of the essential forms of political knowledge, and it recurs throughout the essay. All moral good, he says, "begins and ends in a reverence of right," including the right to be recognized as a "rational creature" with "feeling, will, and judgment."[31] Wordsworth also uses the means/end distinction to frame the broader significance of the conflict. Moving from the "contemplation of their errors in the estimate and application of means, to the contemplation of their heavier errors and worse blindness in regard to ends," he laments that "the British Generals acted as if they had no purpose but that the enemy should be removed from the country in which they were, upon *any* terms."[32] The stakes of the conflict, for Wordsworth, are much higher than "mere riddance" of the French. "We combated for victory in the empire of reason, for strong-holds in the imagination. Lisbon and Portugal, as city and soil, were chiefly prized by us as a *language*; but our Generals mistook the counters of the game for the stake played for." Winning the battle of "mere riddance" means little in the context of a broader spiritual and imaginative war, in which the conquest of cities signifies greater victories in an inexorable "march of Liberty."[33]

Wordsworth understands the treaty as part of a broader drama between liberty and oppression, one that revolves around the definition of knowledge: knowledge may be defined in the service of conflicting interests, and it is crucial for the interests of liberty that it be defined in sufficiently liberal terms. The communication of knowledge provides the justification for the tract: "For all knowledge of human nature leads ultimately to repose"—this would become part of the argument to book 4 of *The Excursion*—"and I shall write to little purpose if I do not assist some portion of my readers to form an estimate of the grounds of hope and fear in the present effort of liberty against oppression."[34] Wordsworth writes that this most sacred cause "calls aloud for the aid of the intellect, knowledge, and love."[35] He goes on: "It is not from any thought that I am communicating new information, that I have dwelt thus long upon this subject, but to recall to the reader his own knowledge, and to re-infuse into that knowledge a breath and life of appropriate feeling." Knowledge, then, is not dead matter, but organic and vital. The inspiring function of the inspired poet is here transferred to the political essayist, as Wordsworth hopes to breathe new life into a kind of unrealized knowledge. The conjunction of knowledge with the "breath and life of appropriate feeling" suggests an associated sensibility that, Wordsworth contends, is the precondition of any solution to the political crisis (what constitutes "appropriate" feeling is not discussed). The conjunction of knowledge and tranquillity, or repose, is repeated in a rejection of the claim that submission to Napoleon's authority would result in peace and happiness: "[P]eace and happiness can exist only by knowledge and virtue; slavery has no enduring connection with tranquillity or security."[36] Wordsworth again implies that knowledge, along with virtue, is the condition of both political security and individual tranquillity, a variation of the claim made in the 1802 Preface that pleasure, represented in his major poetry as a kind of tranquillity, is the condition of all knowledge.

Knowledge is at the center of Wordsworth's political argument in more concrete ways, as he contends that a lack of knowledge was the cause of this national disgrace and that its only solution consists in the establishment of a new form of political knowledge. Inquiring into the causes of the political problem, Wordsworth enumerates, "First; a want, in the minds of the members of government and public functionaries, of knowledge indispensable for this service; and, secondly, a want of power, in the same persons acting in their corporate capacities, to give effect to the knowledge which individually they possess."[37] He stops short of identifying knowledge with power, as he does in the eventually deleted passage on Bacon, but he does assert an intimate connection: power "gives effect" to knowledge. Godwinian optimism in inevitable progress based on human reason is discarded, as Wordsworth argues for the necessity of applying knowledge through political and social institutions, that is, recognized individuals acting in their "corporate capacities." Because the absence of the right kind of necessary knowledge and the power to apply that knowledge are the causes of the problem, the solution must be accordingly epistemic. Considering the possibility of British reparations to the Portuguese, Wordsworth returns to the basis of social freedom in individual and collective knowledge. "We may confidently affirm that nothing, but a knowledge of human nature directing the operations of our government, can give it a right to an intimate association with a cause which is that of human nature. I say, an intimate association founded on the right of thorough knowledge."[38] A science of human nature, and indeed the poetics of human nature that Wordsworth conceived throughout the first decade of the nineteenth century, has real political value.

The British government has a right to interfere in the Portuguese cause only if it proceeds from a thorough knowledge of human nature, which Wordsworth defines in opposition to other foundations of right. He proposes first "to contradistinguish this best mode of exertion from another which might find *its* right upon a vast and commanding military power put forth with manifestation of sincere intentions to benefit our allies." British interference is justified insofar as it proceeds from an understanding of human nature, but not if it proceeds on the basis of military might and noble intentions. He also distinguishes "this best mode of exertion" from a "conviction merely of policy that their liberty, independence, and honour, are our genuine gain." British association with the Portuguese cause, if it is to be founded on true knowledge, can-

not be self-serving, motivated by the assumption that a stable Iberian Peninsula is essential to British interests.

"Knowledge of human nature" is a broad category, though Wordsworth
enumerates many of its possible forms, many of them allied with sensibility: it
includes knowledge of "the instincts of natural and social man," "the deeper
emotions," "the simpler feelings," "the spacious range of the disinterested imagination," "the pride in country for country's sake, when to serve has not been a
formal profession," "the instantaneous accomplishment in which they start up
who, upon a searching call, stir for the land which they love," "the delicacy of
moral honour," "the apprehensiveness to a touch unkindly or irreverent," and
"the power of injustice and inordinate calamity" to bring out what is most noble
in people.[39] For Wordsworth, these are the indispensable forms of political
knowledge, noticeably absent in the British generals, Wellesley and Dalrymple,
who negotiated the treaty. "It is plain *à priori*," Wordsworth writes, "that the
minds of Statesmen and Courtiers are unfavorable to the growth of this knowledge." This is so because they "are in a situation exclusive and artificial," cut off
from the real world in an environment designed to increase their pride, and
because this knowledge is "founded not upon things but upon sensations;—
sensations which are general, and under general influences (and this it is which
makes them what they are, and gives them their importance);—not upon things
which may be *brought*; but upon sensations which must be *met*." Substantive political knowledge comes only from an active, empirical engagement with objective things—in the words of the Preface, the world of "real men," "real life," and
"real events"—and is denied to those whose intellects have been weakened by
inherited wealth, privilege, and the promise of advancement. "Hence, where
higher knowledge is a prime requisite, [practical statesmen] not only are unfur-
nished; but, being unconscious that they are so, they look down contemptuously
upon those who endeavor to supply (in some degree) their want."[40]

Wordsworth is, of course, speaking of himself here, but he is also speaking
of the poet more generally. As he says in the Preface, the poet has a "greater
knowledge of human nature, and a more comprehensive soul."[41] This "greater
knowledge of human nature" is precisely the kind of political knowledge
Wordsworth addresses in *The Convention of Cintra*: knowledge of the passions
of real men. One of his purposes here, he claims, is to guard against unreason-
able expectations of politicians: "That specific knowledge,—the paramount importance of which, in the present condition of Europe, I am insisting upon,—
they, who usually fill places of high trust in old governments, neither do—nor,
for the most part, can—possess: nor is it necessary, for the administration of
affairs in ordinary circumstances, that they should." These, though, are extraordinary circumstances, demanding "that specific knowledge" unfortunately
denied to those accustomed to power. "The fact is certain—that there is an

unconquerable tendency in all power, save that of knowledge acting by and through knowledge, to injure the mind of him who exercises that power."[42] Power corrupts, but not absolutely or necessarily. Power that begins in knowledge and that is exercised through knowledge need not be injurious to those who possess it.

So much for the powerful, but what of the conquered people of Spain and Portugal? Of all possible responses to French aggression, Spanish and Portuguese submission is for Wordsworth the least desirable. Justifications for submission based on the idea that they would benefit materially from French domination are particularly worrisome. Allowing, Wordsworth says, "that the mass of the Population would be placed in a condition outwardly more thriving— would be *better off* (as the phrase in conversation is); it is still true that—in the act and consciousness of submission to an imposed lord and master, to a will not growing out of themselves . . . there would be the loss of a sensation within for which nothing external . . . can make amends."[43] Marginal improvement in economic security is meager recompense for spiritual submission. That this is not abundantly clear to everyone suggests, for Wordsworth, the success of certain elements of eighteenth-century philosophy itself, namely, an uncritical faith in induction and the blind materialism he sees as its consequence. Just as the minds of men have been atrophied to a state of "almost savage torpor" by inferior cultural products, so have the minds of men, especially their imaginations, been atrophied by the narrow pursuits of the experimental philosophy:

> [I]n many parts of Europe (and especially in our own country), men have been pressing forward, for some time, in a path which has betrayed by its fruitfulness; furnishing them constant employment for picking up things about their feet, when thoughts were perishing in their minds. While Mechanic Arts, Manufactures, Agriculture, Commerce, and all those products of knowledge which are confined to gross—definite—and tangible objects, have, with the aid of the Experimental Philosophy, been every day putting on more brilliant colours; the splendour of the Imagination has been fading: Sensibility, which was formerly a generous nursling of rude Nature, has been chased from its ancient range in the wide dominion of patriotism and religion with the weapons of derision by a shadow calling itself Good Sense: calculations of presumptuous Expediency— groping its way among the partial and temporary consequences—have been substituted for the dictates of paramount and infallible Conscience, the supreme embracer of consequences: lifeless and circumspect Decencies have banished the graceful negligence and unsuspicious dignity of Virtue.[44]

Material progress has outpaced spiritual progress, with disastrous moral, political, and religious consequences.[45] To suggest that the benefits of French accommodation compensate for the absence of self-determination is to lose sight of the positive freedom that is afforded only by the unrestrained use of the creative imagination. The "calculations of presumptuous Expediency" can yield only "partial and temporary consequences." (The frequent reference to expediency and fixed principles in *Cintra* reflects perhaps the continued influence of Coleridge, who in the same year was writing on theories of expediency and the principles of political knowledge in *The Friend*.) Recall Wordsworth's professed aim in writing *The Convention of Cintra*, quoted above: "to re-infuse" into the reader's "knowledge a breath and life of appropriate feeling." Here, again, Wordsworth values animated thought. There are at least two kinds of knowledge, then, both with political relevance: indefinite, animated knowledge infused with feeling and definite, inanimate knowledge that is somehow less real, or less important. The failure to distinguish between the two has led to a misunderstanding of liberty, knowledge of which can be gained only in conjunction with the sensibility and the imagination, not through the "calculations of presumptuous expediency." In this respect, Wordsworth departs from Coleridge, exhibiting reservations about the political theory of expediency promoted in *The Friend*.

Wordsworth pursues the distinction between material and spiritual progress in a lengthy passage eventually deleted from the tract. In it, he goes to the origin of the English Enlightenment as part of a larger critique of its eighteenth-century manifestations:

> Lord Bacon two hundred years ago announced that knowledge was power and strenuously recommended the process of experiment and induction for the attainment of knowledge. But the mind of this philosopher was comprehensive and sublime and must have had intimate communion of the truth of which experimentalists who deem themselves his disciples are for the most part ignorant viz. that knowledge of facts conferring power over the combinations of things in the material world has no determinate connection with power over the faculties of the mind. Nay so far is such encrease from being a necessary result that it is scarcely possible to [? strengthen] and unite the two species of power in such a manner that the more noble shall not lag behind in proportion to the rapid and eager advancement of the less noble.[46]

Wordsworth suggests that the project of spiritual, or nonmaterial, enlightenment (what he would broadly define as poetry) cannot employ the same method as the "mechanical arts." Bacon's dictum that knowledge is power is true enough as long as it remains confined to the material world. The knowledge produced by the new science may grant us greater power over the physical world, but it does not guarantee the kind of imaginative power that, Wordsworth argues, is closely related to political affairs.[47] Wordsworth's qualified appropriation of Bacon's formulation is part of *Cintra's* immanent critique of the Enlightenment ("immanent" as opposed to, for example, Coleridge's transcendent and transcendental critiques of empiricism and materialism).

Adorno and Horkheimer would perform a similar maneuver at the beginning of their *Dialectic of Enlightenment* (1944), where the identification of knowledge and power is preserved but knowledge is understood primarily as power over the material world and other people. Technology, for Adorno and Horkheimer, is the essence of this knowledge. It refers not to concepts, but to method: the exploitation of others' work and capital. Wordsworth cannot be said to anticipate precisely this kind of critique of the Enlightenment, but he shares its method: a critique of the Enlightenment undertaken from within its ideological center (Bacon) and that proceeds dialectically outward (progress in technology, or the "mechanical arts," defined in opposition to nondomination or the positive freedom of the imaginative life). Bacon's identification, though, is predicated on a particular notion of causality: "Human knowledge and power come to the same thing, for ignorance of the cause puts the effect beyond reach. For nature is not conquered save by obeying it."[48] Knowledge of causal relationships, denied in Hume's skepticism, is thus the ground of action in the material world. Hume's claim that we cannot know with certainty the necessary connection between two events introduces certain ethical problems, at least when treated in isolation. This was immediately obvious to commonsense philosophers such as Beattie, who argued that the result of Hume's skepticism is "to disqualify man for action, and to render him useless and wretched."[49] Wordsworth's identification of knowledge with power is accepted not so that one may dominate nature, as Bacon suggests ("For Nature is not conquered save by obeying it"), but so that the individual consciousness may realize itself to be the free and unrestricted child of nature. This self-realization of consciousness involves the acquisition of, in the terms of *Cintra*, a "higher knowledge" that subsumes the knowledge provided by inductive reasoning. *The Convention of Cintra* presents an aggressively liberal understanding of this knowledge, grounded in the power to inflict material and symbolic punishment in defense of national liberty against imperial ambition.

Trying French Principles:
Two Addresses to the Freeholders of Westmorland

The *Two Addresses to the Freeholders of Westmorland* (1818) present a special challenge for the Wordsworth critic, at least insofar as he or she possesses even the slightest apologetic tendency. In the *Addresses* and the circumstances surrounding their publication, Wordsworth does more than renounce liberal or revolutionary principles. He acts on the basis of a single, questionable premise: the reelection of the Lowthers is an end justifying practically any means (in the words of the "Second Address," "they who *will* the end *will* the means").[50]

In his legally ambiguous support of the Lowthers, his strong-arming of local newspaper editors, his reporting of rumor and gossip, and in the consummation of his intellectual desertion of Godwin for Burke, he commits many of the same political sins for which he had attacked Bishop Watson in the *Letter to the Bishop of Llandaff*, most seriously the attempt to control public inquiry and vigilance. Wordsworth no doubt felt himself to be engaged in a matter of pure principle—"this attempt is no common affair of county Politics, but proceeds from dispositions and principles, which if not checked and discountenanced, would produce infinite mischief not to Westmoreland only, but to the whole kingdom"[51]—and he very likely was. But his principles here are so dramatically opposed to his earlier principles that one must turn to Wordsworth's long relationship with the House of Lowther to discover their roots and the reasons for their development.[52]

The death of Wordsworth's father, John Wordsworth, in 1783 revealed that he had spent substantial sums of his own money (Dorothy often places it around £4,700) in conducting the business of his employer, Sir James Lowther, for whom John had worked as a law-agent (a bailiff and recorder). Lowther, made Earl of Lonsdale in 1784, was the most powerful man in northwest England, inheriting a portion of his wealth from a family with coal and trading interests and acquiring the rest through marriage. A claim in behalf of the Wordsworths was submitted to Lonsdale in August 1786, which the Lord declined to acknowledge. This was the beginning of a protracted and unpleasant legal battle that was not settled until 1804, two years after the death of Sir James. Stephen Gill, who shows great sensitivity to the importance of the Lonsdale affair, remarks that "the rejection of their claim only intensified the bitterness of children feeling their isolation as orphans and dependants and in Wordsworth the bitterness was sustained in the years to come by a conviction that such tyranny was not an isolated case but a symptom of the essential relationship between governors and the governed in an unjust society." If the rejection of the claim produced in Wordsworth a profound hostility toward the nobility, the settlement of the claim in 1804 coincided with a more amiable attitude. Wordsworth became a close friend of the next Lord Lonsdale, to whom he would owe both his position as distributor of stamps and his Patterdale property (the distributorship legally barred Wordsworth from actively campaigning for the Lowthers). When an opportunity arose to serve the Lowther cause in the 1818 Westmorland elections, he devoted all his energy to it. "One can only speculate," writes Gill, "on how conscious Wordsworth was of satisfaction in reestablishing the place of the Wordsworth family in the affairs of the Lonsdales."[53] The entire Lonsdale affair is perhaps the most significant series of events in Wordsworth's life not mentioned, or even alluded to, in *The Prelude*.

The *Two Addresses to the Freeholders of Westmorland* were part of a broad effort by Wordsworth to get the two Tory sons of Lord Lonsdale, Lord Lowther and Colonel Henry Lowther, reelected to the House of Commons. The Lowthers were opposed by the reform-minded Henry Brougham, whom Wordsworth regarded as "the most prominent Demagogue in the Kingdom."[54] In addition to the *Two Addresses*, the effort included frequent anonymous articles and letters in the local press ("were it only to keep others out"),[55] a sustained and detailed correspondence with Lord Lonsdale on the election, an aborted attempt to have Lowther supporters purchase the *Kendal Chronicle*, and the establishment of the Tory *Westmorland Gazette* (for which Wordsworth appointed De Quincey as editor). Prior to considering a takeover of the *Kendal Chronicle*, Wordsworth visited the editor himself, persuading him to publish a particular account of the Lowthers' entry into Kendal in February and the mob-scene that surrounded it: "The account which you will see in the Kendal paper," Wordsworth writes to Lord Lonsdale, "was drawn up under Lord Lowther's directions, as being better than stating the facts in their naked deformity."[56]

In the *Addresses* themselves, Wordsworth passionately defends the landed interests, argues that democracy threatens social order, defends Britain's wars with France as both just and necessary, advocates emendation of the Poor Laws, and attacks Brougham's push for annual parliaments and universal suffrage. It is his more general statements, though, that reveal the problem at the center of Wordsworth's reevaluation of political principles—that is, their claim to immediate moral judgment and their demand to be tested according to knowledge derived from experience.

The threat of a British reiteration of the French Revolution presides, as it did in much counterrevolutionary rhetoric of the time, over Wordsworth's argument. "French principles," therefore, are on trial once again. It is worth noting here the ambiguity of "French principles," a phrase that refers to no single set of doctrine. The principles of the *philosophes* (themselves far from homogeneous) and the *monarchiens,* the Girondins and the *feuillants,* the sansculottes and the *jeunesse dorée*; the principles of the National and the Legislative Assemblies; the liberal bourgeois revolution of 1789 and the democratic revolution of 1792; the events of Thermidor and of Brumaire—all these signify divergent and even contradictory principles, hardly classifiable under any heading other than "revolutionary" in the broadest sense. This, though, is sufficient for the present purposes of Wordsworth, who contrasts political and aesthetic judgment in the following terms:

> In matters of taste, it is a process attended with little advantage, and often injurious, to compare one set of artists, or writers, with another. But, in estimating the merits of public men, especially of two parties acting in direct opposition, it

is not only expedient, but indispensible, that both should be kept constantly in sight. The truth or fallacy of French principles, and the tendency, good or bad, of the Revolution which sprang out of them; and the necessity, or non-necessity—the policy, or impolicy, of resisting by war the encroachments of republican and imperial France; these were the opposite grounds upon which each party staked their credit: here we behold them in full contrast with each other—To whom shall the crown be given? On whom has the light fallen? and who are covered by shade and thick darkness?[57]

Politicians and political parties can only be judged for Wordsworth in relation to each other. Here the relation is between the party of Fox and the party of Pitt, with the belief in the truth or fallacy of French principles, and their consequences, dividing them. Political judgment can only aspire to relative truth; it requires that two objects be placed before it, of which it then determines the value. Political judgment, moreover, must be founded on knowledge of human nature, which is to be acquired through an active empiricism, an engagement with "real men," or aesthetically, through poetry in its widest Romantic sense.

Wordsworth is thus able to say in the "Second Address" that the frankness with which he admitted the faults of the Revolution "entitles the writer to some regard, when, speaking from an intimate knowledge of the internal state of France at the time, he affirms, that the war against her, was, in a liberal interpretation of the words, *just and necessary*."[58] Here he follows the Spinozistic-Coleridgean line that, in his words, "government is essentially a matter of expediency" and adds to it Burke's faith in the wisdom of tradition and the special qualifications of large property-owners.[59] These, for Wordsworth, "are the general principles of reason which govern law, and justify practice in this weighty matter. The decision is not to take place upon imagination or conjecture."[60] Legislators are to be acquainted with these principles, but, more important, they should have "in the general disposition of the mind . . . a sedate yielding to the pressure of existing things; or carry the thoughts still higher, to religious trust in a superintending Providence, by whose permission laws are ordered and customs established, for other purposes than to be perpetually found fault with."[61] Behind Wordsworth's almost comic impatience with reform is the possibility of the supernatural origin of laws; the poet has come a long way from the rational resistance of the *Letter to the Bishop of Llandaff*.

The disparity between political and aesthetic judgment in the passage quoted above assumes a new shape toward the end of the "Second Address," where conceiving public policy begins to looks something very much like a series of imaginative decisions. In a remarkable political analogy, Wordsworth speaks not of rational resistance but of "rational liberty," which as a living thing ought to be cultivated and which has been impeded by precisely the kind of reform promoted in his earlier political writings:

> Government and civil Society, are things of infinite complexity, and rash Politicians are the worst enemies of mankind; because it is mainly through them that rational liberty has made so little progress in the world. You have heard of a Profession to which the luxury of modern times has given birth, that of Landscape-Gardeners, or Improvers of Pleasure-grounds. A competent practitioner in this elegant art, begins by considering every object, that he finds in the place where he is called to exercise his skill, as having a right to remain, till the contrary be proved. If it be a deformity he asks whether a slight alteration may not convert it into a beauty; and he destroys nothing till he has convinced himself by reflection that no alteration, no diminution or addition, can make it ornamental. Modern Reformers reverse this judicious maxim. If a thing is before them, so far from deeming that it has on that account a claim to continue and be deliberately dealt with, its existence with them is a sufficient warrant for its destruction.[62]

This is an aesthetic defense of conservatism, borrowing heavily from Burke. The state is no longer a body politic to be judged primarily in terms of health, but a natural environment to be judged in terms of beauty, an end to which health is a means and a necessary condition. Generally speaking, the less one interferes with the system, the better. The persistence of certain arrangements is understood as a form of "right," to be violated only when the value of a change has been proven. Proofs such as these are rare, even in the most ambitious systems of political knowledge. In the absence of such proofs, reformers merely have bad taste, or they seem motivated by a perversely nihilistic predisposition.

Wordsworth himself would become increasingly active in the modern art of "landscape-gardening," an interest that begins at least as early as 1803, when Sir George Beaumont gave him a piece of land at Applethwaite, under Skiddaw. Wordsworth accepted after some hesitation, asking simply to be considered "Steward of the land."[63] In light of the passage quoted above, his correspondence with Beaumont about landscape design is especially interesting. Wordsworth writes that one who sets out from Coleridge's recommendation— that "your House will belong to the Country and not the Country to be an appendage to your House"—cannot go wrong. "I see nothing interesting either to the imagination or the heart, and of course nothing which true taste can approve, in any interference with nature grounded upon any other principle." Nature retains its priority, and interference is justified only insofar as it reasserts this priority, the principle behind Wordsworth's landscape/state analogy. "Laying out the grounds, as it is called, may be considered as a liberal art, in some sort like Poetry or Painting," and as such its object is to "assist Nature in moving the affections." Wordsworth thus protests against the efforts of a local grounds-keeper to connect the estate of his employer with an adjacent one. This would be accomplished through a "manufactured Walk" that would cut through "the most beautiful specimen of forest pathway ever seen by human eyes," one that "winds on under the trees with the wantonness of a River or a living Creature."[64] The maligned "manufactured Walk," as it happens, would have connected parts of the Lowther and Brougham estates.

The contest between the Lowthers and Brougham in the 1818 Westmorland elections represented, for Wordsworth, a contest between two opposed sets of principles. He viewed the election, much as he did the Convention of Cintra, as a signifier in a broader struggle between opposing historical forces. It was "no common affair of county politics," but something that obsessed him, as the writing of *Cintra* had. Wordsworth's tendency in political matters is to allegorize events such that he is unable to think or write about much else, as his letters show. The ferocity with which he attacks political issues, and the passion with which he writes about them, is unusual even for the often inflated political rhetoric of the late eighteenth and early nineteenth centuries. His register is consistently high, in the case of *Cintra* across well over a hundred pages. What regularly emerges from his political writings is an insistence that problems of freedom are problems of knowledge, that the division between justice and injustice is as clear as the division between true and false: they are in fact the *same* division. "Power of mind is wanting," he writes in *Cintra*. What is needed is "intellectual courage," the epistemic virtue that allows other kinds of virtues to develop.

In the *Letter to the Bishop of Llandaff,* "Political virtues are developed at the expence of moral ones." *Cintra* is a more sober document, but it does not do away with revolutionary political virtues altogether. It does what his other major political writings do not: it distinguishes between the early and late (postregicide) principles of the French Revolution. "With great profit might the Chiefs of the Spanish Nation look back upon the earlier part of the French Revolution," Wordsworth writes as late as 1809. The *Two Addresses,* written in 1818, would refer dismissively only to "French principles" in general, a conflation that was perhaps necessary for the immediate goal of Lowther reelection. In willing the end, Wordsworth willed the means. The doors of Wordsworth's radicalism were closed not with principles—French or not—but with an act of the will in conjunction with a relentlessly allegorizing vision.

POETRY AND POETICS OF THE
EXCURSIVE AND UNBOUND MIND

CHAPTER SEVEN

The Dwellers of the Dwelling

Wordsworth and the Poetry of Recompense

•

The political liberty of the subject is a tranquillity of mind.
> —*Montesquieu,* De l'esprit des loix

But there is nothing sweeter than to dwell in towers that rise
On high, serene and fortified with teachings of the wise,
From which you may peer down upon the others as they stray
This way and that, seeking the path of life, losing their way;
> —*Lucretius,* De Rerum Natura

And it is this tiny, fragile, powerless, and transitory being, the
human being of whom we are to speak.
> —*Martin Heidegger,* The Essence of Human Freedom

In an 1822 letter to Walter Savage Landor, Wordsworth confesses his limited knowledge of Latin poetry but asserts nevertheless that his "acquaintance with Virgil, Horace, Lucretius, and Catullus is intimate."[1] The influences of Virgil and Horace on Wordsworth's poetry are readily apparent; the influence of Lucretius less so (I shall leave Wordsworth's schoolboy imitations of Catullus aside).[2] Paul Kelley has pursued the influence of, and borrowings from, Lucretius in the poetry of 1792–94—*Descriptive Sketches, Salisbury Plain,* and *An Evening Walk*—and later poems such as "To ——— upon the Birth of Her First-Born Child, March, 1833" and the 1838–39 revisions of *The Prelude*.[3] Martin Priestman remarks on how the recurrent image of Stonehenge in *Salisbury Plain* owes much to Lucretius's account of the sacrifice of Iphigenia (which Wordsworth regarded as "worth the whole of Goethe's long poem" on the same subject) and on Lucretian echoes in "Elegaic Stanzas, Suggested by a Picture of Peele Castle, in a Storm" (1807).[4] The purpose of this chapter is not to map Wordsworth's debt to the Epicurean Lucretius in greater detail but to use it as an initial, direct point of contact between Wordsworth's conception of pleasure and Hellenistic ideas of tranquillity, both Epicurean and Stoic. Through readings of the two major poems associated with—that is, at some point intended to form a part of—Wordsworth's *The Recluse,* namely, *Home at*

Grasmere (composed 1800–1806) and *The Excursion* (1814), I hope to demonstrate how Wordsworth's conception of pleasure is related to both his theory of knowledge and his political thought.

The argument of this chapter moves through four stages. First, I assess Wordsworth's most precise epistemological formulation as stated in the 1802 Preface to the *Lyrical Ballads*—pleasure is the condition of all knowledge—before discussing his frequent and varied uses of "pleasure" in the Preface. I then turn toward *Home at Grasmere*, a poem that represents the relationship between pleasure and tranquillity with greater force than perhaps any other poem by Wordsworth. In the third section, tranquillity reveals itself to be an essentially political concept for the poet, who associates it with a particular response to the French Revolution in books 3 and 4 of *The Excursion*, "Despondency" and "Despondency Corrected." Finally, I place Wordsworth's emphasis on the political value of tranquillity in the context of later accounts of the retreat to the "inner citadel of the spirit," by Arendt, Berlin, and Heidegger. Mental tranquillity, a kind of pleasure, is for Wordsworth both a cause and an effect of knowledge about human nature, social relations, and political arrangements.

Epistemic Hedonism: The 1802 Preface

The shadow of Lucretius, whose didactic poem was intended to persuade readers of the truth of atomism and materialism, hovers over Wordsworth's classic discussion of the Poet and the "Man of science" in the 1802 Preface. Lucretius is the paradigmatic convergence of the two types, surpassing predecessors such as Parmenides and Empedocles and successors such as Alexander Pope and Erasmus Darwin in writing scientific, or pseudoscientific, didactic verse. Lucretius succeeds because he is acutely aware of what makes poetry "the most philosophic of all writing" (a claim Wordsworth falsely attributes to Aristotle, who admits only that poetry is more philosophical than history): "its object is truth, not individual or local, but general and operative; not standing upon external testimony, but carried alive into the heart by passion."[5] Truth, though, is not poetry's only object, if "object" is understood to mean anything like "end" or "purpose." Pleasure, Wordsworth repeats throughout the Preface, is also the object of poetry: "The Poet writes under one restriction only, namely, the necessity of giving immediate pleasure to a human Being possessed of that information which may be expected from him, not as a lawyer, a physician, a mariner, an astronomer, or a natural philosopher, but as a Man." The poet, in the act of *poiesis*, is freer than other men: he operates under only one restriction, while most men under normal circumstances operate under many. The addition of other restrictions—political, material, moral, etc.—would obstruct the poet in his attempt to give pleasure. Pleasure in the Preface is indeed something "given," a gift from the relatively unrestricted individual to the many, and it is freely given, self-willed and without coercion. The tension here between the freedom and necessity of giving—the poet *must* freely give pleasure if he is to write poetry at all—runs throughout English Romanticism, informing its expressive critical orientation and, simultaneously, its professed aims of aesthetic education and moral legislation, what M. H. Abrams would call its "pragmatic" orientation. The transfer of pleasure discussed in the Preface is itself free and unobstructed: the poet gives "immediate" pleasure to others. It is not mediated by contemplation, reflection, memory, or institutions. It is mediated, or conditioned, only by the possession of a certain kind of "information."

What, then, is the information possessed by the poet? Wordsworth says it is not the information of the bourgeois professional (the "lawyer" or "physician") nor is it the information of the scientist (the "astronomer" or "natural philosopher"). Nor, interestingly, is it the information of the "mariner," whose appearance right after the Preface in the *Lyrical Ballads* represents a kind of knowledge most would rather not have at all. The poet is a man speaking to other men who possess the information that may be expected from them as men. Wordsworth defends the pleasure-producing task of poetry on the following grounds:

> Nor let this necessity of producing immediate pleasure be considered a degradation of the Poet's art. It is far otherwise. . . . We have no sympathy but what is propagated by pleasure: I would not be misunderstood; but wherever we sympathise with pain, it will be found that the sympathy is produced and carried on by subtle combinations with pleasure. We have no knowledge, that is, no general principles drawn from the contemplation of particular facts, but what has been built up by pleasure, and exists in us by pleasure alone. The Man of science, the Chemist and Mathematician, whatever difficulties and disgusts they may have had to struggle with, know and feel this. However painful may be the objects with which the Anatomist's knowledge is connected, he feels that his knowledge is pleasure; and where he has no pleasure he has no knowledge. What then does the Poet? He considers man and the objects that surround him as acting and re-acting upon each other, so as to produce an infinite complexity of pain and pleasure; he considers man in his own nature and in his ordinary life as contemplating this with a certain quantity of immediate knowledge, with certain convictions, intuitions, and deductions, which from habit acquire the quality of intuitions.[6]

Pleasure is the condition of all knowledge: where there is no pleasure, there is no knowledge. Poetry gives immediate pleasure, and this pleasure, in turn, is the condition of knowledge, defined here explicitly as the product of induction. Wordsworth thus grounds the art of poetry here on a kind of hedonistic epistemology. Note the social implications of the passage, as sympathy, along with knowledge, is the product of pleasure; the poet, moreover, considers the interaction between man and his environment and in doing so repeats the ordinary man's rudimentary contemplation of his situation, conducted with only "a certain quantity of immediate knowledge." This repetition, though, occurs on a higher level, as the poet, Wordsworth says, "has a greater knowledge of human nature, and a more comprehensive soul." The poet has the ability to see the hidden nature of things, including human nature and invisible social ties, though, as he makes clear elsewhere in the Preface, knowledge of social relations is precarious, susceptible of disappearing under the weight of historical and economic forces. In producing poetic pleasure, the poet reproduces the conditions of knowledge in his reader. There are, then, three cognitive moments in the Preface: the ordinary man's contemplation of his relationship to his surroundings, the poet's more advanced consideration of this relationship, and the reader's pleasurable apprehension of the poet's representation.

An important eighteenth-century precedent for Wordsworth's argument is the criticism of John Dennis, the English dramatist and critic satirized, often unfairly, by Addison, Pope, and others.[7] In *The Advancement and Reformation of Modern Poetry* (1701), Dennis defines "Poetical Enthusiasm" as a "Passion guided by Judgment, whose Cause is not comprehended by us." Enthusiasm, Dennis argues, "must proceed from the Thoughts, as the Passions of all rational creatures must certainly do." Moreover, "most of our Thoughts, are naturally attended with some sort, and some degree of Passion. And 'tis the Expression of this Passion, which gives us so much Pleasure, both in Conversation, and in Human Authors."[8] Wordsworth would have been familiar with the writings of Dennis through, at the very least, De Quincey, who mentions in an 1842 letter that he had "once collected his ridiculous pamphlets to oblige Wordsworth, who (together with S.T.C.) had an absurd 'craze' about him."[9] Wordsworth's craze for Dennis surely had to do with the critic's emphasis on "Passion" and, perhaps more important, with Dennis's conjunction of Passion with the stabilizing guidance of Judgment and Thought. Poetic enthusiasm can, for Dennis, lead to "violent Agitation" of the mind, but it is an exalted kind of agitation insofar as it proceeds from Thought and is guided by Judgment (Dennis, it should be noted, was also one of the first critics to introduce Alpine sublimity into a nascent aesthetic discourse in England). Judgment and Thought do not immediately come to mind when thinking of the manic John Dennis who has been handed down to us in a literary history shaped in large part by Addison and Pope; nor does De Quincey's use of "craze" to describe Wordsworth's fascination with him suggest a cool, disinterested reception. This is a pattern that begins, fittingly, with Lucretius, prone himself to bouts of madness and whose fervor in persuading the reader of the virtues of imperturbable calm led one French critic to speak of "the anti-Lucretius in Lucretius."[10] I shall return to this tension as it relates to Wordsworth later, but the point here is that Wordsworth appears indebted to Dennis and yet goes further than he does in his repeated conjunction of pleasure not merely with "Thought," but with sympathy, truth, and knowledge. This, though, still does not tell us what, exactly, Wordsworth means by "pleasure," much less how pleasure can "build up" knowledge.

"Pleasure" is among the most important terms in the Preface—second only to "language" as the most frequently used keyword in the text—and its varied uses reveal important aspects of pleasure in Wordsworth's poetry in general. Here Wordsworth claims that the poet may "rationally endeavor" to impart a certain kind of pleasure by fitting the real language of men to metrical arrangement; that the kind of pleasure with which he is concerned is "of high importance to our taste and moral feelings"; that there are different forms of pleasure, some more imaginative than others (thus his disparaging remarks about people "who talk of Poetry as a matter of amusement and idle pleasure; who will converse with us as gravely about a *taste* for Poetry, as they express it, as if it were a thing as indifferent as a taste for rope-dancing, or Frontiniac or Sherry"); that it is a "grand, elementary principle," by which man "knows, and feels, and lives, and moves"; that it is, as in the passage quoted above, the shared condition of knowledge and sympathy; and that the pleasure received from metrical language is "the pleasure which the mind derives from the perception of similitude in dissimilitude," and "from this principle the direction of the sexual appetite, and all the passions connected with it, take their origin" (whether this is meant to be in the service or to the detriment of meter is an open question).[11]

Still, though, Wordsworth knows that for some readers he will have failed to communicate or explain the specific kind of pleasure he wishes to cultivate. He ends the Preface by saying, "I know that nothing would have so effectually contributed to the further end which I have in view, as to have shown of what kind the pleasure is, and how that pleasure is produced, which is confessedly produced by metrical composition essentially different from that which I have here endeavored to recommend: for the Reader will say that he has been pleased by such composition; and what more can I do for him?"[12] A more complete representation of the pleasure Wordsworth has in mind would have to wait until the poetry of pleasure and compensation begun shortly after the first edition of the *Lyrical Ballads*. The post–*Lyrical Ballads* poetry would also, significantly, be a poetry of knowledge: "I have completed 1300 lines of a poem," Wordsworth announces of *The Recluse* as early as March 1798, "in which I contrive to convey most of the knowledge of which I am possessed."[13] The transmission of knowledge is, alongside the production of pleasure, an essential component of the poet's art. Instruction and delight are bound together at the core of Wordsworth's poetics, as articulated in the Preface to the *Lyrical Ballads*, and at the core of his poetry, especially the *Recluse* poetry.

Tranquil and Troubled Pleasure: *Home at Grasmere*

The concept of pleasure had undergone a number of substantial transformations by the time Wordsworth articulated his poetics and epistemology of pleasure. In Plato's *Philebus*, there are two kinds of pleasure: pure pleasures of the soul that accompany knowledge and, at times, perceptions (knowledge about the nature of justice is given as an example) and bodily pleasure. The good life consists primarily in the pure pleasures of the soul that accompany knowledge. The association between "true and pure pleasure" and knowledge borders, as it does in Wordsworth's Preface, on identification.[14] Aristotle defines pleasure in the *Nicomachean Ethics* as the unimpeded activity of our natural state.[15] Hellenistic philosophy, Stoic and Epicurean, allies pleasure with mental tranquillity (Greek, *ataraxia*). Augustine emphasized the role of the will in pleasure, an emphasis that continued in medieval Christian thought. Descartes regarded pleasure as thought; Spinoza as an effect of transition to a greater perfection. For Locke, pleasure is synonymous with delight derived from either sensation or reflection; its attachment to certain ideas assists, as it does in the Preface, in attaining knowledge of God.[16] After centuries of Christian debasement, pleasure acquired a new legitimacy in the eighteenth century, as writers like Bernard Mandeville, Joseph Butler, and Adam Smith argued for the social importance of pleasure. The new legitimacy of pleasure in the eighteenth century was rooted in a new rational hedonism, the belief that the pursuit of private pleasure would enhance the public good.[17] This rational hedonism marks the philosophical status of pleasure at the time Wordsworth began to write his greatest poetry: pleasure is finally embraced, but only insofar as it is bound to some moral, social, or economic good.

We are familiar with the pleasures (and, of course, the pains) of "Tintern Abbey," *The Prelude*, and shorter poems like "I Wandered Lonely as a Cloud." We are perhaps less familiar with the pleasures of Wordsworth's more austere poetry, what I am grouping together, according to convention, as the "*Recluse* poetry" of the 1790s and early 1800s. The compositional history of the unfinished *Recluse* is notoriously complex. In his plans for *The Recluse*, Wordsworth cobbles together bits and pieces of *The Ruined Cottage*, "The Old Cumberland Beggar," *Home at Grasmere*, *The Tuft of Primroses*, *The Excursion*, and various other fragments. As the most recent editors of *The Excursion* point out, during the early composition of *The Recluse*, "and possibly until quite late into the process, Wordsworth did not feel himself to be working on one poem entitled *Home at Grasmere*, another *The Tuft of Primroses*, and a third *The Excursion*."[18] Though incomplete, this is a cohesive group of poetry, intended to form a single whole, what Coleridge hoped would be "the first and finest philosophical poem" (one obvious contender for the title, *De Rerum Natura*, fails according to Coleridge because, as he says in a letter to Wordsworth, "whatever in Lucretius is poetry is not philosophical, whatever is philosophical is not poetry.")[19] *The Prelude*, long regarded as the central work of the Wordsworth canon, was intended to be only the "Anti-chapel [*sic*]" of this more immense Gothic cathedral.

In what remains the most thorough reading of *The Recluse* poems to date, Kenneth Johnston sees Coleridge's failure to provide Wordsworth with an adequate philosophy on which to base *The Recluse* as only one reason for its alleged failure (critics like Johnston and Jonathan Wordsworth have argued that *The Recluse* constitutes a significant aesthetic achievement, even in its incomplete form).[20] A more pressing issue, Johnston suggests, is "Wordsworth's own difficulty in accommodating his genius to the third of *The Recluse*'s announced themes, 'On Man, on Nature, and on Human Life'—that is, to society and history," which in turn results in an inability to resolve the tension between the poem's "subjective, artistic motivations and its objective, social intentions." It is for this reason that, as a self-consciously philosophical poem, *The Recluse* is "more moral than metaphysical, more psychological and political than ontological and epistemological."[21] It is true that Wordsworth's major challenge in composing *The Recluse* was how to make the leap from the world of the personal and the subjective (the world of *The Prelude* and *Home at Grasmere*) to the world of the social and the objective (the relatively de-centered world of *The Ruined Cottage* and *The Excursion*). This was a problem already addressed in book 10 of *The Prelude*. And it is a problem that, as Johnston suggests in his reading of *The Excursion*, is prominently thematized in *The Recluse* poetry itself.[22] Rather than being a renunciation of the epistemological in favor of the political, this group of poems, especially the movement from *Home at Grasmere* to *The Excursion* in the plan of *The Recluse*, is precisely about how to move from one category to the other, that is, about how the subjective conditions of freedom and knowledge find objective correlatives in social life, political institutions, and historical events.

Home at Grasmere, composed between 1800 and 1806 but not published until 1877, was conceived of as the introductory first book of *The Recluse* itself. William and Dorothy moved to Grasmere toward the end of 1799, and the poem is a meditation on the place. In typically Wordsworthian fashion, the poet's meditation on the valley becomes the occasion for more wide-ranging reflection and speculation. The blank-verse lyric, like much of Wordsworth's early poetry, has its roots in the tradition of eighteenth-century loco-descriptive, or descriptive-meditative, poetry. It transforms the mode in customarily Romantic ways: the intensity and duration of meditation, the range of speculation, the attitude of surmise and mode of interrogation, the priority given to the creative imagination, and the heightened drama of consciousness and subjectivity. The broad outline of the poem consists of a preamble, a series of alternating descriptions and meditations, and a final climax. In more local terms, its structure consists of a preamble on desire and possession (lines 1–98); a meditation on beauty, repose, and freedom (99–276); a description of the valley's birds (277–357); a meditation on peace and complacency (358–397); a description of the valley's human inhabitants (398–645); a meditation on the valley's abundance and the value of the feelings it produces (646–719); another description of animals (720–805); a meditation on solitude, society, and pleasure (806–958); and a concluding effusion on poetry (959–1049) that would eventually form the "Prospectus" to *The Recluse* and that was prominently prefaced to *The Excursion*.

It is the poem's sustained meditation on pleasure, though, that is most relevant here, as it provides perhaps the most illuminating representation of pleasure in Wordsworth's body of work: pleasure as a form of tranquillity, also called by Wordsworth in this poem "calmness," "stillness," "placidity," "peace," "quiescence," and other words in this family. Given our tendency to associate Wordsworthian pleasure with intense mental or sensual experience, physical and psychic movement, memory, revelation, revolution, and even sublime fear, the frequency with which he depicts pleasure as some form of tranquillity or stasis should give us pause. *Home at Grasmere* is above all about a search for, in the words of the poem, a "home within a home," both Dove Cottage within the Vale of Grasmere and, I suggest, the self-sufficient and protected mind within an often hostile material world. Home and mind, dwelling and thinking, become coextensive. The strength and self-sufficiency of the mind in the midst of variable external circumstances—sometimes pleasant, sometimes intensely painful—is the dominant theme of the poem and at the center of Wordsworth's conception of pleasure.

Near the beginning of the poem, the boy Wordsworth looks at the spot of his future home and pauses: "Long did I halt; I could have made it even / My business and my errand so to halt. / For rest of body 'twas a perfect place" (20–22).[23] The confident and respiratory caesura, the pause of a lifelong walker, near the middle of line 20 and the following enjambment affirm the self-willed character of this halting: the conscious and controlled movement of the lines proceeds according to the poet's own leisure and freedom. As it was for the

Stoics and Augustine, pleasure for Wordsworth is conjoined with the conscious will. Why "business" and "errand," though, to describe what is an evidently pleasurable experience? "Business" and "errand" suggest worldliness, a concern with the activities of "getting and spending" Wordsworth decries in "The World Is Too Much with Us" (1807). That he considers making this pleasure, or rest of body, his "business" is a mark of freedom from worldly affairs; that he considers making it his "errand" does much the same. "Errand," though, has religious and diplomatic senses, lost in modern usage, that elevate and confer nobility on this act of leisure. This pleasurable stasis—the pleasures of halting, of being at rest—recurs throughout the poem. Wordsworth remarks on two missing swans from Grasmere Lake, valued for "their still / And placid way of life," who, like himself and Dorothy ("Emma" in the poem) came to live in this "safe retreat" in "peace and solitude" (322–336). Peace, in fact, comes necessarily to the inhabitants of the valley: "For peace they have; it cannot but be theirs" (371). Wordsworth's apostrophe to the valley itself is framed in terms of "pleasing rest" and "full complacency":

> Hail to the visible Presence! Hail to thee,
> Delightful Valley, habitation fair!
> And to whatever else of outward form
> Can give us inward help, can purify
> And elevate and harmonize and soothe,
> And steal away and for a while deceive
> And lap in pleasing rest, and bear us on
> Without desire in full complacency,
> Contemplating perfection absolute
> And entertained as in a placid sleep.   (388–97)

The breathy caesura of the young walker noted in line 20 gives way over the course of the poem to this breathless polysyndeton. Wordsworth's compounded conjunctions express the restlessness he hopes the valley will remedy. Unable to do it by himself—and thus qualifying the Stoic self-sufficiency I will later associate with him—Wordsworth welcomes the "inward help" of the valley's "outward forms." The desired state is a state without desire or attachment, a *vita contemplativa* marked by placidity. "Pleasing rest," or "full complacency," is the first aspect of Wordsworthian tranquillity in the poem.

The second attribute of Wordsworthian tranquillity in *Home at Grasmere* is safety, already suggested by "lap" (to fold, clasp, embrace) in the above passage and the swans' "safe retreat" in the center of the lake, their "home within a home." Having survived his tumultuous youth (to which we shall return), he remarks, "But I am safe; yes, one at least is safe" (74). In an apostrophe that prefigures the one to the "Delightful Valley," he cries, "Embrace me, then, ye Hills, and close me in; / Now in the clear and open day I feel / Your guardianship; I take it to my heart" (129–31). Shortly afterward, he refers to

> Something that makes this individual Spot,
> This small abiding-place of many men,
> A termination and a last retreat,
> A Centre, come from wheresoe'er you will,
> A Whole without dependence or defect,
> Made for itself and happy in itself,
> Perfect Contentment, Unity entire.   (164–70)

The compression of these lines, achieved through an asyndeton in opposition to the compounded conjunctions of lines 388–97 noted above, follows from what Wordsworth values about this "small abiding-place": a bare minimum that does not need to be conjoined to any further end. It is its own end (a "termination" and "last retreat") that is a sort of felicitous *causa sui*, "Made for itself and happy in itself." The movement of abstraction is quick and direct: this "individual Spot" is at once a "Centre," a "Unity entire," and a "Whole without dependence." The land is a kind of independent substance, standing under the plants, animals, and people that are its attributes.[24] The independence and unity of the place give it the power to protect the exposed mind: "this deep vale as it doth in part / Conceal us from the storm—so here there is / A Power and a protection for the mind" (456–58). This protection from external threats is the second aspect of Wordsworthian tranquillity, a state of nondomination, noninterference, and negative liberty. This is pleasure as the absence of pain (Greek, *aponia*), a necessary condition of happiness (Greek, *eudaimonia*) for Epicurus.

The third aspect of tranquillity in *Home at Grasmere* is the ability of the protected mind to experience the pleasure of its own power. The poet is "exalted with the thought / Of my possessions, of my genuine wealth / Inward and outward" (89–91). He praises "Simplicity of purpose, love intense, / Ambition not aspiring to the prize / Of outward things, but for the prize within" (207–9), which is the condition for the "perpetual pleasure of the sense" (212). The language of wealth and prizes appears again later: "the silent mind / Has its own treasures" (643–44). The emphasis here should be on "silent," as only a silent mind can rejoice in its own strength. This seems to have been apparent even to advocates of the *vita activa* such as Aquinas, who recommends such a life because it exhausts and quiets the "interior passions" and prepares the mind for contemplation.[25] The treasures of the silent mind are a source of pleasure, both in themselves and as agents of transformation: the mind not as mirror but as lamp. "Such pleasure now is mine," Wordsworth writes, even if he is sometimes "forced to cast a painful look / Upon unwelcome things." "Not therefore is my mind / Depressed, nor do I fear what is to come; / But confident, enriched at every glance, / The more I see the more is my delight" (714–17). He goes on to speak of "this deep vale"

> By which and under which we are enclosed
> To breathe in peace; we shall moreover find
> (If sound, and what we ought to be ourselves,
> If rightly we observe and justly weigh)
> The Inmates not unworthy of their home,
> The Dwellers of the Dwelling.   (854–59)

The repetition in the remarkable final phrase borders on tautology—it is strange to imagine dwellers without a dwelling or a dwelling without dwellers—but it is a linguistic and conceptual tension to which Wordsworth was clearly drawn, appearing two years prior to the composition of *Home at Grasmere* in the "vagrant dwellers" of "Tintern Abbey" (1798).

The movement of empowerment, expressed above as Wordsworth recognizes himself and Dorothy to be worthy of their home, continues as the poem nears its climactic, Miltonic conclusion. *Home at Grasmere*, to be placed at the beginning of the epic *Recluse*, announces Wordsworth's high argument:

> Of truth, of grandeur, beauty, love, and hope—
> Hope for this earth and hope beyond the grave—
> Of virtue and of intellectual power,
> Of blessed consolations in distress,
> Of joy in widest commonalty spread,
> Of the individual mind that keeps its own
> Inviolate retirement, and consists
> With being limitless the one great Life—
> I sing; fit audience let me find though few!   (964–72)

The individual mind that keeps its own inviolate retirement is the tranquil mind, not far removed in these lines from virtue and knowledge, or "intellectual power." Intellectual power, and the pleasure that comes from the retired mind's experience of its own power, is the third, final aspect of tranquillity represented in *Home at Grasmere*.

At the middle of Wordsworth's meditation on the pleasures of home and tranquillity is the story of the Scholar. The poem, thematically and structurally, is built around a description of the inhabitants of the valley (lines 398–645). Wordsworth describes a shepherd, laborer, scholar, widower, and widow. The poet characteristically maintains a safe distance from the objects of his contemplation: he begins the story of the widow, "I feel—/ Though in the midst of sadness, as might seem—/ No sadness" (540–42). He spends the most amount of time, though, on the story of the Scholar, which is the story of a man who pursued the wrong type of pleasure. The Scholar, so-called by his neighbors because "he drew much delight from those few books that lay within his reach," was "the Master of a little plot of ground." He was a man of "mild deportment and discourse" (474), "of just and placid mind" (481), leading a family life "which men the wisest and most pure / Might look on with entire complacency" (485–86). And then comes the girl: "A blooming girl," a servant, who brings the Scholar great "distress of mind" (500). "Poor now in tranquil pleasure, he gave way / To thoughts of troubled pleasure" (504–5). This is the end of the Scholar. He becomes "stung by his inward thoughts" (an echo of Macbeth's cry, "O, full of scorpions is my mind," and an anticipation of the "Viper thoughts, that coil around my mind" in Coleridge's "Dejection" ode). Moreover, he loses the placidity of his former mind: "A rational and suffering Man, himself / Was his own world, without a resting-place. / Wretched at home, he had no peace abroad" (515–17). Insufficient virtue causes "tranquil pleasure" to give way to "troubled pleasure"; reason becomes a slave to the passions; the inner citadel of the spirit is forfeited; his home becomes wretched. The poem's anxieties about the Scholar (and scholarship) recur throughout Wordsworth's poetry: in the companion poems "Expostulation and Reply" and the "The Tables Turned" (where the knowledge of books is provisionally opposed to the knowledge of nature); in the early books of *The Prelude* ("Not that I slighted Books; that were to lack / All sense; but other passions had been mine" [3.371–72]); and in the later books of *The Prelude* in which the poet remarks on "how Books mislead us," "how they debase / The Many for the pleasure of those few" (2.207–10). In this poem about finding a "home within a home," the story of the Scholar is a cautionary tale about pursuing the wrong kind of pleasure, forfeiting the virtuous tranquillity promised by reason for the deceptive pleasures promised by the passions.

My language here is Stoic because I think that the Stoic—or, more broadly, the Hellenistic—conception of tranquillity is closely allied to Wordsworth's conception of pleasure. The Latin *tranquillitas* is Cicero's and Seneca's translation of Democritus's *euthymia* (cheerfulness), but it is closer in meaning to the Greek *ataraxia* (freedom from trouble or anxiety). Epicurus was the first philosopher to bring tranquillity into the framework of a *eudaimonist* philosophy of life, in which happiness, or well-being, is the highest good. He did so by arguing that tranquillity is a sort of pleasure. Tranquillity is the pleasant state of mind, corresponding to the state of *aponia*, the absence of pain, in the body.[26] Epicurus argues that happiness consists in both *aponia* and *ataraxia*, freedom from pain and anxiety. *Ataraxia* is similarly important for the Stoics, for whom the goal is a life in agreement with nature, that is, a life of virtue. Such a life, the Stoics contend, necessarily brings with it an inner state of tranquillity.

Seneca writes that serenity and tranquillity "are goods indeed, but consequences of the highest good, not constituents of it."[27] So the Epicureans (for whom the highest good was a life of pleasure) and the Stoics (for whom the highest good was a life of virtue) both agree that tranquillity is not the goal, but the state of mind of the satisfied or virtuous person. There are subtle differences, though, in their conceptions of what this state of mind is. Epicurean tranquillity is a state of contentment and inner calm that arises from the thought that one has or can easily get all that one needs. Stoic tranquillity is based on the knowledge that one already has the only real good (virtue) and on the absence of fear, connected with the thought that one's good cannot be lost. Epicurus holds that the happy person will be unperturbed; the Stoics make the more ambitious claim that the sage will be imperturbable, and this results in a wonderful sense of relief and freedom, a source of unending pleasure.

Pleasure, for Wordsworth, is related to both conceptions of tranquillity. The representations of pleasure I have pointed to in *Home at Grasmere*— variously figured as stasis, safety, peace, a retreat, complacency, inviolate retirement, inner wealth that cannot be taken away, or consciousness of the power of the mind itself—suggest that tranquillity is for Wordsworth a sort of pleasure (the "prize within" that will generate "perpetual pleasure of the sense") and that it is based on the inalienable possession of virtue (the Scholar, we recall, was of "*just* and placid mind" before his fall, which was a moral failure). The first claim is the doctrine of Epicurus, present to Wordsworth through the mediation of Lucretius; the second the doctrine of the Stoics, whose emphasis on virtue as a will in agreement with nature accords with Wordsworth's occasionally asocial ethics (one's relation to nature has ethical priority over one's relation to society).[28]

The poem's compulsion to repeat imagined moments of tranquillity and security—"But I am safe, yes, one at least is safe" (74), the desire for the valley's "guardianship" (131), for "peace and solitude" (327), a "safe retreat" (332), "pleasing rest" (394), "protection for the mind" (458), the "silent mind" (643), "sublime retirement" (723), "stillness" (801), and even for "forgetfulness" (386), the desire, we recall, of Byron's *Manfred*—raises an obvious, much discussed question: from what, or from whom, is the poet running? It requires no act of psychoanalytic acuity to see this as a central Wordsworthian motif, one the poet addresses himself as early as 1798: the boy in "Tintern Abbey" who is "more like a man / Flying from something that he dreads, than one / Who sought the thing he loved" (71–73). David Bromwich, Nicholas Roe, Kenneth Johnston, and others have ably pursued the question, and answers typically bring us back to France: both to Wordsworth's complex, changing attitudes to the Revolution and to his relationship with Annette Vallon; their illegitimate daughter, Caroline; and the Vallon family.[29] The complexity of Wordsworth's psychological state in the 1790s is indicated by his own inability to describe his feelings of political guilt in book 10 of *The Prelude,* one of the significant moments when the poet denies immediate, transparent access to his own mental states or the ability to make them linguistically intelligible (the Penrith Beacon episode in book 11 is another notable example): "Grief call it not, 'twas anything but that, / A conflict of sensations without name" (264–65). As these critics have shown, compelling biographical incidents underlie Wordsworth's preoccupation with peace and tranquillity.

Home at Grasmere, though, offers its own intimations regarding the sources of Wordsworth's interest in tranquillity, with finding a home, physically and mentally, that is impenetrable to change or history. The first is its reference to a youth marked by an inability to harness its own imaginative power. The "thoughtless youth" described in "Tintern Abbey" included "coarser pleasures" (74) and "glad animal movements" (75), but also included moments of sublime fear ("The sounding cataract / Haunted me like a passion" [77–78]). There are of course many such descriptions in Wordsworth's poetry, most famously, perhaps, the boat-stealing episode of *The Prelude.* Wordsworth's youth in *Home at Grasmere* is described in the same primitive terms of "Tintern Abbey:" "I breathed (for this I better recollect) / Among wild appetites and blind desires, / Motions of savage instinct, my delight / And exaltation" (912–15). Wordsworth presents his youthful, animalistic state as one of delight and exaltation, and we have no reason to doubt that this was in some sense true. There is pleasure in this kind of sublimity, what Mary Shelley would call "thrilling horror," but there is also always some degree of displeasure, as Kant argues in the third *Critique,* in experiences of the sublime.[30] More important in Wordsworth's case, these are pleasures that have been encountered once the youth has left his home. The sources of Wordsworth's restlessness—those inclinations or events that cause him from a young age to move more like a man flying from something he dreads than one seeking the thing he loves—are varied and difficult to know. A constitutional and voracious "hunger of the imagination that preys incessantly on life," to borrow Johnson's phrase, is one basic source.[31] The "conflict of sensations" produced by Wordsworth's political and romantic engagements in France explains in part his more mature itinerary.

The "wild appetites" and "blind desires" of his youth and the later desire for "pleasing rest," to use the terms of *Home at Grasmere,* are also related to the death of the poet's father in 1783 and to the entire Lonsdale affair that followed it, discussed in the previous chapter. The death of his father, Stephen Gill writes, "deprived [the Wordsworth children] of a home. From 1784 onwards Wordsworth had no base. . . . [T]he strength of his later reverence for the values of rootedness, continuity, and sustained love, all originate now."[32] And the protracted legal battle that followed did not help to create a sense of security.

The combined effects of the death of John Wordsworth, the consequent itiner-
ancy of the Wordsworth children, and the Lonsdale affair explain, perhaps
more than anything else, Wordsworth's intense preoccupation with finding a
home that promises tranquillity and, at the same time, his feeling that finding
such a home is in some way an act of justice, of fitting recompense.

Home at Grasmere offers another, more purely subjective explanation of
Wordsworth's preoccupation. Finding a home, the end of the poem suggests,
has provided pleasure and tranquillity, but it also demands that some action be
taken: "But 'tis not to enjoy, for this alone / That we exist; no, something must
be done. / I must not walk in unreproved delight . . ." (875–77). The poet feels
that he must give something. Wordsworth makes clear in the Preface, as we
have seen, what the poet may be expected to give: namely, "immediate pleasure." The gift of this pleasure is not, however, given painlessly.

> avow
> That Nature to this favourite Spot of ours
> Yields no exemption, but her awful rights,
> Enforces to the utmost and exacts
> Her tribute of inevitable pain,
> And that the sting is added, man himself
> For ever busy to afflict himself.   (837–43)

This is not the divine curse of Milton's Adam ("In the sweat of thy Face shalt
thou eat Bread") but Nature's demand that an "inevitable tribute of pain" be
exacted from the inhabitants of this spot. The character of this tribute is determined by what the poet already possesses: "Possessions have I, wholly, solely
mine, / Something within, which yet is shared by none" (897–98).

The presence of Milton is more forcefully felt a few lines later, as Wordsworth announces the themes of *The Recluse*, of which "I sing: fit audience let me
find though few" (972). The energy of the passage increases, as the poet appeals
directly to Milton's Urania, or, indeed, "a greater Muse" (975), whose guidance
he will need: "For I must tread on shadowy ground, must sink / Deep, and,
aloft ascending, breathe in worlds / To which the Heaven of heavens is but a
veil" (977–79). The poetry of the supernatural, though, does not really trouble
Wordsworth: "Jehovah, with his thunder, and the quire / Of shouting angels
and the empyreal throne—/ I pass them unalarmed" (982–84; Blake found
these lines blasphemous). This assertion of poetic authority and bravado is immediately followed by a description of what he finds truly terrifying:

> The darkest Pit
> Of the profoundest Hell, chaos, night,
> Nor aught of vacancy scooped out

By help of dreams can breed such fear and awe
As fall upon us often when we look
Into our minds, into the mind of Man,
My haunt and the main region of my song.   (984–990)

The entire passage echoes both Lucretius's description of Epicurus's mental journey (*De Rerum Natura*, 1.68–74) and Satan's flight through Chaos in *Paradise Lost* (2.920–1055). Wordsworth's statement here is remarkable: the darkest pit of Hell does not breed such fear and awe as the act of introspection. The poem's preoccupation with inner tranquillity takes on a new shape at the end of the poem, as preparatory self-examination for *The Recluse*, yielding both *The Prelude* and *Home at Grasmere*, appears to have revealed an intensely painful fact: a retreat to the inner citadel of the spirit—that "Possession I have wholly, solely mine, / Something within, which yet is shared by none"—may offer the pleasurable freedom of nonattachment or inalienable tranquillity ("Without desire in full complacency"), but it also presents the possibility of mental anguish, spiritual penury, or simply the "grief without a pang, void, dark and drear" Coleridge would describe two years later in the "Dejection" ode. Wordsworth's compulsion to find "a home within a home" is not merely a matter of justice, a way of imaginatively settling the Lonsdale claim, but of making the mind of man ("My haunt") a place in which one can live and breathe ("we are enclosed / To breathe in peace").

Home at Grasmere indicates the centrality of tranquillity in Wordsworth's poetic vision, but it only hints at how tranquillity, as a mode or condition of thinking, relates to his social and political vision. Political freedom is for Wordsworth related to the personal freedom that lies at the very root of the concept of tranquillity. As noted, "tranquillity" comes from the Latin *tranquillitas* and means, in its primary sense, "freedom from disturbance or agitation;" its Greek counterpart *ataraxia* means the same thing. Freedom lies at the very root of the concept. *The Prelude* develops the relationship between tranquillity and freedom in books 9 and 10. Book 9 speaks of the combined effects of youthful subservience to "God and Nature's single sovereignty" (tempered in 1850 to "presences of God's mysterious power / Made manifest in Nature's sovereignty"), early fellowship with books, and growing up in "mountain liberty": "It could not be / But that one tutor'd thus . . . should look with awe / Upon the faculties of man, receive / Gladly the highest promises, and hail / As best the government of equal rights / And individual worth" (9.238–49). Wordsworth's self-incurred tutelage to nature, that is, necessarily produced a set of republican beliefs that predisposed the poet to welcome the stirrings of revolution in France. These beliefs are called into question in book 10, when he declares that, after failing to find adequate justification for them, he "yielded up moral questions in despair." But before this, at the height of his infatuation with reason, Wordsworth expresses the potential pleasure of "shaking off / The accidents of nature, time, and place" in order to "Build social freedom on its only basis, / The freedom of the individual mind" (10.821–25). The freedom of the individual mind consists, *Home at Grasmere* suggests, above all in its capacity for tranquillity. How social freedom may be built upon it would become the motivating question behind Wordsworth's mature poetry.

Building Social Freedom: *The Excursion*

Home at Grasmere takes us as far in as any poem by Wordsworth, not only to an isolated physical home close to the place of the poet's birth, but also to a mental "home within a home" that both promises tranquillity and, at once, threatens us with a vision more terrifying than the "darkest pit of the profoundest Hell." *The Excursion*, following *Home at Grasmere* in the plan of the *Recluse*, takes us out, not merely on the one excursion that governs the entire poem but on a series of excursions within excursions. *The Excursion* mirrors and inverts the penetrating impulse of *Home at Grasmere*, taking us, through the Wanderer, out into widening, concentric social circles. *The Excursion* revolves around the story of the dejected, misanthropic Solitary, whom the other characters try to persuade to view the world differently.

Books 3 and 4 of the poem, "Despondency" and "Despondency Corrected," develop the story of the Solitary and will be the focus here. Book 3 contains both a meditation on the two Hellenistic schools we have been considering and a forceful representation of the Solitary's disappointment in the French Revolution. That the two subjects are closely allied in Wordsworth's mind is no coincidence and recalls Coleridge's initial request regarding the poem: "I wish you would write a poem, in blank verse, addressed to those, who, in consequence of the complete failure of the French Revolution, have thrown up all hopes of the amelioration of mankind, and are sinking into an almost epicurean selfishness."[33] As Wordsworth would address in the poem itself, the poetic representation of political disappointment presents particular challenges. To say that the French Revolution "failed" is to say more than that it frustrated one's desires for it, but that radicalism proved to be, in some sense, *false*: you thought you had knowledge of something, but it turns out you did not. The representation in verse of this particular kind of frustration is a prominent concern of book 3. The Solitary, who had seen his hopes for the French Revolution dashed, criticizes the "perpetual warbling" of poetry: the "tedious record" that tells us "night [is] hush'd as night, the day serene as day." Metaphor is merely tautology for the Solitary—he would have no truck with the "Dwellers of the Dwelling"

of *Home at Grasmere*—and poetry offers us no new knowledge. At this point
the Poet interjects:

> My thoughts, agreeing, Sir, with yours,
> Would push this censure farther;—for, if smiles
> Of scornful pity be the just reward
> Of Poesy, thus courteously employed
> In framing models to improve the scheme
> Of Man's existence, and recast the world,
> Why should not grave Philosophy be stiled,
> Herself, a Dreamer of a kindred stock,
> A Dreamer yet more spiritless and dull?   (3.338–46)[34]

The blank verse of *Home at Grasmere* is intensely lyrical and meditative, ema-
nating from a single voice. The form of *The Excursion* allows for greater tonal
shifts (though still not as great as some would like), enacting the kind of enlightened social sympathy it repeatedly imagines. Here, prompted by the Solitary's criticism of poetry, the Poet challenges what he sees as the Solitary's philosophic withdrawal. His thoughts "agree" with the Solitary's, and yet he pushes
his argument further: if philosophical poetry is an impossibility, then why not
reject the dream of philosophy itself? The Poet is especially interested in questioning the value of Epicurean and Stoic philosophy, wondering whether philosophy ought to be placed in "world-excluding groves." This exclusion, he says,
is the "brotherhood" of the "soft Epicureans" who were taught "to yield up their
souls / To a voluptuous unconcern, preferring / Tranquillity to all things" (3.355–59).
(There is a nice paradox in "voluptuous unconcern," and paradox is perhaps one
way of answering the Solitary's charge that poetry is mere tautology.) Is voluptuous indifference, then, the value of philosophy? Or, the Poet asks, is philosophy more exalted when, "for the sake of sterner quiet," it closed the "The Stoic's
heart against the vain approach / Of admiration, and all sense of joy?" (3.362–63).
The Poet's invocation of Hellenistic philosophy—Epicureanism a kind of opening up, Stoicism a kind of closing off, both a withdrawal from the tasks of
poetry and politics—is designed to draw the Solitary out, to unearth the assumptions on which his solitude is based.

The Solitary has little patience for these nice distinctions, and regards the
Epicurean and Stoic schools as two means to the same worthy end: "Security
from shock of accident, / Release from fear" that allows one to cherish "peaceful
days / For their own sakes, as mortal life's chief good, / And only reasonable
felicity" (3.370–73). In conjoining tranquillity and "reasonable felicity," Wordsworth evokes Hobbes, for whom felicity, or "continual prospering," and tranquillity stand at odds. "For there is no such thing," Hobbes writes, "as perpet-

uall Tranquillity of mind, while we live here; because Life it selfe is but Motion, and can never be without Desire, nor without Feare, no more than without Sense."[35] Hobbes's conception of felicity, excluding as it does the possibility of lasting tranquillity, justifies in part the absolute authority of the Sovereign. Wordsworth, in *The Excursion*, is largely sympathetic to the Solitary's project of becoming released from "fear" and, repeating the terms of book 10 of *The Prelude*, "accident," an enterprise joined to those of the Epicureans and the Stoics in "monastic brotherhood" and one that justifies the *rejection* of absolute authority. It is the realization of "the universal instinct of repose / The longing for confirmed tranquillity, / Inward and outward" (3.404–6). The link between inward and outward has not yet been made, though it will be attempted twice in the poem: first through the unsuccessful idealism of the Solitary and then through the active empiricism of the Wanderer.

The Solitary tells us that his turn inward was occasioned by the death of his wife, son, and daughter all within a short space of time: "Then my Soul / Turned inward,—to examine of what stuff / Time's fetters are composed" (3.704–6). The turn outward, he tells us, was occasioned by the French Revolution. "From that abstraction was I roused," says the Solitary, by the fall of the "dread Bastile" (3.715–18). The Solitary's vision is a political vision, in which "war shall cease" (3.732) and all nations shall "Be rich by mutual and reflected wealth" (3.741). "Thus," the Solitary says, was he "reconverted to the world," his "soul diffused" in "wide embrace / Of institutions, and the forms of things" (3.742–47). This reconversion to the world is, however, short-lived—unsurprisingly, given its intensity and what else we know of the Solitary. The Solitary eventually retires back into himself, and it requires the words of the Wanderer to give us a new, more comprehensive perspective, to bring us out fully into the world through a particular type of knowledge.

Book 4 of *The Excursion*, "Despondency Corrected," belongs to the Wanderer, who upbraids the Solitary and presents new grounds for hope. It is an essentially fatalistic response, rooted in the "everlasting purposes" of an infinitely benevolent and powerful God; this, at least, is how he understands his own poverty. His criticism of the Solitary is that the liberty of what he calls the "unimprisoned Mind" is a lower form of freedom, falling short of a more robust, positive conception of liberty:

> to relinquish all
> We have, or hope, of happiness and joy,—
> And stand in freedom loosened from this world;
> I deem not arduous:—but must needs confess
> That 'tis a thing impossible to frame

Conceptions equal to the Soul's desires;
And the most difficult of tasks to *keep*
Heights which the Soul is competent to gain.   (4.132–39)

Killing one's desires may be one way of preserving a certain kind of liberty, but true liberty, for the Wanderer, consists in a twofold act of the imagination and will: framing conceptions equal to the soul's desires and living in a way worthy of these desires.

When he turns his attention to the French Revolution, the Wanderer discerns a noble effort to shake off oppressive accidents of time and place, but little vision as to what a liberated people might do. He awaits a new breed of philosophers, a Christianized inversion of Nietzsche's philosophers of the future, who realize that "Spirit only can redeem Mankind" and that, even if this redemption should fail, "proper peace" may still be maintained:

Yet, should this confidence prove vain, the Wise
Have still the keeping of their proper peace;
Are guardians of their own tranquillity.
They act, or they recede, observe, and feel;
"Knowing"—(to adopt the energetic words
Which a time-hallowed Poet hath employed)
"Knowing the heart of Man is set to be
The centre of this World, about the which
Those revolutions of disturbances
Still roll; where all the aspects of misery
Predominate; whose strong effects are such
As he must bear, being powerless to redress;
And that unless above himself he can
Erect himself, how poor a thing is Man!   (4.321–34)

Knowledge, as the Argument to book 4 announces, is the only true source of tranquillity. The Stoic claimed that tranquillity is based on the knowledge that one already has the only real good, virtue, and the absence of fear, connected with the thought that one's good cannot be lost. The Wanderer adds to this the knowledge that the heart of man resides at the center of revolution (recall the sense of "revolution" as "circular movement").

This circular conception of social life is introduced only to be replaced by a vertical one, as the Wanderer explains how knowledge produces happiness, well-being, or blessedness: "Happy is He who lives to understand! / Not human Nature only, but explores / All Natures,—to the end that he may find / The law that governs each" (4.335–38). This is to be done through "all the mighty Commonwealth of things; / Up from the creeping plant to sovereign Man" (4.345–46). This knowledge, in turn, leads to love:

Such Converse, if directed by a meek,
Sincere, and humble Spirit, teaches love;
For knowledge is delight; and such delight
Breeds love; yet, suited as it rather is
To thought and to the climbing intellect
It teaches less to love, than to adore;
If that be not indeed the highest Love!   (4.347–53)

It is a pious sentiment, one of many that endeared *The Excursion* to the Victorians, but it is a piety born of the Enlightenment, with love bound to knowledge. The identification of knowledge and delight in this passage is not accidental or superfluous; it is a reaffirmation of one of Wordsworth's most fundamental poetic and epistemological principles. As stated in the 1802 Preface: "We have no knowledge, that is, no general principles drawn from the contemplation of particular facts, but what has been built up by pleasure, and exists in us by pleasure alone." This is Wordsworth's most precise epistemological formulation, and it informs his foundational critical principle: "The Poet writes under one restriction only, namely that of the necessity of giving immediate pleasure to a human Being." Pleasure, in turn, is not only the condition of knowledge, but also of sympathy: "We have no sympathy but what is propagated by pleasure."

The Excursion develops this triangulated set of relationships. There are, I have been suggesting, two relevant forms of knowledge in the poem: knowledge of the order of things (knowing, for instance, that political change revolves around the "heart of man") and the related knowledge of social relations, a delight that breeds "love" or, in the words of the Preface, "sympathy." These are precisely the forms of knowledge that Wordsworth accuses British statesmen of lacking in his political tract *The Convention of Cintra*. These lines, spoken by the Poet immediately following the Wanderer's above, might easily have been directed toward them:

The dignity of Life is not impaired
By aught that innocently satisfies
The humbler cravings of the heart; and He
Is a still happier Man, who, for those heights
Of speculation not unfit, descends;
And such benign affections cultivates
Among the inferior Kinds;   (4.355–61)

These passages from *The Excursion* illuminate a central aspect of Wordsworth's social and political poetry: an ideal of a hierarchical, or "organic," society, but one in which social bonds are strong and in which human suffering does not easily go unnoticed. Wordsworth's poetry performs an understanding of social relations from the bottom up and from the inside out. It is famously a poetry of marginal social figures: idiot boys, mad women, beggars, hermits, discharged soldiers, and, the greatest figure in this class, the Wanderer. The Wanderer, Wordsworth admits, is how he conceived of himself had he been placed in different circumstances, and the character represents in a way the truly free individual: not merely the unattached, tranquil self living in "inviolate retirement," but one who has wide exposure to the many aspects of social life. His knowledge is his pleasure, and his pleasure is his sympathy. Things are more difficult for Wordsworth, who, he realizes, finds himself in very different circumstances. For Wordsworth, if he is not to yield up moral questions in despair, there must always be an effort of the imagination and of the will in the movement from the inner citadel of the spirit out into the world. The possibility of building "social freedom on its only basis, / The freedom of the individual mind" exists not simply when the individual mind "shakes off" the accidents of time and place to exert power over itself (although this may be a kind of prerequisite), but when the individual freely exercises what at the end of book 4 Wordsworth calls "the mind's *excursive* power," literally the power of the mind to "run out" of itself, to make a journey from home in the coterminous acquisition of knowledge, pleasure, and sympathy.

The Inner Citadel of the Spirit

If Wordsworth's "pleasure," then, is akin to Hellenistic *ataraxia*, what does this mean for the epistemological claim made in the Preface and for the poet's broader critique of political reason? In asserting that pleasure is the condition of knowledge, Wordsworth proposes a kind of epistemological hedonism few would find politically palatable. Surely there must be ways of knowing the foundation of rights or the principles of justice that have little, if anything at all, to do with pleasure, however it may be conceived. To step back further, it is hard to see how Wordsworth's claim that we have no knowledge "but what has been built up by pleasure, and exists in us by pleasure alone" can be defended on almost any level. Knowing the truth of a mathematical proposition, for example, does not seem to depend on pleasure in any meaningful sense of the term. A feeling of pleasure may follow it, but the actual act of cognition appears to exist independently of pleasure. Wordsworth's epistemological claim becomes not only feasible but also politically relevant once pleasure is understood to mean something like tranquillity.

Epicureanism and Stoicism, in their shared emphasis on inner tranquillity, do not seem to be politically oriented philosophies (and criticisms of their supposed withdrawal from the social or political world closely mirror late-twentieth-century ideological critiques of Wordsworth's poetry). The freedom they purport to offer is, some have argued, not a politically legitimate concept of freedom, but a state of consciousness indifferent to circumstances, a sham model of individual liberty standing in the way of true progress. Stoicism, Isaiah Berlin writes, shares this putatively "positive" doctrine of freedom with Christianity: "The inner citadel of the spirit, according to Christian and Stoic thinkers, is the only true freedom, because it is incapable of invasion."[36] Berlin is unsympathetic to this concept of positive freedom, attracted as he is to models of self-creation and self-realization he associates with Romanticism (models he also views with intense suspicion). Berlin's Romanticism, though, is, as I have noted, essentially German Romanticism, with Fichte as its most representative figure. The Stoic retreat to the "inner citadel of the spirit" he describes more closely corresponds to the "inward turn" of English Romanticism. *Home at Grasmere*—a search, in this reading, for a mental "home within a home" that will guarantee safety, freedom, peace, pleasure, tranquillity, and happiness—represents one important moment in the history of this inward turn.

This still does not, however, redeem the turn from political irrelevance or worse. Berlin's criticism of this inward retreat would be repeated in more forceful terms six years after his Bryn Mawr lectures in Hannah Arendt's *The Human Condition* (1958):

> [T]he "natural" experience underlying the Stoic as well as the Epicurean independence of the world is not labor or slavery but pain. The happiness achieved in isolation from the world and enjoyed within the confines of one's own private existence can never be anything but the famous "absence of pain," a definition on which all variations of consistent sensualism must agree. Hedonism, the doctrine that only bodily sensations are real, is but the most radical form of a non-political, totally private way of life, the true fulfillment of Epicurus' *lathe biosas kai me politeuesthai* ("live in hiding and do not care about the world"). . . . The mental effort required by philosophies which for various reasons wish to "liberate" man from the world is always an act of imagination in which the mere absence of pain is experienced and actualized into a feeling of being released from it.[37]

Arendt's charge against the Epicurean and Stoic schools is that the "liberation" offered by them—the imaginative conversion of the absence of pain into a feeling of pleasure—is merely "world alienation." The charge is part of a larger project to challenge what she sees as the traditional superiority of the *vita contemplativa* to the *vita activa* in Western philosophy. The force of Berlin's and Arendt's critiques, formulated in roughly the same historical moment, is easily felt: withdrawal from the political world (which demands action) into the world of the self (which promises freedom) is a political act that bears some relation to acts of injustice and human cruelty.

The question, again, is not whether Wordsworth ever sought or celebrated such a complete withdrawal—he would remain politically active at least until the Westmorland elections of 1818—but whether the life of tranquillity celebrated in *Home at Grasmere* and then qualified in *The Excursion* has any political value. Wordsworth, I think, believed that it did, that the freedom offered by the contemplative life grounded in a particular place was not a sham freedom but a genuine liberty that was the condition for certain kinds of knowledge. Wordsworthian tranquillity, we have seen, is a consequence of finding a proper home, of making one's own mind a self-sufficient home and of being at home in the world. This is the theme and central preoccupation of *Home at Grasmere*, achieving its greatest linguistic compression in the phrase already noted: "The Dwellers of the Dwelling" (858).

Heidegger offers one way of thinking about the political significance of dwelling, its association with a certain kind of thought, in his lecture "Building, Dwelling, Thinking" (1951). In that lecture, he asks, "in what does the essence of dwelling consist?"

> Let us listen once more to what language says to us. The Old Saxon *wuon*, the Gothic *wunian*, like the old word *bauen,* mean to remain, to stay in a place. But the Gothic *wunian* says more distinctly how this remaining is experienced. *Wunian* means to be at peace, to be brought to peace, to remain in peace. The word for peace, *Friede*, means the free, das *Frye*; and *fry* means preserved from harm and danger, preserved *from* something, safeguarded. To free actually means to spare. The sparing itself consists not only in the fact that we do not harm the one we spare. Real sparing is something *positive* and takes place when we leave something beforehand in its own essence, when we return it specifically to its essential being, when we "free" it in the proper sense of the word into a preserve of peace. To dwell, to be set at peace, means to remain at peace within the free, the preserve, the free sphere that safeguards each thing in its essence. *The fundamental character of dwelling is this sparing.*[38]

One may object to Heidegger's essentialism here, but the comparative, at times imaginative, philology of the essay is worth noting. The original meaning of *bauen* (to build) is *wohnen* (to dwell), that is, to settle a piece of land, to build a home on it. Dwelling, according to Heidegger, is the end of all building: "Building is really dwelling."[39] *Wohnen* derives from the Gothic *wunian* (to remain in peace, to be free, to be spared); *Wohnen* is also related to *Wonne* (delight). Dwelling is *"the basic character* of Being."

As he says in the "Letter on Humanism" (1947), "The reference in *Being and Time* to 'being-in' as 'dwelling' is no etymological game"; dwelling is "the essence of 'being-in-the-world.'" Furthermore, building and thinking are "inescapable for dwelling," but they must "[listen] to each other" which can only happen "if they remain within their limits and realize that the one as much as the other comes from the workshop of long experience and incessant practice." Finally, again from the "Letter on Humanism": "Thinking builds upon the house of Being, the house in which the jointure of Being fatefully enjoins the essence of man to dwell in the truth of Being." Heidegger operates here on a characteristically high level of abstraction. There are, though, two points worth stressing in the context of *Home at Grasmere*: (1) attention to the essence of dwelling results in a kind of thinking that reveals important aspects of living in the world; and (2) there is no such thing as a *pure* inward turn. "Even when mortals turn 'inward,' taking stock of themselves, they do not leave behind their belonging" to what Heidegger calls the "fourfold" (a "*primal* oneness" consisting of earth and sky, divinities and mortals).[40] Wordsworth lingers on the term in "The Dwellers of the Dwelling," and the word carries with it some of the history Heidegger alerts us to (via the Old English *dwellan* and the Old High German *twellan*).[41]

In short, the epistemological hedonism asserted in the Preface—we have no knowledge "but what has been built up by pleasure, and exists in us by pleasure alone"—makes sense only if we associate "pleasure" with "tranquillity," a mental state it is perhaps easy to take for granted or simply dismiss when considering Wordsworth's poetry. A state of mental calm or stillness must precede, and accompany ("build up"), the act of knowing. The *Recluse* poetry, and especially *Home at Grasmere*, consistently represents pleasure as a kind of tranquillity, drawing on an Epicurean tradition that was intimately present to Wordsworth through the poetry of Lucretius. These poems, furthermore, represent tranquillity (*ataraxia*) as a genuine source of positive liberty, a condition in which the self has the freedom to know virtue, as the Stoics did, as a will in agreement with nature.

The search for a "home within a home" in *Home at Grasmere* is the search for both Dove Cottage within the Vale of Grasmere and, at the same time, a self-sufficient and protected mind within an often hostile material world. Wordsworth's preoccupation with tranquillity has circumstantial determining factors, such as the Lonsdale claim, and, as suggested by the Miltonic end of *Home at Grasmere*, determining factors related to the displeasure of the sublime experience of self-consciousness. The inward turn depicted in *Home at Grasmere*, in conjunction with the pleasure-based epistemology of the Preface, does not necessarily pose a threat to the liberal and participatory democracies championed by Berlin and Arendt, respectively; nor does it pose a threat to value-pluralism (Berlin) or plurality (Arendt). As Heidegger suggests, there is no such thing as a *pure* inward turn, as the essence of dwelling is "being-in-the-world." Dwelling, and the kind of meditation on dwelling we see in *Home at Grasmere* and *The Excursion*, derives from freedom and is itself productive of a particular kind of thinking, what I have been placing under the heading "political knowledge." Tranquillity, as it is represented in Wordsworth's poetry, is the condition of sympathy and of knowing the complex network of connections and associations in a given society. For Wordsworth, the task of the statesman is to know these connections more fully; the task of the poet is to re-create them. Far from a withdrawal, the inward turn of Wordsworth's poetry is an attempt to reimagine the shared conditions of objective and subjective freedom. The dream of building social freedom on the freedom of the individual mind recollected in *The Prelude* demanded the kind of meditation conducted in the *Recluse* poetry, in which the tranquillity of the subject is a condition of knowledge and a model of freedom.

CHAPTER EIGHT

P. B. Shelley and the Forms of Thought

•

His mind has no atmosphere, no changes of season and
temperature.
                        —*Michael Oakeshott on "The Rationalist,"*
                        Rationalism in Politics

In the history of every people, there are moments in which,
uncertain of the side they shall choose, and balanced between
political good and evil, they feel a desire to be instructed; in
which the soil, so to express myself, is in some manner prepared,
and may easily be penetrated by the dew of truth.
                        —*Helvétius,* De l'homme

His teeth they chatter, chatter still.
                        —*Wordsworth, "Goody Blake and Harry Gill"*

Nowhere is the Romantic alliance of politics and epistemology more ambitious
than in the poetry and prose of P. B. Shelley. One way to describe Shelley's
accomplishment in verse is to say that he developed a poetry that demands to
be read simultaneously as an allegory of both mind and body politic, an exploration of the structure of human thought that is at the same time an examination of political structures and social institutions. *Prometheus Unbound* (1820)
is perhaps the greatest poem in this mode, though the alliance is present in
shorter lyrics such as "Mont Blanc" (1817) and popular, political poems such as
The Mask of Anarchy (composed 1819). Prose works like *A Philosophical View of
Reform* (composed 1819–20) and *A Defence of Poetry* (composed 1821) similarly
combine intellectual and political history with an astonishing breadth of vision.
In order to account for the centrality of both politics and philosophy (epistemology and metaphysics) in his thought, criticism of Shelley has largely suf-
ficed with a twin set of assumptions: politically, he was an egalitarian reformist
in the tradition of Godwin and, philosophically, he was something called a
"skeptical idealist." Moreover, insofar as we accept some basic notion of the unity
of consciousness, we have also come to accept that these two strains of Shelley's
thought bear some noncontradictory or complementary relation to each other:
skeptical idealism is, in some way, the "appropriate" philosophical attitude for

the project of egalitarian reform. Egalitarianism—the doctrine that all human beings are born equal and that equality ought to be the aim of all social organization—seems to depend, for some critics, on skeptical idealism—a more ambiguous doctrine suggesting both a mind-dependent reality and a mind significantly constrained in its ability to know that reality. There are advantages to such a reading of Shelley, a poet whose passion for formal and political innovation—bordering on pathology, for some—calls for the grounding in intellectual tradition provided by criticism. In stationing him in these specific terms, though, we may have obscured the particularity of his achievement, which substantially transforms the doctrinal materials with which it works.

It is worth recalling briefly how we have arrived at the skeptical-idealist reading. For much of the twentieth century, philosophical critics of Shelley fell into two camps: those who conceived of him as a Platonist and those who conceived of him as a skeptic. The Platonic school, culminating in James A. Notopoulos's *The Platonism of Shelley* (1949), sought to redeem the poet from New Critical and New Humanist debasement by asserting his legitimacy as a poet-philosopher. The skeptical school, as developed in seminal works such as C. E. Pulos's *The Deep Truth: A Study of Shelley's Skepticism* (1954) and Earl Wasserman's *Shelley: A Critical Reading* (1971), emphasized the skeptical solution to doubt as the exegetical key to Shelley. By the end of the twentieth century, a consensus and a compromise seem to have been reached: Shelley is a *skeptical idealist*, that is, one who believes that knowledge of reality does not derive from experience nor is it possible a priori, but is gained through "intuition" loosely defined (or "faith"). Skepticism does what Shelley defined in "On Life" (composed 1819) as the task of philosophy in general: "It leaves, what is too often the duty of the reformer in political and ethical questions to leave, a vacancy. It reduces the mind to that freedom in which it would have acted, but for the misuse of words and signs, the instruments of its own creation."[1] Idealism, or at least some form of moral or aesthetic intuition, fills the vacancy. Knowledge of the objective world, essential to any truly philosophical view of reform, is maintained, often by way of a loose or weak version of idealism. Wasserman's thesis in *Shelley* is representative of the skeptical-idealist compromise: "At the center of the mind in Shelley's collective works are a denial of any self-evident truths that may serve as constructive first principles and a consequent indecision between contradictory desires for worldly perfection and an ideal postmortal eternity."[2] The Shelley of skeptical idealism is able to inhabit two worlds by never fully committing himself to either one.

Subsequent Anglo-American criticism of Shelley has remained more or less committed to this view.[3] It has provided the critic with a flexible way of understanding the poet's divergent commitments: to biblical prophecy and Enlightenment epistemology, to religious doubt and aesthetic necessity, to the public and private selves, and so forth.[4] Indeed, the conjunction of skepticism and idealism in Shelley has been regarded as an essential component of Romantic discourse itself.[5] It is true that critics have long recognized the influence of other philosophical traditions—materialism, dualism, even pragmatism—in Shelley's thought, but it is the doctrine of skeptical idealism to which so many studies of the poet seem wedded.[6] Surveying recent Shelley criticism, Uttara Natarajan is thus able to say in 2007: "Allied to the view of a sceptical idealism, Shelley's political utopianism has been shown to be qualified by his practical engagement in reform."[7] Skeptical idealism has been the means by which critics have reconciled the material and immaterial tendencies in Shelley.

The purpose of this chapter is twofold: to demonstrate why a reexamination of skeptical idealism as Shelley's "default" philosophy is necessary and to suggest other ways of understanding his representations of truth, knowledge, and power, concepts at the core of some of his most ambitious works. I argue first that there are problems with the skeptical-idealist compromise. I do not claim to be exempt from the synthetic impulse it exhibits, but I do wish to suggest that it does not account for the full range of Shelley's thought and that, as a doctrine, skeptical idealism suffers from a degree of incoherence. *A Philosophical View of Reform*—a posthumously published text that is less dogmatic than some of Shelley's other philosophical works, opting instead for a historical understanding of knowledge and its conditions—indicates some of the limits of skeptical idealism as the appropriate attitude for reform. *Prometheus Unbound*, the composition of which overlapped with that of *A Philosophical View of Reform*, deals with many of the same issues. Knowledge, particularly the knowledge of historical necessity, is at the center of *Prometheus Unbound*, which presents the problem of freedom in the context of a constantly changing "atmosphere of human thought" from which the major images of the poem emanate. That Shelley chose to draw the imagery of this political poem from the operations of the human mind, as he claims to do in its preface, is no mistake. Political freedom was for Shelley, as we have seen it was for Wordsworth, inextricably bound to intellectual freedom.

The Case for Skeptical Idealism

The case for skeptical idealism has its merits. The essential principles of Shelley's philosophy are contained in two works: in the first fragment of "Speculations on Metaphysics" and in the fragmentary essay "On Life." The latter grew directly from an early passage in *A Philosophical View of Reform*, and should be read in conjunction with it. Shelley's most definitive philosophical pronouncement, from "On Life," supports the skeptical-idealist view: "I confess that I am one of those who am unable to refuse my assent to the conclusions of those philosophers, who assert that nothing exists but as it is perceived."[8] The strained syntax of the sentence, especially the awkward double negative of "unable to refuse my assent," suggests assent in spite of virtuous inclination. Such resistance to idealism is counterintuitive among philosophers of a certain stripe: Bertrand Russell, for instance, would say only half in jest that every reader knows that idealists are virtuous and materialists are wicked. Shelley's idealism, though, is not a pious Christian idealism, but a negation of the materialism that had tempted him in his youth. "This materialism is a seducing system to young and superficial minds. It allows its disciples to talk, and dispenses them from thinking."[9] The materialism to which the young Shelley was especially attracted was that of Holbach, whose *Système de la nature* (1770) denied the existence of God and argued that the universe is nothing other than matter in motion, governed by inexorable natural laws. Shelley would have been attracted to Holbach's virulent anticlericalism and thoroughgoing materialism. He would also have been attracted to what these views entail: in Holbach's terms, "the moral man is nothing more than this physical being considered under a certain point of view."[10] Human injustice and misery are, for Holbach, the products of ignorance and fear; justice and happiness are gained only by the dissemination of knowledge. Holbach was a major player in the eighteenth-century project of reducing politics to a descriptive science, and his early influence on Shelley should be kept in mind. Holbach was to Shelley what Hartley was to Coleridge: the influence of their materialisms would inflect the poets' later turns to various forms of idealism.

Shelley's circumlocution in the statement from "On Life" aside, the belief that "nothing exists but as it is perceived" is clearly idealist. It is a direct importation of Berkeley's doctrine of *esse est percipi* ("to be is to be perceived"), developed in *A Treatise concerning the Principles of Human Knowledge* (1710) and *Three Dialogues between Hylas and Philonous* (1713). Berkeley's position itself draws from the foundational text of Western epistemology, Plato's *Theaetetus*, which ultimately defines knowledge as "justified, true belief" (a definition that would remain remarkably intact in analytic philosophy until Edmund Gettier's classic 1963 essay, "Is Justified True Belief Knowledge?"). Before this definition of knowledge is reached, however, Socrates elicits from Theaetetus a definition of knowledge as "nothing else than perception," a position Socrates associates with Protagoras's assertion that "man is the measure of all things, of the existence of the things that are and the non-existence of the things that are not."[11] It is important to remember that this is not the position of Platonic idealism as such, but an initial stage in the definition of knowledge, the first birth pang under Socrates's midwifery. In short, Shelley, in the skeptical-idealist view, draws most heavily from Berkeley, who himself assumes the mantle of Protagorean, and not Platonic, idealism.

Pulos and the skeptical school that followed him are therefore correct in refuting or seriously qualifying Shelley's Platonism, at least in the context of his most explicit philosophical statement, "On Life." This does not, however, explain the strange claim that "[t]here is not the slightest evidence that Berkeley had any significant influence on Shelley's rejection of common-sense materialism."[12] Given the direct importation of the *esse est percipi* principle and the contiguous remarks on materialism in "On Life," it is difficult to deny the influence of Berkeley. Pulos is right to note, "In fact, the poet plainly tells us that Berkeley's arguments did not impress him," alluding to a letter from Shelley to Southey, dated July 29, 1812, which states: "I have read Berkeley, & the perusal of his arguments tended more than anything to convince me that immaterialism & other words of general usage deriving all their force from mere *predicates* in *non* were invented by the pride of philosophers to conceal their ignorance even from themselves."[13] It would be a mistake, though, to accept any statement made by Shelley to Southey in 1812 at face value, as Southey was at the time a sort of patron to Shelley, determined to rid him of his "eccentricity," as he puts it in a letter to John Rickman in that year.[14] Southey was an established poet looking to mold the promising, yet directionless and financially precarious, young poet. Six months prior to the July letter to Southey, Shelley says this about him to Godwin: "the paid champion of every abuse and absurdity. . . . I do not feel the least disposition to be Mr. S's proselyte."[15] Even if one were to accept that Shelley rejected Berkeley in 1812, which I do not, this does not mean of course that he rejected him in 1819. He may have differed from him in some important respects, as I hope to show, but the idea that Berkeley—the most immediate source of Shelley's alleged skeptical idealism— had no "significant influence" on the poet seems false.

Berkeley's philosophy, though, is rarely referred to as "skeptical idealism." He called it "immaterialism," and later readers would refer to it as "subjective idealism." The argument for Shelley's immaterialism rests on his assertion of *esse est percipi* and the following passage from "On Life": "The relations of *things*, remain unchanged, by whatever system. By the word *things* is to be understood any object of thought, that is, any thought upon which any other thought is employed, with an apprehension of distinction. The relations of these remain unchanged; and such is the material of our knowledge."[16] An "object of thought" is here a particular kind of mental entity, not a thing in the world. The relations of thoughts may remain unchanged, but this tells us nothing about the external world; there is, it seems, only mind. This, however, is the exception in Shelley's work when viewed in its entirety. "Unless he is directly expressing his epistemological view," Kenneth Neil Cameron observes, "he writes in terms of things and thoughts."[17]

We may grant the momentary confession of immaterialism in "On Life" and weigh it against the preponderance of mind-independent "things" elsewhere in his philosophical writings. In *A Refutation of Deism* (1814), Shelley writes of a universe "subjected to the rigid necessity of inevitable laws" whose effects are "the boundaries of our knowledge." He writes also of the "action of external objects" without which "we should not only be deprived of all knowledge of the existence of mind, but totally incapable of the knowledge of any thing."[18] "Speculations on Metaphysics" states: "By considering all knowledge as bounded by perception, whose operations may be indefinitely combined, we arrive at a conception of Nature inexpressibly more magnificent, simple and true, than accord[s with] the ordinary systems of complicated and partial consideration."[19] There are, of course, many instances of external and extended things, which determine our perception and bound our knowledge, in Shelley's less formally epistemological writings, all of which distance Shelley from Berkeley.[20] Finally, Berkeley's entire system, denominated either "immaterialism" or "subjective idealism," is predicated on a God, the one true substance, whose constant perception perpetuates the existence of the objective world. Shelley's atheism obviously prohibits such a solution to skepticism. The notion that Shelley is a "skeptical idealist" in the Berkeleyan tradition appears untenable.

Where else, then, are we to turn to find the skeptical idealist tradition of which Shelley was supposedly a part? The philosophy of David Hume, which exerted a greater influence on Shelley than that of Berkeley, is adequately described as "empiricism" or "skepticism," or, if one wishes, some combination of the terms.[21] Hume's empiricist vocabulary of "impressions" seems to imply the causal power of external objects, but, as his system demands, the origin of our impressions is *hors de combat*. Our impressions simply exist, and his project is to show how they may be "built up" into ideas. He makes no claim about reality, material or ideal, only about what we can know, which turns out to be very little. This is too modest an epistemological position to assign to Shelley. Even at his most Humean, in *A Refutation of Deism*, Shelley asserts the causal power of external objects in producing our impressions. There are problems, then, with linking Shelley's skeptical idealism to Platonic, Berkeleyan, or Humean epistemology.

The most prominent use of "skeptical idealism" by a major philosopher is, interestingly, in Kant. Frustrated by what he perceived to be misinterpretations of his *Critique of Pure Reason*, Kant distinguished between the various forms of idealism in the *Prolegomena* (1783) and then in the "Refutation of Idealism" inserted into the second edition of the first *Critique* (1787). There are, Kant says, three types of idealism: his own "critical Idealism" (also called "formal" or "transcendental" idealism), the "dogmatic idealism" of Berkeley, and, oddly, the "skeptical idealism" of Descartes (also called "empirical" or "problematic" idealism).[22] Cartesian philosophy is presumably skeptical by virtue of its hyperbolic doubt; idealist insofar as it assumes the indubitable reality of our "immediate experience," that is, our clear and distinct ideas. In his description of Descartes, Kant seems to neglect the Sixth Meditation, in which the existence of objects in space follows from the existence of a God who is not a malevolent deceiver. Descartes's skeptical idealism, according to Kant, "professes only our incapacity for proving an existence outside us from our own by means of immediate experience" and is "rational and appropriate for a thorough philosophic manner of thought." Berkeley's "dogmatic Idealism," on the other hand, "declares things in space to be merely imaginary." Kant's formal idealism "subverts the ordinary idealism" because it grants objective reality to all a priori cognition. This is essentially the project of the Transcendental Deduction, which establishes our entitlement to apply the categories to objects: "[T]he objective validity of the categories, as *a priori* concepts, rests on the fact that through them alone is experience possible (as far as the form of thinking is concerned)."[23]

If Shelley, in his most explicit philosophical formulations, is in fact a skeptical idealist, then it is only in the sense in which Kant describes Descartes's "skeptical idealism": a "rational and appropriate" manner of thought "allowing no decisive judgment until a sufficient proof has been found." The skeptical idealism that has at times been attributed to Shelley—the doctrine that a sufficient proof for the existence of objects in space is not forthcoming, and that any existence we attribute to them is mind-dependent—is, in Kant's terms, a "dogmatic" idealism. This, I have been arguing, is too extreme a position to assign to the general trend of Shelley's thought. The only suitable definition of skeptical idealism is the "problematic" one offered by Kant in reference to, of all things, the philosophy of Descartes. Moreover, it would not be implausible to suggest that the picture of the mind in Shelley's works has greater affinities with "formal," or "transcendental," idealism than with the "skeptical," or "dogmatic," idealism of someone like Berkeley. Shelley, we remember, would have been familiar with Kant through the skeptical *Academical Questions* (1805) of Sir William Drummond. *Prometheus Unbound* presents a picture of the mind closer to the active transcendental subject than to the passive, skeptical or otherwise, empirical subject. Before turning to that poem, it is important that we pivot from Shelley's formal, though often fragmentary, statements about knowledge to his historical view of the conditions under which certain kinds of knowledge, freedom, and art flourish, that is, to the intertwined intellectual and political histories of his longest prose work, *A Philosophical View of Reform*.

Historical Epistemology: *A Philosophical View of Reform*

The case for skeptical idealism, we have seen, has its merits, but it may be best for now to understand Shelley's most formulaic philosophical utterances in the context of a "problematic" idealism, to borrow Kant's term. That said, Shelley is not a systematic philosopher, and it would be a mistake to place a great deal of emphasis on the seemingly definitive statements of "On Life" and the "Speculations on Metaphysics." The originality and value of Shelley's thought lie elsewhere, in the way he adapts philosophic abstraction to the concrete project of reform. Shelley does what neither a Godwin nor a Cobbett is able to do: in Cameron's estimation, "It is this combination of the general and the particular, of vision and practicality, that makes *A Philosophical View of Reform* the most advanced work of political theory of the age."[24]

A Philosophical View of Reform was conceived and largely composed during the Shelleys' stay in Florence, toward the end of 1819 (it remained unpublished until 1920). Political unrest in England was at a high—the Peterloo massacre occurred in August—and the reform movement was divided between Cobbett and Hobhouse in their bids for a seat in the House of Commons. In a letter to Charles Ollier from December 23, 1819, Shelley writes that he is preparing an "octavo on reform," which he hopes will be "an instructive and readable book, appealing from the passions to the reason of men."[25] Shelley divides the work into three chapters: a sweeping historical sketch of the progress of liberty, an argument for the necessity of change in specific British institutions, and, finally, proposals for achieving reform. Shelley's reflections on the history of political philosophy are mostly contained in the first chapter, the focus of this section.

The claim that *A Philosophical View of Reform* is the most advanced work of political theory of the age rests in part on the breadth of its historical perspective. The first chapter begins with the dissolution of the Roman Empire, "that vast & successful scheme for the enslaving [of] the most civilized portion of mankind,"[26] and ends with the current condition of England, which has arrived with the rest of Europe "at a crisis in its destiny." Following the fall of the Roman Empire, Christianity instituted a subtler form of domination, as "a system of liberty & equality (for such was the system preached by that great Reformer) was perverted to support oppression."[27] The republics and municipal governments of Italy managed to maintain some degree of independence, to which we owe the achievements of Dante, Raphael, and Michelangelo. The Reformation, "that imperfect emancipation of mankind from the yoke of priests & kings," represented the next stage in the progress of "philosophy & civilization."[28] Signs of freedom emerged in the republics of Holland and Switzerland. England achieved relative stability and peace, resulting in the genius of Shakespeare and Bacon. The great writers of the Elizabethan and Jacobean eras "were at once the effects of this new spirit in men's minds, & the causes of its more complete development."[29] This is perhaps the clearest articulation of a principle, much discussed by critics of Shelley, that is developed in the *Defence of Poetry* and other writings: poetry—defined in the *View* as any "intense & impassioned power of communicating intense & impassioned impressions respecting man & nature"[30]—is the effect and, at once, the cause of historical circumstances. As stated in *A Philosophical View of Reform*, this principle not only shows that Shelley, like Hume, did not adhere to a skepticism of causation outside of purely epistemological contexts, but also that causation in this case runs both ways: circumstances determine consciousness *and* the other way around.

The radical element of Shelley's vision is his recognition, decades before Marx, of the first direction in this causal relationship, that is, how circumstances determine consciousness. This attitude may be said to be an inheritance from the determinism of French materialists such as Helvétius and Holbach, but Shelley places greater emphasis than they do on artistic production—the works of the imagination, man's most creative and seemingly autonomous faculty—as the effect of historical circumstance. Here and elsewhere, Shelley's anticipation of Marx should not be overlooked. In the historical narrative of *A Philosophical View of Reform*, England's Glorious Revolution marked a compromise between the "unextinguishable spirit of Liberty" (this is the language of, among other things, Wordsworth's *Cintra*) and the "ever watchful spirit of fraud & tyranny."[31] Limits were placed on the power of the three-headed beast: monarchy, aristocracy, and episcopacy. "Unfortunately," Shelley writes, "they lost no more in extent of power, than they gained in security of possession."[32] Shelley sees in this transfer of power the kind of disparity Marx invokes in his distinction between the state and civil society. Formal political emancipation at the level of the state does not entail human emancipation in civil society; changes to the representational superstructure (the loss of political "power") do not entail changes to the base (including ownership, or "security in possession"). But, as it was for Wordsworth and Burke, discussed in previous chapters, this is history viewed in aesthetic, and not merely materialist, terms, in which the "spirit of liberty" is no simple poetic figure, but a symbol in the constitutive, Coleridgean sense, that is, harmonious in itself and "consubstantial" with the truth it conducts.[33] If Shelley is an idealist in more than the "skeptical" or "problematic" sense, it is insofar as he grants reality to what the age called the "spirit of liberty." Such a willingness to grant reality to this kind of abstraction—and the readiness to see it in particular historical events—is the mark, if anything is, of "late" Romantic consciousness in Britain.

The spirit of liberty, for Shelley, took a decisive turn with the Revolution of 1688, the pivotal historical event in *A Philosophical View of Reform*. The settlement of that revolution, he suggests, marked real gains in the progress of liberty, even as it remained fundamentally incomplete in establishing the conditions of emancipation. It formally established the will of the people as the foundation of the state's right to exercise power, from which, he argues, the rule of constitutional law follows. The Glorious Revolution inaugurated a new epoch in the history of the progress of civilization, one accompanied by "deeper enquiries into the forms of human nature."[34] Shelley presents a sketch of the beginning and evolution—it is by necessity teleological and progressive—of modern political philosophy in ways that illuminate his core political and philosophical ideas. Bacon, Spinoza, Hobbes, Bayle, and Montaigne, he argues, "regulated the reasoning powers, criticised the past history, exposed the errors by illustrating their causes and their connection, and anatomized the inmost nature of social man."[35] Of these projects, the anatomy of social man was the most revolutionary; it would become the dream of much eighteenth-century political thought. The goal, as Isaiah Berlin describes it, was "to treat man as if he were a natural object, wholly determined in his bodily behavior, as well as in his thoughts and wishes and imaginative life, by forces which could be studied by the natural sciences." Individuals and societies, in this view, must be studied "like stones and trees, beavers or bees."[36] The group of thinkers including Bacon and Hobbes mentioned above marks the beginning of this new science— indeed an "anatomy"—of social man. That Shelley includes Spinoza in this group is significant, as he was at the time of *A Philosophical View of Reform*'s composition translating parts of the *Tractatus Theologico-Politicus* (1670). Spinoza's tract is also prominently cited in Coleridge's essay "On the Principles of Political Knowledge" (appearing in the 1818 edition of *The Friend*, discussed previously). The influence of Spinoza's pantheism on early Romantic metaphysics has been studied in depth,[37] but his influence on the Romantics' politics, as prominent as Godwin's or Burke's in some of their most systematic political writings, demands greater critical attention. Spinoza's political theory is closest to that of Hobbes, but it has a more expansive conception of the individual's pursuit of "advantage," which goes beyond warding off death and pursuing pleasure. The pursuit of advantage for Spinoza involves the pursuit of knowledge that allows one to participate in the infinite. The significance accorded to Spinoza in both Coleridge's essay "On the Principles of Political Knowledge" and Shelley's *A Philosophical View of Reform* is due, in part, to the philosopher's recognition of the intimate relation between knowledge and liberty—that is, to his robust conception of positive liberty that includes the pursuit of higher forms of knowledge.

Post-Hobbesian empiricism represents for Shelley an unfortunate narrowing of vision. Locke and "the philosophers of his exact and intelligible but superficial school" followed the first group of creative thinkers. Berkeley, Hume, and Hartley followed and "clearly established the certainty of our ignorance with respect to those obscure questions" that had been treated and distorted by religion.[38] Meanwhile, "a crowd of writers in France"—Shelley has in mind, perhaps, the more extreme French materialists—"seized upon the most popular portions of [the doctrines of the "new philosophy"]" but did so with "a limitedness of view." According to Shelley, "they told the truth, but not the whole truth."[39] Skepticism and materialism, it is worth noting, together constitute only one stage in Shelley's progressive intellectual history. They are intermediaries in this narrative, carrying empiricism to its logical conclusion and preparing the way for a philosophy that would be socially useful and artistically productive.

By the middle of the eighteenth century, political philosophy, or "that which considers the relations of Man as a social being," was for Shelley assuming "a precise form,"[40] echoing the sense of many in the period that the science of political knowledge becomes systematized at precisely this time.[41] The writers Shelley invokes "illustrated with more or less success the principles of human nature as applied to man in political society."[42] Knowledge in every field seemed to be growing, with mixed results:

> The mechanical sciences attained to a degree of perfection which, though obscurely foreseen by Lord Bacon, it had been accounted madness to have prophesied in a preceding age. Commerce was pursued with a perpetually increasing vigour, & the same area of the Earth was perpetually compelled to furnish more & more subsistence. The means & sources of knowledge were thus increased together with knowledge itself, & the instruments of knowledge. The benefit of this increase of the powers of man became, in consequence of the inartificial forms into which society continues to be distributed, an instrument of his additional evil. The capabilities of happiness were increased & applied to the augmentation of misery. Modern European society is thus an engine assumed to be for useful purposes, whose force is by a system of subtle mechanism augmented to the highest pitch, but which instead of grinding corn or raising water acts against itself & is perpetually wearing away & breaking to pieces the wheels of which it is composed. The result of the labours of the political philosophers has been the establishment of the principle of Utility as the substance & liberty & equality as the forms according to which the concerns of human life ought to be administered.[43]

The passage as a whole bears a remarkable resemblance to the lengthy footnote Wordsworth eventually deleted from *Cintra*, discussed in chapter 6. There, as here, Bacon is the pure origin of a way of knowing that is fundamentally double-edged: the induction of "experimental" philosophy yields knowledge that gives us power over the world, but at the same time increases our capacity to hurt or destroy one another. This is a familiar theme, running in some form or another through the writings of Vico, Hamann, Herder, Rousseau, Blake, Marx, Adorno, and Foucault. It is, on the face of it, a relatively incontrovertible claim; few people will claim that an increase in knowledge is always and everywhere wholly good.

What separates Shelley and, to varying degrees, these other figures from the common view of the limitations of knowledge is the emphasis on the necessity of domination within such an epistemic structure or process of reasoning (coupled with an emphasis on the necessity of resistance on the other end). This has less to do with a gloomy view of human nature, which acts on some neutral matter called knowledge, than it does with the nature of knowledge itself and the method of its acquisition. The possibility that Shelley and, later, theorists like Adorno and Horkheimer are at least willing to entertain is that there is something about (specifically "Enlightenment") ratiocination itself, beginning with the alienation of subject from object, that necessitates the subject's domination of the object. One may not agree with this view—in a sense, disagreement is practically impossible, given that any rational criticism of it is bound to engage in the practice it finds objectionable—but it is as much of a possibility as Descartes's malevolent deceiver (this time internalized to the mind itself).

The possibility of a faculty of reason that continually and even necessarily leads us astray is not confined to the agitated protests of counter-Enlightenment figures, Marxists, and poststructuralists. As we have seen, Kant himself plainly states in the Transcendental Dialectic that the ideas of human reason, unlike the truth-inclined categories of the understanding, "effect a *mere, but irresistible illusion*, deception by which one can hardly resist even through the most acute criticism."[44] The spectre of a kind of "pathological" reason runs throughout the first *Critique*.[45] The leftist critique of Enlightenment progress, though, is finally justified not on a purely logical basis, but by its social effects: the exploitation of others' labor and capital (this, incidentally, seems to be an extension of Kantian ethical theory and not an argument against it). The "mechanical arts" are to Shelley what "technology" is to Adorno: the "essence" of inductive knowledge (Adorno) that results in "the augmentation of misery" (Shelley). Shelley, though, ultimately places greater emphasis on human agency (increased knowledge as an "instrument" of evil, "applied" to the augmentation of misery); for Adorno, these effects, and their negations, are internal to Enlightenment logic itself.

Shelley is no irrationalist—he is, of course, quite the opposite—but he is ambivalent at times about the role knowledge is to play in the amelioration and liberation of mankind (an attitude achieved through his psychological *agon* with Godwin).[46] Shelley's ambivalence is captured at the end of the quoted passage, where a vision of modern society as a self-consuming machine, "act[ing] against itself and perpetually wearing away or breaking to pieces the wheels of which it is composed," abruptly gives way to the strangely atonal final sentence. His attitude to utilitarianism (the "substance" of contemporary political philosophy), libertarianism, and egalitarianism (its "forms") is not immediately obvious; their value becomes clearer when Shelley's vocabulary is historicized.

The philosophical diction of the passage is no accident. "Substance" had become a loaded term by the end of the eighteenth century. Hume had banished the idea of substance from philosophy altogether, to the great consternation of the Scottish common-sense moralists, by arguing that it has no basis in either sensation or reflection.[47] Kant sought to rescue the idea of substance, that is, "something that could exist as a subject but never as a mere predicate,"[48] by arguing that the perception of simultaneity or succession is possible only if there is something that persists through time. Substance is one of the pure concepts of the understanding, or categories, which make experience possible. In calling the principle of utility the "substance" and liberty and equality the "forms" of political philosophy, Shelley makes no definitive philosophical claim. It is, though, a suggestive formulation, implying that even if the idea of substance has no place in psychology or metaphysics, it still has some use in political philosophy or in the kind of intellectual history he attempts. He reiterates the notion later in the *View*: "public happiness is the substance & the end of political institution."[49] There is perhaps something that persists through time or history, according to which "the concerns of human life ought to be administered." This, for Shelley, is the principle of utility as developed by Spinoza, Bentham, Owen, and others.

The maximization of happiness, then, is the content of political philosophy at the beginning of the nineteenth century; liberty and equality, its forms, follow. The state is justified insofar as it promotes them. "By this test the various institutions regulating political society have been tried and, as the undigested growth of the private passions, errors, and interests of barbarians and oppressors, have been condemned. And many new theories, more or less perfect, but all superior to the mass of evil which they would supplant, have been given to the world."[50] The authority of institutions is something that may be tried, and, if proven illegitimate, overthrown. The great revolutions of the eighteenth century (American, French, and Haitian) challenged the legitimacy of absolute monarchy, feudalism, slavery, and the Church, institutions condemned as the "undigested growth" of barbaric and oppressive impulses. In the juridical language of which the seventeenth and eighteenth centuries were so fond, they were tried by reason—for thinkers like Bayle the "supreme tribunal, the final arbiter of all that is set before us, against which no appeal is possible"[51]—and found guilty ("supreme" tribunals such as Bayle's would themselves be put on trial in the "court of justice" of the first *Critique*). The important point for Shelley is that the state does not derive its authority from any other source than the will of the people and is justified insofar as it meets the demands of reason: the purpose of government is to maximize the happiness of the people while ensuring liberty and equality. All men, if allowed to think freely and rationally, would choose the same things. The principles of utilitarianism, Shelley suggests, persist through time as the measure of how successfully those rational desires are met. Libertarianism and egalitarianism are, at a particular stage in the progress of civilization, the forms of government best suited to satisfy those desires. Shelley sees no conflict between the demands of liberty and equality. Man has been anatomized; politics has been reduced to a descriptive science.

His history of political knowledge having come to an end, Shelley turns to the United States, which he says is the "first practical illustration of the new philosophy."[52] It is a "victorious example" of a "highly civilized community administered according to republican forms."[53] It has no king, oligarchy, established church, or "false representation." Moreover, its constitution is amendable, capable of reforming itself in accordance with advances in political knowledge: "It constitutionally acknowledges the progress of human improvement, and is framed under the limitation of the probability of more simple views of political science being rendered applicable to human life."[54] The republican form of government, then, is not the ideal political arrangement, but the one most suited to particular historical circumstances.

Shelley's is a stadial theory of government, with political evolution occurring in stages. The pattern that emerges from *A Philosophical View of Reform* is roughly the same as the pattern presented in his other political writings: monarchy and feudalism are followed by republicanism and capitalism, which are followed in turn by a kind of libertarianism. The Godwinian termini of the evolution are anarchism and egalitarianism. "Equality in possessions," Shelley writes later in the *View*, "must be the last result of the utmost refinements of civilization," the condition to which "it is our duty to tend."[55] As in Godwin, the whole is driven by necessity. This is the familiar Marxist picture, with one important exception: Shelley is not a revolutionary but, again like Godwin, a gradualist. Arguing against the push for immediate universal suffrage, he remarks that a republic that undergoes "violence & sudden change" incurs a great risk of "being as rapid in its decline as in its growth."[56] It is "patience & reason & endurance" that, for Shelley, coincide with a "calm yet irresistible progress."[57]

The evolution of political institutions depends in large part on the state of political knowledge. An increase in political knowledge, though, is not a sufficient condition of political progress. Some nations appear to be ahead of political philosophy; some behind it. Observing that France in 1819 occupies much the same position that England had at the Restoration, Shelley expresses his hope that France may proceed with greater alacrity: "There remains in the natural order of human things that the tyranny & perfidy of the reigns of Charles the 2^d & James the 2^d . . . perhaps under a milder form and within a shorter period should produce the institution of a government in France which may bear the same relation to the state of political knowledge existing at the present day, as the Revolution under William the 3^d bore to the state of pol[itical] knowledge existing at that period."[58] Recall Wordsworth's immediate reaction to the news of Napoleon's Iberian campaign, discussed in chapter 6: "What rema[rks] do you make on the Portuguese? in what state is knowledge with them?"—questions reflecting a similar sense that the progress of knowledge and the progress of liberty are interdependent.

Shelley is optimistic in *A Philosophical View of Reform* about the state of knowledge across Europe. Germany, he says, "is rising with the fervour of a vigorous youth to the assertion of those rights for which it has that desire arising from knowledge, the surest pledge of victory."[59] Their greatness as a people is proved by, among other things, "the deep passion & the bold & Aeschylean vigour of the imagery of their poetry" and their "subtle and deep philosophy, however erroneous & illogical [in] mingling fervid intuitions into truth with obscure errors" (presumably Leibniz and Wolff, but, again, Shelley would have been familiar with Kant through Drummond).[60] Shelley is, in fact, optimistic about the state of political knowledge around the globe. Much of the rest of the first chapter is devoted to marking the progress made by more remote countries: Spain (which "must of necessity be renovated"), South America (where the people will be "inevitably enfranchised"), India and Egypt (which are being successfully modeled on "European feelings" and culture), Persia (soon to be "infected by the contagion of the good"), the Jews (who, he hopes, "may reassume their ancestral seats"), parts of Asia Minor and Greece (which will be "colonized by the overflowing population of countries less enslaved & debased"), and the West Indies (where the "deepest stain upon civilized man is fading away" under Toussaint L'Ouverture) are all inexorably advancing to higher stages of liberty, equality, and justice.[61] Despite the championing of such noble ends, these passages contain imperialist and orientalist assumptions that require no critical unmasking and that must temper any reflexive association of the poet with free-thinking radicalism in general.[62]

The sweeping historical narrative of *A Philosophical View of Reform* concludes predictably with a turn to England, which "has arrived like the nations which surround it at a crisis in its destiny." It has the advantage, though, of being in the midst of a new Renaissance: the literature of England "has arisen, as it were, from a new birth."[63] Its poets and philosophers surpass any of those in its recent history. Regardless of the system they profess to support individually, "they actually advance the interests of Liberty."[64] Shelley ends his introductory narrative with the first version of his most celebrated critical declaration, the closing paragraph of the *Defence of Poetry*. Here, "poets *and philosophers* are the unacknowledged legislators of the world," a conjunction that would of course collapse in the *Defence*.[65] The intensity of Shelley's rhetoric continues unabated in the other two chapters of the *View*, "On the Sentiment of the Necessity of Change" and "Probable Means," which address more specific political and economic issues: the national debt and paper money, parliamentary reform, working conditions and child labor, the "new aristocracy" of bankers and merchants, universal suffrage, war, and revolution. The principles outlined in the first chapter of the work gain greater shape and force as Shelley merges, elegantly and swiftly, philosophical abstraction with concrete political realities. The philosophical and historical necessity that drives the narrative of *A Philosophical View of Reform* would become the central theme of Shelley's most ambitious poem.

The Atmosphere of Human Thought: *Prometheus Unbound*

Shelley's remark in *A Philosophical View of Reform* that the Germans were developing a poetry of "bold and *Aeschylean* imagery" is telling. Aeschylus was on Shelley's mind at the end of 1819, as Mary Shelley's *Frankenstein; or, The Modern Prometheus* (1818) and Byron's own "Prometheus" (1816) were written not long before. Shelley continued to work on *Prometheus Unbound* through the fall and winter of 1819, the time in which he also began to conceive and draft *A Philosophical View of Reform*. These two works, Shelley's most far-reaching contributions to dramatic poetry and political thought, are best read together, as complementary visions of a historical drama about knowledge and freedom, on one hand, and ignorance and oppression, on the other.

It is only partially true to say that this is how the poem has always been read. While most readings recognize that it is a poem about freedom on some fundamental level, bearing some relation to prose works composed around the same time, *Prometheus Unbound* has occasioned a wide range of commentary, reflecting, as Shelley's works have always done, a variety of critical preoccupations.[66] It is Wasserman, again, who has offered perhaps the most powerful and influential (distinctly idealist) reading of the poem, arguing that Prometheus "must be whatever Shelley's philosophy provides for as eternal and immutable," namely, the "One Mind," the "metaphysical reality" of existence itself.[67] More recently, William Keach has questioned Wasserman's account of the metaphysical premises of the poem but confirms his idea that "all the *dramatis personae* of Shelley's text—'except for Demogorgon'—should be grasped as representations of Prometheus's status as 'the type of the highest perfection of moral and intellectual nature.'"[68] I would like to focus our attention on one group of the *dramatis personae* in particular, the Chorus of Spirits who inhabit the "atmosphere of human thought," as a way to make sense of Shelley's claim in the preface that "the imagery which I have employed will be found in many instances to have been drawn from the operations of the human mind" and as a way to understand how the philosophical and political parts of the poem work together. Wasserman is right to note that, insofar as the Chorus of Spirits is distinct from Prometheus, Prometheus cannot represent human thought as such. It is essential to note, though, the reciprocal, mutually constitutive, and emancipating relationship between Prometheus and the Chorus of Spirits. The entrance of the Chorus marks the pivotal moment of the drama, and the poem's central images derive from the atmosphere they inhabit. The tension at the heart of *Prometheus Unbound* is between the constantly changing, seemingly insubstantial atmosphere of human thought—a mutability Shelley virtuosically delineated in the intellectual history of *A Philosophical View of Reform*—and the eternal and immutable power of historical, even revolutionary, necessity.

Prometheus Unbound is not, Shelley makes clear, *A Philosophical View of Reform* put into verse (nor is it, as Yeats maintained in an early fit of heterodoxy, Godwin's *Political Justice* put into rhyme).[69] It is a mistake, Shelley says in his preface to the poem, "to suppose that I dedicate my poetical compositions solely to the direct enforcement of reform, or that I consider them in any degree as containing a reasoned system on the theory of human life."[70] As it was for Keats, "didactic poetry," he says, "is my abhorrence." Rather, Shelley claims that his purpose is "to familiarize the highly refined imagination" with "beautiful idealisms of moral excellence." The argument that beauty is a symbol of morality had, of course, been revitalized three decades before *Prometheus Unbound* in Kant's third *Critique* (1790), in which aesthetic experience teaches "us to find a free satisfaction in the objects of the senses even without any sensible charm."[71] Beauty is in this way a "symbol" of morality; it "presupposes and cultivates a certain liberality in the manner of thinking, i.e., independence of the satisfaction from mere sensory enjoyment."[72] Kant's phrase, "a certain liberality in the manner of thinking," is apt here, as the liberality (and, one might add, the liberty) of thought in the period frequently consists in its independence from sensory experience (hence the significance accorded to the a priori). Wordsworth and Coleridge would both speak of the tyranny of the senses in general and of the "despotism of the eye" in particular. Among the second-generation Romantic poets, it is Shelley who pushes the idea to its limit.

Prometheus Unbound is many things, but a poem of sensation is not one of them. It is the most perfectly realized expression of the intellectual, ethereal, and abstract tendencies of Shelley's verse, at the furthest possible remove from, as Kant would put it, "any sensible charm" (it is, in this way, a powerful countercurrent to the poetry of sensation Keats was developing in his odes of the same year). This is philosophical poetry in full dress, opting in general for a life of thought over one of sensation. It is also political poetry, concerned with the abstract forms of tyranny, liberty, revolution, and justice. The purpose of what follows is to show how this is possible, to show how Shelley turns this poem about oppression into a poem about the human mind and to show how he turns the seemingly unpromising prospect of a long dramatic poem about the human mind into an aesthetic achievement. As he says in the preface, "poetical abstractions are beautiful and new . . . because the whole produced by their combination has some intelligible and beautiful analogy with those sources of emotion and thought, and with the contemporary condition of them."[73] I trace in this section the course of one such analogical relationship—between the poem's atmospheric imagery and the movement of human thought—by focusing on the constitutive tropes of the poem: collection and dispersion, condensation and evaporation.

Prometheus Unbound, the central work of the Shelley canon, requires no extended paraphrase. In the briefest terms, the poem continues the story of Prometheus developed by Hesiod and Aeschylus; in act 1, Prometheus's curse of Jupiter is repeated to him and it "repents" him; in act 2, Asia and Panthea descend to the world of Demogorgon, the source of Necessity, whose subsequent ascent initiates the overthrow of Jupiter; in act 3, Demogorgon drags Jupiter down into Chaos, and Hercules releases Prometheus, who retires with Asia to a cave to cultivate the arts; finally, in act 4, the Spirits rejoice, and Demogorgon places the story in a historical perspective. Such is the action of *Prometheus Unbound*, a dramatic poem considerably closer to Dante and Milton than to Wordsworth and Coleridge. Other elements of the plot will be introduced when necessary, though my focus will be on the language, images, and tropes of the poem, through which Shelley constructs his analogy between the operations of the human mind and the drama of tyranny and emancipation.

The poem begins in the Indian Caucasus.[74] Prometheus is "Nailed to this wall of eagle-baffling mountain, / Black, wintry, dead, unmeasured; without herb, / Insect, or beast, or shape or sound of life" (1.20–22).[75] The torture of Prometheus is more than being surrounding by death. It is the pain of being at war with the earth itself. Glaciers pierce him with spears, chains eat into his bones with "burning cold," Jupiter's eagle tears his heart apart, and, in the most violent image, the Earthquake fiends "wrench the rivets from my quivering wounds / When the rocks split and close again behind" (1.39–40). The sublime work of the "Earthquake-daemons" in "Mont Blanc," it seems, is not without its victims. All this Prometheus suffers with patience:

> And yet to me welcome is day and night,
> Whether one breaks the hoar frost of the morn,
> Or starry, dim, and slow, the other climbs
> The leaden-coloured East;   (1.44–47)

Here is the first instance of what would be the most common image associated with the poem's dominant trope: the dew, in this case the harsher "hoar frost of the morn," is the crystallization of the poem's movements between collection and dispersion, condensation and evaporation. In these lines, too, is the first appearance of another of the poem's primary symbols, the Morning and Evening Star (for Yeats, the most important and precise of Shelley's symbols).[76] To some things at least, Prometheus is indifferent during his torture ("And yet to me welcome is Day and Night"), an attitude of dispassionate endurance that prepares the way for his forgiveness of Jupiter: "Disdain? ah no, I pity thee." (1.53); a few lines later, "I speak in grief / Not exultation, for I hate no more" (1.56–57).

Sensibility makes no claims on his power of judgment, as his surroundings initially resemble a vacuum: "Black, wintry, dead," and without "shape or sound of life." There is physical torture, to be sure, but this he handles with Stoic detachment (even to the Furies of Hell who promise the most excruciating anguish, he remains "king over myself" [1.492]). In Kantian terms, the freedom of his imagination—and it is an immensely powerful imagination, as free as his body is constrained—is able to act in accord with the lawfulness of his understanding, which is equally vast. The freedom of the imagination in aesthetic judgment, for Kant, prepares the mind for moral judgment, where the freedom of the will acts in agreement with the universal laws of reason. In his essay on "The Philosophy of Shelley's Poetry," Yeats grants the imagination complete cognitive power: "[I] am now certain that the imagination has some way of lighting on the truth that the reason has not, and that its commandments, delivered when the body is still and the reason silent, are the most binding we can ever know."[77] No body is more still than the bound Prometheus's—the only real movement is the quivering of his wounds—and the cries of reason have yet to release him from bondage. At the beginning of the poem, the suffering, heroic Prometheus is, as he is in Aeschylus, the picture of "patience and reason and endurance," the conditions of the "calm yet irresistible progress" Shelley was delineating at the same time in *A Philosophical View of Reform*. His endurance results from his knowledge of the inevitability of Jupiter's downfall: "I know but this, that it must come" (1.413). Three thousand years of bondage have rendered day and night equally welcome; their stars are of course the same, considered from different points of view.

The Morning and Evening Star is one of Shelley's primary symbols, but it is ultimately a non-nuclear relation in the family of images that dominates the entire poem: atmospheric images that are constantly forming and reforming themselves, first gathering together and then dissipating away. This set of images, some combination of which occurs in practically every significant utterance, includes dew, frost, and mist; clouds, thunder, and lightning; ether, vapor, and atmosphere. These three image clusters constitute the core of the poem. It is not the images themselves that differentiate the poem—Shelley's poetry is, with few exceptions, always ethereal and atmospheric—but the extraordinary movement of the images, the constant and overlapping cycles of condensation and evaporation, that separates *Prometheus Unbound*. It is, perhaps, the most *humid* poem in the language. I bring our attention to this not as a curiosity of literary history, but because the imagery of the poem is crucial to Shelley's attempt to "familiarize the highly refined imagination" with "beautiful idealisms of moral excellence." Were he to have spoken with greater candor, he might have added "political excellence," as the poem finally emphasizes not the virtuous endurance of Aeschylus's Prometheus, but the objective necessity of the overthrow of Jupiter. The relevance of meteorological imagery to the political concerns of the poem remains obscure unless we keep in mind what Shelley says in his preface: "The imagery which I have employed will be found in many instances to have been drawn from the operations of the human mind," a principle most clearly at work in the "atmosphere of human thought" in the poem but present throughout.

In act 1, then, the bound Prometheus complains to his mother, Earth ("Gaia" in Hesiod's *Theogony*), that she and her sons, the other Titans, have "vanished like thin *mist* / Unrolled on the morning *wind*" (1.116–17; emphasis added, here and throughout, to highlight the relevant set of images). The Earth responds by reflecting on his birth, "When thou didst from [my] bosom, like a *cloud* / Of glory, arise, a spirit of keen joy!" (1.157–58).[78] He arises like a cloud; his family vanishes like a mist. Their colloquy is interrupted by the Phantasm of Jupiter, whom Prometheus has called to repeat the curse. A spirit seizes the Phantasm, who is unable or unwilling to repeat the curse himself, tearing him apart "as fire tears a thunder-cloud" (1.255). The fire that "tears" thunder-clouds appears again in the body of the curse: with a "calm, fixed mind" (1.262), Prometheus invites Jupiter to inflict him with "frost and fire" (1.268), "Lightning, and cutting hail" (1.270). Lightning represents, throughout the poem, an accumulation of creative energy that must necessarily be discharged, usually violently. It figures prominently in the preface, where Shelley associates it with the mental activity of the innovative artist. A number of writers in any given age, he says, possess a "form" that is the endowment of the age, but lack "spirit,"[79] which must be "the uncommunicated lightning of their own mind."[80]

Shelley's position in the preface is far less Platonic than it is in the *Defence of Poetry*, where poets are the "hierophants of an unapprehended inspiration," and creation is a "fading coal which some invisible influence, like an inconstant wind, awakens to transitory brightness."[81] Here inspiration is not merely "unapprehended" but "uncommunicated." The great writers of Shelley's age are the "companions and forerunners of some unimagined change" in social conditions or political philosophy: "The cloud of mind is discharging its collected lightning, and the equilibrium between institutions and opinions is now restoring, or is about to be restored."[82] The equilibrium between institutions and opinions, we recall, was the concept through which Shelley constructed the intellectual and political histories of *A Philosophical View of Reform*. Clouds, in the symbolism of *Prometheus Unbound*, are mind; lightning, the mind's creative energy. Creation is cotemporaneous with social change, the causality, again, running both ways: poets, he says in the preface, are "in one sense, the creators, and, in another, the creations, of their age."[83]

After hearing the curse repeated to him—including the wish that Jupiter's omnipotence become a "crown of pain / To *cling* like burning gold round thy *dissolving* brain" (1.290–91)—Prometheus repents. Or, rather, the curse "re-pents" *him* ("It doth repent me" [1.303]), an archaic construction that persists as late as Swinburne's Shelleyan "Triumph of Time" ("Will it not one day in heaven repent you?").[84] Prometheus's repentance does not prevent Mercury and his Furies from torturing him, the occasion for Earth to summon the Spir-its "whose homes are the dim caves of human thought / And who inhabit, as birds wing the wind, / Its world-surrounding ether" (1.659–61). The Chorus of the Spirits, delivering the only kind of absolution Prometheus will receive for his repentance, directly addresses the atmosphere of human thought at the center of the poem's imagery:

> From unremembered ages we
> Gentle guides and guardians be
> Of Heaven-oppressed mortality;
> And we breathe, and sicken not,
> The atmosphere of human thought:
> Be it dim and dank and grey
> Like a storm-extinguished day
> Travelled o'er by dying gleams;
> Be it bright as all between
> Cloudless skies and windless streams,
> Silent, liquid, and serene—
> As the birds within the wind,
> As the fish within the wave,
> As the thoughts of man's own mind
> Float through all above the grave,
> We make there our liquid lair,
> Voyaging cloudlike and unpent
> Through the boundless element—
> Thence we bear the prophecy
> Which begins and ends in thee!   (1.672–91)

The Chorus presents two atmospheres of human thought: one "dim and dank and grey," the other "silent, liquid, and serene." In both of these the spirits make their home ("liquid lair") as fluidly as birds inhabit the air, fish inhabit the water, and thoughts float through the mind (recall the "everlasting universe of things" that flows through the mind in "Mont Blanc"). The lyric passage as a whole is extremely fluid, employing a rhyme scheme that would be copied, with some variation, in each of the Spirits' shorter speeches: typically a mixture of couplets and tercets, with one line near the middle (always the *d* rhyme) that contains an internal rhyme, but does not rhyme with any other (in this passage, "there" and "lair"). This more extended passage includes eight lines of alternating rhymes near the middle. While the rhyme schemes in the lyric passages lack the balance of the *terza rima* of "Ode to the West Wind" (1820) or "The Triumph of Life" (composed 1822), they reflect a vertical stratification appropriate for a poem that moves rapidly through atmospheric layers. The poem achieves, with more complex rhyme patterns, the Miltonic sublimity of movement Wordsworth aspires to, and intends to surpass, in the Prospectus to *The Recluse*, where he recognizes that he must "sink / Deep, and, aloft ascending, breathe in worlds / To which the Heaven of Heavens is but a veil." Shelley's Spirits breathe easily, "but sicken not," in the atmosphere of human thought. They inhabit, the Earth tells us, the world-surrounding ether as effortlessly as birds "wing the wind." As they would say a few lines later, "In the atmosphere we breathe,—As buds grow red when snow-storms flee" (1.790–91). The poem is all growth and decay, happening on many levels, simultaneous and overlapping.

It is worth pausing here at the end of act 1 to note that it is the introduction of the forms of human thought that marks the major turn of Shelley's Prometheus narrative. Prometheus is as close to despair as he will be, owing to the torturous visions of human suffering presented to him by the Furies, when the Earth bids the Spirits to ascend from the caves of human thought and gather like flocks of clouds before him. The Spirits of human thought bear the prophecy of Prometheus's emancipation. There is an important reciprocity here: Prometheus liberates man by providing him with knowledge, and human thought liberates Prometheus through its highest, most prophetic form of knowledge. Thus the refrain of the Spirits of human thought: "Thence we bear the prophecy / Which begins and ends in thee."

Act 2 opens with the visitation of Asia by Panthea, who like joy rises up from the earth "clothing with golden clouds / The desert of our life" (2.1.10–12). The imagery we have been tracing continues in widening morns, fading waves, unraveling clouds, cloudlike snow, wind-divided mists, mists of silver dew, and mountain mists condensing at the sound of Panthea's and Asia's voices (2.1.58). Panthea communicates to Asia two dreams she has had predicting the liberation of Prometheus and the renewal of the world. In the first, one of the poem's most lyrical passages, Prometheus appears in "that form / Which lives unchanged within" (2.1.64–65). His love

Steamed forth like vaporous fire; an atmosphere
Which wrapped me in its all-dissolving power,
As the warm ether of the morning sun
Wraps ere it drinks some cloud of wandering dew.
I saw not, heard not, moved not, only felt
His presence flow and mingle through my blood
Till it became his life, and his grew mine,
And I was thus absorbed—until it passed,
And like the vapours when the sun sinks down,
Gathering again in drops upon the pines,
And tremulous as they, in the deep night
My being was condensed; and as the rays
Of thought were slowly gathered, I could hear
His voice . . .   (2.1.75–87)

Love, the "great secret of morals" in the *Defence*, is the essence or "form" of Prometheus, what makes him the friend of mankind, as he is in Aeschylus (where Prometheus speaks of his "excessive love for Man"). Love pours forth in this passage like a "vaporous fire," a permeating warmth that comes like the morning sun, drinking in clouds of dew, and passes away like the setting sun, allowing moisture to collect again in drops on the trees. Panthea, in this extraordinary conceit, collects like evening vapor upon Prometheus's departure, her being "condensed" and her thoughts "slowly gathered."

Love is a radiating, diffusive power, dispersing thought so that sympathetic identification may take place: Panthea's self dissolves ("I saw not—heard not—moved not") as she completely merges with Prometheus (her blood "became his life and his grew mine"). This recalls the just mentioned "great secret of morals" passage in the *Defence*, where love is defined as "a going out of our own nature, and an identification of ourselves with the beautiful which exists in thought, action, or person, not our own." It is an act of the imagination, the "great instrument of moral good," the circumference of which is enlarged by poetry. The language of Panthea's speech even more closely resembles Shelley's description in the *Defence* of Petrarch's sonnets, which express delight in the grief of love: "It is impossible to feel them without becoming a portion of that beauty which we contemplate: it were superfluous to explain how the gentleness and the elevation of mind connected with these sacred emotions can render men more amiable, more generous, and wise, and lift them out of the dull *vapours* of the little world of self."[85] Vapor appears twice in Panthea's speech, first as the "vaporous fire" of Prometheus's love and then as the evening vapors that condense, like her "being" and "rays of thought," into drops of dew. The little world of self is one kind of vapor, real but "dull" and finally insubstantial; the dissolving power of love another, equally real but more powerful.

Panthea and Asia descend in the next scene into the underworld of Demogorgon through a path completely shielded from the sun, moon, wind, and rain. Only two things are able to penetrate it: a cloud of dew that hangs pearls of moisture on the green laurel and a star that "scatters drops of golden light, / Like lines of rain that ne'er unite" (2.2.20–21). The Lucretian echo is fitting, for Demogorgon is the source of Necessity, but here there is no *clinamen*: lines of rain fall down in parallel lines, with no deviation. The only intimations of human freedom and creativity on the path leading to him are the drops of dew on the laurel. Deviation may be impossible on the path leading to Necessity, but once in Demogorgon's realm Asia and Panthea witness, in the drama's pivotal moment, the cause of change and revolution:

> —Hark! The rushing snow!
> The sun-awakened avalanche! whose mass,
> Thrice sifted by the storm, had gathered there
> Flake after flake: in Heaven-defying minds
> As thought by thought is piled, till some great truth
> Is loosened, and the nations echo round,
> Shaken to their roots: as do the mountains now.   (2.3.36–42)

In contrast to the "mere anarchy" and the "blood-dimmed tide" that would be loosed upon the world in the darkened vision of Yeats's "The Second Coming," the loosening of *Prometheus Unbound* heralds a time when conviction and passionate intensity will be restored to the world. And, again, it is to the materialist Lucretius (the only Roman poet considered a "creator" in the "highest sense" in the *Defence*) that Shelley alludes in this climactic moment. Lucretius held that change is possible only if there is some slight deviation in the path of an atom to the ground. Shelley echoes Lucretius's description of the fall of atoms, but his description is shot through with necessity: the lines of rain never unite. He accounts for change in the above passage with the accumulation of precipitation. Flakes pile upon flakes, as thoughts pile upon thoughts, until an avalanche becomes inevitable. In his prose, Shelley, like Godwin and unlike Marx, does not assert the necessity of actual revolution, only in the intellectual revolution that tends to coincide with social change. As represented here, the avalanche is nevertheless "sun-awakened," precipitated by the same fire-giving, Promethean energy Panthea had described in her dream.

Acts 1 and 2 introduce and condense the three image clusters of the poem, bringing them to a head in the intellectual avalanche and revolution of the second act. Acts 3 and 4 consist of joyous dispersion and the release of creative energy. Act 3 opens with Jupiter ironically rejoicing in how his curses "Like snow on herbless peaks, fall flake by flake" (3.1.12) on the soul of man, unaware that an avalanche has already been triggered. Demogorgon drags Jupiter down into Chaos, and Hercules unbinds Prometheus. Prometheus announces that he will retire with Asia and Ione to a cave (the haunt, of course, of the witch Poesy in "Mont Blanc"), where they will practice philosophy and—like the childlike souls in "On Life" who "feel as if their nature were dissolved into the surrounding universe" and are "conscious of no distinction"[86]—make "strange combinations out of common things" (3.3.32):

> And lovely apparitions—dim at first
> Then radiant, as the mind, arising bright
> From the embrace of beauty whence the forms
> Of which these are the phantoms, casts on them
> The gathered rays which are reality—
> Shall visit us, the progeny immortal
> Of Painting, Sculpture, and rapt Poesy,
> And arts, though unimagined, yet to be.   (3.3.49–56)

This is the closest Shelley comes to idealism in the poem, as the mind assumes its exalted, Romantic role as lamp: it casts on the arts the "gathered rays which *are* reality." The mind here dwells with beauty and arises from its embrace.

In the utopian vision that dominates the second half of *Prometheus Unbound*, the Earth itself becomes rejuvenated, and natural processes are allowed to follow their course without interference: as she says, "The dew-mists of my sunless sleep shall float / Under the stars like balm" (3.3.100–101). The imagery of "dew-mingled rain" and "aerial dew" continues until the Spirit of the Hour announces what changes have happened in the world of men. The poem—which had until this point operated, politically, through such abstractions as necessity, tyranny, revolution, and liberation as they relate to immortals—now represents the culmination of utopian politics on earth. Thrones are kingless; men cease to be fearful of one another; the twin mind-forged manacles of self-love and self-contempt release their grip; men no longer gaze on the "eye of cold command" until "the subject of the tyrant's will / Became, worse fate, the abject of his own" (3.4.138–40); virtue is freely chosen and not commanded; "None talked that common, false, cold, hollow talk / Which makes the heart deny the *yes* it breathes" (lines that surely impressed the Yeats of 1900 [3.4.149–50]); and women, freed from custom's tyranny, speak the "wisdom once they could not think" and feel "emotions once they feared to feel" (3.4.157–58). Finally, man, "Equal, unclassed, tribeless, and nationless," becomes, as Prometheus had declared he himself was to the Furies, "the King / Over himself" (3.4.195–97).

The vision of an ideal earthly society that concludes act 3 marks the end of the action. Act 4 consists, like act 1, of a single scene, here devoted to a hymn of rejoicing. Dew is again the predominant image; mutability emerges as the predominant theme. The specific kind of mutability under consideration—the way things gather together and then disperse—receives greater emphasis here than it had in previous acts. The Voice of Unseen Spirits appears and then "melt[s] away, / Like dissolving spray" (4.24–25). It then reappears, marking the movements of dew on the land, clouds in the sky, and waves on the sea (mirroring the basic image pattern of "Ode to the West Wind," written in Florence during the same period as act 4). A Chorus of Hours punctuates its song with the refrain: "Break the dance, and scatter the song; / Let some depart, and some remain" (4.159–60). Their departure prompts a discussion of change between Ione and Panthea, but "Even whilst we speak / New notes arise (4.184–85). The Earth rejoices in the "*vaporous exultation*" that wraps around her like an "*atmosphere* of light" (4.321–23); the Moon, recalling the avalanche of act 2, proclaims, "The snow upon my lifeless mountains / Is loosened into living fountains" (4.356–57). Panthea's words "fall like the clear soft *dew*" (4.508); the Earth is "as a drop of *dew* that dies!" (4.523). Demogorgon, echoing the Moon's earlier enraptured statement, " 'Tis Love, all Love!" (4.369), concludes the drama with a panegyric on Love, which has left its throne to fold its healing wings over the world.

With its multiple, high-pitched effusions on Love, the conclusion as presented in act 4 is unsatisfying. The real ending of the drama occurs with the egalitarian vision of act 3. Such is the end of Shelley's radicalism, a vision of the world in which unjustifiable political obligation is supplanted by self-legislation and self-knowledge. The contemptuous dismissal of Shelley's politics by the world-weary critics of the early twentieth century (Babbitt, Eliot, and Leavis) sees in this vision nothing but adolescence, banality, and moral corruption. Shelley's politics is, for them, all vegetables and free love. But even in his most visionary poetic mode, Shelley works from an idea of what a just and free society ought to look like *in concreto*.

The political epistemology of *Prometheus Unbound*—its atmospheric conflation of mental and political phenomena—is in many ways distinct to Shelley, but its theme is not. It is a poem in the tradition of Spenser's *Mutabilitie* cantos. Everything related to human experience, especially the atmosphere of human thought, morphs and changes in the poem, though two things remain constant: Prometheus and Demogorgon. "Indeed," Wasserman argues, "except for Demogorgon, Prometheus is the only reality actually present in the poem." Prometheus is not human knowledge, but the source of human knowledge (just as Demogorgon is not historical or philosophical necessity itself, but the source of necessity). Human knowledge is discontinuous and radically indeterminate; its source, for Shelley, is not. As Panthea recounts her dream to Asia in act 1, Prometheus appears and "the azure night / Grew radiant with the glory of that form / Which lives unchanged within," an idea echoed in act 3, when Prometheus proposes to Asia that they retire to "talk of time and change, / As the world ebbs and flows, ourselves unchanged" (3.3.23–34). "What can hide man," he asks, "from Mutability?" Nothing, of course. If *A Philosophical View of Reform* traces the histories of knowledge and freedom to show their interdependence, *Prometheus Unbound* undermines any dogmatic faith in the progress of human knowledge by contrasting its beautiful, at times hypnotic, shape-shifting with its sublime, immutable source. The power of the poem consists in the reciprocal relationship noted above, Shelley's major modification of the Aeschylus narrative: Prometheus, the source of knowledge, liberates humanity just as human knowledge—in its highest, most prophetic mode— liberates the bound Prometheus. This poem about tyranny, revolution, and freedom is, in the end, a sustained response to Demogorgon's emancipating directive to Asia: "Ask what thou wouldst know."

Afterword

I have tried in the preceding chapters to give some indication of how a group of British writers in the Romantic period responded to the challenges of reform and revolution by thinking in new, imaginative ways about the scope of political reason and the principles of political knowledge. The French Revolution, the terror that followed it, and the prospect of revolution at home occasioned an extraordinary set of responses in Britain: a scathing critique of "political metaphysics" at the origin of modern conservatism in Burke and powerful redemptions of "political reason" on the left in the vindications of Wollstonecraft and the inquiries of Godwin; a synthesis of political and epistemological concerns in the intellectual histories of Coleridge and Shelley; a nuanced, fluid reconsideration of revolutionary principles in Wordsworth's political prose and a correspondent emphasis on tranquillity at the heart of his verse; and a virtuosic representation of tyranny, liberty, and necessity in Shelley's most ambitious poem. All of these figures—with the exception of Burke, whose exceptionality determines the contours of this work—responded positively to the challenge that so captivated the young Wordsworth: in the words of *The Prelude* that could function as an epigraph to this entire study, the project to "Build social freedom on its only basis, / The freedom of the individual mind." There are no doubt other figures relevant to this story, as discussed in the introduction: Paine, Thelwall, De Quincey, and Hazlitt, among others. The figures studied here are only nodes of a larger discursive network that, I am suggesting, took shape toward the end of the eighteenth century and the beginning of the nineteenth: a discourse of political epistemology that sought to bring together questions of freedom and questions of knowledge in the service of both—a mode of thought, speech, and writing, in other words, that sought to advance the project of enlightenment, which is the project of emancipation ("freedom from self-incurred tutelage" in Kant's famous formulation), after revolution.

Any subsequent elaboration of this book's line of argument would locate other relevant figures in the emerging field of political epistemology that I have attempted to sketch in the context of British Romanticism. It would also, I think, have to develop a more thorough account of what is here only a suggestion: that the a priori in the decades following the French Revolution was a political as well as epistemological problem. Independence from experience—and the possibility of knowledge that could properly be described as independent from experience—was a profoundly consequential issue not only for revolutionary philosophers such as Kant, but also, we have seen, for postrevolutionary poets such as Wordsworth, who associates the project of building social freedom with the ability of the rational subject to shake off "the accidents of nature, time, and place / That make up the weak being of the past" (presented as a forsaken wish in *The Prelude*, though never, I think, truly given up). Wordsworth's wish may be explained, as it typically has been, on biographical grounds—that is, in relation both to his formative preoccupation with Godwin and to his wish to run from certain elements of his past—but there is also an important philosophical issue at play here, which I have tried to bring to the surface. In the most direct terms, the passive empirical subject, forever closed off from knowledge that does not derive from experience, is doomed to a life of ignorance and servitude; the active rationalist or transcendental subject, for whom a priori knowledge is within reach, is offered the possibility of enlightenment and emancipation (the "Romantic subject," insofar as it exists at all, would fall under the latter category, though I have noted some important qualifications). This, at least, is the premise from which I have proceeded. Whether it serves as a satisfactory premise about the status of the a priori as a political concept at the end of the eighteenth century remains to be seen.

The kind of study I have attempted here represents one possible direction of philosophical criticism in Romanticism. "Philosophical criticism," which Coleridge himself claimed to have an inclination toward in his lectures on Shakespeare, has remained a vibrant part of Coleridge studies; its status in Romantic studies on the whole has, since the decline of theory, not always been so secure. After a period of preeminence that constitutes one of the great movements in the history of criticism, philosophical approaches to Romanticism have been eclipsed in recent decades by various kinds of historicism, for reasons too numerous and too varied to consider here and that have been studied at length elsewhere. As I see no reason why the history of ideas and the history of non-ideal things ought to exclude each other, there is perhaps no necessary conflict between philosophical and historicist approaches to literature. I have tried to suggest their compatibility and mutual dependence. Ideas, like everything else, have their own histories, their origins in material circumstances, institutional practices and norms, and individual human lives; they develop according to particular laws and logics, which we can observe. To see the drama of the history of ideas—to see, for instance, how our humanity seemed to stand or fall on the status of a priori knowledge or the association of ideas—is to see the history of ideas as the Romantics saw it, which is the first step in seeing Romanticism clearly.

There are, finally, a few things that should be said about the relationship between Romanticism as it is presented in this book and our own political circumstances. Each of the figures studied here provides us with a model of what political rhetoric can look like. This need not, it must be emphasized, translate into a nostalgic yearning for an impossibly enlightened past, in which politics was a purely rational enterprise consistently serving the interests of freedom: political discourse in the Romantic period was often as irrational, short-sighted, vindictive, or otherwise compromised as it has been before or since. We can freely admit that political rhetoric has always contained elements that were vicious, self-serving, or manipulative at the same time that we can lament its current state and wish it to be better. One would be hard pressed to find someone with Burke's rhetorical powers on the right—if, in fact, Burke would be recognized on the right as it presently exists at all—or someone with Wollstonecraft's rhetorical powers on the left. Again, none of this is to be mistaken with a mere call for grace or civility in political discourse. It is part of a stronger claim, allied to a reformation of thought, speech, and writing that the major Romantics saw as a precondition of human emancipation. The attention I have paid to a particular set of literary texts stems in large part from the belief that there exists an intimate connection between linguistic and political debasement: if one gets rid of certain bad habits in writing and speech, Orwell wrote in "Politics and the English Language," "one can think more clearly, and to think clearly is a necessary first step towards political regeneration." I have tried to show how a group of Romantic writers, each equipped with a command of language and an active imagination, sought to think in a new kind of way about the shared conditions of knowledge and freedom and, in doing so, created a literature in which philosophical and political concerns are closely linked. Attention to figures such as Burke, Wollstonecraft, Godwin, Coleridge, Wordsworth, and Shelley is important, then, because they provide us with models of thought and speech through and against which we may define our own; they articulate conceptions of truth and freedom that we have, in large measure, inherited. There are, in other words, discursive reasons for studying them.

There are also historical reasons for attending to them. Together, these figures constitute one of the earliest and most significant responses to the problem introduced at the very beginning of this study: the possibility of enlightenment after revolution and terror. It is instructive, I think, to refer back to their response as we make sense of present conditions. If the French Revolution is the defining event of political modernity, then we remain Romantics insofar as we attempt to realize the earliest and purest of revolutionary motives in the midst of violence, disorder, and irrationality and insofar as we see popular struggles around the globe as part of a larger advance of what the Romantics called the "spirit of liberty." In the West, the revolutionary decades of the 1960s and 1970s have been followed by decades in which the gulf between those with and without power has widened and in which existing political institutions seem increasingly incapable of addressing our most pressing problems. In much of the rest of the world, the conditions for a decent human existence remain largely elusive, and the logics of revolution and counter-revolution are lived, daily realities. So we remain in an era of revolution and reaction—the "end of history" predicted by some has not been realized—and we live, in some ways, in the midst of a new enlightenment. More people have access to more information than at any other point in human history, with technological advances making this access easier every day. There are repressive forces, to be sure, both from the state and from private concentrations of wealth, but the possibility of a new kind of popular enlightenment exists. Whether, as the major Romantic poets and philosophers had hoped, the project of enlightenment necessarily coincides with the project of emancipation remains an open question. Though we can learn, perhaps, from their sense that either one, fully conceived, is impossible without the other.

Introduction

1. The best work in literary history and the history of ideas resists these oversimplifications. The definitive treatment of the imagination in the eighteenth century and the Romantic period remains Engell, *The Creative Imagination*. The literature on Romantic and eighteenth-century faculty psychology is immense, though useful points of reference include Wellek, *Immanuel Kant in England*; Richards, *Coleridge on Imagination*; Bullitt and Bate, "Distinctions between Fancy and Imagination in Eighteenth-Century English Criticism"; Frye, *Fearful Symmetry*; Cassirer, *The Philosophy of the Enlightenment*; Abrams, *The Mirror and the Lamp*; McFarland, *Coleridge and the Pantheist Tradition*; and Perry, *Coleridge and the Uses of Division*.

2. Wordsworth, *The Thirteen-Book Prelude* (AB-Stage Reading Text), 13.170. Subsequent references to *The Prelude* refer to this text.

3. Kant, *Critique of Pure Reason*, 101. Subsequent references to Kant's first *Critique* (hereafter *CPR*) refer to the Cambridge edition, unless otherwise noted.

4. *CPR*, 101.

5. Wordsworth, *The Borderers* (early version), 30–33; and "Essay Prefaced to the Early Version," 65.

6. Berlin, *The Roots of Romanticism*, 1.

7. For more on Romantic periodization, see Lovejoy, "On the Discrimination of Romanticisms"; Wellek, "The Concept of Romanticism in Literary History"; and Ferguson, "On the Number of Romanticisms."

8. Godwin, *Considerations on Lord Grenville's and Mr. Pitt's Bills*, 2.

9. Wollstonecraft, *An Historical and Moral View of the Origin and Progress of the French Revolution*, 295.

10. Coleridge, *A Moral and Political Lecture, Delivered at Bristol*, 13.

11. Hume, "Of the Original Contract," 279.

12. "Epistemology," like "Romanticism," is a term that must be understood as a kind of shorthand here. As discussed in the Coleridge chapter, "epistemology" enters the English language near the middle of nineteenth century, in Ferrier's *Institutes of Metaphysic: The Theory of Knowing and Being* (1854). I use it in its original and broadest sense, denoting the theory or science of the method or grounds of knowledge. I do not, that is, use it in the strict sense of much twentieth- and twenty-first-century Anglo-American analytic philosophy. It refers here to a general theory of knowledge: a theory about the conditions under which it is possible, what categories it might be divided into, how these categories relate to each other,

who is in a position to attain it, what its social or political effects might be, and so forth. Whereas epistemology in the analytic tradition is largely concerned with what properties a proposition must have if it to be considered knowledge, the "epistemology" I retroactively attribute to the Romantics goes beyond the objective characteristics of the proposition to consider knowledge in relation to both the constitution of the subject (in the Romantic period, typically the division of the mind into various faculties) and the constitution of the state (the conditions of freedom and obligation in which the subject finds itself).

13. Hume, "That Politics May Be Reduced to a Science," 13–24.

14. *Dictionary of National Biography*, 2:349.

15. Bacon, *De Augmentis*, 9:298.

16. Locke, *Elements of Natural Philosophy, to Which Are Added Some Thoughts concerning Reading and Study for a Gentleman*, 52.

17. Eighteenth Century Collections Online, http://www.galegroup.com/ecco.

18. Fellow of the Royal Society, *A Short Specimen of a New Political Arithmetic; Containing, Some Considerations Concerning Public Roads*, 4.

19. Postlethwayt, *Great-Britain's True System*, xlviii.

20. Hume, *Essays and Treatises on Several Subjects*, vol. 3. Hume refers to Montesquieu.

21. Anon., *The Politician's Dictionary*.

22. Paley, *The Principles of Moral and Political Philosophy*, 119.

23. Temple, "To The North Briton,", 184.

24. Anon., *The Sequel to the Congress of the Beasts*, 4.

25. Priestley, *An Essay on a Course of Liberal Education for a Civil and Active Life*, 71.

26. Dempster, *Reasons for Extending the Militia Acts to the Disarmed Counties of Scotland*, 12.

27. Johnson, *The Idler*, 2:221.

28. Rev. Mr. Pattensen, *A Sermon, Preached in Halifax Church, on the Twenty-third of April, 1789*, 13.

29. Coxe, *Observations on the Agriculture, Manufactures and Commerce of the United States*, 4.

30. Williams, *Lectures on Education*, 2:138.

31. Beddoes, *Essay on the Public Merits of Mr. Pitt*, 11.

32. Edgeworth, *Practical Education*, 423.

33. Mathias, *The Shade of Alexander Pope*, 14.

34. Penn, *Further Thoughts on the Present State of Public Opinion*, 140–41.

35. Bancroft, *The Danger of Political Innovation and the Evils of Anarchy*, 11.

36. Hamilton, *The Federalist*, 1:192.

37. Wortman, *A Treatise, concerning Political Enquiry, and the Liberty of the Press*, 58.

38. Godwin, *An Enquiry concerning Political Justice, and Its Influence on Morals and Happiness*, 1:273.

39. Sinclair, *Specimens of Statistical Reports*, viii.

40. Ibid., viii n.

41. Shelley, *A Philosophical View of Reform* in *Shelley and His Circle*, 6:981.

42. Macaulay, *Rudiments of Political Science, Part the First*, iii.

43. Hume, "That Politics May Be Reduced to a Science," 15.

44. Valpy, *Two Assize Sermons*, 58.

45. Anon., *Modern Politics*, 14.

46. Society for Constitutional Information (London), *Society for Constitutional Information*, ii.

47. Society of the Friends of the People, *At a Meeting Held at the Three Turns Tavern*, 1.

48. Birmingham Society for Constitutional Information, *Birmingham Society for Constitutional Information*, 13.

49. Revolution Society, *The Correspondence of the Revolution Society in London*, 5.

50. York Society for Political Information, *An Address to the People of York, by the York Society for Political Information*, 3.

51. Price, *Observations on the Nature of Civil Liberty, and the Principles of Government*, 10.

52. London Corresponding Society, *The Correspondence of the London Corresponding Society, Revised and Corrected*, 58.

53. Paine, *Letter Addressed to the Addressers*, 20. The causes of this opposition, to the French Revolution itself and to revolutionary societies in Britain, are various. As R. K. Webb notes: "Mob violence in Paris reminded Englishmen of their own endemic unrest and of the Gordon Riots. When Louis XVI was executed, they were horrified, forgetting what had happened to Charles I a century and a half before; and highborn French refugees were in London, sedulously cultivating the makers of opinion and policy, and putting in the worst possible light events they could neither understand nor forgive" (*Modern England*, 135).

54. Duigenan, *A Speech Spoken in the House of Commons of Ireland on Monday February 4, 1793*, 56.

55. Anon., *Report of Committee of Secrecy of the House of Commons*, 28.

56. Parkinson, *Knave's-Acre Association*, 14.

57. Anon., *Comments on the Proposed War with France*, 67; Knox, *The Spirit of Despotism*, 39.

58. Anon., *The Proceedings in Cases of High Treason*, 56.

59. Ibid., 69.

60. London Corresponding Society, *The Moral and Political Magazine of the London Corresponding Society*, 29.

61. Thompson, "Disenchantment or Default? A Lay Sermon," 33–74; Mahoney, *Romantics and Renegades*.

62. Foucault, *The Essential Works of Foucault, 1954–1984*, vol. 3, 298.

63. Chomsky and Foucault, *The Chomsky-Foucault Debate*, 16.

64. I use the terms "intellectual history" and "history of ideas" more or less interchangeably, though they refer, of course, to distinct disciplines: intellectual history is a subset or outgrowth of the history of ideas, which, as formulated by figures like Arthur Lovejoy, emphasized an autonomy of ideas of the sort invoked by Mannheim in his notion of the "free-floating" intellectual. Intellectual history is typically a kind of corrective to this presumed independence, stressing the location of ideas in particular historical contexts.

65. Russell, *The History of Western Philosophy*, 678.

66. Ibid., 681.

67. Shelley, *A Philosophical View of Reform*, 974.

68. Berlin, *Political Ideas in the Romantic Age*, 31; ibid., 10.

69. Oakeshott's essay first appeared in *Cambridge Journal* 1 (1947). It was later published, along with other essays, as a book under the same name in 1962 (*Rationalism in Politics*, London: Methuen, 1962).

70. Oakeshott, *Rationalism in Politics and Other Essays* (Indianapolis: Liberty Fund, 1991), 6–7.

71. Ibid., 36.

72. Ibid., 6.

73. Just as those sympathetic to Burke inevitably point, as he did, to the Reign of Terror as a clear example of "political rationalism" in action, so does Timothy Fuller, Oakeshott's editor in the early 1990s, say, with little explanation, that "one can safely say that many Soviet, Eastern European, and Chinese citizens today know by hard experience what 'rationalism in politics' is all about." The possibility that arguments such as these never seem to consider is that the political conditions to which they ominously allude might have as little to do with "rationalism" properly defined as, say, the tyranny of Lenin had to do with socialism in theory or practice. One seeking to advance the project of the Enlightenment might just as easily say that the people Fuller has in mind had, regrettably, far too little experience of "rationalism in politics." The equation of political reason with coercion, injustice, and terror—among the most significant legacies of Burke—is an unjustifiably narrow view, one that ignores the affirmative critiques of political reason presented in this work.

74. Horkheimer, "Vernunft und Selbsterhaltung," in "Walter Benjamin zum Gedachtnis" (unpub., 1942), 43 (Friedrich Pollock collection, Montagnola). Cited in Jay, *The Dialectical Imagination*, 258 and 347n.

75. Horkheimer, *Eclipse of Reason*, 174.

76. Jay, *The Dialectical Imagination*, 279–80.

77. Debray, *Critique of Political Reason*, 37.

78. Ibid., 39.

79. Ibid.

80. Glaeser, *Political Epistemics*, xxv.

81. Ibid., xxvi.

82. Glaeser, it should be remarked, notes the roots of political epistemology in other eighteenth-century contexts, namely, in Herder and Vico: "The sociology of knowledge has never really made good of the full Vico-Herderian idea to explore the co-constitution between institutions and understandings" (*Political Epistemics*, xxviii).

83. P. Hamilton, *Metaromanticism*; Jarvis, *Wordsworth's Philosophic Song*; and Tim Milnes, *The Truth about Romanticism*.

84. *CPR*, 101.

85. Godwin, *An Enquiry concerning Political Justice*, 2:279.

Chapter 1 · Kant and the Revolutionary Settlement of Early Romanticism

1. It was during the Romantic period in Germany, in Wilhelm Tennemann's *History of Philosophy* (1798–1819), that Mirandola's reputation began to be revived as a proto-Kantian advocate of human freedom and dignity. Pomponazzi's reputation was revived throughout the seventeenth and eighteenth centuries, when radical thinkers showed new interest in his distinction between natural reason and faith and in his attempt to reconcile freedom with divine foreknowledge.

2. In this way, this study is part of an ongoing Kantian tradition (broadly conceived) within Romantic criticism, including the work of Christoph Bode, Monika Class, Frances Ferguson, Paul Hamilton, Simon Jarvis, Steven Knapp, Gian N. G. Orsini, Thomas Weiskel, and René Wellek, among many others. Ferguson has made particularly strong cases for

Kantian Romanticism in *Solitude and the Sublime* and "On the Number of Romanticisms," where she argues that "the romantic 'discovery' of nature that Kantian aesthetics epitomizes"—a discovery that is not empirical but formal and idealist—is central to the project of Romanticism in Britain. But whereas much of the interest in Kant over the past few decades has been in his aesthetics—and especially in how the *Critique of Judgment* provides a model for Romantic aesthetics at the same time that it informs or resists current critical paradigms—the emphasis of this work is on the epistemological and ethical dimensions of Kant's system in relation to Romanticism.

3. R. Williams, *Keywords*, 270–74.

4. *CPR*, 110.

5. *CPR*, 111.

6. *CPR*, 20.

7. Wordsworth, *Home at Grasmere* (MS. B), 1006–14.

8. Wordsworth, *The Thirteen-Book Prelude* (AB-Stage Reading Text), 13.18–19. All subsequent quotations from *The Prelude* in this chapter come from this text.

9. See, for instance, book 13 of *The Prelude*, in which Wordsworth continues the distinction between "higher" and "grosser" minds to describe the suitability of both to nature:

> The Power which these
> Acknowledge when thus moved, which Nature thus
> Thrusts forth upon the senses, is the express
> Resemblance, in the fullness of its strength
> Made visible, a genuine Counterpart
> And Brother of the glorious faculty
> Which higher minds bear with them as their own. (13.84–90)

10. The relevant passages are book 11 of *The Prelude* (75–95) and Prospero's speech in act 4 of *The Tempest* (4.1.146–63).

11. *CPR*, 110.

12. *CPR*, 101.

13. *CPR*, 109.

14. *CPR*, 485.

15. See Caygill, *A Kant Dictionary* (Malden: Blackwell, 1995), 75–78.

16. *CPR*, 219–20.

17. Stewart, ed., *A Documentary Survey of the French Revolution*, 114.

18. Ibid., 113.

19. Ibid., 32.

20. Ibid., 88, 91.

21. Ibid., 92.

22. Ibid., 49.

23. Ibid., 50.

24. Ibid., 51.

25. Ibid., 199.

26. Ibid., 430.

27. Translated in Rudé, *Robespierre*, 59.

28. O'Connor, *The Measures of Ministry to Prevent a Revolution Are the Certain Means of Bringing It On*, ii.

29. Old Member of Parliament, *A Looking-Glass for a Right Honourable Mendicant*, 49.

30. Blake, *The Complete Poetry and Prose of William Blake*, 617. On Blake and prophecy, see David Erdman, *Blake: Prophet against Empire* and Ian Balfour, *The Rhetoric of Romantic Prophecy*, 127–72.

31. Kant, "What Is Enlightenment?," in *Practical Philosophy*, 18.

32. Kant, *The Metaphysics of Morals*, in *Practical Philosophy*, 464n.

33. Kant, *Conflict of the Faculties*, in *Religion and Rational Theology*, 301.

34. Ibid., 302.

35. Ibid.

36. Kant, "What Is Enlightenment?," 18.

37. Kant, *Conflict of the Faculties*, 297.

38. Ibid., 297.

39. Ibid., 298.

40. Ibid., 300.

41. Thompson, "Disenchantment or Default? A Lay Sermon," 152.

42. Badiou, "The Courage of the Present."

43. Kant, *Conflict of the Faculties*, 301.

44. See Mary J. Gregor's commentary in Kant, *Practical Philosophy*, 276.

45. See, for instance, Boghossian and Peacocke, *New Essays on the a Priori*; and Shaffer and Veber, *What Place for the a Priori?*

46. Boghossian and Peacocke, *New Essays on the a Priori*, 8.

47. Russell, *Human Knowledge*, quoted in Chomsky, *Problems of Knowledge and Freedom*, 8.

48. Chomsky, *Problems of Knowledge and Freedom* 9–10.

49. Ibid., 10.

50. Ibid., 49.

51. Ibid., 49–50.

52. Coleridge, *Lectures 1808–1819: On Literature*, 1:494.

53. Schlegel, *Ueber dramatische Kunst und Literatur*, 2.2.8.

54. Coleridge, *Biographia Literaria* (hereafter *BL*), 2.15–16.

55. Wordsworth, *Poems, in Two Volumes*, 133.

56. Kant, *Groundwork of the Metaphysics of Morals*, 94.

57. *CPR*, 533.

58. Kant, *Critique of Pure Reason*, trans. Norman Kemp Smith, rev. 2nd ed. (New York: Palgrave Macmillan), 312.

59. Chomsky, *Problems of Knowledge and Freedom*, 50.

60. *BL*, 1:22.

61. *Collected Letters of Samuel Taylor Coleridge*, 3:360. The editors of the *Biographia* note that "to exemplify a psychological approach to criticism C could have picked many other writers, including Lord Kames, Joseph Priestley, Hugh Blair, Alexander Gerard, James Beattie, Daniel Webb, Lessing, Herder, or Schiller" (*BL*, 1:22n).

62. Russell, *Roads to Freedom*, 154.

63. Caygill, *Kant Dictionary*, 208.

64. Hegel, *Phenomenology of Spirit*, 360.

65. Ibid., 363.

66. Nietzsche, *Genealogy of Morals*, ed. and trans. Walter Kaufmann (New York: Random House, 1967), 65.

Chapter 2 · *Burke and the Critique of Political Metaphysics*

1. Coleridge, *Biographia Literaria*, 1:191–92.

2. Blake, *Complete Poetry and Prose of William Blake*, 617. Blake's often-invoked definition of prophecy comes from his annotations to Richard Watson's *An Apology for the Bible* (1797). It is the same Richard Watson, bishop of Llandaff, to whom Wordsworth addresses his first formal political statement (see chapter 6).

3. Coleridge, *The Friend*, 1:449.

4. Lord North's Regulating Act in 1773 provided the first in a series of loans designed to prevent bankruptcy.

5. See Burke, *On Empire, Liberty, and Reform*, ed. David Bromwich, 282. Bromwich's commentary is excellent throughout.

6. Burke, "Speech on Fox's East India Bill," 289.

7. Ibid., 289.

8. Ibid., 309–12 passim.

9. Ibid., 311–12.

10. Ibid., 312.

11. Burke, *A Philosophical Enquiry into the Origins of Our Ideas of the Sublime and Beautiful*, in *The Writings and Speeches of Edmund Burke*, ed. T. O. McLoughlin and James T. Boulton (Oxford: Clarendon Press, 1997), 1:233.

12. Ibid.

13. Burke, "Speech on Fox's East India Bill," 312.

14. According to Bromwich, under the treaty the wazir "agreed to pay an annual subsidy of seventy-four lakhs of rupees in exchange for the company's maintaining of two regiments in Oudh to uphold his rule. Even as the Wazir fell into arrears, Hastings required ever larger sums to pay for the company's wars with Mysore, the Marathas, and Chait Singh. The Wazir sent Hastings to the Begams of Oudh [the mother and grandmother of al-Daula] for the necessary money. . . . The company gathered many affidavits, with a slender body of evidence, to argue that the Begams were in rebellion." Hastings ordered the money be taken by force (*On Empire, Liberty, and Reform*, 312–20n).

15. Burke, "Speech on Fox's East India Bill," 313–15, passim.

16. Ibid., 315.

17. Campbell, *The Philosophy of Rhetoric*, 100.

18. Burke, "Speech on Fox's East India Bill," 319, 316, 332, 338.

19. Ibid., 345.

20. Burke, *Reflections on the Revolution in France*, in *The Writings and Speeches of Edmund Burke*, ed. L. G. Mitchell (Oxford: Clarendon Press, 1989), 3:111.

21. "Hence, in order that the social pact shall not be an empty formula, it is tacitly implied in that commitment—which alone can give force to all others—that whoever refuses to obey the general will shall be constrained to do so by the whole body, which means nothing other than that he shall be forced to be free." Rousseau, *The Social Contract*, 64.

22. Burke, *Reflections*, 111, original emphasis.

23. Auerbach, *Mimesis*, 70.

24. Hampsher-Monk, *The Impact of the French Revolution*, 59.

25. Ibid.

26. Price, *A Discourse on the Love of Our Country*, 53.

27. Ibid., 41–45.

28. Hampsher-Monk, *The Impact of the French Revolution*, 58.

29. Burke, *Reflections*, 112.

30. Ibid., 111.

31. Ibid., 111–12.

32. Ibid., 112.

33. Hume, "That Politics May Be Reduced to a Science," 15.

34. Burke, *Reflections*, 112.

35. The professed alliance of modern conservatism with the recognition of complexity remains one of Burke's most enduring legacies. David Brooks, then, can say in 2009 that "Obama sees himself as a Burkean" insofar as "he sees his view of the world as a view that understands complexity and the organic nature of change." As Brooks's essay reveals, the idea of Burke, as opposed to the actual content of his political thought, has come to signify, in some contexts, thoughtful moderation itself. As he says of the administration, "David Axelrod walks into a meeting with me, carrying the *Reflections On The Revolution In France* by Edmund Burke. They're not without manipulation" (*New Republic*, August 2009).

36. Burke, *Reflections*, 102, 110, 111, 142.

37. Ibid., 127.

38. Ibid.

39. Ibid., 137.

40. Ibid., 138.

41. Marx, "For a Ruthless Criticism of Everything Existing," 14.

42. Marx, *Capital*, 1:925–26n.

43. For an excellent discussion of the controversy surrounding Burke's pension, see Blakemore, "Paine and the Myth of Burke's Secret Pension," in *Intertextual War*, 84–96.

44. Paine, *The Rights of Man*, 51.

45. Boswell, *Life of Johnson*, 696.

Chapter 3 · *Wollstonecraft and the Vindication of Political Reason*

1. Bromwich, "Wollstonecraft as a Critic of Burke," 617–18.

2. Fennessy, *Burke, Paine, and the Rights of Man*, 68. Conniff, "Edmund Burke and His Critics," 311.

3. See Tomaselli's introduction to Wollstonecraft, *"A Vindication of the Rights of Men" and "A Vindication of the Rights of Woman,"* xvi.

4. Wollstonecraft, "Thoughts on the Education of Daughters," 4:7.

5. Wollstonecraft, *A Vindication of the Rights of Men* (hereafter *Rights of Men*), 6.

6. Ibid., 7.

7. Ibid., 23–24.

8. Ibid., 9.

9. Ibid., 12.

10. Ibid., 26.

11. Ibid., 27 ("Where then was the infallibility"), 34 ("I reverence the rights of men").

12. Ibid., 30.

13. Ibid., 15 and 41.

14. Ibid., 64.

15. Ibid., 59.

16. Skolnik, "Wollstonecraft's Dislocation of the Masculine Sublime: A Vindication." Skolnik cites the following studies as examples of the tendency to disparage Wollstonecraft's prose style: Janet Todd, *Mary Wollstonecraft: A Revolutionary Life*, 168, 184, 186; Mary Poovey, *The Proper Lady and the Woman Writer*, 80, 81; and Blakemore, *Intertextual War*, 60.

17. Walpole, *Correspondence*, letter to Hannah Moore, January 24, 1795; Godwin, *Memoirs*, 94; Burke, *Correspondence*, 6:214.

18. Allen, "The Uses and Problems of 'Manly' Rhetoric."

19. *Rights of Men*, 27

20. Ibid., 7–8.

21. Coleridge, *The Friend*, 1:449.

22. *Rights of Men*, 5.

23. Ibid., 25.

24. Ibid., 29.

25. Ibid.

26. Ibid.

27. Ibid., 28.

28. Ibid.

29. Ibid., 63.

30. Orwell, "Politics and the English Language," 955.

31. *Rights of Men*, 9.

32. See Skolnik, "Wollstonecraft's Dislocation of the Masculine Sublime"; and Allen, "The Uses and Problems of 'Manly' Rhetoric."

33. *Rights of Men*, 6. See Conniff, "Edmund Burke and His Critics." Conniff argues that, in contrast to Burke, Wollstonecraft "rejected any suggestion that reason could not control and direct the passions" (311).

34. *Rights of Men*, 6.

35. Ibid., 8.

36. Burke was not, in fact, an ancient constitutionalist, as his fragmentary *History of England* shows, though he frequently refers reverentially to the wisdom of English "antiquity" in general terms, e.g., ". . . our old settled maxim, never entirely or at once to depart from antiquity" (*Reflections*, 150).

37. *Rights of Men*, 62.

38. Burke, *Enquiry*, 275–76.

39. Ibid., 270.

40. *Rights of Men*, 25.

41. Ibid., 47–48.

42. Burke, *Enquiry*, 238.

43. *Rights of Men*, 21.

44. Ibid., 20.

Chapter 4 · *The Government of the Tongue*

1. Godwin, *Political Justice*, 1:250. All quotations from *Political Justice* in this chapter come from the third edition of 1798 (reproduced in Priestley's 1946 photographic facsimile), as this was the last version Godwin saw through the press.

2. Ibid., 2:271.

3. Hume, "Of the First Principles of Government," 32.

4. Godwin, *Political Justice*, 1:252.

5. Ibid., 2:549.

6. Ibid., 1:25.

7. Ibid., 1:26.

8. Ibid., 1:4.

9. Ibid., 1:xxvi.

10. Ibid.

11. Ibid., 2:341.

12. Ibid., 2:358 and 473.

13. Ibid., 1:55.

14. Ibid., 1:177 and 2:94.

15. Ibid., 1:73.

16. Ibid., 1:74.

17. Ibid., 2:132–33.

18. Burke, *Reflections on the Revolution in France*, 138.

19. Godwin, *Political Justice*, 1:306.

20. Ibid., 1:94.

21. Ibid., 1:174.

22. Ibid., 1:273.

23. Ibid.

24. Ibid., 1:256.

25. Ibid., 2:227.

26. Ibid., 1:66.

27. Ibid., 1:298.

28. Ibid., 2:486–87.

29. Ibid., 1:275.

30. Ibid., 1:276.

31. Ibid.

32. Ibid., 2:315.

33. Ibid., 2:447.

34. Ibid., 2:55.

35. Ibid., 1:278.

36. Ibid., 1:114n.

37. Ibid.

38. Burke, *A Philosophical Enquiry into the Origin of Our Ideas of the Sublime and Beautiful*, 1:310.

39. Ibid., 311.

40. Ibid., 312–13.

41. Godwin, *Political Justice*, 1:115.

42. Ibid.

43. Ibid., 1:119.

44. Ibid., 1:24–25n, 80–81, 258.

45. Ibid., 2:80.

46. Ibid., 1:195.

47. Ibid.

48. Ibid., 1:294.

49. Ibid., 2:275.

50. Ibid., 1:294.

51. Ibid., 1:291.

52. Ibid., 1:292.

53. Ibid., 2:204.

54. Ibid., 2:201.

55. Ibid., 2:205.

56. Ibid., 2:245.

57. Ibid., 2:260.

58. Ibid., 2:266.

59. Ibid., 2:267.

60. Ibid., 1:363.

61. Ibid., 1:385.

62. Ibid.

63. Ibid., 2:278.

64. Ibid., 2:276.

65. Ibid., 2:278.

66. Ibid., 2:279–80.

67. *The Diary of William Godwin*, ed. Victoria Meyers, David O'Shaughnessy, and Mark Philp (Oxford: Oxford Digital Library, 2010), August 20, 1795, http://godwindiary .boldeian.ox.ac.uk.

68. Allestree, *The Government of the Tongue*, 3–4.

69. Kramnick, introduction to Godwin, *Political Justice*, 26.

70. Godwin, *Cursory Strictures*, 67. All quotations in this chapter from *Cursory Strictures* and from Eyre's "Charge" come from *The Political and Philosophical Writings of William Godwin*, ed. Philp, vol. 2.

71. Ibid., 72–73.

72. Ibid., 87.

73. Ibid., 70.

74. Godwin, *Considerations on Lord Grenville's and Mr. Pitt's Bills, concerning Treasonable and Seditious Practices, and Unlawful Assemblies*, 4–5.

75. Godwin, *Cursory Strictures*, 80.

76. Ibid., 85.

77. Ibid.

78. Ibid., 86.

79. Ibid.

80. Ibid., 88.

81. Ibid.

82. Hume, *History of England*, vol. 6, quoted in Godwin, *Cursory Strictures*, 90.

83. Godwin, *Cursory Strictures*, 90 (Godwin's emphasis).

84. Ibid., 91.

85. Ibid.

86. Ibid., 92.

87. Ibid., 92–96.

88. Ibid., 96 and 98.

89. Ibid., 98.

90. Godwin, *Political Justice*, 2:538.

91. Ibid., 2:281.

92. Ibid., 2:230.

93. Ibid., 1:290.

Chapter 5 · Coleridge and the Principles of Political Knowledge

1.   This is not to say that the focus in Romanticism on the dialectic between reason and imagination is not without its own justification. I have already noted Wordsworth's claim in the Mt. Snowdon episode of *The Prelude* that the imagination is "reason in her most exalted mood" (13.170). Of the many instances in Coleridge's philosophical development, one might note his fascination with Lessing during his 1798 stay in Germany, when it was precisely the "mingling and *interpenetration* of reason and imagination" that attracted him to the German writer. The understanding may fit uneasily into the conflict of the mental faculties as it has been traditionally understood, but this incongruity is among the most interesting and distinctive aspects of Coleridge's political thought.

2.   Coleridge, *The Friend*, in *The Collected Works of Samuel Taylor Coleridge*, vol. 1:176. Unless noted otherwise, all quotations from *The Friend* (hereafter *F*) come from the 1818 version (vol. 1 of *The Friend* in the *Collected Works*), as this was the last edition Coleridge saw through the press.

3.   *Oxford Dictionary of English Etymology*, ed. C. T. Onions (Oxford: Clarendon Press, 1966).

4.   *F*, 2:13.

5.   *F*, 16.

6.   *F*, 19.

7.   *F*, 21.

8.   *F*, 157.

9.   *F*, 462.

10.   *F*, 97.

11.   *F*, 166.

12.   *F*, 446.

13.   *F*, 487.

14.   *F*, 513.

15.   *F*, 112.

16.   Kant, *Critique of Practical Reason* (hereafter *CPrR*), 153. See also Kant's discussion of "principles" in the *Critique of Pure Reason*, 387–88.

17.   *CPrR*, 153.

18.   *CPrR*, 153.

19.   This "Kantian/Coleridgean" version of Romanticism is hardly the result of a generation of philosophically minded critics. It extends to some of Coleridge's earliest critics, such as J. S. Mill: "Now the Germano-Coleridgean doctrine is, in our view of the matter, the result of such a reaction. It expresses the revolt of the human mind against the philosophy of the eighteenth century. It is ontological, because that was experimental; conservative, because that was innovative; religious, because so much of that was infidel; concrete and historical, because that was abstract and metaphysical; poetical, because that was matter-of-fact and prosaic. In every respect it flies off in the contrary direction to its predecessor" (Mill, "Coleridge," in *Complete Works of John Stuart Mill*, 10:125).

20. Cavell, *In Quest of the Ordinary*, 41.

21. Craig, "Coleridge, Hume, and the Chains of the Romantic Imagination," 32.

22. Perry, "Enlightened Romantics," 7–8.

23. Coleridge, *Collected Letters of Samuel Taylor Coleridge* (hereafter *CL*), 2:928.

24. Coleridge, *Biographia Literaria* (hereafter *BL*), 1:291.

25. Coleridge, *The Statesman's Manual* (hereafter *SM*), 22.

26. Hume, *Dialogues concerning Natural Religion* (1779), pt. 7. Philo, the hard-lined skeptic, relates to Cleanthes, the more cautious skeptic, the Brahmin theory that the "world arose from an infinite spider, who spun this whole complicated mass from his bowels, and annihilates afterwards the whole or any part of it, by absorbing it again, and resolving it into his own essence." The argument that a possible world exists wholly inhabited by these spiders prompts Philo to assert, "Why an orderly system may not be spun from the belly as well as from the brain, it will be difficult for [Cleanthes] to give a satisfactory reason" (56). The argument did not convince Cleanthes, nor did it convince Coleridge.

27. *BL*, 1:121.

28. *SM*, 32.

29. Hume, *A Treatise of Human Nature* (hereafter *THN*), 112.

30. Coleridge, *The Notebooks of Samuel Taylor Coleridge* (hereafter *CN*), 2:2370.

31. *BL*, 1:140–41.

32. *BL*, 1:141–42.

33. *BL*, 1:141–42n.

34. *BL*, 1:142–43.

35. See the discussion of necessity in *SM*: "Suffer me to inform or remind you, that there is a threefold Necessity. There is a logical, and there is a mathematical, necessity; but the latter is always hypothetical, and both subsist *formally* only, not in any real object. Only by the intuition and immediate spiritual consciousness of the idea of God, as the One and Absolute, at once the Ground and the Cause, who alone containeth in himself the ground of his own nature, and therein of *all* natures, do we arrive at the third, which alone is a real *objective, necessity*. Here the immediate consciousness decides: *the idea is its own evidence*, and is insusceptible of all other" (32, final emphasis mine).

36. *SM*, 114.

37. Hume, *THN*, 7n. For Locke, ideas are those things furnished to the understanding through either sensation or reflection (*Essay concerning Human Understanding*, 1.2.3–4). Knowledge is "nothing but the perception of the connexion and agreement, or disagreement and repugnancy of any of our Ideas" (*EHU*, 4.1.2).

38. *SM*, 113–14.

39. R. J. White, *SM*, 114n.

40. The *OED* cites Coleridge as the first to use "educt" in this way (*Oxford English Dictionary*, 2nd ed. 1989; *OED Online*, April 2000).

41. I use this phrase, used by Kant in *The Critique of Judgment* to signify the feeling of aesthetic pleasure, in the more general sense of an "interaction" among the various faculties. It is significant, though, that the language used by Kant to describe aesthetic pleasure may apply equally well to the formation of the Coleridgean idea. In both cases, there is a reaction against the perceived rigidity of dogmatic rationalism or empiricism and a willingness to recognize the reality of certain mental events that would ordinarily be subordinated to propositional or discursive reasoning.

42. In the now classic definition from *SM*: the symbol "always partakes of the Reality which it renders intelligible; and while it enunciates the whole, abides itself as a living part in that Unity, of which it is the representative" (30).

43. *BL*, 1:96.

44. *BL*, 1:96–97.

45. *BL*, 1:97.

46. *SM*, 23–24. As R. J. White notes in his edition of the *Lay Sermons*, the idea is untraced in Bacon.

47. *SM*, 101.

48. *SM*, 102.

49. See John Guillory's widely influential analysis in *Cultural Capital*, 85–133.

50. *CN*, 2:2193.

51. *CN*, 2:2598.

52. Coleridge, *Marginalia*, 4:75.

53. Ibid., 1:74–75.

54. Coleridge, *Collected Letters*, 4:667. The phrasing here is reminiscent of Coleridge's claim, derived from Schelling, in the *Biographia* that "[m]atter has no *Inward*" (1:133). The language of surface and depth, appearance and reality, to describe both the Scottish and matter is suggestive: it was Hume, after all, who banished the ideas of substance, self, and essence from philosophy altogether. Scots like Hume, then, appear to be all surface and no depth, acutely aware of their own ideas but resolutely determined not to inquire into their origin.

55. Dyce, *Reminiscences*, 178.

56. Coleridge, *Lectures 1818–1819: On the History of Philosophy* (hereafter *LHP*), 1:258–59.

57. *LHP*, 1:260.

58. Knud Haakonssen, "The Structure of Hume's Political Theory," 182.

59. Hume, "That Politics May Be Reduced to a Science," in *Political Essays* (hereafter *PE*), 13.

60. "Of the Original Contract," in *PE*, 46.

61. Ibid., 48.

62. Hume, *Enquiry concerning the Principles of Morals* (hereafter *EPM*), in *Enquiries concerning Human Understanding and concerning the Principles of Morals*, 196.

63. "Of the Original Contract," 50.

64. *EPM*, 197n.

65. Hume would revise his position in "Of the Origin of Government" (1777), where he contends, much as he does in "Of the Original Contract," that authority is established first by force, then gradually by a mixture of force and consent, and maintained by habits of submission.

66. *EPM*, 196–97.

67. *THN*, 319.

68. *CN*, 2:2074.

69. *CL*, 2:1036.

70. *F*, 2:13.

71. Spinoza, *Tractatus Theologico-Politicus* in vol. 4 of *The Chief Works of Benedict de Spinoza*, 1.1.1–6.

72. *F*, xcviii–xcix.

73. See, for example, Milnes, *The Truth about Romanticism*, 145–89.

74. *F*, 166.

75. See Morrow, *Coleridge's Political Thought*, 79.

76. *F*, 167.

77. *F*, 159.

78. *F*, 171.

79. *F*, 174.

80. *BL*, 1:304.

81. *F*, 176.

82. Coleridge, letter to Rev. Joseph Hughes, November 24, 1819, in *Collected Letters*, 4:1049 (app. B).

83. *F*, 177n.

84. Kant, *Prolegomena to Any Future Metaphysics*, 291.

85. Ibid., 304.

86. Kant, *Critique of Pure Reason* (hereafter *CPR*), 242–43.

87. *CPR*, 387.

88. *CPR*, 389.

89. *F*, 156–57.

90. *F*, 177n.

91. *F*, 156.

92. *F*, 156; *Hamlet*, 1,2. 50.

93. *CPR*, 387.

94. *F*, 154–61. It should be noted that Kant, in the Analytic of Principles, suggests something similar to Coleridge's subordination of the understanding to reason: the "Understanding-in-General" (*Verstandes überhaupt*) consists of the understanding (*Verstand*), the power of judgment (*Urteilskraft*), and reason (*Vernunft*). Kant's "Understanding-in-General" does not, however, perform the intuitive acts of apprehension and identification that Coleridge assigns to the "discourse of reason," or the understanding enlightened by reason.

95. *F*, 157.

96. *F*, 178.

97. *F*, 192.

98. *F*, 193.

99. Morrow, *Coleridge's Political Thought*, 88–99.

100. *F*, 200, emphasis added.

101. Coleridge, letter to George Coleridge, March 10, 1798, in *Collected Letters*, 1:238.

102. *F*, 199, emphasis added.

103. *F*, 196.

104. *F*, 194.

105. *F*, 195.

106. Constitution of 1791 in Stewart, ed., *A Documentary Survey of the French Revolution*, 234.

107. *F*, 194.

108. Lockridge, review of Coleridge's *Opus Maximum*, 133.

109. *F*, 103.

110. *F*, 166–68 passim; following quotation, from section on "Virtue and Knowledge," *F*, 100–101.

111. Lockridge, *Coleridge the Moralist*, 268.

112. *F*, 194–95.

113. In upholding this distinction, Coleridge most clearly diverges from the kind of pragmatist ethics suggested by his repeated endorsement of a prudential politics of expediency.

114. Morrow, *Coleridge's Political Thought*, 79.

115. *F*, 173–74.

116. *THN*, 105–18.

117. *LHP*, 2:572.

118. *THN*, 11, 16, 27.

119. *LHP*, 2:572–73.

120. *LHP*, 1:332–33.

121. Craig, "Coleridge, Hume, and the Chains of the Romantic Imagination," 32.

122. *LHP*, 1:332.

123. Carlyle, *The Life of John Sterling*, 56.

124. Hazlitt, "My First Acquaintance with Poets," 17:113.

Chapter 6 · The State of Knowledge

1. Wordsworth, Advertisement (1798) to the *Lyrical Ballads*, in *Prose Works of William Wordsworth*, 1:116.

2. Wordsworth, Preface (1802) to the *Lyrical Ballads* (as presented in the variants to the 1850 version), in *Prose Works of William Wordsworth*, 1:139. All quotations from the Preface are from this edition.

3. Preface, 122.

4. Preface, 128.

5. Preface, 128.

6. Wordsworth, *The Convention of Cintra*, in *Prose Works of William Wordsworth*, 1:305. All quotations from *Cintra* are from this edition.

7. Preface, 126.

8. Godwin, *Political Justice*, 1:281.

9. Ibid.

10. *Prose Works of William Wordsworth*, 1:50.

11. Wordsworth, *Letter to the Bishop of Llandaff*, in *Prose Works of William Wordsworth*, 1:32. All quotations from *Llandaff* are from this edition.

12. Chandler, *Wordsworth's Second Nature*, 23.

13. *Llandaff*, 33.

14. *Llandaff*, 33.

15. *Llandaff*, 34.

16. *Llandaff*, 48.

17. *Llandaff*, 48.

18. *Llandaff*, 36.

19. See Gill, *William Wordsworth*, 71–73.

20. *Llandaff*, 44–45.

21. Liu, *Wordsworth: The Sense of History*, 184.

22. Wordsworth, letter to William Mathews, February 17, 1794, in *Letters of William and Dorothy Wordsworth (The Early Years: 1787–1805)*, 113.

23. *Cintra*, 293.

24. See Chandler, *Wordsworth's Second Nature*, 42–44; Cobban, *Edmund Burke and the Revolt against the Eighteenth-Century*, 140–52; and Gill, *William Wordsworth*, 274–77.

25. Thomas, *Wordsworth's Dirge and Promise*, 59–84, 151–65.

26. Baugh, *A Literary History of England*, vol. 4; Chew, *The Nineteenth Century and After*, 145.

27. *Cintra*, 298.

28. *Cintra*, 318.

29. *Cintra*, 232–34 passim.

30. *Cintra*, 343.

31. *Cintra*, 331. There is a tension in Wordsworth's recognition of the Spanish and Portuguese people as "rational creatures," worthy to be treated as ends themselves, and his view of the conflict as a mere signifier in a broader historical drama.

32. *Cintra*, 261–62 passim.

33. *Cintra*, 331.

34. *Cintra*, 237.

35. *Cintra*, 248 passim.

36. *Cintra*, 258.

37. *Cintra*, 302–3.

38. *Cintra*, 304 passim.

39. *Cintra*, 304–7 passim.

40. *Cintra*, 304–5.

41. Preface, 138.

42. *Cintra*, 306–8.

43. *Cintra*, 323–24.

44. *Cintra*, 324–25.

45. Shelley makes exactly the same point in *A Philosophical View of Reform* and *A Defence of Poetry*, as noted in chapter 8.

46. *Cintra*, 324–25n.

47. Shelley, for whom the moral and the imaginative are virtually synonymous, takes a more optimistic view in the notes to *Queen Mab*: "there is no great extravagance in presuming . . . that there should be a perfect identity between the moral and physical improvement of the human species," *Complete Works of Shelley*, 1:143.

48. Bacon, *The Instauratio Magna, Part II: Novum Organon and Associated Texts*, 65.

49. Beattie, *An Essay on the Nature and Immutability of Truth, in Opposition to Sophistry and Scepticism*, 4.

50. Wordsworth, *Two Addresses to the Freeholders of Westmorland*, in *The Prose Works of William Wordsworth*, 3:165. All quotations from *Two Addresses* are from this edition.

51. Wordsworth, letter to Lord Lonsdale, January 18, 1818, in *Letters of William and Dorothy Wordsworth (The Middle Years)*, part 2 (1812–1820), 411.

52. Wordsworth's relationship with the Lonsdales has been examined in detail by his biographers. See Gill, *William Wordsworth*, 34–35, 51, 260–61, 274–76, 301–2, 328–31; and Moorman, *William Wordsworth, a Biography*, vol. 2, *The Later Years, 1803–1850*, 60–63, 242–44, 344ff.

53. Gill, *William Wordsworth*, 35.

54. Wordsworth, letter to Lord Lonsdale, March 14, 1818, in *Letters of William and Dorothy Wordsworth (The Middle Years)*, part 2 (1812–1820), 439.

55. Wordsworth, letter to Lord Lonsdale, February 10, 1818, in *Letters of William and Dorothy Wordsworth (The Middle Years)*, part 2 (1812–1820), 425.

56. Wordsworth, letter to Lord Lonsdale, February 13, 1818, in *Letters of William and Dorothy Wordsworth (The Middle Years)*, part 2 (1812–1820), 427.

57. *Two Addresses*, 3:166.

58. *Two Addresses*, 3:165.

59. Ibid.

60. *Two Addresses*, 3:176.

61. *Two Addresses*, 3:181.

62. *Two Addresses*, 3:185.

63. See Moorman, *William Wordsworth, a Biography*, vol. 1, *The Early Years, 1770–1803*, 408.

64. Wordsworth, letter to Sir George Beaumont, October 17, 1805, in *Letters of William and Dorothy Wordsworth (The Early Years: 1787–1805)*, 623–27 passim.

Chapter 7 · The Dwellers of the Dwelling

1. Wordsworth, letter to Walter Savage Landor, April 20, 1822, in *Letters of William and Dorothy Wordsworth (The Later Years: 1821–1828)*, 125.

2. See Graver, "Wordsworth's Translations from Latin Poetry," 21–28, and Wu, *Wordsworth: The Earliest Poems, 1785–1790*, 87.

3. Kelley, "Wordsworth and Lucretius' *De Rerum Natura*," 219–22.

4. Priestman, "Lucretius in Romantic and Victorian Britain." For more on Lucretian echoes in Wordsworth, see Spiegelman, "Some Lucretian Elements in Wordsworth," 27–49.

5. Wordsworth, Preface to *Lyrical Ballads*, 1:139.

6. Preface, 140.

7. See Owen and Smyser's commentary in *The Prose Works of William Wordsworth*, 1:170.

8. Dennis, *The Advancement and Reformation of Modern Poetry*, 1:217.

9. Cited in Owen and Smyser, *The Prose Works of William Wordsworth*, 1:171; and in Edward Hooker's introduction to *The Critical Works of John Dennis*, 2:lxxiii. Hooker notes that this passage comes from an unpublished letter from De Quincey to Alexander Blackwood, dated August 30, 1842.

10. Henri Patin, "L'Anti-Lucrèce chez Lucrèce."

11. Preface, 119–59 passim.

12. Ibid., 157.

13. Wordsworth, letter to James Tobin, March 6, 1798, cited in Beth Darlington's introduction to *Home at Grasmere*, 3.

14. Plato, *Philebus*, 398–457.

15. Aristotle, *Nicomachean Ethics*, 7.12.

16. Locke, *Essay concerning Human Understanding*, 2.7.

17. See Porter and Roberts, eds., *Pleasure in the Eighteenth Century*; and Boyson, *Wordsworth and the Enlightenment Idea of Pleasure*.

18. Bushell et al., eds., *The Excursion*, 9.

19. S. T. Coleridge, letter to Wordsworth, May 30, 1815, in *Collected Letters of Samuel Taylor Coleridge*, 4:574.

20. Johnston, *Wordsworth and "The Recluse"*; and Jonathan Wordsworth, *Wordsworth and the Borders of Vision*.

21. Johnston, *Wordsworth and "The Recluse,"* xiii–xiv.

22. Johnston argues that "it was not until the publication of *The Excursion* in 1814 that Wordsworth publicly affirmed the anthropological value of his imagination's location, prin-

cipally by a dialectical examination of its easily misunderstood appearance of escapism, dramatized in the character of the Solitary" (*Wordsworth and "The Recluse,"* 268).

23. Wordsworth, *Home at Grasmere* (MS. B), ed. Darlington. All subsequent quotations from *Home at Grasmere* come from this edition.

24. For one account of the "substantialist" view of the environment in the Romantic period, see Morton, *Ecology without Nature*; and his chapter, "Nature and Culture" in *The Cambridge Companion to Shelley*. "Substantialism," with which Morton associates Burke, asserts that nature is a "squishy thing in itself" and tends to promote a monarchist or authoritarian view, in which there is an external thing to which the subject should bow; by contrast, "essentialism," with which Morton associates Kant and Shelley, asserts an abstract principle that transcends the material realm and is allied with revolutionary republicanism.

25. Aquinas, *Summa Theologiae*, 2.2.182.3.

26. See Striker, *Essays on Hellenistic Epistemology and Ethics*.

27. Seneca, translated and quoted by Striker in *Essays on Hellenistic Epistemology and Ethics*, 186.

28. Wordsworth, it should be noted, grants less importance to the will than do contemporaries such as Coleridge and Blake. As Lockridge argues, Wordsworth "gives the affective life greater prominence as both norm and fact, and hesitates to treat the conative life as its equal" (*Ethics of Romanticism*, 206).

29. Bromwich, *Disowned by Memory*; Roe, "Politics, History, and Wordsworth's Poems"; and Johnston, *The Hidden Wordsworth*.

30. According to Kant's *Critique of Judgment*, in the case of the mathematically sublime, this displeasure comes from an awareness of the inadequacy of our imagination. In the case of the dynamical sublime, it comes from an awareness of our physical powerlessness in the face of nature's might.

31. Johnson, *Rasselas*, 78.

32. Gill, *William Wordsworth*, 35.

33. Coleridge, letter to Wordsworth, September 10, 1799, in *Collected Letters of Samuel Taylor Coleridge*, 1:527.

34. Wordsworth, *The Excursion*, ed. Bushell, et al. All quotations from *The Excursion* come from this edition.

35. Hobbes, *Leviathan*, 37.

36. Berlin, *Political Ideas in the Romantic Age*, 168.

37. Arendt, *The Human Condition*, 113.

38. Heidegger, "Building, Dwelling, Thinking," in *Basic Writings*, 350–51.

39. Ibid., 350.

40. Heidegger, "Letter on Humanism," in *Basic Writings*, 217–65 passim.

41. *Oxford Dictionary of Etymology*, ed. C. T. Onions (Oxford: Clarendon Press, 1996).

Chapter 8 · P. B. Shelley and the Forms of Thought

1. Shelley, "On Life," in *The Complete Works of Percy Bysshe Shelley*, 6:195. All subsequent quotations from "On Life" come from this edition.

2. Wasserman, *Shelley*, ix; Pulos, *The Deep Truth*; and Notopoulos, *The Platonism of Shelley*.

3. See, for example, Curran, *Shelley's Annus Mirabilis*; Hall, *The Transforming Image*; and Rajan, *Dark Interpreter*.

4. See, respectively, Hoagwood, *Prophecy and the Philosophy of Mind*; Leighton, *Shelley and the Sublime*; and Clark, *Embodying Revolution*.

5. For a theoretically sophisticated treatment of the subject, see Rajan, *Dark Interpreter*.

6. For a useful overview of Shelley's philosophy—in its materialist, idealist, dualist, and skeptical dimensions—see Cameron, *Shelley: The Golden Years*, 150–63. On Shelley and pragmatism, see Milnes, *The Truth about Romanticism*, 105–45. On Shelley and materialism, see Ruston, *Shelley and Vitality*; and P. Hamilton, *Percy Bysshe Shelley*. Hamilton's essay on "Literature and Philosophy," in *The Cambridge Companion to Shelley*, 166–84, is also illuminating in the way it counters the idealist reading. Shelley and skeptical idealism have been addressed in previous notes, but for more on Shelley and skepticism, see Reiman, *Intervals of Inspiration*; Lockridge, *The Ethics of Romanticism*, 284–96; and Harding, *The Reception of Myth in English Romanticism*. For more on Shelley and idealism (philosophical and political), see McNiece, *Shelley and the Revolutionary Idea*; Robinson, *Shelley and Byron*; and Engell, *The Creative Imagination*, 256–64.

7. Natarajan, ed., *The Romantic Poets*, 243.

8. Shelley, "On Life," 194.

9. Ibid.

10. Holbach, *Système de la nature*, 1:7.

11. Plato, *Theaetetus*, 39–41.

12. Pulos, *The Deep Truth*, 105–12.

13. Shelley, *The Letters of Percy Bysshe Shelley*, 1:316.

14. Southey, letter to Rickman, January 6, 1812, in *The Collected Letters of Robert Southey: Part Four, 1810–1815*.

15. Shelley, letter to Godwin, January 16, 1812, in *The Complete Works of Percy Bysshe Shelley*, 8:244.

16. Shelley, "On Life," 196.

17. Cameron, *Shelley: The Golden Years*, 154.

18. Shelley, *A Refutation of Deism*, in *The Complete Works of Percy Bysshe Shelley*, 6:48–56.

19. Shelley, "Speculations on Metaphysics," in *The Complete Works of Percy Bysshe Shelley*, 7:60.

20. See Cameron, *Shelley: The Golden Years*, 150–88.

21. It is true that Hume ultimately refers in the *Treatise* to his philosophy as a "mitigated skepticism," an attitude of cautious moderation that knows when to set skepticism aside and act on the basis of ordinary, everyday belief. This, though, is essentially an ethical recommendation about *when not to practice philosophy*, a statement made when he has concluded the innovative part of his work. What makes Hume unique and interesting *as a philosopher* is his epistemology, which carries the empiricism of Locke and Berkeley to its skeptical conclusion.

22. Kant, *Prolegomena to Any Future Metaphysics*, 288–89, 293, 336–37, 373–75; *Critique of Pure Reason* (hereafter *CPR*), 326.

23. *CPR*, 224.

24. Cameron, *Shelley: The Golden Years*, 149.

25. Shelley, *Letters*, 2:760.

26. Shelley, *A Philosophical View of Reform*, in *Shelley and His Circle*, 6:963. All subsequent quotations from *Philosophical View* come from this edition and volume.

27. Ibid.

28. Ibid., 965.

29. Ibid., 967.

30. Ibid., 992.

31. Ibid., 967.

32. Ibid., 968.

33. Coleridge, *The Statesman's Manual* in *The Collected Works of Samuel Taylor Coleridge*, 29.

34. Shelley, *Philosophical View*, 970.

35. Ibid.

36. Berlin, *Political Ideas in the Romantic Age*, 42.

37. See, for example, McFarland, *Coleridge and the Pantheist Tradition*, and Levinson, "A Motion and a Spirit."

38. Shelley, *Philosophical View*, 971.

39. Ibid., 972.

40. Ibid.

41. See introduction, 6–17.

42. Shelley, *Philosophical View*, 973.

43. Shelley, *Philosophical View*, 973–74. Compare with *A Defence of Poetry*: "There is no want of knowledge respecting what is wisest and best in morals, government, and political oeconomy. . . . We want the creative faculty to imagine that which we know; we want the generous impulse to act that which we imagine; we want the poetry of life" (502).

44. *CPR*, 590, emphasis added.

45. Compare, for example, with the language of the preface to the second edition: "Why then has nature afflicted our reason with the restless striving for such a path [speculative metaphysics], as if it were one of reason's most important occupations? Still more, how little cause have we to place trust in our reason if in one of the most important parts of our desire for knowledge it does not merely forsake us but even entices us with delusions and in the end betrays us!" (*CPR*, 110). Also, the introduction to the Transcendental Dialectic: "For what we have to do with here is a natural and unavoidable illusion [*eine natürlichen un unvermeidlichen Illusion*], which itself rests on subjective principles and passes them off as objective. . . . Hence there is a natural and unavoidable dialectic of pure reason, not one in which a bungler might be entangled through lack of acquaintance, or one that some sophist has artfully invented in order to confuse rational people, but one that irremediably attaches to human reason, so that even after we have exposed the mirage [*Blendwerk*] it will still not cease to lead our reason on with false hopes, continually propelling it into momentary aberrations that always need to be removed" (*CPR*, 386–87).

46. Shelley's ambivalence toward knowledge is related to his views of reason itself, developed in the "Speculations on Metaphysics," "On Life," *A Defence of Poetry*, and the intellectual poetry. James Engell notes that in *Prometheus Unbound* (2.4.10–11), for instance, "Asia reports that the living world contains 'passion, reason, will / Imagination,' and the order here seems to be roughly ascending" (*Creative Imagination*, 263). Shelley's position on reason and imagination, somewhere in between Blake's and Wordsworth's, suggests that reason is not the antithesis of all creative energy nor is it the same in kind as the imagination. The knowledge it produces, political or not, must cohere with a broader poetic vision and not merely correspond to the state of the world.

47. Hume, *Treatise of Human Nature*, bk. 1, sec. 6. See, for example, James Beattie, *An Essay on the Nature and Immutability of Truth* (1770): "I had reason to believe that his

arguments, and his influence as a great literary character, had done harm, by subverting or weakening the good principles of some, and countenancing the licentious opinions of others. Being honored with the care of the British youth; and considering it my indispensable duty to guard their minds against impiety and error, I endeavored . . . to form a right estimate of Mr. Hume's philosophy." The tenor of Beattie's estimate is evident in the following statement: "Scepticism is now the profession of our fashionable enquirers into human nature . . . divesting the mind of every principle, and of all conviction; and consequently, to disqualify man for action, and to render him useless and wretched."

48. *CPR*, 256.

49. Shelley, *Philosophical View*, 1022.

50. Ibid., 974.

51. Bayle, *Commentaire philosophique* (1686), pt. 1, *Oeuvres diverses de Mr. Pierre Bayle*, 2:368, col. 1.

52. Shelley, *Philosophical View*, 974.

53. Ibid., 975.

54. Ibid., 976.

55. Ibid., 1044.

56. Ibid., 1040.

57. Ibid., 1041–42.

58. Ibid., 981.

59. Ibid.

60. Ibid.

61. Ibid., 982–90.

62. On orientalism and imperialism in Shelley, see Leask, *British Romantic Writers and the East*.

63. Shelley, *Philosophical View*, 991.

64. Ibid., 993.

65. Ibid., emphasis added.

66. Northrop Frye, in *A Study of English Romanticism*, for instance, reads *Prometheus Unbound* as comedy, with affinities to Shakespearean comedy. For M. H. Abrams, in *Natural Supernaturalism*, Shelley's play is "a psycho-drama about the re-integration of the split personality." For Barbara Charlesworth Gelpi, in *Shelley's Goddess*, it is a poem about patriarchal control, matriarchal fantasies, and tabooed sexual energies. In *British Romantic Writers and the East*, Nigel Leask notes that the poem unsettles "the norms of both 'orientalist' and 'assimilationist' discourse." And for Kim Wheatley (*Shelley and His Readers*), the poem undercuts Shelley's hostile reviewers through its construction of a nonpartisan aesthetic realm divorced from the political.

67. Wasserman, *Shelley*, 255.

68. Keach, "The Political Poet," 128.

69. Yeats, "The Philosophy of Shelley's Poetry," 51.

70. Shelley, *Prometheus Unbound* (hereafter *PU*), in *The Poems of Shelley*, 2:475 passim. All subsequent quotations from *Prometheus Unbound* come from this edition and volume.

71. Kant, *Critique of Judgment*, 228.

72. Ibid., 151.

73. *PU*, 474.

74. As Everest and Matthews note, Shelley's relocation of the myth from the Georgian to the "Indian" Caucasus (the Hindu Kush) "plac[es] his action in a region traditionally associated with the birth of civilisation, and away from an area tainted by the presence of reactionary political forces in S.'s contemporary milieu" (*Poems of Shelley*, 2:477n). See also Curran, *Shelley's Annus Mirabilis*, 61ff.

75. References to *Prometheus Unbound* will hereafter consist of act, scene (for acts with more than one), and line numbers.

76. "The most important, the most precise of all Shelley's symbols, the one he uses with the fullest knowledge of its meaning, is the Morning and Evening Star. It rises and sets for ever over the towers and rivers, and is the throne of his genius" (Yeats, *Early Essays*, 67).

77. Ibid., 51.

78. I refer here to the lines as they were originally published in 1820 and then in subsequent editions. See Shelley, *PU*, 487n.

79. The distinction also appears in the *Defence of Poetry*: "Yet it is by no means essential that a poet should accommodate his language to this traditional form [meter], so that the harmony which is its spirit, be observed" (484).

80. *PU*, 474.

81. *Defence of Poetry*, 508 and 504.

82. *PU*, 474.

83. *PU*, 474–75.

84. Swinburne, "The Triumph of Time," in *Major Poems and Selected Prose*. See McGann's introduction for other affinities between the two poets.

85. *Defence of Poetry*, 487–97 passim.

86. "On Life," 195.

Abrams, M. H. *The Mirror and the Lamp: Romantic Theory and the Critical Tradition.* New York: Oxford University Press, 1953.

———. *Natural Supernaturalism: Tradition and Revolution in Romantic Literature.* New York: Norton, 1971.

———. "Structure and Style of the Greater Romantic Lyric." In *Romanticism and Consciousness: Essays in Criticism.* New York: Norton, 1970.

Adorno, Theodor, and Max Horkheimer. *Dialectic of Enlightenment* (1944). Translated by John Cumming. London: Verso, 1997.

Aeschylus. *Prometheus Bound.* Translated by David Grene. In *Aeschylus II*, edited by David Grene and Richmond Lattimore. Chicago: University of Chicago Press, 1956.

Allen, Julia. "The Uses and Problems of 'Manly' Rhetoric: Mary Wollstonecraft's Adaptation of Hugh Blair's Lectures in Her Two Vindications." In *Listening to Their Voices: The Rhetorical Activities of Historical Women*, edited by Molly Meijer Wertheimer, 320–36. Columbia: University of South Carolina Press, 1997.

Allestree, Richard. *The Government of the Tongue.* Oxford, 1674.

Anon. *Modern Politics; or, the Cat Let out of the Pock: A Dialogue.* Edinburgh: J. Simpson, 1793.

———. *The Politician's Dictionary; or, a Summary of Political Knowledge.* London: Geo. Allen, 1775.

———. *The Proceedings, at Large, on the Trial of John Horne Tooke, for High Treason.* London: J. S. Johnson, 1795.

———. *The Proceedings in Cases of High Treason.* London: James Ridgeway; H. D. Symonds, 1794.

———. *Report of Committee of Secrecy of the House of Commons.* London: John Stockdale, 1799.

———. *The Sequel to the Congress of the Beasts; or, the Northern Election.* London: W. Webb; J. Bull, 1749.

Aquinas, Thomas. *Summa Theologiae.* 60 vols. London: Blackfriars, 1964–81.

Arbuthnot, John. *An Essay on the Usefulness of Mathematical Learning.* Oxford, 1701.

Arendt, Hannah. *The Human Condition.* 2nd ed. Chicago: University of Chicago Press, 1958.

Aristotle. *The Nicomachean Ethics.* Translated by H. Rackham. Cambridge, MA: Harvard University Press, 1934.

————. *Politics*. Translated by H. Rackham. Cambridge, MA: Harvard University Press, 1932.

Auerbach, Erich. *Mimesis: The Representation of Reality in Western Literature* (1953). 50th anniversary ed. Princeton, NJ: Princeton University Press, 2003. First German ed., 1946.

Bacon, Francis. *De Augmentis Scientiarum* (1623). In *The Works of Francis Bacon*. Edited by James Spedding, Robert Leslie Ellis, and Douglas Denon Heath. Boston: Taggard and Thompson, 1864.

————. *The Instauratio Magna, Part II: Novum Organon and Associated Texts*. Edited by Graham Rees with Maria Wakely. Oxford: Clarendon Press, 2004.

Badiou, Alain. "The Courage of the Present." *Le Monde*, February 13, 2010.

Balfour, Ian. *The Rhetoric of Romantic Prophecy*. Stanford, CA: Stanford University Press, 2002.

Bancroft, Thomas. *The Danger of Political Innovation and the Evils of Anarchy*. Chester, 1792.

Baugh, Albert C., ed. *A Literary History of England*. 2nd ed. 4 vols. New York: Appleton-Century-Crofts, 1967.

Bayle, Pierre. *Commentaire philosophique* (1686). Part 1, *Oeuvres diverses de Mr. Pierre Bayle*. The Hague, 1737.

Beattie, James. *An Essay on the Nature and Immutability of Truth, in Opposition to Sophistry and Scepticism* (1770). Bristol: Thoemmes Press, 1999.

Beddoes, Thomas. *Essay on the Public Merits of Mr. Pitt*. London: Joseph Johnson, 1796.

Berkeley, George. *Three Dialogues between Hylas and Philonus* (1713). Edited by Robert Adams. Indianapolis, IN: Hackett, 1979.

Berlin, Isaiah. *Political Ideas in the Romantic Age: Their Rise and Influence on Modern Thought*. Edited by Henry Hardy. Princeton, NJ: Princeton University Press, 2006.

————. *The Roots of Romanticism*. Edited by Henry Hardy. Princeton, NJ: Princeton University Press, 1999.

Birmingham Society for Constitutional Information. *Birmingham Society for Constitutional Information: First instituted November 20, 1792*. Birmingham, 1792.

Blair, Hugh. *Lectures on Rhetoric and Belles Lettres*. Dublin, 1783.

Blake, William. *The Complete Poetry and Prose of William Blake*. Edited by David Erdman. New York: Random House, 1965.

Blakemore, Steven. *Intertextual War: Edmund Burke and the French Revolution in the Writings of Mary Wollstonecraft, Thomas Paine, and James Mackintosh*. Madison, NJ: Fairleigh Dickinson University Press, 1997.

Bode, Christoph. "Coleridge and Philosophy." In *The Oxford Handbook of Samuel Taylor Coleridge*, edited by F. Burwick, 588–619. Oxford: Oxford University Press, 2009.

Boghossian, Paul, and Christopher Peacocke, eds. *New Essays on the a Priori*. Oxford: Clarendon Press, 2000.

Bolingbroke, Lord. *The Idea of a Patriot King*. London, 1740.

Boswell, James. *A Letter to the People of Scotland, on the Alarming Attempt to Infringe the Articles of the Union, and Introduce a Most Pernicious Innovation, by Diminishing the Number of the Lords of Session*. London: Charles Dilly, 1785.

————. *Life of Johnson* (1791). Edited by R. W. Chapman. Oxford: Oxford University Press, 2008.

Boyson, Rowan. *Wordsworth and the Enlightenment Idea of Pleasure*. Cambridge: Cambridge University Press, 2012.

Bradley, F. H. *Ethical Studies* (1876). Cambridge: Cambridge University Press, 2012.

Bromwich, David. *Disowned by Memory: Wordsworth's Poetry of the 1790s*. Chicago: University of Chicago Press, 1998.

———. "Wollstonecraft as a Critic of Burke." *Political Theory* 23, no. 4 (1995): 617–34.

Bullitt, John, and W. J. Bate. "Distinctions between Fancy and Imagination in Eighteenth-Century English Criticism." *Modern Language Notes* 60, no. 1 (1945): 8–15.

Burke, Edmund. *The Correspondence of Edmund Burke*. Chicago: University of Chicago Press, 1958.

———. *A Philosophical Enquiry into the Origin of Our Ideas of the Sublime and Beautiful* (1757). In vol. 1 of *The Writings and Speeches of Edmund Burke*. Edited by T. O. McLoughlin and James T. Boulton. Oxford: Clarendon Press, 1997.

———. *Reflections on the Revolution in France* (1790). In vol. 8 of *The Writings and Speeches of Edmund Burke*. Edited by L. G. Mitchell. Oxford: Clarendon Press, 1989.

———. "Speech on Fox's East India Bill" (1783). In *On Empire, Liberty, and Reform: Speeches and Letters*. Edited by David Bromwich. New Haven, CT: Yale University Press, 2000.

———. *A Vindication of Natural Society* (1756). In vol. 1 of *The Writings and Speeches of Edmund Burke*. Edited by T. O. McLoughlin and James T. Boulton. Oxford: Clarendon Press, 1997.

Butler, Marilyn *Romantics, Rebels, and Reactionaries: English Literature and Its Background, 1760–1830*. New York: Oxford University Press, 1982.

Cameron, Kenneth Neill. *Shelley: The Golden Years*. Cambridge, MA: Harvard University Press, 1974.

———. *The Young Shelley: Genesis of a Radical*. New York: Collier Books, 1962.

Campbell, George. *The Philosophy of Rhetoric* (1776). New York: Harper and Brothers, 1849.

Carlyle, Thomas. *The Life of John Sterling* (1851). London: Chapman and Hall, 1897.

Cassirer, Ernst. *The Philosophy of the Enlightenment*. Princeton, NJ: Princeton University Press, 1951.

———. *The Renaissance Philosophy of Man*. Chicago: University of Chicago Press, 1948.

Cavell, Stanley. *In Quest of the Ordinary: Lines of Skepticism and Romanticism*. Chicago: University of Chicago Press, 1988.

Caygill, Howard. *A Kant Dictionary*. The Blackwell Philosopher Dictionaries. Malden: Blackwell, 1995.

Chandler, James K. *England in 1819: The Politics of Literary Culture and the Case of Romantic Historicism*. Chicago: University of Chicago Press, 1998.

———. *Wordsworth's Second Nature: A Study of the Poetry and Politics*. Chicago: University of Chicago Press, 1984.

Chew, Samuel C. *The Nineteenth Century and After*. New York: Appleton-Century-Crofts, 1948.

Chomsky, Noam. *Problems of Knowledge and Freedom*. New York: New Press, 1971.

Chomsky, Noam, and Michel Foucault. *The Chomsky-Foucault Debate: On Human Nature*. New York: New Press, 2006.

Clark, Timothy. *Embodying Revolution: The Figure of the Poet in Shelley*. New York: Oxford University Press, 1989.

Class, Monika. *Coleridge and Kantian Ideas in England, 1796–1817*. London: Bloomsbury, 2014.

Cobban, Alfred. *Edmund Burke and the Revolt against the Eighteenth Century*. 1st AMS ed. New York: AMS Press, 1978.

Coleridge, Samuel Taylor. *Biographia Literaria*. In *The Collected Works of Samuel Taylor Coleridge*. Edited by James Engell and W. Jackson Bate. 2 vols. Princeton, NJ: Princeton University Press, 1983.

———. *Collected Letters of Samuel Taylor Coleridge*. Edited by Earl Leslie Griggs. Oxford: Clarendon Press, 1956–71.

———. *The Friend*. In *The Collected Works of Samuel Taylor Coleridge*. Edited by Barbara Rooke. Princeton, NJ: Princeton University Press, 1969.

———. *Lectures*. In *Shakespeare Criticism*, edited by D. Nichol Smith. London: Oxford University Press, 1946.

———. *Lectures (1808–1819): On Literature*. In *The Collected Works of Samuel Taylor Coleridge*. Edited by R. A. Foakes. Princeton, NJ: Princeton University Press, 1987.

———. *Lectures (1818–1819): On the History of Philosophy*. In *The Collected Works of Samuel Taylor Coleridge*. Edited by J. R. de J. Jackson. Princeton, NJ: Princeton University Press, 2000.

———. *Marginalia*. In *The Collected Works of Samuel Taylor Coleridge*. Edited by H. J. Jackson and George Whalley. Princeton, NJ: Princeton University Press, 1980–98.

———. *A Moral and Political Lecture, Delivered at Bristol*. Bristol: George Routh, 1795.

———. *The Notebooks of Samuel Taylor Coleridge* (1804–8). Edited by Kathleen Coburn. Vol. 2. London: Routledge and Kegan Paul, 1961.

———. *The Statesman's Manual*. In *Lay Sermons*, in *The Collected Works of Samuel Taylor Coleridge*. Edited by R. J. White. Princeton, NJ: Princeton University Press, 1972.

Colmer, John. *Coleridge: Critic of Society*. Oxford: Clarendon Press, 1959.

Conniff, James. "Edmund Burke and His Critics: The Case of Mary Wollstonecraft." *Journal of the History of Ideas* 60, no. 2 (1999): 299–318.

Cox, Jeffrey. "The Dramatist." In *The Cambridge Companion to Shelley*, edited by Timothy Morton. Cambridge: Cambridge University Press, 2006.

———. *Poetry and Politics in the Cockney School: Keats, Shelley, Hunt, and Their Circle*. Cambridge: Cambridge University Press, 1998.

Coxe, Tench. *Observations on the Agriculture, Manufactures and Commerce of the United States*. New York: Francis Childs and John Swaine, 1789.

Craig, Cairns. "Coleridge, Hume, and the Chains of the Romantic Imagination." In *Scotland and the Borders of Romanticism*, edited by Leith Davis, Ian Duncan, and Janet Sorensen. Cambridge: Cambridge University Press, 2004.

Curran, Stuart. *Shelley's Annus Mirabilis: The Maturing of an Epic Vision*. San Marino, CA: Huntington Library, 1975.

Day, Thomas. *Reflections on the Present State of England*. London: J. Stockdale, 1782.

Debray, Régis. *Critique of Political Reason*. Translated by David Macey. London: Verso, 1981.

Dempster, George. *Reasons for Extending the Militia Acts to the Disarmed Counties of Scotland*. Edinburgh: Gavin Hamilton and John Balfour, 1760.

Dennis, John. *The Advancement and Reform of Modern Poetry* (1701). In *The Critical Works of John Dennis*. Edited by Edward Niles Hooker. 2 vols. Baltimore, MD: Johns Hopkins University Press, 1943.

Duigenan, Patrick. *A Speech Spoken in the House of Commons of Ireland on Monday February 4, 1793*. Dublin: W. McKenzie, 1793.

Dyce, Alexander. *The Reminiscences of Alexander Dyce.* Edited by Richard J. Schrader. Columbus: Ohio University Press, 1972.

Edgeworth, Maria. *Practical Education.* London: Joseph Johnson, 1798.

Engell, James. *The Creative Imagination.* Cambridge, MA: Harvard University Press, 1981.

Erdman, David. *Blake: Prophet against Empire.* Princeton, NJ: Princeton University Press, 1954.

Fellow of the Royal Society. *See* Royal Society, Fellow of the.

Fennessy, R. R. *Burke, Paine, and the Rights of Man: A Difference of Political Opinion.* The Hague: M. Nijhoff, 1963.

Ferguson, Frances. "On the Numbers of Romanticisms." *ELH* 58, no. 2 (Summer 1991): 471–98.

———. *Solitude and the Sublime: Romanticism and the Aesthetics of Individuation.* New York: Routledge, 1992.

Ferrier, James Frederick. *Institutes of Metaphysic: The Theory of Knowing and Being.* Edinburgh: Blackwood, 1856.

Fielding, Henry. *The Works of Henry Fielding, Esq.; with the Life of the Author.* 5th ed. Vol. 12. Edinburgh: Alexander Donaldson, 1771.

Foucault, Michel. *The Essential Works of Foucault, 1954–1984.* Edited by James D. Faubion and Paul Rabinow. Vol. 3. New York: New Press, 1994.

Frend, William. *Principles of Taxation.* London: A. Hamilton, 1799.

Frye, Northrop. *Fearful Symmetry: A Study of William Blake.* Princeton, NJ: Princeton University Press, 1947.

———. *A Study of English Romanticism.* New York: Random House, 1968.

Galloway, Joseph. *Historical and Political Reflections on the Rise and Progress of the American Rebellion.* London: J. Paramore, 1780.

Gelpi, Barbara Charlesworth. *Shelley's Goddess.* New York: Oxford University Press, 1992.

Gibbon, Edward. *The History of the Decline and Fall of the Roman Empire.* London: Strahan and Cadell, 1788.

Gill, Stephen. *William Wordsworth: A Life.* Oxford: Oxford University Press, 1989.

Glaeser, Andreas. *Political Epistemics: The Secret Police, the Opposition, and the End of East German Socialism.* Chicago: University of Chicago Press, 2010.

Godwin, William. *Considerations on Lord Grenville's and Mr. Pitt's Bills, concerning Treasonable and Seditious Practices, and Unlawful Assemblies.* London: Joseph Johnson, 1795.

———. *Cursory Strictures on the Charge Delivered by Lord Chief Justice Eyre to the Grand Jury.* In vol. 2 of *Political and Philosophical Writings of William Godwin.* Edited by Mark Philp. London: William Pickering, 1993.

———. *Enquiry concerning Political Justice, and Its Influence on Morals and Happiness.* Edited by F.E.L. Priestley. Photographic facsimile of the 3rd ed., 1798. 3 vols. Toronto: University of Toronto Press, 1946.

———. *Memoirs of the Author of the Vindication of the Rights of Woman.* London: G. G. and J. Robinson, 1798.

Graver, Bruce Edward. "Wordsworth's Translations from Latin Poetry." Ph.D. diss., Chapel Hill: University of North Carolina, 1983.

Guillory, John. *Cultural Capital: The Problem of Literary Canon Formation.* Chicago: University of Chicago Press, 1993.

Haakonssen, Knud. "The Structure of Hume's Political Theory." In *The Cambridge Companion to Hume*, edited by David Fate Norton and Jacqueline Taylor. Cambridge: Cambridge University Press, 1993.

Hall, Jean. *The Transforming Image: A Study of Shelley's Major Poetry*. Urbana: University of Illinois Press, 1980.

Hamilton, Alexander. *The Federalist*. Vol. 1. New York: J. and A. McLean, 1787.

Hamilton, Paul. "Literature and Philosophy" in *The Cambridge Companion to Shelley*, edited by Timothy Morton. Cambridge: Cambridge University Press, 2006.

———. *Metaromanticism: Aesthetics, Literature, Theory*. Chicago: University of Chicago Press, 2003.

———. *Percy Bysshe Shelley*. Tavistock: Northcote House, 2000.

Hampsher-Monk, Iain, ed. *The Impact of the French Revolution*. Cambridge: Cambridge University Press, 2005.

———. "Rhetoric and Opinion in the Politics of Edmund Burke." *History of Political Thought* 9, no. 3 (1988): 455–84.

Harding, Anthony. *The Reception of Myth in English Romanticism*. Columbia: University of Missouri Press, 1995.

Hazlitt, William. "My First Acquaintance with Poets" (1823). In vol. 17 of *The Complete Works of William Hazlitt in Twenty-One Volumes*. Edited by P. P. Howe. London: J. M. Dent and Sons, 1933.

Hegel, G.W.F. *Phenomenology of Spirit* (1807). Translated by A. V. Miller. Oxford: Oxford University Press, 1977.

———. *Science of Logic* (1817). Translated by A. V. Miller. London: G. Allen and Unwin, 1976.

Heidegger, Martin. "Building, Dwelling, Thinking" (1954). In *Basic Writings*. Edited by David Farrell Krell. San Francisco: Harper Collins, 1977.

———. *The Essence of Human Freedom* (1930). Translated by Ted Sadler. London: Continuum, 2002.

———. "Letter on Humanism" (1947). In *Basic Writings*. Edited by David Farrell Krell. San Francisco: Harper Collins, 1977.

Helvétius, Claude-Adrien. *De l'homme, or a Treatise on Man* (1773). Translated by W. Hooper. New York: Franklin, 1969.

Hoagwood, Terence Allan. *Prophecy and the Philosophy of Mind: Traditions of Blake and Shelley*. Tuscaloosa: University of Alabama Press, 1985.

Hobbes, Thomas. *Leviathan* (1651). Edited by Richard E. Flathman and David Johnston. New York: Norton, 1997.

Holbach, Paul-Henri Thiry, Baron d'. *Système de la nature* (1770). Adapted from the original translation by H. D. Robinson, 1868. Manchester: Clinamen Press, 1999.

Horkheimer, Max. *Eclipse of Reason* (1947). Rev. ed. London: Continuum, 2004.

Hume, David. *Dialogues concerning Natural Religion and Other Writings*. Edited by Dorothy Coleman. Cambridge: Cambridge University Press, 2007.

———. *Enquiries concerning Human Understanding and concerning the Principles of Morals*. Edited by L. A. Selby Bigge. 3rd ed. Oxford: Clarendon Press, 1975.

———. *Essays and Treatises on Several Subjects*. Vol. 3. London: Andrew Millar, 1753.

———. *Essays, Moral, Political, and Literary*. Edited by Eugene F. Miller. Indianapolis, IN: Liberty Fund, 1985.

————. *History of England* (1754–62). 6 vols. Indianapolis, IN: Liberty Fund, 1985.

————. "Of the Original Contract" (1748). In *Selected Essays*. Edited by Stephen Copley and Andrew Edgar. Oxford: Oxford University Press, 1993.

————. *Political Essays*. Edited by Charles W. Hendel. New York: Liberal Arts Press, 1953.

————. "That Politics May Be Reduced to a Science" (1742). In *Selected Essays*. Edited by Stephen Copley and Andrew Edgar. Oxford: Oxford University Press, 1993.

————. *A Treatise of Human Nature* (1739–40). Edited by David Fate Norton and Mary J. Norton. Oxford: Oxford University Press, 2000.

Information, Societies for. *See* Birmingham Society for Constitutional Information; Society for Constitutional Information (London); and York Society for Political Information.

Inwood, Brad, and L. P. Gerson, eds. and trans. *Hellenistic Philosophy: Introductory Readings*. 2nd ed. Indianapolis, IN: Hackett, 1988.

Jarvis, Simon. *Wordsworth's Philosophic Song*. Cambridge: Cambridge University Press, 2007.

Jay, Martin. *The Dialectical Imagination: A History of the Frankfurt School and the Institute of Social Research, 1923–1950* (1973). Berkeley: University of California Press, 1996.

Johnson, Samuel. *The Idler*. Vol. 2. London: John Newberry, 1761.

————. *Rasselas*. In *Rasselas and Other Tales*. Edited by Gwin J. Kolb. New Haven, CT: Yale University Press, 1990.

Johnston, Kenneth. *The Hidden Wordsworth: Poet, Lover, Rebel, Spy*. New York: Norton, 1998.

————. *Wordsworth and "The Recluse."* New Haven, CT: Yale University Press, 1984.

Kant, Immanuel. *The Conflict of the Faculties* (1798). Translated and edited by Allen W. Wood and George Di Giovanni. In *Religion and Rational Theology*. Cambridge: Cambridge University Press, 1996.

————. *Critique of the Power of Judgment* (1790). Edited by Paul Guyer and translated by Guyer and Eric Matthews. Cambridge: Cambridge University Press, 2000.

————. *Critique of Practical Reason* (1788). Translated and edited by Mary J. Gregor. In *Practical Philosophy*. Cambridge: Cambridge University Press, 1996.

————. *Critique of Pure Reason* (1781). Translated and edited by Paul Guyer and Allen Wood. Cambridge: Cambridge University Press, 1998.

————. *Groundwork of the Metaphysics of Morals* (1785). In *Practical Philosophy*. Translated and edited by Mary J. Gregor. Cambridge: Cambridge University Press, 1996.

————. *The Metaphysics of Morals* (1797). In *Practical Philosophy*. Translated and edited by Mary J. Gregor. Cambridge: Cambridge University Press, 1996.

————. *Practical Philosophy*. Translated and edited by Mary J. Gregor. Cambridge: Cambridge University Press, 1996.

————. *Prolegomena to Any Future Metaphysics* (1783). Translated by Paul Carus. Indianapolis, IN: Hackett, 1977.

————. "What Is Enlightenment?" (1784). In *Practical Philosophy*. Translated and edited by Mary J. Gregor. Cambridge: Cambridge University Press, 1996.

Keach, William. "The Political Poet." In *The Cambridge Companion to Shelley*, edited by Timothy Morton. Cambridge: Cambridge University Press, 2006.

Kelley, Paul. "Wordsworth and Lucretius' *De Rerum Natura*." *Notes and Queries* 30, no. 3 (1983): 219–22.

Knapp, Steven. *Personification and the Sublime: Milton to Coleridge*. Cambridge, MA: Harvard University Press, 1985.

Knox, Vicesimus. *The Spirit of Despotism*. London, 1795.

Kramnick, Isaac, ed. Introduction to William Godwin, *Enquiry concerning Political Justice and Its Influence on Modern Morals and Happiness*. Harmondsworth, UK: Penguin, 1985.

La Mettrie, Julien Offray de. *Machine Man and Other Writings*. Translated and edited by Ann Thomson. Cambridge: Cambridge University Press, 1996.

Leask, Nigel. *British Romantic Writers and the East: Anxieties of Empire*. Cambridge: Cambridge University Press, 1992.

Leighton, Angela. *Shelley and the Sublime*. Cambridge: Cambridge University Press, 1984.

Levinson, Marjorie. "A Motion and a Spirit: Romancing Spinoza." *Studies in Romanticism* 46, no. 4 (Winter 2007): 367–408.

Liu, Alan. *Wordsworth: The Sense of History*. Stanford, CA: Stanford University Press, 1989.

Locke, John. *Elements of Natural Philosophy, to Which Are Added Some Thoughts concerning Reading and Study for a Gentleman*. London, 1750.

———. *An Essay concerning Human Understanding* (1689). Edited by Peter H. Nidditch. Oxford: Oxford University Press, 1975.

Lockridge, Laurence. *Coleridge the Moralist*. Ithaca, NY: Cornell University Press, 1977.

———. *The Ethics of Romanticism*. Cambridge: Cambridge University Press, 1989.

———. Review of *Opus Maximum* by S. T. Coleridge. *Wordsworth Circle* (Fall 2002): 132–34.

London Corresponding Society. *The Correspondence of the London Corresponding Society, Revised and Corrected*. London, 1795.

———. *The Moral and Political Magazine of the London Corresponding Society*. London: John Ashley, 1796.

Lovejoy, Arthur. "On the Discrimination of Romanticisms." In *English Romantic Poets*, edited by M. H. Abrams. Oxford: Oxford University Press, 1975.

Lover of Peace. *See* Peace, Lover of.

Lucretius. *The Nature of Things*. Translated by Richard Jenkyns. London: Penguin, 2007.

Macaulay, Angus. *Rudiments of Political Science, Part the First; Containing Elementary Principles: With an Appendix*. London, 1796.

Macaulay, Catharine. *Observations on the Reflections of the Rt. Hon. Edmund Burke*. London: C. Dilly, 1790.

Mackintosh, James. *Vindicae Gallicae* (1791). In *Miscellaneous Works of the Right Honorable Sir James Mackintosh*. 2nd ed. London: Longman, 1851.

Mahoney, Charles. *Romantics and Renegades: The Poetics of Political Reaction*. New York: Palgrave Macmillan, 2003.

Marx, Karl. *Capital* (1867). Translated by Ben Fowkes. Vol. 1. London: Penguin, 1976.

———. "For a Ruthless Criticism of Everything Existing" (1843). In *The Marx-Engels Reader*, edited by Robert C. Tucker. New York: Norton, 1978.

Mathias, Thomas James. *The Shade of Alexander Pope on the Banks of the Thames: A Satirical Poem*. London: T. Becket, 1799.

McFarland, Thomas. *Coleridge and the Pantheist Tradition*. Oxford: Clarendon Press, 1969.

McGann, Jerome. *The Romantic Ideology: A Critical Investigation*. Chicago: University of Chicago Press, 1983.

McKusick, James C. *Coleridge's Philosophy of Language*. Yale Studies in English. New Haven, CT: Yale University Press, 1986.

McNeice, Gerald. *Shelley and the Revolutionary Idea*. Cambridge, MA: Harvard University Press, 1969.

Mill, John Stuart. "Coleridge." In *The Complete Works of John Stuart Mill*. Edited by J. M. Robson. Toronto: University of Toronto Press, 1969.

Milnes, Tim. *The Truth about Romanticism: Pragmatism and Idealism in Keats, Shelley, Coleridge*. Cambridge: Cambridge University Press, 2010.

Milton, John. *The Riverside Milton*. Edited by Roy Flannagan. Boston: Houghton Mifflin, 1998.

Montesquieu, Charles de Secondat. *De l'esprit des lois, or the Spirit of Laws* (1748). Translated by Thomas Nugent. Littleton, CO: F. B. Rothman, 1991.

Moorman, Mary. *William Wordsworth, a Biography*. Vol. 1, *The Early Years, 1770–1803*. Oxford: Clarendon Press, 1957.

———. *William Wordsworth, a Biography*. Vol. 2, *The Later Years, 1803–1850*. Oxford: Clarendon Press, 1965.

Morrow, John. *Coleridge's Political Thought: Property, Morality, and the Limits of Traditional Discourse*. New York: St. Martin's Press, 1990.

Morton, Timothy, ed. *The Cambridge Companion to Shelley*. Cambridge: Cambridge University Press, 2006.

———. *Ecology without Nature: Rethinking Environmental Aesthetics*. Cambridge, MA: Harvard University Press, 2007.

———. *Shelley and the Revolution in Taste*. Cambridge: Cambridge University Press, 1994.

Natarajan, Uttara, ed. *The Romantic Poets: A Guide to Criticism*. Malden: Blackwell, 2007.

Nietzsche, Friedrich Wilhelm. *On the Genealogy of Morals* (1887). Edited and translated by Walter Kauffman. New York: Random House, 1967.

Notopoulos, James A. *The Platonism of Shelley*. Durham, NC: Duke University Press, 1949.

Oakeshott, Michael. *Rationalism in Politics and Other Essays*. Edited by Timothy Fuller. Indianapolis, IN: Liberty Fund, 1991.

O'Connor, Arthur. *The Measures of Ministry to Prevent a Revolution Are the Certain Means of Bringing It On*. London, 1794.

Old Member of Parliament. *See* Parliament, Old Member of.

Orsini, Gian N. G. *Coleridge and German Idealism*. Carbondale: Southern Illinois University Press, 1969.

Orwell, George. "Politics and the English Language" (1946). In *Essays*. New York: Knopf, 1968.

Paine, Thomas. *Letter Addressed to the Addressers, on the Late Proclamation*. London: H. D. Symonds; Thomas Clio Rickman, 1792.

———. *The Rights of Man* (1791). London: Penguin, 1984.

Paley, William. *The Principles of Moral and Political Philosophy*. Dublin: Exshaw, White, H. Whitestone, Ryrne, Cash, Whitebank, and McKenzie, 1785.

Parkinson, James. *Knave's-Acre Association*. London: T. Spence, 1793.

Parliament, Old Member of. *A Looking-Glass for a Right Honourable Mendicant*. London, 1794.

Patin, Henri Joseph Guillaume. "L'Anti-Lucréce chez Lucréce." In vol. 1 of *Études sur la poésie latine*. Paris: Librairie Hachette, 1868.

Pattensen, Rev. Mr. *A Sermon, Preached in Halifax Church, on the Twenty-Third of April, 1789, the Day of Thanksgiving, for His Majesty's Happy Recovery.* Halifax: E. Jacob, 1789.

Paulson, Ronald. *Representations of Revolution, 1789–1820.* New Haven, CT: Yale University Press, 1983.

Peace, Lover of. *Comments on the Proposed War with France.* London, 1793.

Penn, John. *Further Thoughts on the Present State of Public Opinion.* London: J. Hatchard; W. Bulmer and Co., 1800.

Perry, Seamus. *Coleridge and the Uses of Division.* Oxford: Clarendon Press, 1999.

———. "Enlightened Romantics." *Times Literary Supplement,* August 20, 2004.

Plato. *Philebus.* In *Plato: Complete Works.* Edited by John M. Cooper and D. S. Hutchinson. Indianapolis, IN: Hackett, 1997.

———. *The Republic.* Translated by Paul Shorey. 2 vols. Cambridge, MA: Harvard University Press, 1937.

———. *Theaetetus.* Translated by Harold N. Fowler. Cambridge, MA: Harvard University Press, 1921.

Pocock, J.G.A. *Politics, Language, and Time: Essays on Political Thought and History.* Chicago: University of Chicago Press, 1989.

Poovey, Mary. *The Proper Lady and the Woman Writer: Ideology as Style in the Work of Mary Wollstonecraft, Mary Shelley, and Jane Austen.* Chicago: University of Chicago Press, 1984.

Pope, Alexander. *The Poems of Alexander Pope.* Edited by John Butt. New Haven, CT: Yale University Press, 1963.

Porter, Roy, and Marie Mulvey Roberts, eds. *Pleasure in the Eighteenth Century.* New York: New York University Press, 1996.

Postlethwayt, Malachy. *Great-Britain's True System.* London: Andrew Millar, 1757.

Price, Richard. *A Discourse on the Love of Our Country* (1789). In *The Impact of the French Revolution,* edited by Iain Hampsher-Monk. Cambridge: Cambridge University Press, 2005.

———. *Observations on the Nature of Civil Liberty, and the Principles of Government, from Dr. Price's Much Esteemed and Popular Essay, Published Anno 1776. With the Declaration of Principles, and Regulations of the Friends of Liberty, United for Promoting Constitutional Information.* London, 1795.

Priestley, Joseph. *An Essay on a Course of Liberal Education for a Civil and Active Life.* London: Johnson and Davenport, 1765.

———. *Letters to the Right Honorable Edmund Burke.* Birmingham: Thomas Pearson, 1791.

Priestman, Martin. "Lucretius in Romantic and Victorian Britain." In *The Cambridge Companion to Lucretius,* edited by Stuart Gillespie and Philip Hardie. Cambridge: Cambridge University Press, 2007.

Pulos, C. E. *The Deep Truth: A Study of Shelley's Skepticism.* Lincoln: University of Nebraska Press, 1954.

Rajan, Tilottama. *Dark Interpreter: The Discourse of Romanticism.* Ithaca, NY: Cornell University Press, 1980.

Reiman, Donald H. *Intervals of Inspiration: The Skeptical Tradition and the Psychology of Romanticism.* Greenwood, FL: Penkevill Publishing, 1988.

Revolution Society. *The Correspondence of the Revolution Society in London, with the National Assembly, and with Various Societies of the Friends of Liberty in France and England.* London, 1792.

Richards, I. A. *Coleridge on Imagination*. New York: Harcourt, Brace, 1935.

Robinson, Charles. *Shelley and Byron: The Snake and Eagle Wreathed in Flight*. Baltimore, MD: Johns Hopkins University Press, 1981.

Roe, Nicholas. "Politics, History, and Wordsworth's Poems," in *The Cambridge Companion to Wordsworth*, edited by Stephen Gill. Cambridge: Cambridge University Press, 2003.

———. *Wordsworth and Coleridge: The Radical Years*. Oxford: Clarendon Press, 1988.

Rorty, Richard. *Contingency, Irony, and Solidarity*. Cambridge: Cambridge University Press, 1989.

Rousseau, Jean-Jacques. *The Social Contract* (1762). London: Penguin, 1968.

Royal Society, Fellow of the. *A Short Specimen of a New Political Arithmetic; Containing, Some Considerations concerning Public Roads*. London: F. Jefferies, 1734.

Rudé, George, ed. *Robespierre*. Englewood Cliffs, NJ: Prentice Hall, 1967.

Russell, Bertrand. *The History of Western Philosophy*. New York: Simon and Schuster, 1945.

———. *Human Knowledge: Its Scope and Limits*. New York: Simon and Schuster, 1948.

———. *Roads to Freedom*. London: George Allen and Unwin, 1977.

Ruston, Sharon. *Shelley and Vitality*. Basingstoke: Palgrave Macmillan, 2005.

Sapiro, Virginia. *A Vindication of Political Virtue: The Political Theory of Mary Wollstonecraft*. Chicago: University of Chicago Press, 1992.

Schlegel, August Wilhelm von. *Ueber dramatische Kunst und Literatur*. Heidelberg: Mohr und Zimmer, 1809–11.

Scrivener, Michael Henry. *Radical Shelley: The Philosophical Anarchism and Utopian Thought of Percy Bysshe Shelley*. Princeton, NJ: Princeton University Press, 1982.

Sewell, George. *A Vindication of the English Stage*. London: W. Mears, 1716.

Shaffer, Michael J., and Michael L. Veber, eds. *What Place for the a Priori?* Chicago: Open Court, 2011.

Shelley, Percy Bysshe. *The Complete Works of Percy Bysshe Shelley*. Edited by Roger Ingpen and Walter E. Peck. 10 vols. New York: Gordian Press, 1965.

———. *A Defence of Poetry*. In *Shelley's Poetry and Prose*. Edited by Donald H. Reiman and Sharon B. Powers. New York: Norton, 1977.

———. *The Letters of Percy Bysshe Shelley*. Edited by Frederick Jones. 2 vols. Oxford: Clarendon Press, 1964.

———. *A Philosophical View of Reform*. In vol. 6 of *Shelley and His Circle: 1772–1822*. Edited by Donald H. Reiman. Cambridge, MA: Harvard University Press, 1973.

———. *Prometheus Unbound*. In vol. 2 of *The Poems of Shelley*. Edited by Kelvin Everest and Geoffrey Matthews. Harlow: Longman, 2000.

———. *A Vindication of Natural Diet*. In vol. 1 of *The Prose Works of Percy Bysshe Shelley*. Edited by E. B. Murray. Oxford: Clarendon Press, 1993.

Sinclair, Sir John. *Specimens of Statistical Reports; Exhibiting the Progress of Political Society from the Pastoral State, to That of Luxury and Refinement*. London: Printed for T. Cadell, Strand; J. Debrett, Picadilly; and J. Sewell, Cornhill, 1793.

Skolnik, Christine M. "Wollstonecraft's Dislocation of the Masculine Sublime: A Vindication." *Rhetorica* 21, no. 4 (2003): 205–23.

Smith, Charlotte Turner. *Emmeline, the Orphan of the Castle*. London: Thomas Cadell, 1788.

Smollett, Tobias. *The History of England from the Revolution to the Death of George the Second*. London, 1785.

Society for Constitutional Information (London). *Society for Constitutional Information*. London, 1790.

Society of the Friends of the People. *At a Meeting Held at the Three Turns Tavern*. London, 1792.

Southey, Robert. *The Collected Letters of Robert Southey: Part Four, 1810–1815*. Edited by Ian Packer and Lynda Pratt. Romantic Circles, http://www.rc.umd.edu/editions/southey_letters/Part_Four.

Spiegelman, Willard. "Some Lucretian Elements in Wordsworth." *Comparative Literature* 37, no. 1 (1985): 27–49.

Spinoza, Benedict de. *Tractatus Theologico-Politicus* (1670). Translated by R.H.M. Elwes. In *The Chief Works of Benedict De Spinoza*. London: George Bell and Sons, 1889.

Sterne, Laurence. *A Political Romance*. York, 1759.

Stewart, John Hall, ed. *A Documentary Survey of the French Revolution*. New York: Macmillan, 1951.

Striker, Gisela. *Essays on Hellenistic Epistemology and Ethics*. Cambridge: Cambridge University Press, 1996.

Swift, Jonathan. *A Vindication of Isaac Bickerstaff*. London, 1709.

Swinburne, Algernon Charles. "The Triumph of Time." In *Major Poems and Selected Prose*. Edited by Jerome McGann and Charles L. Sligh. New Haven, CT: Yale University Press, 2004.

Taylor, Thomas. *A Vindication of the Rights of Brutes*. London, 1792.

Temple, William. "To the North Briton." *North Briton* 1, no. 19 (1763): 173–84.

Thelwall, John. *Political Lectures*. London, 1795.

Thomas, Gordon Kent. *Wordsworth's Dirge and Promise*. Lincoln: University of Nebraska Press, 1971.

Thompson, E. P. "Disenchantment or Default? A Lay Sermon." In *Power and Consciousness*, edited by C. C. O'Brien and W. D. Vanech. London: University of London Press; New York: New York University Press, 1969.

Todd, Janet. *Mary Wollstonecraft: A Revolutionary Life*. New York: Columbia University Press, 2000.

Trenchard, John. *The Sixth Collection of Cato's Political Letters, in the London Journal*. Vol. 2. London: Printed for J. Peele, 1722.

Valpy, Richard. *Two Assize Sermons*. Reading, 1793.

Wakefield, Priscilla. *Reflections on the Present Condition of the Female Sex*: London: J. Johnson, 1798.

Walpole, Horace. *The Yale Edition of Horace Walpole's Correspondence*. 48 vols. New Haven, CT: Yale University Press, 1937–83.

Warburton, William. *A Vindication of the English Stage*. London: J. Robinson, 1716.

Wasserman, Earl R. *Shelley: A Critical Reading*. Baltimore, MD: Johns Hopkins University Press, 1971.

———. *Shelley's "Prometheus Unbound": A Critical Reading*. Baltimore, MD: Johns Hopkins University Press, 1965.

Webb, R. K. *Modern England*. 2nd ed. New York: Harper and Row, 1980.

Weiskel, Thomas. *The Romantic Sublime: Studies in the Psychology and Structure of Transcendence*. Baltimore, MD: Johns Hopkins University Press, 1976.

Wellek, René. "The Concept of Romanticism in Literary History." In *Romanticism: Points of View*, edited by Robert F. Gleckner and Gerald E. Enscoe. Englewood Cliffs, NJ: Prentice-Hall, 1970.

———. *Immanuel Kant in England, 1793–1838*. Princeton, NJ: Princeton University Press, 1931.

Wentworth, Anne. *A Vindication of Anne Wentworth*. London, 1679.

Wheatley, Kim. *Shelley and His Readers*. Columbia: University of Missouri Press, 1999.

Williams, David. *Lectures on Education*. Vol. 2. London: John Bell, 1789.

Williams, Raymond. *Keywords: A Vocabulary of Culture and Society*. New York: Oxford University Press, 1976.

Wollstonecraft, Mary. *An Historical and Moral View of the Origin and Progress of the French Revolution; and the Effect It Has Produced in Europe*. London: Joseph Johnson, 1794.

———. "Thoughts on the Education of Daughters." In *The Works of Mary Wollstonecraft*. Edited by Emma Rees-Mogg, Janet Todd, and Marilyn Butler. London: Pickering, 1989.

———. *"A Vindication of the Rights of Men" and "A Vindication of the Rights of Woman."* Edited by Sylvana Tomaselli. Cambridge: Cambridge University Press, 1995.

Wordsworth, Jonathan. *Wordsworth and the Borders of Vision*. Oxford: Oxford University Press, 1984.

Wordsworth, William. *The Borderers*. Edited by Robert Osburn. In *The Cornell Wordsworth*. Ithaca, NY: Cornell University Press, 1982.

———. *The Convention of Cintra*. In *The Prose Works of William Wordsworth*. Edited by W.J.B. Owen and Jane Worthington Smyser. Oxford: Clarendon Press, 1974.

———. *The Excursion*. Edited by Sally Bushell, James A. Butler, and Michael C. Jaye. In *The Cornell Wordsworth*. Ithaca, NY: Cornell University Press, 2007.

———. *Home at Grasmere*. Edited by Beth Darlington. In *The Cornell Wordsworth*. Ithaca, NY: Cornell University Press, 1977.

———. *The Letters of William and Dorothy Wordsworth*. Edited by Mary Moorman and Alan G. Hill. 8 vols. Oxford: Clarendon Press, 1967–93.

———. *Letter to the Bishop of Llandaff*. In *The Prose Works of William Wordsworth*. Edited by W.J.B. Owen and Jane Worthington Smyser. Oxford: Clarendon Press, 1974.

———. *Poems, in Two Volumes*. Edited by Jared Curtis. In *The Cornell Wordsworth*. Ithaca, NY: Cornell University Press, 1983.

———. *The Poetical Works of William Wordsworth*. Edited by E. De Selincourt. Oxford: Clarendon Press, 1940–49.

———. Preface to the *Lyrical Ballads*. In *The Prose Works of William Wordsworth*. Edited by W.J.B. Owen and Jane Worthington Smyser. Oxford: Clarendon Press, 1974.

———. *The Thirteen Book Prelude*. Edited by Mark L. Reed. In *The Cornell Wordsworth*. Ithaca, NY: Cornell University Press, 1991.

———. *Two Addresses to the Freeholders of Westmorland*. In *The Prose Works of William Wordsworth*. Edited by W.J.B Owen and Jane Worthington Smyser. Oxford: Clarendon Press, 1974.

Wortman, Tunis. *A Treatise, concerning Political Enquiry, and the Liberty of the Press*. New York: George Forman, 1800.

Wu, Duncan. *Wordsworth: The Earliest Poems, 1785–1790*. New York: Routledge, 2002.

Yeats, W. B. "The Philosophy of Shelley's Poetry." In *Early Essays*. Edited by George Bornstein and Richard J. Finneran. In *The Collected Works of W. B. Yeats*. New York: Scribner, 2007.

York Society for Political Information. *An Address to the People of York, by the York Society for Political Information; with the Resolutions and Laws for the Government of the Society*. York, 1795.

Zimmermann, Eberhard August Wilhelm von. *A Political Survey of the Present State of Europe, in Sixteen Tables*. London: C. Dilly, 1787.